TEACHING STRATEGIES
FOR ETHNIC STUDIES

James A. Banks

University of Washington, Seattle

ALLYN AND BACON, INC. BOSTON • LONDON • SYDNEY

To my parents
Lula Holt Banks and Matthew Banks, 1909–1964
and to my daughter
Angela Marie Banks

Copyright© 1975 by Allyn and Bacon, Inc.
470 Atlantic Avenue, Boston, Massachusetts 02210.

Library of Congress Cataloging in Publication Data

Banks, James A.
    Teaching strategies for ethnic studies.

    Bibliography: p.
    Includes index.
    1. Ethnic studies—United States.   I. Title.
E184.A1B24   301.45'1'071073   74–31149
ISBN 0–205–04674–6 (hardbound)
ISBN 0–205–04673–8 (paperbound)

Second printing . . . August, 1976

Contents

iii

Part II

TEACHING ETHNIC CULTURES: CONCEPTS, STRATEGIES,
AND MATERIALS **137**

Preface

In recent years vigorous attempts have been made in school districts throughout the nation to eliminate the "great lie of silence" that has haunted the American public school curriculum for centuries. These efforts have resulted from the belated realization by educators that students attain only a partial education when they learn little about American ethnic groups and the cogent role of ethnicity in American life. Despite serious attempts by teachers and curriculum specialists to incorporate ethnic content into the curriculum in recent years, the tremendous dearth of materials depicting ethnicity within a broad social context has frustrated their most noble and diligent efforts. Because of the nature of American society and the plight of American ethnic groups in the last decade, most published materials on ethnic groups understandably focused on specific groups and their unique problems. There are many excellent books about Afro-Americans, but few which relate their experiences to those of other American ethnic groups such as Asian Americans, Mexican Americans, and European Americans. Even fewer books describe multiethnic teaching strategies and materials.

This book is based on the assumption that we have reached a point in our history in which multiethnic approaches to the teaching of ethnic studies is not only appropriate but essential. Specialized ethnic heritage programs such as Native American Studies and Mexican American Studies are necessary. However, they cannot give students the global view of ethnicity in America which they need to become effective change agents in contemporary society. Students must be exposed to a curriculum which will enable them to develop valid comparative generalizations and theories about American ethnic groups. Students need to know that Irish immigrants in colonial America, Italian immigrants in the 1880s, and Filipino immigrants in the 1920s experienced rejection, hostility, and psychological shock upon their arrival in America. However, they should also be aware of the significant ways in which the immigration of these groups was different. This book is designed to help present and future teachers attain the content, strategies, concepts, and resources needed to teach comparative ethnic studies and to integrate ethnic content into the regular curriculum.

This book is divided into two major parts. Part I presents a rationale for teaching comparative ethnic studies. An argument is made for a broader definition of ethnicity and the need to include all American ethnic groups in ethnic studies programs. The problem of goals in ethnic studies, key concepts for ethnic studies programs, and practical ways to organize ethnic studies lessons and units are also discussed in Part I. The author contends that the main goal of ethnic studies should be to help students develop the ability to make effective decisions so that they can, through intelligent social action, influence public policy.

Part II consists of a chapter on each major American ethnic group. Each of these chapters contains: (1) a chronology of key events, (2) a historical overview of the group discussed, (3) illustrative key concepts and teaching strategies, (4) an annotated bibliography for teachers, and (5) an annotated bibliography for elementary and secondary school students. While the bibliographies are selective, we found it necessary, because of the paucity of books on some groups, to include books which would have been omitted had better books been available.

The final chapter is designed to highlight and summarize the major points discussed in the book and to illustrate how the teacher can use the information and strategies described in earlier chapters to implement and evaluate multiethnic units which focus on two or more ethnic groups. The major components of a sample multiethnic unit are presented to illustrate the steps in unit construction. The Appendixes are designed to help the teacher obtain information and materials which he or she can use in the classroom. They consist of (a) a chronology of key events in the history of ethnic groups, (b) a list of films and filmstrips, (c) a selected list of ethnic periodicals, and (d) criteria for evaluating textbooks and other learning materials.

I am deeply grateful to a number of friends and colleagues who helped in various ways with the preparation of the manuscript. Charles F. Diaz greatly enriched the book by contributing Chapter 11, which discusses Cuban Americans and Native Hawaiians. A group of academic specialists on the various ethnic groups prepared perceptive and scholarly reactions to the Chapters in Part II. I wish to thank each of the following people for reacting to the chapters indicated: Willard Bill, Chapter 5; Charles O. Burgess, Chapter 6; Carlos E. Cortés, Chapter 8; Lowell K.Y. Chun-Hoon, James K. Morishima, and Stanley Sue, Chapter 9; and Francesco Cordasco, Chapter 10. Gwendolyn C. Baker, Dale L. Brubaker, Geneva Gay, Anna S. Ochoa, and Richard Wisniewski prepared extremely helpful general comments on the manuscript. While all of the comments on the manuscript were valuable and informative, I assume total responsibility for the contents of this book.

I wish to thank Sharon A. Giese and Betty Thomsen for perceptively typing and editing the manuscript. Professor Clifford D. Foster, chairman of Curriculum and Instruction, and Dean Frederic T. Giles helped make it possible for me to take a leave from the University of Washington to complete the manuscript. I am very grateful for their support and encouragement. I would like to thank Joan Augerot, Obdulia Castillo, P. Raaze Garrison, Mildred German, and Barbara Knaflich, of the Multi-Ethnic Curriculum, Human Relations Task Force, Seattle Public Schools, for help in compiling the list of multimedia resources in Appendix B, and for help in field testing some of the ideas in this book. I am indebted to the National Academy of Education for providing financial assistance in the form of a Spencer Fellowship, which enabled me to work on the manuscript full time and covered the expenses involved in its preparation.

My deepest indebtedness is to my wife, Cherry A. Banks, who wrote the annotations for the "Books for Students" sections in Chapters 5 through 10, prepared the index, and perceptively criticized each chapter in manuscript form. She also gave me the moral support and encouragement that an author must have to write.

J. A. B.

PART I

Goals, Concepts, and Instructional Organization

Introduction to Part I

Part I of this book discusses the basic instructional problems in the teaching of ethnic studies. Chapter 1 reviews some of the major trends in the teaching of ethnic studies and argues for a need to expand the definition of ethnic studies and to include content about all ethnic groups in school ethnic studies programs. The problem of goals in ethnic studies is explored in Chapter 2. The author argues that the main goal of ethnic studies should be to help students develop decision-making skills so that they can become effective change agents in contemporary society.

To help students develop effective decision-making skills, ethnic studies must help them to master higher level concepts and generalizations. Chapter 3

discusses key concepts from the various social science disciplines which should be major components of sound ethnic studies programs. The final chapter in Part I, Chapter 4, considers some practical ways to plan, organize, and teach ethnic studies units and lessons.

The actual steps to follow to gain the needed content background, to identify key concepts and generalizations, and to choose ethnic content are discussed. Valuing strategies and social action projects are also discussed in Chapter 4.

Teaching Ethnic Studies: Significance and Trends

Beyond the Melting Pot: Ethnicity in American Society

When *The Melting Pot*, a play written by the English Jewish author Israel Zangwill, was staged in New York City in 1908, it became an overwhelming success. The great ambition of the play's composer-protagonist, David Quixano, was to create an American symphony that would personify his deep conviction that his adopted land was a nation in which all ethnic differences would amalgamate and a novel man would emerge from this new ethnic synthesis. The play, considered an inferior one by drama critics, was eagerly embraced by Americans because it embodied an ideology that was pervasive in the United States at the turn of the century.

However, even when the play was first performed there were salient indications, even if Americans preferred to ignore them, that ethnic communities and cultures were deeply interwoven into the American social fabric and that the theme portrayed in Zangwill's play did not accurately reflect the status of ethnicity in America. The protagonist completes his symphony by the play's end. "Individuals, in very considerable numbers to

A version of this chapter was originally published as James A. Banks, "Teaching for Ethnic Literacy: A Comparative Approach," Social Education 37 (December 1973), pp. 738–50. It is reprinted here with permission of the National Council for the Social Studies.

be sure, broke out of their mold, but the groups remained. The experience of Zangwill's hero and heroine was *not* general. The point about the melting pot is that it did not happen."[1] Despite the blatant inconsistencies between the play's theme and American social reality, Americans held tenaciously to the idea that ethnic cultures would vanish in the United States.

However, as reality boldly confronted the melting pot ideology, many Americans began to embrace it less enthusiastically. "It was an idea close to the heart of the American self-image. But as a century passed, and the number of individuals and nations involved grew, the confidence that they could be fused waned, and also the conviction that it would be a good thing if they were to be."[2] It is significant that later in his life, Zangwill was very much the antithesis of the melting pot prototype. "He was a Zionist. He gave more and more of his energy to this cause as time passed, and retreated from his earlier position on racial and religious mixture."[3]

Despite the facts that the architect of the melting pot concept later reversed his earlier position and that ethnic cultures are endemic in the American social order, today many Americans still believe that ethnic groups should and will eventually abandon their unique cultural components and acquire those of Anglo-Americans. Contemporary melting pot advocates, unlike David Quixano, rarely envision a true cultural systhesis, but rather a domination of Anglo-Saxon culture traits in America. A classical example in the 1960s were the educators who formulated compensatory education programs. One of the major goals of these programs was to acculturate Afro-Americans, Mexican Americans, and other lower-class ethnic minority groups so that they would become colored Anglo-Americans. That these programs were largely a failure is due in no small part to the lack of respect and recognition which the architects gave to the importance of ethnicity in their formulation of programs for minority groups.

1.   Nathan Glazer and Daniel P. Moynihan, *Beyond the Melting Pot: The Negroes, Puerto Ricans, Jews, Italians and Irish of New York City* (Cambridge: M.I.T. Press, 1970), p. 290.

2.   Ibid., pp. 288–89.

3.   Ibid., p. 290.

Social science specialists in ethnic relations have abundantly documented the fact that ethnicity and ethnic cultures are integral parts of our social system and that these aspects of American life are exceedingly resistant to change or eradication.[4] As Glazer and Moynihan have perceptively stated, ethnicity "is fixed deep in American life generally; *the specific pattern of ethnic differentiation, however, in every generation is created by specific events*"[5] [emphasis added].

In recent years, we witnessed a number of events which reinforced and intensified ethnic identification and allegiance. During the Ocean Hill-Brownsville controversy in the New York Public Schools in 1968, Blacks and Jews formed antagonistic coalitions. Most members of these two ethnic groups interpreted the event in ethnic terms because the majority of teachers in the city schools were Jewish, and most of the students involved in the controversy were Afro-American.

Ethnicity also strongly influences American politics. When John F. Kennedy was a presidential candidate in 1960, Catholics throughout America went to the polls and supported him overwhelmingly partly because he was Catholic. A large percentage of the public officials in Chicago are Irish Catholic because of the number of Irish Catholics in that city who vote or sanction political appointments. Politicians often take advantage of their ethnic names when they are campaigning for political office in predominantly ethnic neighborhoods. When Senator Edmund S. Muskie made an aborted attempt to become the Democratic presidential candidate in 1972, he emphasized his feelings of ethnic kinship when soliciting support in Polish-American communities. The overwhelming Black vote was largely responsible for the election of Black mayors in Gary, Indiana; Cleveland, Ohio; and Newark, New Jersey in the 1960s.

Politics is only one significant area in American life in which ethnicity looms large. While many upwardly mobile members of other ethnic groups acquire Anglo-Saxon culture traits, they tend to confine their primary social relationships to

4. This proposition is thoroughly documented in Milton M. Gordon, *Assimilation in American Life: The Role of Race, Religion, and National Origins* (New York: Oxford University Press, 1964), and in Glazer and Moynihan, *Beyond the Melting Pot.*

5. Glazer and Moynihan, *Beyond the Melting Pot,* p. 291.

their ethnic communities.[6]   The reasons why this is the case are highly complex; some of which we will explore in later chapters. Institutional racism and discrimination have been major factors, especially in the cases of ethnic minorities.   However, some ethnic group members prefer to socialize with members of their own groups even when they have other options.   Historically, this has been to some extent true of European immigrants. However, prejudice and discrimination often have also limited their social options.   Nevertheless, especially in recent years with the emergence of ethnic pride among minorities, many of their most vocal spokesmen have frequently expressed a desire to limit many of their primary social contacts to members of their ethnic groups.   This is true for many of the more militant spokesmen among Afro-Americans, Mexican Americans, Asian Americans, Puerto Rican Americans, and Native Americans.

Participation in close social relationships and marriage are two areas in which ethnic divisions and cleavages are steep in American society.   Jewish-Americans usually marry other Jews,* Blacks most often marry Blacks, and Catholics usually marry Catholics.   To some extent a kind of pan-Catholicism has developed in America since the various ethnic groups who are predominantly Catholic such as Italian Americans, Polish Americans, and Slovak Americans often intermarry.   However, Spanish-speaking Americans, who are also predominantly Catholic, rarely intermarry or participate in the primary social groups with Catholics of European descent.   Thus Catholic society, too, has extreme ethnic divisions, despite the fact that some degree of pan-Catholicism has emerged.[7]

Since the Black Revolt of the 1960s, we have witnessed an intensified movement among ethnic minority groups to glorify their ancient pasts and to develop ethnic pride within group mem-

---

*A National Jewish Population Study conducted by the Council of Jewish Federation and Welfare Funds indicated that 69 percent of the Jews who married between 1966 and 1971 married other Jews.   Thirty-one percent married gentiles.   These figures show that while Jews now marry out of their ethnic group more often than in the past, the majority still marry others Jews. See Dorothy Rabinowitz, "The Trouble with Jewish-Gentile Marriages," New York 6, no. 34 (August 20, 1973), p. 26.

6.   Gordon, Assimilation, pp. 51–59.

7.   Ibid., pp. 201–202.

bers. Especially among the intellectuals and social activists within these groups, there has emerged a tremendous interest in ethnic foods, history, values, and other unique cultural components. A greater sense of what Gordon calls a *sense of peoplehood* has also developed within these groups.[8] Those of the small Black middle class, pejoratively dubbed the "Black bourgeoisie" by the late sociologist E. Franklin Frazier partly because he felt that they despised the Black lower classes,[9] have developed a great deal of interest in their more humble brothers in recent years. These groups are now undergoing a process which Sizemore has conceptualized as nationalism.[10] Whenever an ethnic group intensifies its search for identity and tries to build group cohesion and solidarity, some degree of ethnocentrism and rejection of "out-groups" emerges.

In a perceptive and seminal historical and sociological analysis, Sizemore documents how European ethnic groups also experienced this stage at various points in American history. This "stage is the *nationalist* stage, in which the excluded group intensifies its cohesion by building a religio-cultural community of beliefs around its creation, history, and development. The history, religion, and philosophy of the nation from which the group comes dictates the rites, rituals, and ceremonies utilized in the proselytization of the old nationalism. Because of rejection by white Anglo-Saxon Protestants and the ensuing exclusion from full participation in the social order, the excluded group embraces its former or future nation. For the Irish Catholics, it becomes Ireland; for the Polish Catholics it is Poland; and for the Jews it is Zion-Israel. The intense nationalistic involvement increases separatism."[11] During this stage, ethnic groups also reject "out-groups," and "projects its negative identities toward other groups."[12]

8. Ibid., pp. 28–29.

9. E. Franklin Frazier, *Black Bourgeoisie* (Glencoe, Illinois: Free Press, 1957).

10. Barbara A. Sizemore, "Is There a Case for Separate Schools?" *Phi Delta Kappan* 53 (January 1972), p. 282.

11. Ibid., p. 282.

12. Ibid.

Ethnicity, then, is an integral and salient part of the American social order. A sophisticated understanding of our society cannot be grasped unless the separate ethnic communities (which exist regionally as well as socially) that constitute American society are seriously analyzed from the perspectives of the various social sciences and the humanities. To treat *ethnicity* in America like the "invisible man," or to contend that ethnic groups in the United States have "melted" into one, is both intellectually indefensible and will result in a gross misinterpretation of the nature of American life. It is also insufficient to conceptualize ethnicity in America only in terms of ethnic minority groups. While these groups, because of institutional racism and discrimination, are the most socially and regionally isolated, and physically identifiable groups in America, ethnic divisions also exist among Americans of European origin.

Irish Catholics rarely marry Jewish Americans, and many first generation Greek Americans would find it difficult to accept their daughter's marriage to a White Anglo-Saxon Protestant. It is true, especially among later generation White ethnic groups, that inter-marriage and social mixture often occur. However, Polish Americans, Greek Americans, Italian Americans, and White Anglo-Saxons culture groups still confine many of their intimate social relations to their own ethnic group and have a strong sense of ethnic identification. The prophecy that these ethnic cleavages would disappear has been made throughout American history. However, ethnic enclaves continue to exist partly because events evoke them anew in each generation.

Because ethnicity is a salient part of our social system, it is essential that students master the facts, concepts, generalizations, and theories needed to understand and interpret events which are related to intergroup and intragroup interactions and tensions. This book is designed primarily to help equip classroom teachers with the information, strategies, and materials needed to help students to become more *ethnically literate*, and consequently more tolerant of cultural differences.

Recent Trends in Ethnic Studies

In recent years, educators have begun to realize the importance of ethnicity in American society and the need to help students develop more sophisticated understandings of the diverse ethnic groups that make up America and a greater tolerance and acceptance of cultural differences. Responding largely to student demands and community pressure groups, educational institutions at all levels have made some attempts to put more information about ethnic groups into the social studies, language arts, and humanities curricula.

The pressure to implement ethnic studies programs has come largely from America's oppressed ethnic minority groups such as Afro-Americans, Mexican Americans, Native Americans (Indians), and Puerto Rican Americans. Because these groups have taken the lead in pushing for ethnic studies programs, (White ethnics are increasingly making similar demands), educators created ethnic studies programs largely in response to their demands and needs as they perceived them. Consequently, *ethnic studies* has been conceptualized rather narrowly. Most of the programs that have been devised and implemented are parochial in scope, fragmented, and structured without careful planning and clear rationales. Typically, school ethnic studies programs focus on one specific ethnic group such as Afro-Americans, Native Americans, or Mexican Americans. The ethnic group upon which the program focuses is either present or dominant in the local school population. A school district which has a large Puerto Rican population is likely to have a program in Puerto Rican Studies, but not one which teaches about the problems and sociological characteristics of other ethnic groups.

The result of these kinds of narrowly conceptualized programs, even though the information they teach students is essential, is that they rarely help students develop scientific generalizations and concepts about the characteristics ethnic groups have in common, about the unique status of each ethnic group, and about why ethnicity is an integral part of our social system. Ethnic studies must be conceptualized more broadly, and ethnic studies programs should include information about *all* of America's diverse ethnic groups to enable students to develop valid comparative generalizations and to fully grasp the complexity of ethnicity in American society.

An Expanded Definition of Ethnicity

The fragmentation in ethnic studies programs has resulted largely from the ways in which ethnicity and ethnic groups in

America have been defined by curriculm specialists. Usually when a curriculum committee is formed to create an ethnic studies guide, the group does noes not deal with ethnicity in a broad sociological sense, but rather limits its conceptualization of an ethnic group to an ethnic minority group, and often to one specific group. We need to formulate a more meaningful and inclusive definition of an ethnic group in order to create more intellectually defensible ethnic studies programs.

What is an *ethnic group?* Individuals who constitute an ethnic group share a sense of group identification, a common set of values, political and economic interests, behavior patterns, and other culture elements which differ from those of other groups within a society. Writes Rose, "Groups whose members share a unique social and cultural heritage passed on from one generation to the next are known as *ethnic groups.* Ethnic groups are frequently identified by distinctive patterns of family life, language, recreation, religion, and other customs which cause them to be differentiated from others. Above all else, members of such groups feel a sense of identity and an 'interdependence of fate' with those who share the customs of the ethnic tradition" [13] [emphasis added]. If we accept these definitions of an ethnic group, as do sociologists who specialize in ethnic relations, then all Americans are members of an ethnic group, since each of us belongs to a group which shares a sense of peoplehood, behavior patterns, and cultural traits which differ from those of other groups.

Not only are Greek Americans, Jewish Americans, Italian Americans, and Polish Americans members of ethnic groups, but those individuals who are descendants of the earliest European settlers in New England also belong to an ethnic group. This group is the dominant ethnic group in the United States: White Anglo-Saxon Protestants. We often do not think of White Anglo-Saxon Protestants as members of an ethnic group because they constitute our dominant ethnic group. However, because a group which shares a common culture and a sense of group identification is culturally dominant within a society does not mean that it is not an ethnic group. Writes Anderson, "white

13. Peter I. Rose, *They and We: Racial and Ethnic Relations in the United States* (New York: Random House, 1964), p. 11.

Protestants, like other Americans, are as much members of an ethnic group as anyone else, however privileged the majority of them might be."[14]

In this book, ethnic studies is conceptualized more broadly than is often the case. Information, materials, and strategies for teaching about White ethnic groups (such as White Anglo-Saxon Protestants and Jewish Americans), as well as the experiences of ethnic minority groups such as Mexican Americans, Asian Americans, and Native Americans are included. To conceptualize ethnic studies more narrowly will result in curricula programs which are too narrow in scope, and which will fail to help students fully understand both the important similarities and differences in the experiences of the groups that constitute America. An ethnic studies program which omits treatment of the great migrations from Southern and Eastern Europe that took place in the late nineteenth and early twentieth centuries will not provide students with the perspective needed to grasp the complexity of the Chinese immigrations in the 1800s. There were many similarities in the experiences of these two groups of immigrants, as well as significant differences. Both groups were uprooted, physically and psychologically, and were seeking opportunities in a nation which, in myth if not in fact, offered unlimited social mobility. Both groups experienced shock and alienation in their new country. However, while the Southern and Eastern European immigrants were often the victims of racist ideologies, they never reached the alarming proportions as on the West Coast with the coming of the Chinese sojourners. Also, the Europeans came to America intending to stay; the Chinese came hoping to earn their fortunes in the promised land and to return to China. The Europeans brought their wives and families, while the Chinese did not. This latter fact profoundly shaped the social development of the Chinese-American community.

A vital ethnic studies program should enable students to derive valid generalizations about the characteristics of all of America's ethnic groups and to learn how they are alike and different, in both their past and present experiences.

14. Charles H. Anderson, *White Protestant Americans: From National Origins to Religious Group* (Englewood Cliffs, N. J.: Prentice-Hall, 1970), p. xiii.

Ethnic Minority Groups

While an ethnic group shares a common set of values, behavior patterns and culture traits, and a sense of peoplehood, an ethnic minority group can be distinguished from an ethnic group because it is characterized by several unique attributes. Although an *ethnic minority group* shares a common culture and a sense of peoplehood, it also has unique physical and/or cultural characteristics which enable persons who belong to dominant ethnic groups to easily identify its members and thus treat them in a discriminatory way. This type of group is also a numerical minority and makes up only a small proportion of the population. In 1970, the non-White ethnic minorities made up about 15 percent of the total national population. Table 1.1 contains selected demographic, income, and employment characteristics of the major non-White ethnic groups in the United States.*

As in most societies, ethnic minority groups in America are victims of racism, stereotypes, and are disproportionately represented in the lower socioeconomic classes, which are heavily concentrated in the blighted sections of rural and urban areas. The color of American ethnic minorities is one of their salient characteristics and is a significant factor which has decisively shaped their experiences in the United States. Any comparisons of European immigrants and America's ethnic minorities that do not deal realistically and seriously with this exceedingly important variable are invidious and misleading. These kinds of comparisons are often found in social science literature. While a Polish-American immigrant can Anglicize his surname, acquire Anglo-Saxon culture traits, and move into almost any White neighborhood without evoking much animosity, no matter how culturally assimilated an Afro-American becomes, his skin color remains a social stigma of immense importance to *all* White ethnic groups.

A special comment about color is warranted. Color attains most of its significance from the perceptions people have of it rather than from biological realities. Most Puerto Rican Amer-

---

* *The U. S. Census defines Cuban Americans and Mexican Americans as White. Sociologically, these groups share many characteristics with Filipino Americans, Chinese Americans, and other non-White ethnic minorities. Non-White is used here sociologically.*

icans, for example, are Caucasians. However, since about 10 percent of them have Negroid physical characteristics,[15] most White Americans consider all Puerto Ricans "non-Whites" and consequently treat them just as they treat other colored Americans such as Chinese Americans, Samoan Americans, Filipino Americans, and Korean Americans. Thus, to be socially defined as colored does not necessarily mean that an individual's skin color is "non-White." An individual acquires his color status in the United States from his group identification and not necessarily from the color of his skin (although some light-skinned ethnic minorities "pass" as White). Many Afro-Americans are genetically and in physical appearance quite Caucasoid. However, any person with any degree of known African descent, regardless of his physical appearance or genotype, is socially defined as *Black.*

Ethnic Studies and Ethnic Minorities: Recent Developments

In the 1950s, a vigorous protest movement known as the Black Revolt emerged within Black communities and culminated in the late 1960s. Black Americans fought an unprecedented battle to achieve social and economic equality during this period. By using such tactics as sit-ins, freedom rides, and boycotts, they succeeded in eliminating legal discrimination in interstate transportation, voting, and in public accommodation facilities. As the Black Revolt progressed, Black people tried to shape a new identity and to shatter old and pervasive stereotypes about their culture and the contributions Afro-Americans have made to American life.

Written history is an important factor that influences both how a group sees itself and how others view it. Keenly aware of this fact, Afro-Americans demanded that school history books be rewritten so that their role in shaping our nation's destiny would be more favorably and realistically portrayed. Civil rights groups such as the National Urban League and the National Association for the Advancement of Colored People pressured educators to ban schoolbooks they considered racist and to buy books that accurately depicted the experience of African people in the

15. Glazer and Moynihan, *Beyond the Melting Pot*, p. xxv.

Table 1.1

Selected Demographic, Income, and Employment Characteristics of Ethnic Minority Groups in the United States*

	Afro-Americans	American Indians	Japanese Americans	Chinese Americans	Filipino Americans	Mexican Americans	Cuban Americans	Puerto Rican Americans	Native Hawaiians
Total Number	22,549,815	763,594	588,324	431,583	336,731	4,532,435	544,600	1,429,396	99,958
Percent of Total Population (203,211,926)	11%	.4%	.3%	.2%	.2%	2%	.3%	.7%	.05%
Mean income of those 25 and over	$3,766.	$3,636.	$6,277.	$5,597.	$4,984.	$3,968.	$4,495.	$4,132.	$6,682.
Median school years completed for those 25 years and over	9.8	9.8	12.5	12.4	12.2	8.1	10.3	8.7	12.1
Percent of those employed, 16 and over, who are professional, technical, and kindred workers	8%	10%	19%	25%	24%	6%	11%	6%	(NA)**

14

Table 1.1 (continued)

	Afro-Americans	American Indians	Japanese Americans	Chinese Americans	Filipino Americans	Mexican Americans	Cuban Americans	Puerto Rican Americans	Native Hawaiians
Percent of those employed, 16 and over, who are laborers, except farm	9%	9%	6%	2%	5%	10%	4%	6%	(NA)**

* This table is based on data reported in Bureau of the Census, *Subject Reports: Ethnic Groups*, 7 vols. (Washington, D. C.: U. S. Government Printing Office, 1973).

** Data not available.

United States. As the pressure on school districts mounted, they encouraged publishers to include more information about Afro-Americans in schoolbooks.

As the ruckus created by the demand for Afro-American studies intensified and spread, other ethnic minority groups initiated protest movements that had as one of their main goals the implementation of ethnic studies school programs which reflected their cultures. Mexican Americans, Native Americans, Asian Americans, and Puerto Rican Americans argued that their histories had been written primarily from a White Anglo-Saxon Protestant point of view, which often described them insensitively, perpetuated stereotypes, or completely omitted discussion of them. A number of special publications, some of which were sponsored by civil rights organizations and others by state departments of education, documented the validity of the claims made by these groups.[16]

The response to the demands for new instructional materials and programs by ethnic minorities other than Afro-Americans has varied widely. Factors influencing the kinds of responses school districts and publishers have made to their demands include their proportion within a local school population, the intensity with which the demands have been made, and the ethnic sensitivity of local educators. The responses by publishers have been determined primarily by economic factors, i.e., whether they felt that including more information about a particular minority group would increase book sales.

School districts and publishers have responded more to the demands for Black Studies programs and materials than to demands by other ethnic minority groups. This is primarily because Black demands have been more intensive and consistent, and Blacks constitute our largest ethnic minority. However, in some regions and school districts such as in the Southwest and parts of the West, other ethnic minorities such as Chicanos and Asian

16. Examples are Michael B. Kane, *Minorities in Textbooks: A Study of Their Treatment in Social Studies Textbooks* (Chicago: Quadrangle Books, 1970); L. P. Carpenter and Dinah Rank, *The Treatment of Minorities: A Survey of Textbooks Used in Missouri High Schools* (Jefferson City: Missouri Commission on Human Rights, 1968); Task Force to Reevaluate Social Science Textbooks Grades Five through Eight, *Report and Recommendations* (Sacramento: California State Department of Education, 1971).

Americans exceed the number of Afro-Americans in the school population. In these districts, educators have been more sensitive to the need for programs which deal with other minorities.

Criteria for Selecting Ethnic Minority Content

The dominant trend, however, is for educators to implement ethnic studies programs in schools and districts which have a high proportion of ethnic minority students, and for the ethnic studies programs within a school or district to focus only or primarily on the minority group which is either dominant or present within the school or district. Most ethnic studies programs have been formulated on the tenuous assumptions that ethnic content is needed primarily by ethnic minorities and that a particular ethnic studies program should focus on the problems and contributions of the particular minority group found in the local school or district. These assumptions, while widespread, are myopic and intellectually indefensible and relegate ethnic minority studies to an inferior status in the school curriculum.

When the author often asks educators in various regions of the nation about the kinds of ethnic studies programs they have implemented, they often respond by saying that there are no Blacks in their schools and thus no need for an ethnic studies program. When other teachers are asked whether they include content about Puerto Rican Americans or Asian Americans in their ethnic studies programs, they often say, "No, because we have no Puerto Ricans or Asian students in our schools." However, they often hastily add that they have Black studies units in the fifth and eighth grades because there are a large number of Black students in their schools. Perhaps unknowingly, educators who feel that ethnic minority content should only be studied by ethnic minorities and that minorities only need to study about their own cultures have a condescending attitude toward ethnic minority studies and do not consider the ethnic minority experiences to be a significant part of American life.

At several points in their schooling, all American students learn something about classical Rome and Greece, Medieval Europe, and the Italian Renaissance. Information about these cultures is included in the curriculum because most teachers believe that they have profoundly influenced the Western world, and that a sophisticated understanding of them is necessary to interpret American society. The criterion used to determine whether these cultures should be taught is not whether there are students in the class who are descendents of ancient Rome and Greece, of Italy or Medieval Europe. Such a criterion would not be intellectually sound. For the same reasons, it should not be used to select content about other cultures, such as the minority cultures in America.

The criterion used to identify content for inclusion into the curriculum should be the same for all topics, cultures and groups, i.e., whether the content will enable students to develop valid generalizations and concepts about their social world and the skills and abilities to influence public policy. To use one criterion to select content about European cultures and another to select ethnic minority content is discriminatory and intellectually indefensible.

Who Needs Ethnic Studies?

Afro-American students, whether they live in New York City or in the Watts district of Los Angeles, as well as White students, regardless of their ethnicity or geographical region, need to seriously study *all* ethnic minority cultures because they are an integral part of American life. They should study about the Puerto Rican cultures found primarily in New York City, but also in Chicago and other regions of the United States. To fully understand American society, Jewish students in the suburbs of New York City should be exposed to information about Japanese Americans and the dehumanizing and shocking experience which they endured in the so-called relocation camps during World War II, and about the 75,000 Mexicans who suddenly became a minority in the United States when this nation annexed a large chunk of Mexico's land in 1848 in the fateful Treaty of Guadalupe Hidalgo.

Indian students should study their history in this nation from a Native American perspective. However, if they learn that during the 1800s many White Southern and Eastern European immigrants in America also inhabited ghettos which contemporary social scientists said resulted from their inferior genetic nature (similar arguments are made about ethnic minorities today by such social scientists as Banfield, Jensen, and Shockley),[17] they will understand that their present situation in America does bear some similarities to the histories of other American groups. This kind of knowledge will help students to gain needed perspective and to better understand, but not necessarily accept, their own social situations.

By arguing that students need to study both their own and other cultures in order to fully comprehend American society, we are not suggesting that students who are members of specific minority groups should never study their cultures in specialized courses or that such specialized knowledge is not vitally important, especially for oppressed minority students who have been denied the opportunity to learn about the problems and contributions of their peoples. We are not suggesting, for example, that Indian children, who often know little about their cultures, except myths invented and perpetuated by White social scientists, should not gain knowledge about their groups prior to studying other peoples and cultures. However, we are strongly arguing that only knowledge about one's own ethnic group is insufficient to help students to attain a liberating education and to fully grasp the complexity of the experience of their own ethnic group or the total human experience. A Chinese student who only studies the sociology of the Chinese-American ghetto may conclude that the urban ghetto is a Chinese-American invention. However, he will be better able to make valid generalizations about the formation of ghettos if he studies White immigrant communities in the 1800s and the contemporary urban experiences of Afro-Americans, Puerto Rican Americans, Indians, and lower-class Whites, many of whom still live their entire lives within ethnic enclaves in cities such as New York, Chicago, and Boston.

Expanding Students' Concepts of Humans with Ethnic Minority Content

Ethnic minority studies are needed by all students to help them to understand themselves and the social world in which

17. Edward C. Banfield, *The Unheavenly City* (Boston: Little, Brown 1970); Arthur R. Jensen, "How Much Can We Boost IQ and Scholastic Achievement," *Harvard Educational Review* 39 (Winter 1969), pp. 1–123; William Shockley, "Dysgenics, Geneticity, Raceology: Challenges to the Intellectual Responsibility of Educators," *Phi Delta Kappan* 53 (January 1972), pp. 297–307.

they live.[18] The minority experience is part of the human experience, and education should deal with the total experience of
humankind. Units and lessons on Indians, Chicanos, Blacks,
Asian Americans, and Puerto Rican Americans, if approached
from an anthropoligical perspective, can help students broaden
their understanding and conception of what it means to be human
and enable them to better understand their own cultures and lifestyles. Students must be helped to discover that while people are
born with the physical capacities to become human, individuals
become human only by learning the culture of their group.

Since cultures are made by people, there are many ways of
being human. By studying this important generalization, students will hopefully develop an appreciation for the great capacity of people to create a diversity of lifestyles and to adapt to
a variety of social and physical environments. Weingrod writes,
"It is at once a humbling and widening experience to learn that
others have met and resolved some universal problems in a manner other than the familiar ones." [19]

During their study of minority cultures, students can learn
that while human beings have many of the same basic needs
such as love, protection, and security, different cultures within
our society have devised a great variety of means to satisfy these
needs. The religious ceremonies of the Native Americans, Black
values and spirituals, and Mexican American literature can illustrate the wide range of culture elements within our society.

Most dominant ethnic groups tend to think that their cultures
are superior to all others. Chauvinist ethnocentrism is especially
acute among dominant White ethnic groups in America. When
students study and understand the cultures of ethnic minorities,
they will be more likely to consider ethnic minority persons as
humans. Research suggests that, with understanding, tolerance
sometimes follows.[20]

18. Parts of this section are adapted from James A. Banks, "Teaching
Ethnic Minority Studies with a Focus on Culture," *Educational Leadership*
29 (November 1971), pp. 113–17. Used with permission of the Association for Supervision and Curriculum Development.

19. Alex Weingrod, "Anthropology and the Social Studies," in Martin
Feldman and Eli Seifman, eds., *The Social Studies: Structure, Models and
Strategies* (Englewood Cliffs, N. J.: Prentice-Hall, 1969), p. 268.

20. For a summary of this research see: James A. Banks, "Racial Preju-

Anthropological concepts and ethnic minority content can also help students to better understand their own cultures. As Kluckhohn, the perceptive anthropologist, wrote, "Studying [other cultures] enables us to see ourselves better. Ordinarily we are unaware of the specialized lens through which we look at life. . . . *Anthropology holds up a great mirror to man and lets him look at himself in his infinite variety.*"[21] We can best view our own behavior from the perspective of another culture. By studying about other ways of being and living, students will see how bound they are by their own values, perceptions, and prejudices. The cultures of our powerless ethnic minority groups, and the oppressive and devastating experiences of America's Black, Brown, Red, and Yellow peoples, are shocking testimony to the criminal effects of racism on its victims. Ethnic minority content can serve as an excellent lens to help White ethnic group students to see and truly know themselves since White racism is deeply implicated in the cultures of America's ethnic minorities.

Ethnic minority content can also help students expand their conceptions of what it means to be human, to accept the fact that minority cultures are functional and valid, and that a culture can be evaluated only within a particular social context. A culture trait that is functional in one social setting may be quite dysfunctional in another. It is especially important for ethnic studies to help White students to expand their definitions of who is human, since many Whites seem to believe that they are the only humans on earth. The differential reactions to the Kent State and Jackson State tragedies by the majority of White Americans suggest that many Whites did not include the Jackson State victims, which were Black, within their conceptions of humanity.

The Challenge

It is imperative that we take decisive steps to help students to develop ethnic literacy and a better understanding of ethnicity within America in these racially troubled times. Intergroup

dice and the Black Self-Concept," in James A. Banks and Jean D. Grambs, eds., *Black Self-Concept: Implications for Education and Social Science* (New York: McGraw-Hill, 1972), pp. 5–35.

21. Clyde Kluckhohn, *Mirror for Man* (Greenwich, Connecticut: Fawcett Publications, 1965), p. 19.

conflict poses a serious threat to our nation and the ideals of American democracy. Blatant racism, which was harshly condemned by influential commission reports in the sixties, raised its ugly head unabashedly in the seventies and became a powerful political weapon that was used advantageously by both political demagogues and America's most esteemed political leaders. Implementing sound, comparative ethnic studies programs will be an exceedingly difficult task. Such programs will be vehemently resisted by diverse pressure groups which are staunch enemies of those who advocate a culturally pluralistic curriculum and society. In the early 1970s, these groups vigorously escalated their activities and attacks on teachers throughout the nation. Their growth was greatly facilitated by the ominous political climate that pervaded the United States. However, these groups must be adamantly resisted by teachers with vision, courage, and commitment. The challenge is Herculean. The odds are against us. The hour is late. However, what is at stake is priceless: the liberation of the hearts and minds of all American youth.

Questions and Activities

1. The author takes the position that ethnicity is an integral part of American life and that the melting pot did not occur. React to this position by stating whether you agree or disagree with it and why.

2. Make a list of the different ethnic backgrounds which constitute your ethnic heritage. Compare your list with similar lists made by other individuals in your class or workshop. What conclusions can you make about ethnicity in American society by analyzing this data?

3. Study the results of the last national or local election. Note particularly the voting patterns of predominantly ethnic communities. What generalizations can you make on the basis of this data? What are the limitations of your generalizations?

4. Interview a curriculum coordinator in one or two local school districts. Ask this individual to describe the school's ethnic studies program. If the school focuses on some ethnic groups and not on others, ask for an explanation of this practice.

How do your findings compare to the trends described in this chapter?

5. In this chapter, the author states what he feels should be the proper goals of ethnic studies programs. Write, in one sentence or more, what *you* feel should be the goals of ethnic studies programs. Compare your statement with that made by the author. In what ways are they alike and different? Why? How are your assumptions about ethnic studies and ethnicity similar and different from those of the author?

6. The author argues for a comparative approach to ethnic studies. What are the advantages and disadvantages of this approach? Do you prefer a comparative or a noncomparative approach to ethnic studies? Why?

7. Define each of the following terms and tell why each is important:

> Israel Zangwill
> the melting pot concept
> nationalism
> ethnic group
> ethnic minority group
> sense of peoplehood
> Pan-Catholicism
> ethnic studies (broadly defined)
> color (socially defined)

Annotated Bibliography

Banks, James A., ed. *Teaching Ethnic Studies: Concepts and Strategies.* Washington, D. C.: National Council for the Social Studies 43rd Yearbook, 1973.

This book includes chapters on all American ethnic groups and women's rights. Concrete methods and annotated bibliographies are key features of the book. Illustrated with "teachable" photographs.

Banks, James A. and William W. Joyce, eds. *Teaching Social Studies to Culturally Different Children.* Reading, Mass.: Addison-Wesley, 1970.

This anthology provides the classroom teacher with the perceptions and strategies which can help him or her to make the social studies more meaningful and exciting for Black, Chicano, Puerto Rican American, Native American, and other children who are members of ethnic minority groups.

Carlson, Ruth Kearney. *Emerging Humanity: Multi-Ethnic Literature for Children and Adolescents.* Dubuque, Iowa: William C. Brown, 1972.

Although occasionally flawed by White bias, this book contains many useful suggestions and resources which the teacher can use to enrich his or her teaching with ethnic literature.

Daniels, Roger and Harry H. L. Kitano. *American Racism: Explorations of the Nature of Prejudice.* Englewood Cliffs, N. J.: Prentice-Hall, 1970.

By using the experiences of ethnic minority groups, the authors document how racism is endemic in the United States. The book focuses on racism directed against Asian Americans.

Epstein, Charlotte. *Intergroup Relations for the Classroom Teacher.* New York: Houghton Mifflin, 1968.

A direct and forthright book which discusses the diverse cultures of students and strategies for improving interethnic relations in the classroom.

Gittler, Joseph, ed. *Understanding Minority Groups.* New York: John Wiley, 1964.

The essays in this book grew out of an Institute on Minority Groups in the United States held in 1955. Six ethnic groups, including Catholics and Jews, are treated. However, the Mexican American is notably absent from the book. This is a serious omission. Oscar Handling, Clarence Senior, and Ira de A. Reid are among the noted contributors.

Glazer, Nathan and Daniel P. Moynihan. *Beyond the Melting Pot: The Negroes, Puerto Ricans, Jews, Italians, and Irish of New York City.* 2nd ed. Cambridge: The M. I. T. Press, 1970.

Although this book is flawed by many insensitive statements about various ethnic minority groups, the authors' initial and final chapters which deal with ethnicity as an integral part of American life merit serious thought. . Many of their comments about specific groups, however, will justifiably evoke outrage.

Gordon, Milton. *Assimilation in American Life: The Role of Race, Religion and National Origins.* New York: Oxford University Press, 1964.

This award-winning book contains a brilliant explication of the concept of ethnicity in America, and sets forth a seminal theory of assimilation in American life. It is must reading for the teacher who wants to plan sound comparative ethnic studies units.

Grambs, Jean D. *Intergroup Education: Methods and Materials.* Englewood Cliffs, N. J.: Prentice-Hall, 1968.

This book includes a rationale for teaching ethnic studies, describes promising teaching strategies, and discusses a flood of resources which will be quite helpful to the teacher. The open-ended stories in the book are highly recommended for use in ethnic studies programs.

Henderson, George. *To Live in Freedom: Human Relations Today and Tomorrow.* Norman: University of Oklahoma Press, 1972.

This book is a useful and readable overview of problems involved in human relations and strategies which may be used to resolve them. The emphasis is on self-examination and introspection. It is recommended for teachers who wish to examine their attitudes and perceptions of different ethnic groups. Beautifully illustrated with photographs and perceptive cartoons.

Jacobs, Paul, Saul Landau with Eve Pell, eds. *To Serve the Devil.* Vols. 1 and 2. New York: Vintage Books, 1971.

This is an excellent documentary history, with an extensive text by the authors on each major ethnic minority group. The tone of the book is hard-hitting and refreshingly candid. A good introductory source.

Leacock, Eleanor B., ed. *The Culture of Poverty: A Critique.* New York: Simon and Schuster, 1971.

A group of noted educators and social scientists shatter many pervasive myths about the cognitive styles and cultures of the poor. They present new conceptual frameworks for viewing the lifestlyes of the poor which are more compassionate and fruitful than most.

McWilliams, Carey. *Brothers Under the Skin.* Rev. ed. Boston: Little, Brown, 1951.

This is a highly readable and interesting treatment of America's non-White minority groups and Jewish Americans. These chapters are good introductions to the various ethnic groups.

Marden, Charles E. and Gladys Meyer. *Minorities in American Society.* 3rd ed. New York: American Book Company, 1968.

This basic text on minorities in American society sets forth theories of intergroup and intragroup relations as well as discusses specific minority groups such as Indians, Blacks, European immigrants, Asian Americans, and Mexican Americans. The attention given to dominant-minority relations in a world context merits careful study.

Rose, Peter I. *They and We: Racial and Ethnic Relations in the United States.* 2nd ed. New York: Random House, 1974.

This easily readable book is valuable primarily because of the clear distinctions which the author makes between such concepts as race, ethnic groups, prejudice, and discrimination. It can be profitably read by high school students as well as teachers.

Santa Barbara County Board of Education. *The Emerging Minorities in America: A Resource Guide for Teachers.* Santa Barbara, Calif.: American Bibliographical Center—Clio Press, 1972.

Although the historical overviews in this book are scanty, the brief biographical sketches of outstanding members of various ethnic groups might prove helpful. Puerto Rican Americans are notably omitted in the book.

Simpson, George E. and J. Milton Yinger. *Racial and Cultural Minorities.* 3rd ed. New York: Harper and Row, 1965.

An excellent, comprehensive introduction to race and ethnicity in American life. The chapters on the causes and consequences of prejudice and discrimination are especially noteworthy.

Social Science Staff of the Educational Research Council of America. *Prejudice and Discrimination.* Teachers' Guide. Boston: Allyn and Bacon, 1973.

This book includes some useful suggestions for teaching concepts related to *prejudice* and *discrimination.* A student book with the same title is also available.

Steinfield, Melvin. *Cracks in the Melting Pot.* 2nd ed. New York: Glencoe Press, 1973.

An excellent collection of documents on American ethnic relations which exposes the melting pot myth in the United States. A wide range of interesting readings are included.

Stone, James C. and Donald P. DeNevi, eds. *Teaching Multi-Cultural Populations: Five Heritages.* New York: Van Nostrand Reinhold, 1971.

This anthology contains a number of insightful and valuable readings on various aspects of ethnic minority cultures.

Valentine, Charles A. *Culture and Poverty: Critique and Counter-Proposals.* Chicago: University of Chicago Press, 1968.

This book contains one of the most perceptive critiques of prevailing theories of poverty and perceptions of the poor that is available. It will provide the teacher with new ways to view the experiences of ethnic minorities who are victimized by poverty and racist social science ideologies.

Vander Sanden, James W. *American Minority Relations: The Sociology of Race and Ethnic Groups.* New York: Ronald Press, 1966.

A noted sociologist uses the sociological perspective to analyze such issues as the nature of minority relations, race, segregation, assimilation, and minority reactions to dominance. The teacher will find this book helpful when looking for sociological concepts to include in ethnic studies curricula and units.

Wisniewski, Richard, ed. *Teaching About Life in the City.* Washington, D. C.: National Council for the Social Studies 42nd Yearbook, 1972.

The problems of ethnic minorities in the cities, life in the Black community, and creative learning experiences about the city are some of the topics discussed in this useful book. Teachers will find the chapter on teaching strategies especially valuable. Strikingly illustrated with sixty photographs and seventeen diagrams, many of which can be used for inquiry lessons.

The Goal of
Ethnic Studies Instruction

Ethnic Studies: The Problem of Goals

Despite the recent attempts to implement ethnic studies programs, few of them are sound because their goals remain confused, ambiguous, and conflicting.[1] Many ethnic studies programs have been structured without careful planning and clear rationales. Divergent goals for ethnic studies programs are often voiced by experts of many different persuasions and ideologies. Larry Cuban, a leader in ethnic education, argues that "the only legitimate goals for ethnic content [in the public schools] are to offer a balanced view of the American past and present."[2] Nathan Hare, another innovator in ethnic studies, believes that the ethnic studies should be taught from the perspective of the particular ethnic group and should emphasize the struggles and aspirations of that group.[3]

1. Parts of this section are adapted from James A. Banks, "Teaching Black History with a Focus on Decision-Making," *Social Education* 35 (November 1971), pp. 740–45 ff., 820–21. Used with permission of the National Council for the Social Studies.

2. Larry Cuban, "Black History, Negro History, and White Folk," in James A. Banks and William W. Joyce, eds., *Teaching Social Studies to Culturally Different Children* (Reading, Mass.: Addison-Wesley, 1971), p. 318.

3. Nathan Hare, "The Teaching of Black History and Culture in the Secondary Schools," *Social Education* 33 (April 1969), p. 388.

Many young ethnic group activists feel that the main goal of ethnic studies should be to equip oppressed students with an ideology which is imperative for their liberation. Some ethnic spokesmen who belong to the over-thirty generation (such as Martin Kilson and Bayard Ruskin) think that education designed to develop a commitment to a fixed ideology is antithetical to sound scholarship and has no place in public institutions. Writes Kilson, "I don't believe it is the proper or most useful function of a [school] to train ideological or political organizers of whatever persuasion. A [school's] primary function is to impart skills, techniques, and special habits of learning to its students. The student must be free to decide himself on the ideological application of his training." [4] The disagreement over the proper goals of ethnic studies reflects the widespread ethnic tension and polarization within American society.

Classroom teachers are puzzled about strategies to use in teaching ethnic studies and have serious questions about who can teach ethnic studies because of the disagreement over goals among curriculum experts and social scientists. Effective teaching strategies and sound criteria for judging materials cannot be formulated until goals are identified and explicitly stated. In the past, most social studies teachers emphasized the mastery of factual information and tried to develop a blind commitment to "democracy" as practiced in the United States. Unless a sound rationale for ethnic studies programs can be stated and new approaches to the teaching of ethnic studies implemented, students will get just as sick and tired of ethnic content as they have become with White chauvinistic schoolbook history. Some students already feel that Black history has been "oversold." Many teachers who teach in ethnic studies programs use new materials but traditional strategies because multiethnic materials, although necessary for sound social studies programs, do not in themselves solve the classroom teacher's pedagogical problems.

Without both new goals and novel strategies, ethnic studies will become just another fleeting fad. Isolated facts about Crispus Attucks and Crazy Horse do not stimulate the intellect any more than isolated facts about Thomas Jefferson and Abraham Lincoln. In this chapter, we present a rationale for an ethnic

4. Martin Kilson, "Black Studies: A Plea for Perspective," *The Crisis* (October 1969), p. 330.

studies program which focuses on decision-making and social action skills and examine one major component of such a program: the knowledge component.

The Purpose of Ethnic Studies Instruction

Environmental pollution, poverty, war, deteriorating cities, and ethnic conflict are the intractable social problems which Americans must resolve if we are to survive and create a just, humane society. Because of the personal and social problems which are pervasive within our society, the main goal of ethnic studies should be to help students develop the ability to make *reflective decisions* so that they can resolve personal problems, and through social action, influence public policy and develop a sense of political efficacy. It is especially important to help students make intelligent decisions and participate in social action in times when rhetoric is often substituted for reason and when simplistic solutions are often proposed as answers to complicated social problems. The type of ethnic studies program proposed in this book is designed to create students who can make intelligent decisions on social issues and take affirmative actions to help resolve them. Thus the program is decision-making focused.

THE KNOWLEDGE COMPONENT OF DECISION-MAKING

Knowledge is one essential component of the decision-making process. There are many kinds of knowledge and ways of attaining it. To make reflective decisions, however, the student must use the scientific method to attain knowledge. The knowledge on which reflective decisions are made must also be powerful and widely applicable so that it will enable students to make the most accurate predictions possible. There are several categories of knowledge, and they vary in their predictive capacity and in their ability to help us to organize our observations and thus make sound judgments. We will now discuss the characteristics of the major knowledge categories and the contribution which each can make to a vital ethnic studies program.

Facts

Facts are low level, specific empirical statements about limited phenomena. Facts may be considered the lowest level of knowledge and have the least predictive capacity of all of the knowledge forms. In ethnic studies, as in all academic areas and disciplines, facts are the building blocks of knowledge. Students must master facts in order to learn higher levels of knowledge.

Examples of facts are:

The first Blacks to arrive in England's North American colonies came on a Dutch ship that landed at Jamestown, Virginia in 1619.

The Chinese immigrants who came to San Francisco in the 1800s established the *hui kuan*.

There were four million Mexican Americans in the United States in 1960.

In 1969, 2,112,264 Puerto Ricans migrated to the United States from Puerto Rico.

The League of the Five (Indian) Nations was made up of the Seneca, Onondaga, Cayuga, Oneida, and Mohawk tribes.

Responding to a court order, 110,000 Japanese Americans on the West Coast had left their homes and gone to federal evacuation camps by August 7, 1942.

In the period 1820–80, 8,718,271 Northern and Western Europeans immigrated to the United States.

A careful study of the facts above about America's ethnic groups will reveal several characteristics of factual statements. First, facts are empirical statements, or statements which can be tested with available data or data which can be obtained. By carefully studying and analyzing historical documents and statistical data, a social scientist can determine whether the Chinese immigrants who came to the United States in the 1800s actually established *hui kuan* societies, and whether 110,000 Japanese Americans had left their homes and were in federal camps by

August 7, 1942. It is important to stress that factual statements are capable of verification or testing because many statements presented as facts, especially in the area of ethnic studies, are upon closer scrutiny *normative* or *value* statements which cannot be scientifically tested or can only be tested with great difficulty.

"The Chinese immigrants who came to San Francisco in the 1800s established the eccentric *hui kuan*" is an example of a normative or value statement which both students and teachers may classify as a factual proposition. The addition of the word *eccentric* to this statement makes it a value proposition because eccentric is a normative term. Whether a person would judge the Chinese *hui kuan* society eccentric would depend upon his culture, biases, background, and familiarity with this type of Chinese association. Statements and concepts are scientific only when members of the scientific community can agree upon their meaning. Few statements have exactly the same meaning to any two individuals. However, an empirical statement must have the capacity to convey a similar meaning to all informed persons. It is incumbent upon teachers to help students distinguish between *scientific* facts and *normative* statements which purport to be facts, either implicitly or explicitly.

Another distinguishing characteristic of empirical factual statements is that they are quite limited in the data which they reveal, encompass, or contain, and are very limited in their ability to explain and predict behavior. In our example about Mexican Americans, we only learn the number of Mexican Americans who were in the United States in 1960. This statement does not reveal the regions in which they were concentrated, nor the social and economic conditions under which they lived. By merely mastering this statement, the student will not know *why* there were not more or fewer Mexican Americans in the United States in 1960. In our exemplary factual statement about European immigrants, we merely learn the number of Northern and Western Europeans who immigrated to the United States during a particular period, but nothing about why the number of Northern and Western European immigrants was considerably higher than the number of immigrants from Southern and Eastern Europe during this same period. Because factual statements are highly limited in explaining causal relationships, students need to master higher levels of knowledge in addition to facts.

The attributes of factual statements which we have delineated above suggest why they should not be the end goal of instruction, as is often the case in the social studies, language arts, and humanities school programs. Many teachers end instructional units by testing students primarily for their mastery of facts. Because facts, in and of themselves, do not encompass a large quantity of data, they have little transfer value, are quickly forgotten by students, and do not, if they are the end goal of instruction, help students to gain in-depth understanding of social phenomena.

However, to say that facts are limited in the contribution which they can make to students' understanding of social events and problems is not to say that they are not important and that they do not have a proper role in the instructional process. Quite the contrary. Factual statements are very important in the teaching act. If the teacher keeps their limitations in mind and uses them judiciously, they can contribute greatly to student learning. Facts are the foundations of the higher levels of knowledge: *concepts, generalizations,* and *theories.* Without learning facts, as we will later illustrate, students will not be able to master concepts and generalizations. However, the teacher is justified in teaching facts only if they are used to help students to develop and master concepts, generalizations, and theories. Thus, for every fact that the teacher selects for inclusion in the ethnic studies program, he or she should have a concept, generalization, or theory in mind which the fact is intended to help the students develop. Facts taught randomly and in isolation have little instructional value. However, they can become powerful instructional tools if used intelligently by the teacher.

Concepts

Concepts are words or phrases which enable us to categorize or classify a large class of observations and thus to reduce the complexity of our social environment. In structure and function, concepts differ from facts, generalizations, and theories. Both facts and generalizations are empirical *statements;* a theory consists of a system of interrelated generalizations. However, concepts are very special constructs because they are necessary for the formulation of the other categories of knowledge and are contained in all facts, generalizations, and theories. Because concepts are contained in all of the other forms of knowledge, a student cannot understand a fact, generalization, or theory unless the concepts contained within them are meaningful to him. In our factual statements illustrated above, these are among the concepts within them:

Blacks	evacuation camps
hui kuan	immigrants
West Coast	migrated
colonies	tribes
Mexican Americans	Europeans
Puerto Ricans	

Here are a list of concepts which relate to ethnic studies that are discussed in later chapters:

ethclass	economic exploitation
cultural assimilation	region
race	cultural diversity
sinophobia	slavery
structural assimilation	values
acculturation	

While concepts are contained in all facts, generalizations, and theories, they are unique because they can also encompass a large range of facts and generalizations, and a complete theory can be formulated about a single concept, such as discrimination. Some concepts are rather concrete, such as street; others are much more abstract, such as megalopolis. Some concepts are somewhere in between these two extremes. We might call these kinds of concepts *intermediate-level* concepts, such as city. Thus, if we arrange these concepts into a hierarchy, it would look like this:

megalopolis
city
street

In this example, megalopolis is the highest level concept because it consists of a region made up of several cities and their surrounding areas. City is the next level because a city contains many streets. Of course, there are parallel concepts which are more concrete than street.

Concepts encompassing generalizations are usually more abstract (or at a higher level) than concepts which are contained in the generalizations encompassed. Also, the concepts which are contained in facts are often less abstract than those which are used to classify those facts. The same is true for theories. In our example below, we illustrate how a higher-level concept, immigration, can be used to categorize a number of facts. The facts, of course, contain many concepts.

HIGHER-LEVEL CONCEPT: Immigration

Facts being categorized or grouped under concept:

1. After 1820, millions of Europeans came to the United States.
2. By 1860, there were 34,933 Chinese in the United States.
3. In 1900, 24,326 Japanese had arrived in the United States.
4. In 1932, 1,674 Mexicans came to the United States.

Higher-level concepts can also encompass or classify generalizations (see discussion below for definition of a generalization). In the example below, the concept, culture, is used to categorize a number of generalizations at varying levels of abstractions:

CONCEPT: Culture

Generalizations being categorized or grouped under concept:

1. An ethnic minority group usually acquires some of the values, behaviors, and beliefs of the dominant ethnic groups within a society.
2. Dominant ethnic groups usually attain some of the traits and artifacts of ethnic minority groups.
3. Afro-Americans have made a number of contributions to American music.
4. Indian institutions have influenced the development of American lifestyles.

We should comment more about the abstractness or levels of concepts. In many cases, some concepts are clearly at a higher level than others. For example, city is a higer-level concept than street because a city contains many streets. However, because a concept appears in a factual statement does not necessarily mean that it is a lower-level or concrete concept. Study this factual statement:

Over one thousand Mexican immigrants arrived in the United States in 1932.

This factual statement contains the higher-level concept, immigrant. As we illustrated above, the concept immigration* can be used to categorize a number of facts. The distinguishing characteristic of a higher-level concept is that it is able to categorize a number of facts and generalizations. This is true even though that same concept may sometime appear within factual statements. By identifying higher-level concepts in the social sciences, the teacher will be able to help students to relate discrete facts and data to form broad generalizations about ethnicity which they can apply when studying ethnic groups both within the United States and in other nations.

Generalizations

A generalization contains two or more concepts and states the relationship between them. Like empirical facts, generalizations are scientific statements which can be tested and verified with data. Generalizations are very useful tools in instruction because they can be used to summarize a large mass of facts and to show the relationship between higher-level concepts which students have mastered. Like concepts, generalizations vary greatly in their level of inclusiveness; there are low-level generalizations, which are little more than summary statements, and there are very high-level generalizations, which are universal in applicability. To illustrate levels of generalizations, we will study one of the facts listed earlier in this chapter and state generalizations at various levels which encompass it.

FACT: The Chinese immigrants who came to San Francisco in the 1800s established the *hui kuan.*

Lower-Level
Generalization: Chinese immigrants in America established various forms of social organizations.

Intermediate-Level
Generalization: All groups that have immigrated or migrated to the United States have established social organizations.

---

* *Both* immigrant *and* immigration *are derivatives of the concept* immigrate.

Highest-Level   In all human societies, forms of social or-
or Universal   ganizations emerge to satisfy the needs of
Generalization: individuals and groups.

A study of our examples will indicate that a generalization is a higher-level statement than a fact because a generalization encompasses a number of facts. The fact noted above tells us only that Chinese Americans established one kind of social organization, the *hui kuan.* The lower-level generalization in our example reveals that Chinese Americans established a variety of social organizations. Thus our lower-level generalization not only encompasses the fact about the *hui kuan,* but also the following facts:

1. Chinese immigrants in America formed organizations called clans.
2. The Chinese Benevolent Association is a confederation of clans and secret societies.
3. Secret societies emerged within Chinese communities in the United States.
4. The Chinese secret societies provided help to Chinese Americans and obtained control of gambling in Chinese American communities.

The next generalization in our example, called an *intermediate-level generalization,* not only encompasses facts about Chinese Americans, but about all immigrants and migrants in the United States. Thus this generalization is at a higher level of abstraction because it encompasses more facts than the lower-level generalization. For example, our intermediate-level generalization, in addition to encompassing the facts about Chinese-American organizations, also encompasses the following facts:

1. Puerto Rican Americans established the Puerto Rican Forum to help solve the problems of Puerto Rican migrants in New York City.
2. Jewish Americans founded the Anti-Defamation League of B'nai B'rith to help mitigate anti-Semitism in the United States.
3. In 1921, Spanish-speaking Americans formed the Orden Hijos de America [Order of the Sons of America] to train its members for American citizenship.

4. Japanese immigrants in America created the Japanese American Association to provide services for its members.

5. The National Urban League was founded in 1911 to help Black southern migrants adjust to city life.

The last generalization in our example is the highest form of generalization possible because it encompasses all of the other facts and generalizations above it, and it applies to all human societies in the past and present. Note that it does not contain a reference to any particular people, region, or culture. One way to determine whether a generalization is written at the highest possible level is to ascertain whether it is limited to a particular people, culture, or historical era. A generalization of wide applicability contains few or no exceptions and can be tested and verified, to varying degrees, within any human culture. The high-level generalization in our example states that in every past and present human society, one can find examples of social organizations. This generalization has been tested and verified by social scientists. Whether they studied a preliterate tribe in New Zealand or the cultures in Medieval Europe, social scientists have found that they have types of social organizations such as the family and some kind of kinship system. It is true that the forms these organizations take vary greatly both within and between cultures, but they nevertheless exist.

It is necessary for the teacher to be able to identify and write generalizations at various levels in order to plan and implement a sound ethnic studies program. During initial planning, the teacher should identify generalizations of the highest order so that he or she can then select content samples from a variety of cultures to enable students to *test* them. If the teacher starts his or her planning by identifying lower-level or intermediate-level generalizations, he or she will be greatly limited in the content that can be selected to exemplify the generalizations. For example, if a teacher identified this generalization as one upon which to organize instruction,

Chinese immigrants in America established various forms of social organization,

he or she would not be able to help students derive generalizations related to the organizations that other ethnic groups, such as White Anglo-Saxon Protestants, Mexican Americans, Puerto Rican Americans, and Afro-Americans have formed in America.

The teacher should begin his or her planning by identifying high-level concepts and generalizations (often called *key* or *organizing* generalizations in this book), and then select lower-level concepts and generalizations (often called *subconcepts* and *subgeneralizations* in this book) related to the *content samples* he or she has chosen. This type of planning is necessary in order to help students develop higher level statements—one of the ultimate goals of instruction. In Chapter 4, we discuss procedures the teacher can use to identify high-level concepts and generalizations that can form the core of a sound ethnic studies program.

We have noted that generalizations range from very concrete ones to those that are universal in application. We chose a fact related to a Chinese-American institution, the *hui kuan*, to illustrate how a single fact can be encompassed by generalizations at three different levels. The choice of three levels was an arbitrary decision; we could have easily written generalizations at fewer or more levels. For example, Hilda Taba has identified four levels (or orders, as she calls them) of generalizations.[5] Since generalizations exist at many different levels, it is not necessary for the teacher to spend undue time trying to devise elaborate schemes for classifying levels of generalizations.

However, in order to plan effective units and lessons, the teacher should know that generalizations exist at many different levels, that all generalizations are at a higher level than facts, and that the highest-order or -level generalization should be identified during the initial stages of unit planning.

Generalizations have other distinguishing characteristics that merit discussion. When we first introduced the construct, generalization, we noted that it contains two or more concepts and shows how they are related. Generalizations may contain a number of concepts, but usually a relationship is stated between two major ones, which can be identified as the *independent concept* (or variable) and the *dependent concept* (or variable). The independent concept acts upon or influences the dependent concept. This generalization, "In all human societies, some

5. James A. Banks, with Ambrose A. Clegg, Jr., *Teaching Strategies for the Social Studies: Inquiry, Valuing and Decision-Making* (Reading, Mass.: Addison-Wesley, 1973), pp. 95–96.

forms of social organizations emerge to satisfy the needs of individuals and groups," contains a number of concepts, including human socities, forms, social organizations, needs, and groups. However, the statement contains two major concepts. They are human societies and social organizations. The independent concept is human societies and the dependent concept (or variable) is social organizations. We can think of the generalization this way: "Wherever there is a human society, there is some kind of social organization." Thus human societies "cause" or "create" social organizations.

Another characteristic of scientific generalizations is that they can be stated as an "if-then" proposition. This does not mean that generalizations are necessarily written in this form, but that they can be stated as "if-then" statements. Our example above can be stated this way: "*If* there are human societies, *then* there are social organizations." If we think of a generalization as an "if-then" proposition, and *A* and *B* as the two major concepts or variables, then we can say that a generalization takes the form, "If *A*, then *B*."

Earlier we said that a generalization is a statement capable of being tested or verified. While this is true, because the social sciences are so new and because human behavior is so complex, generalizations in the behavioral sciences are always *tentative* statements and can never be proven 100 percent correct. Almost always, social science generalizations will have some exceptions. Because social science generalizations tend to be tentative and nonconclusive, they often have qualifying statements.

Study this generalization: When an ethnic minority group is oppressed, and it sees no legitimate ways to alleviate its problems, rebellions will sometimes occur. The word *sometimes* qualifies this generalization because in many situations an ethnic minority group may feel oppressed and see no legitimate ways to alleviate its problems, yet ethnic rebellions may not occur. Japanese Americans, when they were forced to leave their homes during World War II and were sent to concentration camps, did not resist or rebel as a group, although some individuals did resist internment. One social scientist has hypothesized that most Japanese Americans cooperated with the federal government during this colossal human tragedy because of the norms within their culture toward authority and because they did not believe that resistance would succeed.[6] On the other hand, many Afro-Americans who felt oppressed in our cities in the late 1960s violently rebelled. The particular times, the culture of a group, and the group's perceptions of its social and economic status profoundly influence how it will respond to an oppressive situation. We use this example merely to illustrate that students should be taught how tentative social science conclusions and generalizations are and should learn that social knowledge is constantly changing and is never absolute. This point is exceedingly important.

Like facts, many generalizations purporting to be scientific statements are actually normative statements or value propositions. Teachers and students should be keenly aware of these kinds of statements in all subject areas, but they are especially abundant in ethnic studies because much of the writing in this area is highly emotional and nonscientific. Such statements as "The Indians were defeated by European immigrants because their cultures were inferior" and "Prostitution became widespread in Chinese ghettos because of their immorality" are the types of statements teachers and students will find in books which are presented as empirical generalizations. These statements are normative because they involve *subjective judgments* by their authors. Whether an individual would judge Indian cultures in 1492 "inferior" would depend upon what aspects of a culture he valued. For example, while the cultures of the Europeans were more technologically advanced than the cultures of most Native Americans, some Native American writers argue that Native American cultures were superior because of the value they attached to the land and to the democratic process in making societal decisions.[7] Both claims are obviously value judgments.

The statement about prostitution in early Chinese-American communities is also a value proposition because "immorality" can only be defined subjectively and according to one's cultural

6. Harry H. L. Kitano, *Japanese Americans: The Evolution of a Subculture* (Englewood Cliffs, N. J.: Prentice-Hall, 1969), pp. 31–42.

7. See, for example, Jack D. Forbes, "Teaching Native American Values and Cultures," in James A. Banks, ed., *Teaching Ethnic Studies: Concepts and Strategies* (Washington, D. C.: National Council for the Social Studies 43rd Yearbook, 1973), pp. 201–225.

biases. Prostitution emerged within Chinese-American communities because most of the immigrants were males who left their wives in China. They were usually unable to socialize with White females. Whether they were immoral because they sought the most available outlet for their sex drives involves a value judgment of major proportions. One could argue that prostitution emerged within the Chinese community to satisfy a universal biological need of man.

As we noted when discussing empirical facts, an empirical statement must, as least potentially, have a similar meaning to informed individuals. Our discussion should not be interpreted to mean that normative generalizations should not be written or that they should not be analyzed by students. Quite the contrary is true, as we will indicate when we discuss *value inquiry*. However, empirical rather than normative generalizations should be used to organize ethnic studies curricula. When value statements are encountered by students and teachers, they should be treated as such and should not be confused with scientific generalizations. They have a different structure and function. The failure to distinguish between them or to treat them the same can result in gross misunderstandings by students.

Womack has made a useful summary of high-level generalizations:

1. Generalizations are derived from social studies content, but they are not content themselves. They not only have content as their source, but their substantiation and proof for being generalizations also come from content.
2. Generalizations have universal application and admit no major exceptions.
3. Generalizations contain no specific references to any particular peoples, places, or times.
4. Generalizations have a thesis; that is, they make a point about the subject of the sentence.
5. Generalizations, as principles or rules, comprise the underlying structure for each social science discipline.
6. Generalizations are best discovered by inductive reasoning.
7. Generalizations are abstractions which can be broken down into gradations of complexity and completeness

so that they can be understood and mastered, to some extent, even by primary grades students.

8. Definitions and concepts are not themselves generalizations, but may be incorporated into a generalization.[8]

Generalizations are very important in instruction because they enable students to make predictions; the predictive capacity of generalizations varies directly with their degree of applicability and amount of empirical support. Generalizations which describe a large class of behavior and which have been widely verified are the most useful for making predictions. We have called these types of generalizations *high-level* or *organizing* generalizations. Generalizations not only enable students to predict behavior with a fairly high degree of accuracy but to solve problems in novel situations.

Theory

Theory is the highest form of knowledge and is the most useful for predicting human behavior. We stated that a *concept* was a word or phrase that was used to categorize or classify facts, data, and other forms of information and knowledge. We defined a *generalization* as a statement showing the relationship between two or more concepts that could be empirically verified. We are reviewing the definitions of these terms because a theory consists of a number of related generalizations. The generalizations within a theory constitute a deductive system and are logically interrelated. The generalizations contained within a theory are also *high-level* and *universal-type* generalizations; they are not low-level ones. A theory is called a *deductive* system because when several generalizations within a theory are stated, the concluding ones can be logically derived. In other words, when given some propositions within a theory, a conclusion can be derived from the stated generalizations. Below we present an example of a theory and illustrate how this process can work in a theoretical system.

8. James G. Womack, *Discovering the Structure of Social Studies* (New York: Benziger Brothers, 1966), p. 2. Reprinted with the publisher's permission.

Elsewhere I have summarized the characteristics of an empirical theory as follows:

1. A theory consists of a set of interrelated lawlike propositions or generalizations that are testable.
2. The propositions must show the relationship between variables or concepts that are clearly defined.
3. The propositions must constitute a deductive system and be logically consistent; unknown principles must be derivable from known ones.
4. The propositions must be a source of testable hypotheses.[9]

Gordon's theory of cultural and structural assimilation has heavily influenced the field of ethnic studies. Here are the major generalizations within this theory:

1. With regard to *cultural behavior,* differences of social class are more important and decisive than differences of ethnic group.
2. With regard to *social participation* in primary groups and primary relationships, people tend to confine these to their own social class segment within their own ethnic group—that is, the *ethclass.*
3. With a person of the same social class but of a different ethnic group, one shares behavioral similarities but not a sense of peoplehood.
4. With those of the same ethnic group but of a different social class, one shares a sense of *peoplehood* but not behavioral similarities [emphasis added].[10]

Gordon's theory satisfies our criteria of a theory: a system of high-level interrelated generalizations that constitute a deductive system. In the first generalization in the theory, Gordon hypothesizes that, in terms of cultural behavior, social class is more important than ethnicity. By cultural behavior, he means the values which a person holds, his or her speech patterns, occupational aspirations, clothing, and foods.

This generalization suggests that an upper-class Black indi-

9. Banks (with Clegg), *Teaching Strategies,* p. 106.

10. Milton M. Gordon, *Assimilation in American Life* (New York: Oxford University Press, 1964), pp. 52–53.

vidual's clothing, values, and foods are likely to be more similar to those of an upper-class White than those of a lower-class Black. The second generalization in the theory suggests that an upper-class Mexican-American individual, while he or she shares cultural characteristics with White Anglo-Saxons, is more likely to participate in the private clubs and cliques of other upper-class Mexican Americans than he or she is to participate in White Anglo-Saxon private clubs and social cliques. The theory hypothesizes that while upper-status individuals within different ethnic groups share similar values and behavior, their close, primary group relationships are highly confined to members within their ethnic group of the same social class. This is also true for lower-class members of ethnic groups. Gordon presents much compelling evidence in his book to support the generalizations that make up his theory.

Gordon's theory meets the criteria of a theory because when given generalizations 1 and 2 above, one can logically derive generalizations 3 and 4. To do so, however, it might be necessary to know how he defines two key concepts in his generalizations: ethclass and sense of peoplehood. He defines *ethclass* as the "subsociety created by the intersection of the vertical stratifications of ethnicity with the horizontal stratifications of social class."[11] Thus lower-middle-class Puerto Rican American is an example of ethclass. By *sense of peoplehood,* Gordon means an individual's identification with a group that shares a common culture, religious beliefs, and values.[12] He contends, for example, that Blacks in all social classes have some sense of ethnic identification. This assumption, however, can be challenged.

To help students to fully understand the ethnic experience in America, the teacher should, whenever possible, help them to relate generalizations to a theoretical system. Generalizations have much more meaning when they are studied within a theoretical framework than when studied in isolation. However, since theories, especially complete and verified ones, are not abundant in the social sciences (because these disciplines are so new), the teacher often will not be able to help students to relate generalizations to theories. This book deals primarily with teaching key concepts and generalizations.

11. Ibid., p. 51.

12. Ibid., p. 23.

Earlier, when we discussed the distinguishing attributes of concepts, we noted that concepts could be very concrete, highly abstract, or somewhere in between these two extremes. We also noted that while concepts are contained *within* the generalizations that constitute theories, because of their specialized structure and function, a complete theory could be structured around a single concept. Gordon's theory of cultural and structural assimilation is an example of a theory formed around the concept of assimilation. Cultural assimilation occurs when one ethnic group attains the values and behavior patterns of another ethnic group (usually the ethnic minority group attains the cultural characteristics of the dominant ethnic groups), and structural assimilation occurs when one ethnic group participates in the primary groups, such as private clubs and social cliques, of another ethnic group.[13] Gordon concludes that while widespread cultural assimilation has taken place in American society, little structural assimilation has occurred because ethnic groups within our society, including dominant ethnic groups and ethnic minority groups, participate mainly in the primary groups of their own ethnic communities. He maintains that our society has a high degree of cultural assimilation, but that it may be said to possess *structural pluralism*.[14]

Making Decisions on Social and Ethnic Issues

We have discussed the four categories of knowledge: facts, concepts, generalizations, and theories—at considerable length because students must be able to use the scientific method to derive higher-level generalizations and theories to make reflective decisions, since these forms of knowledge will enable them to make the most accurate predictions possible. The most predictive generalizations and theories are those related to the structures of the social science disciplines. The structure of a discipline consists of its key (or organizing) concepts, generalizations, and theories, unique modes of inquiry, and the central questions it asks. The identification of the structures of the disciplines enables the decision-maker to use the most powerful generalizations which constitute the behavioral sciences and which

13. Ibid., pp. 19–59.

14. Ibid.

can make the greatest contribution to the resolution of personal and social problems and can facilitate the influencing of public policy. In the next chapter, we discuss the structures of the various behavioral sciences and illustrate ways in which the teacher can identify key concepts and generalizations from the social science disciplines in order to structure a sound program in ethnic studies. Chapter 4 discusses the other essential components of a decision-making-focused ethnic studies program: valuing, decision-making, and social action. The contributions that the humanities can make to the development of students' decision-making skills are illustrated in the teaching strategies in Part II.

Questions and Activities

1. Label each of the following a *fact, concept,* or *generalization* and justify each label:
   a) Acculturation. _____
   b) In every human society there is a conflict between unlimited wants and limited resources. _____
   c) Assimilation. _____
   d) In 1827 Vincente Guerrero became president of Mexico. _____
   e) Ethnic cultures, values, and behavior are undergoing constant change. _____
   f) On September 22, 1862, President Lincoln issued a statement that has been called the Preliminary Emancipation Proclamation. _____
   g) In 1960, 28,108 Puerto Ricans lived in the state of California. _____
   h) In recent years, ethnic minority groups have strived less for cultural assimilation and more for cultural pluralism. _____
   i) Cultural pluralism. _____
   j) Ethnic group. _____
2. Here is a higher-level generalization: Most foreigners who voluntarily immigrated to the United States were seeking better economic, political, and social opportunities. Examine several of the books on ethnic groups contained in the

bibliography in Chapter 1 and write several factual statements and lower-level generalizations which this generalization will encompass.

3. Examine several of the books in the bibliography in Chapter 1 and find a number of factual statements and generalizations which these concepts will encompass: resistance to oppression, region, cultural assimilation, structural assimilation.

4. Rewrite the following generalizations as "if-then" statements:

   a) Great diversity exists both within and between various ethnic minority groups.

   b) Color distinctions and evaluations perpetuated by the larger society often exist in ethnic minority communities.

5. Tell whether each of these statements is normative or empirical and why:

   a) The American colonists should not have taken land away from the Native American Indians.

   b) Irresponsible Blacks rioted in many American cities in the 1960s.

   c) Many Mexican immigrants entered the United States illegally.

   d) Japanese Americans should not have been sent to relocation camps in 1942.

   e) Many Puerto Ricans migrate to the United States mainland each year.

   f) Many Chinese Americans live in ghettos in American cities.

6. What do you think should be the role of the following categories of knowledge in a sound ethnic studies program and why?

   a) Facts

   b) Concepts

   c) Generalizations

   d) Theories

7. Examine several books dealing with ethnic minority groups (many such books are listed in the annotated bibliographies found in various chapters of this book) and identify a theory related to ethnic groups. Can this theory be taught to a group of elementary or high school students? Why or

why not? If you think that it can be taught to a group of students, develop a plan for teaching it. If you are a classroom teacher or a student teacher, implement your teaching plan and evaluate its effectiveness.

8. Make a list of your close friends. Note their ethnic, religious, and racial backgrounds. Compare your list with similar lists made by other individuals in your class or workshop. What conclusions can you make about structural assimilation in American society on the basis of the responses made by you and your classmates or fellow workshop participants?

9. If your parents are first or second generation American immigrants, make a list of their values and lifestyles that are different from your own. If your parents are not first or second generation immigrants, interview individuals whose parents are and compare their values and lifestyles with those of their parents. What tentative generalizations can you make about cultural assimilation in American society by studying this data?

10. Define each of the following terms and tell why each is important:

knowledge	ethclass
reflective decision	cultural assimilation
fact	structural assimilation
concept	intermediate level generalization
generalization	high-level generalization
theory	high-level concept
normative statement	low-level concept
empirical statement	

Annotated Bibliography

Banks, James A., with Ambrose A. Clegg, Jr. *Teaching Strategies for the Social Studies: Inquiry, Valuing, and Decision-Making.* Reading, Mass. Addison-Wesley, 1973.

Chapter 3 of this book is a detailed discussion, with illustrations, of the nature and teaching of facts, concepts, generalizations, and theories.

Hunkins, Francis P. *Questioning Strategies and Techniques.* Boston: Allyn and Bacon, 1972.

This useful book discusses and illustrates ways in which questioning techniques can be used to help students master higher levels of knowledge.

Hunt, Maurice P. and Lawrence E. Metcalf. *Teaching High School Social Studies.* 2nd ed. New York: Harper and Row, 1968.

Two chapters in this reflective and perceptive book are "How To Teach A Concept" and "Teaching Generalizations."

Martorella, Peter H. *Concept Learning in the Social Studies: Models for Structuring Curriculum.* Scranton, Penn.: Intex Educational Publishers, 1971.

A sophisticated and somewhat technical treatment of the role of concepts in social studies instruction.

Morrissett, Irving, ed. *Concepts and Structure in the New Social Studies Curricula.* New York: Holt, 1967.

A group of eminent social scientists and educators discuss the roles of concepts and generalizations in social studies teaching.

Taba, Hilda et al. *A Teacher's Handbook to Elementary Social Studies: An Inductive Approach.* 2nd ed. Reading, Mass.: Addison-Wesley, 1971.

This perceptive book is must reading for the teacher interested in conceptual approaches to instruction.

Tanck, Marlin L. "Teaching Concepts, Generalizations and Constructs." In Dorothy McClure Fraser, ed., *Social Studies Curriculum Development: Prospects and Problems.* Washington, D. C.: National Council for the Social Studies 39th Yearbook, 1969, pp. 99–138.

A useful and helpful discussion of the various categories of knowledge.

Womack, James G. *Discovering the Structure of Social Studies.* New York: Benziger Brothers, 1966.

Womack's discussion of the nature of generalizations and their application in the classroom is lucid and practical.

Key Concepts for Ethnic Studies

Ethnic Studies: A Conceptual Approach

Ethnic studies programs should help students to master higher levels of knowledge so that they can understand ethnicity in America and develop the skills and abilities needed to make effective personal and public decisions. Factual knowledge is necessary for the mastery of higher levels of knowledge, but it is insufficient for the development of decision-making skills. A decision-making-focused ethnic studies program stresses higher-level concepts and generalizations and uses facts only to develop these forms of knowledge. A curriculum that focuses on higher-level concepts and generalizations is called a *conceptual* curriculum. A decision-making curriculum is not only characterized by the sequential development of higher-level ideas, it is also *interdisciplinary*. It helps students to view ethnic problems from the perspectives of several disciplines such as anthropology, political science, sociology, and geography.

The Need for an Interdisciplinary Perspective

It is necessary for students to learn to view ethnic events from the perspectives of several disciplines because any one discipline gives them only a partial understanding of intergroup and intragroup problems. Let us suppose that an individual attempts to understand why race riots occurred in many American cities in the 1960s. He tries to understand why the riots took place by using key ideas and questions only from political science. In studying the causes of the riots from the perspective of political science, he uses key political science concepts such as power, legitimacy, and authority to determine what questions to ask about riots. His answers, of course, will be directly related to the questions which he poses. He might conclude that Blacks rioted because they were powerless, felt that those in power did not have legitimate power, and believed that policymakers used their authority ruthlessly.

While these conclusions may partially reveal why urban riots took place in the 1960s, they do not completely explain their emergence. There were also economic, social, and regional factors involved in these rebellions. Our hypothetical inquirer would need to use key concepts and questions from economics, sociology, and geography, respectively, to derive these explanations. Figure 3.1 summarizes why an ethnic problem must be viewed from an interdisciplinary perspective to be fully understood.

The Structures of the Disciplines

To be able to identify the key concepts and generalizations needed to plan and organize an interdisciplinary conceptual ethnic studies curriculum, the teacher must be familiar with the nature of each discipline. The structure of a discipline consists of its (1) key concepts, generalizations, and theories, (2) unique modes of inquiry, and (3) the key questions asked. In the race riot example above, we illustrated how each of the social sciences views human behavior from a different perspective and thus explains the causes of events in different ways.

When the teacher or curriculum committee designs an ethnic studies program, he (or they) should make sure that it includes key concepts and generalizations from each of the major disciplines. Otherwise, students will gain, at best, a partial understanding of ethnicity in America. The key concepts and generalizations identified should have the characteristics discussed in Chapter 4. We will now outline some of the major characteristics of each of the social science disciplines, and discuss selected key concepts that can greatly contribute to an effective ethnic

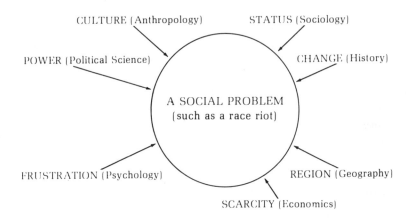

FIGURE 3.1 This figure illustrates how a social problem such as a race riot can be sufficiently understood and therefore reflectively acted upon only after the social actor has viewed it with concepts and generalizations from a number of social science disciplines. Any one discipline gives only a partial understanding of a social problem or issue. Thus ethnic studies programs must be interdisciplinary.

studies program. Each discipline contains key concepts and generalizations, and asks questions, that are essential for understanding American ethnic groups.

ANTHROPOLOGY

Anthrolopology is a diverse discipline consisting of many subfields such as physical, social, and cultural anthropology. However, *cultural anthropology* can offer most to a comparative ethnic studies program. The key concept in cultural anthropology is culture. Although anthropologists have advanced many different definitions of culture, most agree that it consists of the behavior patterns, values, beliefs, symbols, and other people-made elements structured to solve the problems of survival.

Culture is a very powerful and useful concept that is invaluable in ethnic studies. Students should learn, for example, that while all American ethnic groups share elements of a common culture, each group possesses unique cultural characteristics. The Chinese New Year, Rosh Hashanah (Jewish), and St. Patrick's Day (Irish) illustrate the range of ethnic holidays celebrated in the United States. Ethnic foods, dialects, and most importantly, values, also exist within our society. Culture, if studied from a nonethnocentric point of view, can help students understand why these cultural elements emerged and still exist, and develop a respect for cultural differences.

Almost all of the concepts in cultural anthropology are related to, or are subconcepts of, culture. Below are selected key (organizing) anthropological concepts that can contribute greatly to students' understandings of the diverse ethnic groups in America, and the problems that exist within and between groups.

Culture Diversity

Students should learn that there are many different culture elements in our society, and that these differences are not likely to vanish. Events cause them to emerge in each new generation. This concept is the antithesis of melting pot. When studying about cultural differences in the United States, students should be helped to understand that while we have not experienced a true melting pot, most ethnic groups have acquired many culture traits of the dominant ethnic group: White Anglo-Saxon Protestants.

Ethnic individuals, however, tend to be *bicultural;* i.e., they usually acquire culture traits of the dominant group but also retain many of their ethnic characteristics. While the more upward mobile members of ethnic groups tend to be less "ethnic" than lower-class members, this generalization is nevertheless valid. A highly acculturated Sansei,* for example, will often marry a Japanese, eat Japanese foods, and belong to Japanese social organizations. Many ethnic youths attend the public schools during the day and a language or ethnic school after regular school hours or on the weekend. Most Afro-Americans who obtain college degrees speak "standard" English on their

---

*Sansei *refers to a third generation Japanese American. While our claim above is valid, recent evidence indicates that the rate of outmarriages among Japanese Americans has increased substantially in recent years. In 1924, 2 percent of the Japanese Americans residing in Los Angeles County married outside of their ethnic group. In 1972, 49 percent of them married outside of their ethnic group. See Akemi Kikumura and Harry H. L. Kitano, "Interracial Marriage: A Picture of the Japanese Americans,"* The Journal of Social Issues, 29 (No. 2, 1973), p. 69.

jobs and in other settings where it is appropriate to conform to the dominant society's norm. However, when socializing with less assimilated relatives and friends, they often use many words and phrases that linguists call "Black English." Upward mobile Mexican Americans will eat "Anglo-Saxon steak" at fancy Anglo restaurants with their Anglo friends, but they often drive to Spanish-speaking neighborhoods to eat foods such as enchiladas and chiles rellenos, which have a much more spicy taste than "bland" Anglo steak.

In other words, American ethnic groups acquire those dominant cultural traits necessary for them to survive in the wider society, but retain many of the elements of their ethnic culture. The more upward mobile an individual is, the more likely he is to acquire cultural traits of the dominant group. The acquisition of Anglo-Saxon speech, behavior, and values is necessary for upward mobility in the United States because Anglo-Saxons are the dominant ethnic group and control entry to most social, economic, and political institutions.

When studying about cultural differences, students should learn that cultural differences exist within as well as between various ethnic groups. Too many Americans think of ethnic groups as monolith, and find it difficult to understand why conflict exists within ethnic groups. It is exceedingly important for students to study about the differences which exist within ethnic groups. When many members of dominant groups are introduced to an Afro-American or an Asian American, certain stereotypic images immediately come to their minds. They often assume that all Afro-Americans know something about the Black ghetto because of their personal experiences, and can tell them how the Black "community" feels about busing, interracial marriage, and the "riot" which occurred last week. Many people assume that all Asian-Americans are Stoic, shy, and have a high scientific aptitude.

It is true, as stated in Chapter 1, that we can associate certain general characteristics with the various American ethnic groups. However, within these groups, individuals embrace these characteristics to varying degrees. Some *deliberately* attempt to reject them. When we meet an individual and only know that he or she is a Mexican American, and nothing else, there are but a few conclusive statements we can accurately make about him or her.

Mexican Americans, like Asian Americans and Afro-Americans, are a highly diverse group. Some Mexican Americans identify strongly with this group's liberation movement and wish to be called Chicanos. Others, especially those in the upper classes, tend to identify more strongly with their Spanish heritage and consider the word *Chicano* pejorative and insulting. Such individuals are much more likely to prefer the term *Latin American* or *Spanish American* and to reject their Indian heritage. Some Mexican Americans will tell you that they are Spanish, even though their biological traits may be identical to others who call themselves Chicanos or Mexican Americans.

I have heard some Black Americans say that they have never seen a ghetto and they wonder what they are like. One Seattle Black lady told me that she was going to visit some friends in New York City and that she was very excited because they were going to take her to a "Black ghetto." You can imagine how insulted this person would be if a White asked her what life is like in the Black ghetto. Whether this lady lived in a region which some Whites might label a *ghetto* is irrelevant here. The point is, she saw herself as separate and apart from ghetto Blacks and thus shared little "sense of peoplehood" with them. She apparently had grown up in a West Coast neighborhood that was predominantly non-Black.

The gross differences that exist within various ethnic groups often make it exceedingly difficult for an ethnically illiterate person to understand why many Japanese Americans are anti-Chinese, why the Nisei* often express disappointment about the values and lifestyles of the Sansei, or why some upward mobile Mexican Americans disdain Mexican migrant workers. Intragroup differences and conflict exist within dominant ethnic groups as well as within minority groups. However, Americans tend to understand why a German-American corporation president might disdain a German-American dishwasher. The Afro-American, however, who openly wonders about what life is like in the Black inner-city may be considered a freak by many White Americans.

Cultural Assimilation

When a member of an ethnic minority group acquires the behavior patterns, lifestyles, values, and language of the domi-

---

* Nisei *refers to a second generation Japanese American.*

nant ethnic group we say that he or she has become culturally assimilated. *Cultural assimilation* is the process by which an individual or group acquires the culture traits of a different ethnic group. Since the dominant group controls most of the social, economic, and political institutions in a society, members of ethnic minority groups must acquire its cultural traits to move up the social and economic ladder. When studying this concept, it is very important for students to learn that although non-White ethnic minorities may become totally assimilated culturally (i.e., in cultural characteristics they may become indistinguishable from White Anglo-Saxon Protestants), they will still be victims of discrimination and racism because of their different physical characteristics.

A widespread myth is that Mexican Americans and Afro-Americans experience discrimination because they often have meager educations and live in ghettos and barrios. While it is true that many Blacks and Mexican Americans are members of the lower socioeconomic classes, and that all lower-class individuals are treated differently from middle- and upper-class persons, it is also true that Blacks and Chicanos with high educations and incomes frequently experience discrimination *because of their color*. Since American racism is based largely on skin color, no degree of cultural assimilation eliminates it.

Some discussion of forced assimilation and cultural genocide should take place when students study cultural assimilation. Assimilation often occurs when a minority group "voluntarily" acquires the behavior patterns and lifestyles of the dominant group to attain social mobility and occupational success. We use the word *voluntarily* here somewhat reluctantly because without some degree of cultural assimilation a group that is very different culturally may not be able to survive in a particular culture. However, in the history of the United States, some forms of cultural assimilation which took place were totally nonvoluntarily and might be called *forced assimilation* because the cultures of certain groups were deliberately destroyed (*cultural genocide*). These groups were forced to acquire the language, lifestyles, and values of the dominant culture.

Individuals and groups who refused to accept the dominant culture were sometimes the victims of severe punishments such as death. The cultures of African groups were deliberately destroyed by the slave masters. This cultural destruction began on the slave ships. It seems that systematic and deliberate attempts were made to destroy the cultures of Native Americans. These efforts were highly successful since many of the cultural elements of these groups now exist only in the pages of history, and sometimes not even there since they were often destroyed before they could be recorded. Forced assimilation and cultural extinction (genocide) must be dealt with candidly in an honest ethnic studies program.

Acculturation

When a White Anglo-Saxon Protestant eats chow mein and a Chinese American goes to see a Shakespearean play, we say that *acculturation* is taking place because two different ethnic groups are exchanging cultural elements and complexes. Although the exchange of cultural traits is widespread within our society, we often think of the cultural traits that ethnic minorities acquire from dominant ethnic groups, but we hear too little about the cultural traits that dominant groups have acquired from ethnic minorities. Since this is the case, the teacher should stress the ethnic minority cultural traits that have been acquired by dominant groups.

Students should study about the contributions Blacks have made to American music, especially their spirituals, blues, and jazz. American culture traits of Indian origin are rarely mentioned in schoolbooks. As Vogel has noted, "As Rome hid its debt to the Estruscans, we have obscured our inheritance from the red men. Anthropologists know that acculturation proceeds in both directions when two societies are in any kind of contact, and that even a conquered people helps to shape the destiny of their overlords."[1] Indian contributions to American culture include the selection of sites for many American cities, dress styles, tobacco, foods, and values related to the veneration and preservation of the earth.

When teaching about acculturation and the contributions ethnic groups have made to American life, the teacher should avoid the "Who's the Greatest Approach?" All American ethnic

1. Virgil J. Vogel, "The Indian in American History," reprinted in James A. Banks & William W. Joyce, eds., *Teaching Social Studies to Culturally Different Children* (Reading, Mass.: Addison-Wesley, 1971), p. 161.

groups, including White ethnics, have made invaluable contributions to American life.   Thus it is not necessary to minimize the
contributions of one group in order to teach those of another.
It is intellectually counterproductive to ask "Which ethnic group
has made the greatest contributions to American life?"   To answer that question, we would have to agree upon criteria for
making such a judgment.   Since criteria always reflect values, our
answers would be highly conflicting and value laden.

The point the teacher should try to convey to the students
is that all American ethnic groups, including the non-White
ethnics, have contributed material (such as foods and fashions)
elements as well as nonmaterial traits (such as values and norms)
to American culture.   Students can use a *data retrieval chart* to
record examples of contributions that various groups have made
to American life, as illustrated in Figure 3.2.   These categories
are not all inclusive and others might be added; also, they are not
mutually exclusive.   However, this type of chart is a convenient
tool for studying cultural contributions.

Ethnocentrism

Most ethnic groups within a society tend to think that their
culture is superior to the culture of other groups.   This is especially true of the most powerful and dominant groups.   In our
society, White Anglo-Saxon Protestants are the dominant ethnic
group.   Many White Americans not only feel that their culture is
superior to the cultures of other groups, but define "culture" as
those aspects of *their* culture which they value highly such as
classical music and paintings by the European masters.

Civilization is another very ethnocentric term.   Americans
tend to think that cultures are civilized only when they have
social and technological characteristics that are identical or
highly similar to their own.   However, civilization can best be
defined as the total culture of a people or nation.

Students must understand *ethnocentrism* to fully comprehend the complex dimensions of American racism and the separatist movements which have emerged within ethnic minority
groups.   Although many minority persons, because of their socialization, tend to have low self-concepts and to value the dominant
culture over their own, we have seen an escalation of ethnocentrism among minorities in recent years.   Many Afro-Americans,
Mexican Americans, and Asian Americans are now extolling the

Ethnic Contributions to American Culture (Data Retrieval Chart)

Contributions	American Indians	Mexican Americans	Afro- Americans	European Americans	Asian Americans	Puerto Rican Americans
Technological						
Social						
Economic						
Political						
Cultural						
Historical						

FIGURE 3.2

virtues of their cultures and are demanding *separatism* and independent institutions. It may be that some degree of ethnocentricism is necessary for a group to attain cohesion and a strong identity, and that separatism is, as Sizemore had suggested, a necessary step toward inclusion within the larger society.[2] However, a question the teacher can raise with his or her students is: How much cultural and political separatism can a society experience and yet remain a cohesive and functional unit? If this question is raised, several related ones should also be posed: If a society needs some common goals in order to survive, what groups within it should determine those goals? How might we change our society so that each ethnic group can influence policy that shapes common societal goals? At present, dominant groups determine both societal goals and the means to attain them. However, ethnic groups have made it clear in recent years that they will not accept this kind of power arrangement without protest and conflict. These kinds of questions and problems, related to ethnocentrism, should constitute a vital part of ethnic studies.

Other Anthropological Concepts

Cultural diversity, cultural assimilation, acculturation, and ethnocentrism can greatly contribute to students' understandings of ethnic problems and issues, as we have illustrated above. However, this list of concepts by no means includes all of the key anthropological ideas that can play a significant role in a sound ethnic studies program. Race, racial mixture, subculture, syncretism (the synthesis of cultural traits), and melting pot are other anthropological concepts that should, at some point, be studied in a comparative ethnic studies curriculum. We discussed the importance of teaching about *race* in Chapter 1. We emphasized that students should become aware of its social significance because the biological basis of race does not have much meaning in society.

ECONOMICS

Economics is the study of the production of goods and services. The key concept in the discipline is scarcity. This con-

2. Barbara A. Sizemore, "Is There A Case for Separate Schools?" *Phi Delta Kappan* 53 (January 1972), pp. 281–84.

cept conveys the idea that while people have unlimited wants, there are limited resources with which they can satisfy them. In every human society, people have unlimited wants and limited resources. Because of scarcity, each society must solve three related economic problems: What goods and services shall be produced? How shall they be produced? For whom shall they be produced? Each society must also determine who shall produce what goods and services, what rewards will be distributed for their production, and what rewards will go to whom.

Who solves these economic problems for a society is political because those who make up the dominant powerful group (the power elite) determine what goods and services are produced, who will produce them, and for whom they will be produced.[3] They also determine the rewards that will be given for the production of various goods and services and how these rewards will be distributed. The reward structure of a nation's economy is highly related to other aspects of its social system. Thus those who get the greatest share of the economic rewards also have the widest opportunities to participate in the social system and to attain more social mobility. Individuals and groups who get the least economic rewards can only participate in the social system to a limited extent. Thus an individual's or group's economic situation is highly related to his or her social status.

Most ethnic minority groups belong to the lower socioeconomic classes. Economic concepts, especially the concept of scarcity, is necessary to help students understand why ethnic minorities are concentrated in society's lower strata. White Anglo-Saxon Protestants control most of the production industries in the United States. Jobs having the highest economic and social rewards are given to people who are similar to themselves in values, skin color, and lifestyles. The least desirable jobs, those with the lowest economic and social rewards, are reserved for groups which the dominant ethnic group defines as "undesirable" and "nonhuman." These groups are *least* like the powerful group in culture and physical characteristics. In the United States, Blacks, Chicanos, Puerto Rican Americans, and Native Americans constitute the bulk of this group. They work primarily in ser-

3. C. Wright Mills, *The Power Elite* (New York: Oxford University Press, 1956), pp. 4, 9.

vice occupations such as domestic work, restaurants, hotels, farming, and factories. While these groups are assigned jobs primarily in low-paying, laboring occupations, White Anglo-Saxon male Protestants with money own most of the production industries and are the corporation presidents and major economic decisionmakers.[4] These jobs have lucrative economic rewards and high social status.

The groups in our society doing the most arduous work receive the least economic and social rewards. This is a very deliberate policy created and maintained by the dominant group in America because such a delineation of work roles is necessary for them to maintain power and affluence. Concepts related to scarcity that students might study in ethnic studies are discussed below.

Production and Consumption

The creation of goods and services is called *production*. We refer to the use of these goods and services as *consumption*. Students can use these two concepts in ethnic studies to determine the extent to which ethnic minorities own the means of production producing most of the goods and services they consume. When studying these concepts, they can also discuss the extent to which ethnic minorities determine what goods and services are produced and the role they play in determining their distribution.

A study of data on the American economy will reveal that while ethnic minorities consume millions of dollars worth of goods and services each year, they actually own few production industries. Most ethnic businessmen own small service businesses such as restaurants, funeral homes, barber shops, and insurance companies. Students should be asked to hypothesize about why this is the case. In testing their hypotheses, they will need to explore such questions as "What kind of capital does it take to set up a large production company?" and "Why have ethnic minorities usually been unable to get the kind of loans needed to start these kind of industries?"

4. James A. Banks, *Ethnic Studies in the Social Context* (New York: National Urban League, 1972), pp. 3–4.

Other Economic Concepts

A discussion of why few ethnic minorities own large corporations can lead students to a consideration of the nature of capitalism, and why this kind of economic system often militates against the small business and facilitates the growth of conglomerates that monopolize large segments of the market. The concept of economic exploitation can be used to view the economic situation of groups such as ethnic minorities who own few production industries, but perform the most arduous jobs and receive the least economic and social rewards. Not only do most members of these groups receive low wages, they often work under the worst conditions and are usually the last hired and first fired. An honest look at our economic system will reveal that a small elite profits from the labors and hard work of the masses. Economic exploitation, of course, leads to poverty and all of its related characteristics such as poor housing, social pathologies, low aspirations, and political alienation. Viewing the experience of ethnic groups from the perspectives of economics is absolutely essential.

GEOGRAPHY

Geography is concerned with the *location* of peoples and places, the ways in which the physical environment influences human behavior, and how people shape their physical world. While recognizing that the physical environment influences the ways in which people live, modern geographers reject the old notion of environmental determinism, which held that the physical environment actually determines the forms and structure of human institutions. Social science research reveals that while the physical environment affects the ways in which human groups live, people have the ability to drastically change their physical surrounding so that they can meet their survival needs.

Region

Region is a key geographical concept. *Region* may be defined as "(1) an area of any size which is (2) homogeneous in terms of specific criteria and which is (3) distinguished from bordering areas by a particular kind of association of areally related features. [A region] possesses some kind of internal cohesion." [5] Region is a conceptual tool structured by the geographer to enable him to study a particular location and to make generalizations about it. Thus a region exists more in the mind of the geographer than in the real world.

In other words, a particular location can be conceptualized differently as a region depending upon the purposes and concerns of the geographer. Census officials once defined an incorporated place of 2,500 as an urban region. "In 1950, the definition was changed to include unincorporated settlements, if they had predominantly "urban" characteristics as well as a number of incorporated and unincorporated places having populations of less than 2,500." [6] Regions geographers have conceptualized that have special relevance to ethnic studies include inner-city (or ghetto), ethnic enclave (or ethnic neighborhood) and megalopolis. We will now discuss several geographical concepts related to region that can help students profitably study ethnicity in the United States.

Environmental Perception

The attitudes, feelings, and ideas that people have about their physical and cultural environment are referred to as *environmental perception.*. When studying this concept, the teacher should help students discover how different people who inhabit various regions often have very different and conflicting perceptions of the same geographical regions. Many Whites who live in the outlying regions of a metropolitan area often consider the barrio a dilapidated and dangerous slum that should be avoided if at all possible. Many such persons, on their way to other parts of the city, will take routes around the barrio because they consider it dangerous. The Spanish-speaking people who live in the barrio may have very positive feelings toward their neighborhood and consider it a safe place in which to live and work. Many people, whose entire lives have been confined within their ethnic com-

5. Malcolm P. Douglass, *Social Studies: From Theory to Practice in Elementary Education* (Philadelphia: J. B. Lippincott, 1967), p. 231.

6. Noel P. Gist and Sylvia F. Fava, *Urban Society: Fifth Edition* (New York: Thomas Y. Crowell, 1964), p. 42.

munities, might be shocked to learn that others consider their home neighborhood a ghetto and even more shocked to learn that some believe that it is a dangerous place in which to live.

When studying about the various perceptions that different people have of the same geographical locations, the students might explore what causes divergent perceptions. Many Puerto Rican Americans who live in the barrio know little about any other world and have had few experiences which would cause them to feel that their community is "deviant" or dangerous. On the other hand, many Whites who live in suburbs obtain most of their information about the barrio from the news media, which tends to publish highly sensationalized stories about life in the barrio and to emphasize the criminal events that take place within it. While it is true that certain kinds of crimes occur more often in lower-class neighborhoods than in higher-status ones, it is also true that most inhabitants of ethnic neighborhoods feel relatively safe in them and do not consider them jungles. Unlike the stranger in the neighborhood, they know how to best survive in their communities.

Crime occurs in all types of neighborhoods—including upper-status ones. However, most inhabitants of a community rarely consider it so unsafe that they are too afraid to walk to the local store or school. Many students who grew up in ethnic communities are very surprised to "discover" in introductory sociology college courses that they are *ghetto* youths who are *culturally deprived*. These are labels imposed on minority cultures by dominant groups. Almost no one considers his culture deprived and his home a ghetto. This is an extremely important idea for teachers to incorporate into ethnic studies.

Ethnic Enclave (Ethnic Community)

Most Americans grow up in communities in which ethnic values, lifestyles, language modes, and behavior patterns differ from those of other groups. This is as true for Puerto Ricans who grow up in East Harlem as it is for White Anglo-Saxon Protestants who are raised in wealthy suburban neighborhoods such as Mercer Island, Washington, or Forest Park, Illinois. We usually do not think of middle-class or wealthy White suburbs as ethnic neighborhoods because the culture within them constitutes the dominant one in the United States. However, as we pointed out in Chapter 1, because a group is dominant does not mean that it is not an ethnic group having an identifiable ethnic culture. Alice Miel in *The Shortchanged Children of Suburbia,* and Jules Henry in *Culture Against Man* and *Pathways to Madness,* delineate some of the unique cultural traits of middle-class, White American communities.[7]

Because most Americans grow up in ethnic enclaves, they are *culturally encapsulated.* Ethnic minority groups, in order to attain social and economic mobility, are usually forced out of their ethnic encapsulation. However, majority ethnic groups, who control entry to most social, economic, and political institutions, spend their entire lives within their ethnic communities. The cultures of other groups remain foreign, nonhuman, and exotic to them. Blacks who grow up in small southern rural communities often think that everyone eats sweet potato pie, chitterlings, and hog head and black-eyed peas to celebrate New Year's Day. Without this kind of New Year's meal, bad luck will be eminent. When such Blacks migrate to northern and western cities and begin to participate in social institutions that have other ethnic group norms and values, they discover, sometimes abruptly, that their world is not the entire world, and that not only do many people not eat sweet potato pie, but they have serious questions about people who eat hog intestines!

A sound ethnic studies program should help all students— from both majority and minority groups—to break out of their ethnic enclaves and learn that there are many ways to live and survive and that because an individual has a different lifestyle, he or she is not necessarily inferior or superior. Many minority youths tend to devalue their ethnic cultures when they begin to participate in the dominant society. Majority students should learn that there are different ways of living that are as legitimate and functional as their own. I am not suggesting that the school should attempt to force different lifestyles upon students. However, I am strongly arguing that the school should help to release students from *ethnic captivity* so that they can learn to appreciate

7. Alice Miel with Edwin Kiester, Jr., *The Shortchanged Children of Suburbia,* Pamphlet no. 8 (New York: Institute of Human Relations Press, 1967); Jules Henry, *Culture Against Man* (New York: Vintage Books, 1963), Jules Henry, *Pathways to Madness* (New York: Random House, 1971).

cultural differences and thus how to live with people who speak a different dialect, eat different types of foods, and value things they may not value. We can learn to respect and appreciate different cultures without choosing to participate in them. Participation should be an individual decision. However, cultural acceptance should be a goal fostered by the school community.

Migration-Immigration

When individuals or groups move within a nation in which they are natives or citizens, we say that they are *migrants*. Individuals or groups who settle in a foreign country are called *immigrants*. Thus migration describes the movement of individuals and groups within a nation, while immigration describes the settlement of people in a foreign nation. These two concepts must be studied in ethnic studies because all groups that make up the United States, except American Indians, immigrated to this country from a foreign nation or migrated from Puerto Rico. We call Puerto Ricans migrants rather than immigrants because they became United States citizens with the passage of the congressional Jones Act of 1917. Archeological theories and evidence indicate that American Indians immigrated to the Americas from Asia via the Bering Strait. Although this evidence is strongly endorsed by anthropologists, it is inconclusive. Many American Indians believe that they were created in the Americas by the Great Spirit. Because of the inconclusiveness of the Bering Strait theory and the traditional beliefs of many American Indians, American Indians are considered *Native Americans* in this book.

When studying these two concepts, students can formulate hypotheses about why masses of immigrants entered the United States in the nineteenth century. Between 1820 and 1930, about 38 million immigrants came to the United States, most of them from Europe.[8] Students might hypothesize that many individuals and groups came to the United States to avoid religious and political persecution and to improve their economic conditions. When studying statistics on immigration to the United States, students can be asked to note the countries from which most of our immigrants came and why. For example, between 1820 and

8. William Bridgwater, editor-in-chief, *The Columbia-Viking Desk Encyclopedia, Volume One* (New York: The Viking Press, 1968), p. 503.

1971, 6,925,736 German immigrants entered the United States. During the same period, only 1,782,711 immigrants came from the entire continent of Asia, while 35,630,398 came from Europe. A mere 82,317 came from Africa.[9] An investigation into why many more immigrants came from Europe than from Asia and Africa will lead students to discover that our immigration policies, until they were reformed in 1965, were designed to keep this country largely White and to keep out non-Whites. Table 3.1 gives the numbers and countries of origin of people immigrating to the United States between 1820 and 1971. This table can be the source of numerous inquiry exercises such as the one suggested above.

During their study of the immigration and migration of ethnic groups, students can profitably compare and contrast the reasons why the various groups migrated and the kinds of experiences they had in their new country. The special case of African immigrants to the United States should be highlighted. This group differed from all of the other immigrant groups because their immigration was *forced*. They were also the only group enslaved upon their arrival in the Americas. All the other groups of immigrants voluntarily came to the Americas. When studying about the Southern and Eastern European immigrants to the United States, students can note how each of these groups experienced discrimination, lived in urban ghettos, and how many of them eventually became culturally assimilated, attained social mobility, and moved to the suburbs of cities such as New York, Boston, and Chicago. Groups like Italians and Poles discriminated against Afro-Americans and Mexican Americans when these non-White groups started migrating to large cities after the two great world wars.

While European immigrant groups, especially the Southern and Eastern ones, were often the victims of discrimination and racist ideologies, the racism they experienced never reached such alarming proportions as it did in the South against Black Americans or on the West Coast when Asian immigrants started arriving there in the 1800s. It is important for students to realize that while certain classes of European immigrants such as lunatics, convicts, and idiots, were prevented from entering the United

9. Dan Perkes and Laurence Urdang, eds., *The Official Associated Press Almanac 1973* (New York: Almanac Publishing Company, 1972), p. 140.

Table 3.1

Immigration by Countries: 1820–1971

Countries	Total (1870 to 1971)
All countries	45,533,116
Europe	35,630,398
Albania	2,286
Austria[1]	4,304,302
Hungary[1]	–
Belgium	198,738
Bulgaria[4]	66,998
Czechoslovakia	133,285
Denmark	361,095
Estonia	1,071
Finland	31,544
France	733,009
Germany[1]	6,925,736
Great Britain (England	3,095,191
(Scotland	813,348
(Wales	94,306
(Not specified	801,675
Greece	588,160
Ireland	4,715,041
Italy	5,199,304
Latvia	2,442
Lithuania	3,708
Luxembourg	2,671
Netherlands	352,594
Norway[2]	853,783
Poland[3]	487,778
Portugal	369,665
Rumania	162,278
Spain	229,235
Sweden[2]	1,267,574
Switzerland	343,421
USSR	3,347,118
Yugoslavia[4]	90,234
Other Europe	52,808
Asia	1,782,711
China	450,900
India	53,852
Japan	370,033
Turkey in Asia	376,842
Other Asia	531,084
America	7,641,268

Table 3.1 (Cont.)

Countries	Total (1820 to 1971)
Canada & Newfoundland	3,991,417
Mexico	1,642,916
West Indies	1,156,552
Central America	225,770
South America	515,393
Other America	109,220
Africa	82,317
Australia & New Zealand	101,762
Pacific Islands	23,207
Not Specified	271,453

[1] Data for Austria-Hungary were not reported until 1861; Austria and Hungary have been recorded separately since 1905. From 1938 to 1945 inclusive, Austria was included with Germany. [2] From 1820 to 1868, the figures for Norway and Sweden were combined. [3] Poland was recorded as a separate country from 1820 to 1898 and again since 1920. [4] Bulgaria, Serbia, and Montenegro were first reported in 1899. Bulgaria has been reported separately since 1920, while the Serb, Croat, and Slovene Kingdom has been recorded as Yugoslavia since 1922.

*Reprinted with permission from Dan Perkes and Laurence Urdang, eds., *The Official Associated Press Almanac, 1973* (New York: Almanac Publishing Company, 1972), p. 140.

States in the 1800s, the first national group that was totally excluded from the United States was non-White. The Chinese exclusion act of 1882 completely stopped Chinese immigration to the United States for several decades. In the 1920s, the number of Southern and Eastern European immigrants entering the United States was reduced to a trickle because discrimination against them became intense and widespread. Non-White groups were virtually excluded from the United States. Only groups from Northern and Western Europe were favored by the "national origins" quota system that was set up by Congress in 1921 and tightened in 1924. "Quota was based on percentage of residents of a particular nationality in the United States in

1920." [10] The McCarran Act of 1952 relaxed some of the earlier restrictions, but made the "national origin" parts of the law even more severe.   Immigration reform did not come until the Immigration Act of 1965, which became effective in 1968.   The 1965 act removed the national origin quotas and liberalized American immigration policy.   Because the United States, except for the important case of the Native Americans, consists of a "nation of immigrants," ethnicity within our society must be viewed from the geographical perspective in order to be understood adequately.

HISTORY

We suggested that it is necessary to identify key disciplinary concepts and related generalizations to plan a curriculum that focuses on decision making and incorporates the experiences of America's diverse ethnic groups.   Identifying the key concepts within history poses special problems.   While the behavioral sciences use unique conceptual frameworks to view human behavior, history's uniqueness stems from the fact that it views behavior of the past, is interested in the totality of the past of humankind, and uses a modified mode of scientific inquiry.[11] While the sociologist and the political scientist are primarily interested in socialization and power respectively, the historian may be, and sometimes is, interested in how each of these concepts is exemplified in the past behavior of humankind.   History, then, is an interdisciplinary field since historians, in principle, are interested in all aspects of the human past.   It is difficult to speak about unique historical concepts.   Every discipline makes use of the historical perspective and has historical components.   When a sociologist studies norms and sanctions during the period of slavery, and the economist describes how the slaves produced goods and services, they are both studying history.

While history, in principle, is concerned with the totality of

10.   Bridgwater, *Columbia Viking*, p. 503.

11.   Parts of this discussion are adapted from James A. Banks, "Teaching Black History with a Focus on Decision-Making," *Social Education* 35 (November 1969), pp. 740–45. ff., 820–21.   Reprinted with permission of the National Council for the Social Studies.

the human past, in practice history is largely political because most of the concepts which it uses, such as revolution, government, war, and nationalism, belong to political science. History, as it is usually written, focuses on great political events and leaders and largely ignores the experiences of the common person, non-Western people, ethnic minority groups, and key concepts from most of the other social sciences. However, since history, in principle, is concerned with the totality of the human past, it is potentially the most interdisciplinary of all of the social disciplines and for that reason can serve as an excellent framework for incorporating the ethnic experience into the curriculum from an interdisciplinary perspective, as illustrated in Table 3.2.

Although historians have largely ignored concepts from most of the behavioral sciences and the struggles and aspirations of the common and non-Western people, a modern program in historical studies can and should incorporate these knowledge components. In recent years, historians have become acutely aware of how limited and parochial written history is, and they have taken steps (but still inadequate ones) to include both the contributions and struggles of ethnic groups in their accounts and to use more concepts from the behavioral sciences. Change, a concept related to historical content, and historical bias, a concept about historical method, are key ideas that can help students better comprehend ethnicity within the United States.

Change

Although ethnic communities are identifiable entities, they are undergoing constant change. One of the teacher's greatest problems will be to find instructional materials dealing with the current characteristics and status of ethnic communities. Many books and resources describe ethnic groups such as Blacks and American Indians as they existed decades and sometimes centuries ago. Prior to World War II, most Black Americans lived in the rural areas in the Deep South. Today, most Black Americans are urban dwellers. In some American cities, Blacks make up the dominant group in terms of numbers, although they are still largely politically and economically powerless. Like other American ethnic groups, Indians are becoming increasingly urbanized. Although 500,000 out of 792,000 American Indians lived on or near reservations in 1970, about 200,000 lived in cities or towns.[12] Even though 200,000 American Indians lived in urban areas in 1970, many Americans still think that almost all Indians live on reservations.

Not only are the population characteristics and location of ethnic groups undergoing change, their occupations are also changing. In 1940, only 2.9 percent of Chinese Americans worked in professional and technical occupations. In 1960, 17.9 percent of them worked in these types of fields. On the other hand, 30.1 percent of Chinese Americans held service jobs in 1940. In 1960, this figure had dropped to 18.0 percent.[13] The number of Black and other ethnic minorities who are white-collar workers has increased markedly in recent years. In 1957, 12.8 percent of this group were white-collar workers; that number had increased to 27.9 percent in 1970.[14] Change in the status of ethnic minorities in many areas such as education and income is much too slow. However, change is a fact of their lives, as well as a fact of American life generally. Students need to be aware of, and understand, this type of constant change.

Historical Bias

A historian's view of the past is influenced by his or her personal biases, purposes for writing, availability of data, and the society and times in which he or she lives and writes. Because the historian can never totally reconstruct past events and is unable to report all of the data he or she uncovers about particular events,. he or she must use some criteria to determine which aspects of an event to report. The historian must also interpret historical events. History cannot be written without presenting interpretations and points of view. Because this is the case, it is exceedingly important for teachers to teach students about the biases inherent in all historical writing and how to recognize and analyze them.

It is especially important for teachers to teach students how

12. Perkes and Urdang, *Almanac 1973*, p. 143.

13. Betty L. Sung, *The Story of the Chinese in America* (New York: Macmillan, 1967), p. 189.

14. *Statistical Abstract of the United States* (Washington, D.C.: U. S. Government Printing Office, 1971), p. 223.

Table 3.2

Studying the Ethnic Experience from an
Interdisciplinary Perspective
within a Historical Framework

Discipline	Analytical Concepts	Key Questions
Sociology	Values, Norms	What unique values and norms have emerged within ethnic communities?
Political Science	Power	What power relationships have existed within ethnic communities?
Anthropology	Acculturation	What kind of culture exchange has taken place between ethnic groups in the United States?
Psychology	Self-Concept	How have the various ethnic experiences affected the individual's feelings and perceptions of himself or herself?
Geography	Region	Where have different ethnic groups usually lived within our cities, and why?
Economics	Goods, Services, Production	What goods and services have been produced in various ethnic communities? Why?
History	Change	How have various ethnic communities changed in recent years? Why?

to analyze historical materials that are related to America's ethnic minority groups. The histories of minority groups have been written largely by members of the dominant groups. They usually write histories of ethnic minorities that legitimize their dominant social and economic positions and that often depict minorities negatively. Anglo-Saxon writers and social scientists often invent myths and stereotypes about ethnic minorities to explain why they "deserve" the low status in society to which they are most often assigned. Such stereotypes and myths are rampant within our society; e.g., Blacks were enslaved because they were uncivilized and lazy; slavery would not only civilize them, but would deliver their souls to God; Indians were savages who had to be civilized by Whites in order to survive; Asian Americans were a threat to "national survival" during World War II and thus had to be confined to "relocation" camps for national security. Many social scientists and other scholars are gatekeepers of the status quo; they generate research legitimizing the myths and stereotypes that the ruling group creates about exploited groups to justify their oppression.[15]

Throughout human society, history has been written by the victors and not by the vanquished. Thus most students in our schools study histories of American Indians and Afro-Americans that were written by White historians who most often had little empathy or understanding of their cultures. Since this is the case, the teacher should help students view the experiences of ethnic minority groups from *their perspectives*. I am not suggesting that the histories of ethnic minorities written by dominant groups should be banned from the schools. The point I am trying to emphasize is that the study of America must be seen through the eyes of the vanquished, since students now study it primarily from the viewpoints of the victors. While both views can add to our understanding of the American experience, we must stress other viewpoints since the Anglo-Saxon view of American history is so distorted and widespread within our school and the larger society. Only by trying to see this nation from the viewpoints of oppressed peoples will we be able to fully understand its complexity.

Histories and social science accounts written by ethnic minorities writers, like the writings of dominant groups, reflect particular points of view and biases. However, students need to seriously study these writings in order to gain a "balanced" perspective on American life. In recent years, a number of histories presenting ethnic minority viewpoints have been published. The following books are recommended for inclusion in an ethnic studies program:

15. Banks, *Ethnic Studies*, p. 406.

Acuña, Rodolfo. *Occupied America: The Chicano's Struggle Toward Liberation.* San Francisco: Canfield Press, 1972.

Banks, James A. and Cherry A. Banks, *March Toward Freedom: A History of Black Americans,* 2nd ed. Belmont, Calif.: Fearon Publishers, 1974.

Cordasco, Francesco, and Eugene Bucchioni, eds. *The Puerto Rican Experience.* Totowa, New Jersey: Littlefield and Adams, 1972.

Forbes, Jack D., ed. *The Indian in America's Past.* Englewood Cliffs, N. J.: Prentice-Hall, 1965.

Franklin, John Hope. *From Slavery to Freedom: A History of Negro Americans.* New York: Vintage Books, 1969.

Kitano, Harry H. L. *Japanese Americans: The Evolution of a Subculture.* Englewood Cliffs, N.J.: Prentice-Hall, 1969.

Sung, Betty L. *The Story of the Chinese in America.* New York: Macmillan, 1967.

This list by no means exhausts the recommended books for inclusion in an ethnic studies program. However, they are effective "beginning" books. Many other recommended books are found in the annotated bibliographies in Part II. The point emphasized here is that students should read books presenting points of view that differ or extend those they encounter in their basal textbooks. Many of the books in social studies series have improved their treatments of ethnic minorities in recent years. However, most still omit treatments of many groups such as Mexican Americans, Puerto Rican Americans, and Asian Americans, and present the Black experience from an Anglo-Saxon point of view.[16]

POLITICAL SCIENCE

Within every society and institution, some individual or group is authorized to make decisions, rules, and laws that other

16. The following books contain excellent discussions of the treatment of ethnic minorities in textbooks: Rupert Costo and Jeanette Henry, *Textbooks and the American Indian* (San Francisco: American Indian Historical Society, 1970); Jean D. Grambs and John C. Carr, eds., *Black Image: Education Copes with Color* (Dubuque, Iowa: Wm. C. Brown Company Publishers, 1972); and Michael B. Kane, *Minorities in Textbooks: A Study of Their Treatment in Social Studies Texts* (Chicago: Quadrangle Books, 1970).

individuals and groups are required to obey. The individuals or groups who make these types of binding laws and decisions have varied widely throughout history. Kings and presidents, and bodies such as councils, parliaments, and congresses are among the types of individuals and groups that have made binding decisions in different societies at various points in history. Groups and individuals who make binding decisions for a society exercise power because they control and/or influence the behavior of other persons and groups. Political scientists are primarily interested in the processes by which power is exercised in a society.

Power

The ethnic experience within the United States cannot be understood without considering the role that the struggle for power among competing ethnic groups has played in shaping American history. History and contemporary social science teaches us that in every past and present culture individuals have had, and still have, widely unequal opportunities to fully share in the reward systems and benefits of their society. The basis for unequal distribution of rewards is determined by elitist groups in which power is centered.

Almost every decision made by those in power, including economic policy, is made to enhance, legitimize, and reinforce their power. Powerful groups not only make laws, but determine which traits and characteristics are necessary for full societal participation. They determine necessary traits on the basis of the similarity of such traits to their own values, physical characteristics, lifestyles, and behavior. At various periods in history, celibacy, sex, ethnicity, race, religion, as well as many other variables, have been used by ruling groups to determine which individuals and groups would be given or denied opportunities for social mobility and full societal participation.

In colonial America, White Anglo-Saxon male Protestants with property controlled most social, political, economic, and military institutions. These were the men who wrote the Declaration of Independence and the United States Constitution. They excluded from full participation in decision making those people such as Blacks and American Indians who were different from themselves. Our "founding fathers" had a deep suspicion and contempt for individuals who were culturally and racially different. They invented and perpetuated stereotypes and myths about excluded groups to justify their oppression.

The United States, like all other nations, is still controlled by a few powerful groups who deny individuals opportunities to participate in society on the basis of how similar such individuals are to themselves. White Anglo-Saxon Protestants with money are the most valued persons in modern America; an individual who may be so classified has maximum opportunities to participate in America's social, economic, and political institutions. He is the "ideal" person in the United States, and all other individuals and groups are judged on the basis of their similarity to him. Black females without money are probably the least valued individuals in the United States.[17]

When studying about power relationships in American society, students can be asked to hypothesize about ways in which we can make our nation an open society and thus more consistent with our national ideology. They can define an *open society* as one in which rewards and opportunities are not necessarily evenly distributed, but are distributed on the basis of the knowledge and skills that each person, regardless of his or her ethnic characteristics, can contribute to the fullfillment of the needs of society. Their hypotheses might suggest that we can create an open society either by (1) redistributing power so that different ethnic groups will control entry to various social, economic, and political institutions, or (2) by modifying the perceptions and attitudes of those who now hold most of the power in this country. Students should be asked to discuss which of their hypotheses is more sound, how actions based upon them might be implemented, and to state their limitations. Two excellent books that can give students acute perceptions related to power relationships in America are G. William Domhoff, *Who Rules America?* and C. Wright Mills, *The Power Elite.*[18] When studying about power, students should also be introduced to these related

17. Barbara A. Sizemore, "Social Science and Education for a Black Identity," in James A. Banks and Jean D. Grambs, eds., *Black Self-Concept: Implications for Education and Social Science* (New York: McGraw-Hill, 1972), pp. 141–70.

18. Mills, *Power Elite;* G. William Domhoff, *Who Rules America?* (Englewood Cliffs, N. J.: Prentice-Hall, 1967).

concepts: oppression, political alienation, colony, colonized, and separatism.

Many ethnic minority leaders compare the social and political conditions of minority groups in this country to the situations of developing nations that were colonies of Western empires. Such writers argue, with some validity, that ethnic communities, like colonized nations, are economically and politically powerless and are almost totally dependent upon powerful groups in America in order to survive. To gain more political and economic power, separatist movements have emerged within many ethnic minority communities. The primary goal of such movements is to create social, economic, and political institutions that are controlled by the ethnic group, thus making it less dependent upon other groups for jobs, shelter, and the satisfaction of other survival needs. One of the most successful of such movements is the Nation of Islam. E. U. Essien-Udom, *Black Nationalism: A Search for an Identity in America,* and C. Eric Lincoln, *The Black Muslims in America,* are two excellent books describing this group.[19] A conceptual understanding of Black power and separatism can be gained from Stokely Carmichael and Charles V. Hamilton, *Black Power: The Politics of Liberation in America.* George Breitman, *The Last Year of Malcolm X: The Evolution of a Revolutionary,* describes the actions of a late important figure in the Black separatist movement.[20]

Social Protest

Throughout American history, movements have emerged within ethnic communities to protest social conditions, political policies, and economic practices which ethnics considered unjust and unconstitutional. The types of protest have varied widely, from the actions of individual Japanese Americans to resist the internment during World War II to the massive racial rebellions (riots) that took place in our cities in the 1960s. Groups tend to resort to extreme methods of protest such as riots and rebellions

19. E.U. Essien-Udom, *Black Nationalism: A Search for an Identity in America* (New York: Dell Publishing Company, 1962); C. Eric Lincoln, *The Black Muslims in America* (New York: Beacon Press, 1961).

20. Stokely Carmichael and Charles V. Hamilton, *Black Power: The Politics of Liberation in America* (New York: Vintage Books, 1967); George Breitman, *The Last Year of Malcolm X* (New York: Merit Publishers, 1967).

when they feel that the political system is very oppressive, that there are no legitimate channels for the alleviation of their grievances, that there is some cause for hope, or that their protest movement might succeed. When studying about social protest, it is very important for students to understand that such movements only occur when oppressed people feel that there is a cause for *hope*. For example, students can derive this generalization when studying the Black protest movements of the 1960s. This movement emerged partly because prior policies aimed at reducing discrimination had occurred. These included the desegregation of the armed forces by President Harry S. Truman, the laws which desegregated many Southern state universities, and the historic *Brown* vs. *Board of Education* Supreme Court Decision in 1954 which legally outlawed school segregation. These events were necessary precedents to the Black Revolt of the 1960s.

Many people think the ethnic protests of the 1960s were the first of their kind in our history. While it is true that protest by ethnic minority groups reached their acme during these years, ethnic groups have protested discrimination and racism throughout American history. Black protest actually began on the slave ships—on the journeys from West Africa to the Americas. Slave uprisings and mutinies often occurred on these ships. Many slaves also committed suicide by throwing themselves into the Atlantic rather than acquiescently accepting bondage. Protests by Blacks continued during and after slavery. Slave uprisings, led by such individuals as Denmark Vesey, Gabriel Prosser, and Nat Turner often resulted in the mass murder of Whites.

Around the turn of the century, Black organizations emerged to systematically fight for civil rights, including the National Association for the Advancement of Colored People and the National Urban League. Other ethnic groups have also continually fought for their rights. Such organizations as the Anti-Defamation League of B'nai B'rith, the Japanese American Citizenship League, the League of United Latin-American Citizens, and the Puerto Rican Forum were organized to fight for the civil rights of various ethnic groups in a systematic way. Oppression of any human group is likely to lead to organized protest and resistence. Such protest and resistence has emerged within all of America's ethnic groups, although the forms and styles which protest has taken has reflected the unique cultural values and lifestyles of the particular groups.

Teachers should help students to learn that ethnic protest did not suddenly appear in the 1960s. Rather they should view the sixties as a period in which ethnic protest reached one of its highest points in our history. As of this writing, ethnic protest, because of numerous political and sociological reasons, has again subsided. However, we can expect other periods of intense protest as long as ethnic minorities inculcate the American ideology of equality taught in textbooks and are denied equality of opportunity in their daily lives.

SOCIOLOGY

Sociology is primarily concerned with the process by which people become human. A basic assumption of the discipline is that while people are born with the physical capacities to become human, they are capable of becoming many things, including animal-like. The point is dramatically made in William Golding's *Lord of the Flies* and in a more subtle way in Jack London's *Call of the Wild*. Sociologists assume that people acquire human traits and characteristics only by interacting with the human group. The discipline uses the concept of socialization to describe the process which makes individuals human. The group makes use of norms and sanctions to make sure that the individual acquires the attitudes, values, and behavior patterns it deems appropriate.

The sociological perspective is very important in ethnic studies because it provides useful insights that help us understand how individuals acquire prejudices, ethnocentric values, and how people learn to discriminate against other groups. Sociology teaches us that children are not born with racial antipathies. These attitudes are learned. Children learn them from the adults in their environment early in life. Modern sociological research and theory dispels old notions such as the racial and cultural difference theory, which held that "man has an instinctive fear and dislike of individuals who are physically and culturally different from him," and the traumatic experience theory, which states that "racial prejudice emerges in an individual following a traumatic experience involving a member of a minority group during early childhood."[21] Negative attitudes toward certain ethnic groups are institutionalized within our culture and children acquire them by interacting with "significant others" in their environment and from reading books in school, watching television, and going to church. All institutions within our society, including the schools, reinforce and teach negative lessons about America's ethnic minority groups. Students need to understand the relationship between socialization, prejudice, racism, and discrimination.

Prejudice and Discrimination

Prejudice is a set of rigid and unfavorable attitudes toward a particular group or groups which is formed in disregard of facts. The prejudiced individual responds to perceived members of these groups on the basis of his or her preconceptions, tending to disregard behavior or personal characteristics that are inconsistent with his or her biases. The individual who is anti-Semitic will argue that Jews are loud and rudely aggressive no matter how many Jews he or she meets who do not have these characteristics. The prejudiced person sees the world through a set of blinders and refuses to perceive persons, incidents, and groups that fail to reinforce his or her negative attitudes and stereotypes.

Although prejudice and discrimination are highly related and are usually associated, they are conceptually different constructs. Prejudice is a set of *attitudes*, while discrimination consists of differential *behavior* directed toward a stigmatized group. Rose has defined discrimination "as the differential treatment of individuals considered to belong to particular groups or social categories." [22] Discrimination is normally used to describe negative and not positive behavior. Ethnic minority groups are often the victims of discrimination in housing, employment, and education. Although a number of laws have been passed in recent years to ban discrimination in these areas, as well as in voting and public accommodation facilities, such laws are infrequently

21.   Arnold M. Rose, "The Causes of Prejudice," in Milton L. Barron, ed., *American Cultural Minorities: A Textbook of Readings in Intergroup Relations* (New York: Alfred A. Knopf, 1962), pp. 77–80.

22.   Peter I. Rose, *They and We: Racial and Ethnic Relations in the United States* (New York: Random House, 1964), p. 79.

enforced. However, minority groups probably experience less discrimination in public accommodation facilities than in any of the other areas. Discrimination in education is rather blatant. Housing discrimination is insidious in most regions of the United States, but it tends to be subtle and sophisticated. When studying this concept, students should learn that while many laws have been enacted to ban discrimination in all areas of American life, and while much progress has been made in eradicating it, discrimination is endemic in American life. During an inquiry exercise, students can study areas of American life where discrimination exists, laws which have been passed to ban it, the ways in which the laws have been enforced, and formulate strategies which might be used to further reduce American discrimination. When they formulate strategies, they should state how feasible they are to implement and their possible consequences.

Racism

Racism, a concept related to prejudice and discrimination, was popularized by the *Report of the National Advisory Commission on Civil Disorders* (1968), popularly known as the Kerner Report. One of the major conclusions of the commission was: "Race prejudice has shaped our history decisively; it now threatens to affect our culture. . . . White *racism* is essentially responsible for the explosive mixture which has been accumulating in our cities since the end of World War II"[23] [emphasis added]. Despite the fact that many writers have freely used this concept since it was popularized by the commission, there exists little agreement about its meaning among social scientists and popular writers. Notes Gay, "Definitions of racism are as numerous and varied as are the people who have studied this social disease."[24] Gay has provided a useful definition of *racism*. She defines it *"as any activity, individual or institutional, deliberate or not, predicated upon a belief in the superiority of Whites and*

23. *Report of the National Advisory Commission on Civil Disorders* (New York: Bantam Books, 1968), pp. 1, 10.

24. Geneva Gay, "Racism in America: Imperatives for Teaching Ethnic Studies," in James A. Banks, ed., *Teaching Ethnic Studies: Concepts and Strategies*, 43rd Yearbook of the National Council for the Social Studies. (Washington, D. C.: The Council, 1973), p. 30.

the inferiority of ethnic minorities, which serves to maintain White supremacy through the oppression and subjugation of members of ethnic minority groups. It is an extension of an attitude into an action. Although the focus of attention is on *behavior,* attitudes are of crucial importance for they are the motivating forces which determine the nature of the actions one takes." [25] When studying this concept, the teacher can ask the students to study definitions of it that have been given by various writers, formulate a working knowledge of it for their purposes, compare their definition with others, and identify examples of the concept (using the definition they have derived) in the nation, their community, and school. The following books present definitions and analyses of racism and are useful resources:

> Stokeley Carmichael and Charles V. Hamilton, *Black Power: The Politics of Liberation in America* (New York: Vintage Books, 1967)

> Roger Daniels and Harry H. L. Kitano, *American Racism: Exploration of the Nature of Prejudice* (Englewood Cliffs: Prentice-Hall, 1970)

> James M. Jones, *Prejudice and Racism* (Reading, Massachusetts: Addison-Wesley, 1972)

> Louis L. Knowles and Kenneth Prewitt, *Institutional Racism in America* (Englewood Cliffs: Prentice-Hall, 1969)

> *Racism in America and How to Combat It* (Washington, D. C.: U. S. Government Printing Office, 1970)

> Barry N. Schwartz and Robert Disch, *White Racism: Its History, Pathology and Practice* (New York: Dell, 1970)[26]

Values

Those elements within a culture to which individuals and groups attach a high worth are called *values.* Within a social system, there are values that influence the group's feelings toward foods, human life, behavior patterns, and attitudes toward people who belong to out-groups. Sociologists have studied the ways in which values develop within societies and how they

25. Ibid.

26. Ibid., pp. 47–48.

are inculcated by individuals in a community. Values, like attitudes and beliefs, are learned from the groups in which the individual is socialized; we are not born with a set of values and do not derive them independently. Groups use norms and sanctions to assure that the individual inculcates the pervasive values within his or her culture or subculture.

While there are some broad and general values embraced by most American communities (such as a respect for the lives of those regarded as human and kind treatment of children), these general values are often defined and perceived differently within various ethnic subcultures, or they take diverse forms. Other values are very important in some ethnic communities and largely absent in others.

The Nisei usually endorse many traditional Japanese values, including etiquette, personal control, the samurai ethic, a high respect for authority, the achievement ethic, and a strong sense of family obligation. Family obligation in traditional Japanese cultures was often considered more important than personal freedom. Writes Lyman, "The *ie* system [the physical house and permanent family household] was . . . far more important than the individuals who at any one time composed it, and hence if for the sake of the *ie* the personal wishes and desires of those individuals had to be ignored or sacrificed, this was looked on as only natural."[27] Although many of the Nisei values have eroded among the Sansei because the Sansei are highly culturally assimilated, important vestiges of these values remain in Japanese communities today, especially among the aged. Some of these values, such as a high respect for authority and a strong sense of family obligation, conflict with dominant Anglo-Saxon values. In Anglo society, there is often little respect for authority, and it is rarely concentrated in one family member.

Values in other ethnic minority communities are often different from those in Anglo society. In the traditional Puerto Rican family, the girl was highly protected, and father was the undisputed head of the family. The family was also a highly interdependent unit. Uncles, aunts, and other relatives were often considered integral parts of the family unit. This type of extended family was also common among Blacks in the Deep South. As Blacks and Puerto Ricans become more urbanized

27. Stanford M. Lyman, *The Asian in the West* (Reno: Desert Research Institute, 1970), Special Science and Humanities Publication no. 4, p. 90.

and more heavily represented in the middle classes, these aspects of their cultures diminish. However, the extended family is still very much a part of these ethnic cultures. Puerto Rican girls in New York City often do not have the same freedom to come and go with boys as their Anglo peers.

When American Indians are usually studied in school, students are introduced to certain stereotypic components of their cultures such as tipis, baskets, canoes, or moccasins. While these physical elements were parts of the cultures of certain Native American groups, they were by no means the most essential parts of them. Thus students gain only a superficial view of Indian cultures when they only study tangible cultural elements. The essence of a culture can be understood only by studying its central values and the relationships of them to the daily lives of the people. Notes Forbes, "The meaning or significance of the Native American way of life basically revolves around *values* and it is this subject-area which should dominate curriculum-building. This is not to say that Native American cooking, dancing, music, and art should be ignored, but rather that stress should be placed upon the central dynamic *élan* of Native cultures."[28]

The Native American view of people and their relationship to the universe must be studied to understand Indian values toward people and nature. Indian groups tended to look upon the universe as a whole, with every object having a sacred life; to separate people from nature was antithetical to the Great Spirit, for to the Great Spirit all was life. A feeling for the Indian's unity with nature can be gained from the following passage in which an old holy Wintu woman speaks poignantly about the destruction of land by Whites.

The White People Never Cared for Land or Deer or Bear.

When we Indians kill meat, we eat it all up. When we dig roots we make little holes. When we built houses, we make little holes. When we burn grass for grasshoppers, we don't ruin things. We shake down acorns and pinenuts. We don't chop down the trees. We only use dead wood. But the White people plow up the ground, pull down the trees, kill everything. The tree says, "Don't. I am sore. Don't hurt me." But they chop it down and cut it up. The spirit of the land

28. Jack D. Forbes, "Teaching Native American Values and Cultures," in Banks, ed., *Teaching Ethnic Studies: Concepts and Strategies*, p. 202.

hates them. They blast out trees and stir it up to its depths. They saw up the trees. That hurts them. The Indians never hurt anything, but the White people destroy all. They blast rocks and scatter them on the ground. The rock says, "Don't. You are hurting me." But the White people pay no attention. When the Indians use rocks, they take little round ones for their cooking. . . . How can the spirit of the earth like the White man? . . . Everywhere the White man has touched it, it is sore.[29]

It is the values and related lifestyles of ethnic communities that constitute their essence, not chow mein, basket weaving, sombreros, or soul food. These values should be emphasized in the curriculum, not exotic cultural elements whose major outcome is the reinforcement of stereotypes. However, I am not suggesting that tangible cultural elements should not be studied, but that they should not be emphasized. While the study of ethnic values should constitute a large part of an ethnic studies curriculum, it is important to realize, however, that the values of all of America's ethnic groups are changing, especially in urban areas. Ethnic minorities are becoming urbanized at a higher rate than Anglos. It is also important to remember that highly assimilated and higher status members of ethnic minority groups may share few, if any, characteristics with their more humble brothers and sisters. Despite these caveats, ethnic values are endemic in American life. They add strength and diversity to our national culture. This significant message should be communicated to students in all grades.

Ethnic Studies and the Disciplines

To develop ethnic literacy and acquire a sophisticated understanding of ethnic cultures in the United States, students must view ethnic problems from the perspectives of the social sciences. Students must also master higher-level concepts and generalizations and view ethnic groups from an interdisciplinary perspective to formulate effective solutions to ethnic problems. While each of the disciplines contains key concepts and generalizations that can contribute to students' understandings of ethnic prob-

29. T. C. McLuhan, ed., *Touch The Earth: A Self-Portrait of Indian Existence* (New York: Pocket Books, 1971), p. 15. Reprinted with the publisher's permission.

lems, any one discipline can give them only a partial understanding of ethnicity in the United States. The humanities can also be used to help students develop ethnic literacy. Examples showing how to incorporate ethnic literature into the curriculum are presented in Part II. The next chapter discusses ways to organize ethnic studies units around key social science concepts and generalizations.

Questions and Activities

1. Identify an ethnic problem in your community, such as a controversey over busing, the question of open housing, or discrimination in employment. List concepts and generalizations from several social sciences that might help students to understand the problem. What strategies and materials would you use to teach the problem to students?

2. State the advantages of an interdisciplinary ethnic studies program. What problems might you encounter in trying to structure this type of curriculum? How might you resolve them?

3. Examine several of the books dealing with specific ethnic groups listed in the bibliographies of this book. Identify and list *culture traits* which are unique to different ethnic communities. What is the origin of these culture traits? Why do they continue to exist? Are they unique to particular ethnic groups or merely associated with lower-class status? Explain your response.

4. After reading a book on each of the major ethnic groups, make a list of the types of cultural and physical *differences* existing *within* them. Explain why these differences emerged and why they still exist.

5. What kinds of contributions can each of the social science disciplines make to ethnic studies? Why?

6. Make a list of the major occupations in which most American Indians, Mexican Americans, Asian Americans, Puerto Rican Americans, and Black Americans work. Note the percentages of each group working in the major occupations identified. Carefully study the data you have gathered. What generalizations and conclusions can you make about the occupational status of ethnic minority groups in American society? What factors explain their occupational status?

7. Using a map of your city or community, pinpoint the regions where the various ethnic groups live with different colored markers to represent each major ethnic group. What conclusions and generalizations can you make about where different ethnic groups are concentrated in your city or community? What factors explain their location patterns?

8. Conduct a small scale field study in which you gather data about the ways in which people within an ethnic community view their neighborhood and the ways in which outsiders view it. What conclusions can you make? What factors explain your findings?

9. Locate several conflicting accounts of slavery or the Mexican American War and develop an inquiry lesson to teach students the ways in which personal biases influence the writing of history.

10. Study the treatments of the major ethnic groups in your basal social studies and language arts textbooks. What conclusions can you make? What materials and strategies can you use to extend textbook treatments of ethnic groups? How?

11. The author suggests that a small elite actually makes most of the major political and economic decisions in the United States. Defend or refute this assertion. Give ample evidence to support your position.

12. List examples of racial and ethnic discrimination you have seen and/or experienced. Why did the discrimination occur? How might this type of discrimination be reduced?

13. Define each of the following terms and tell why each is important:

interdisciplinary	culturally encapsulated
conceptual curriculum	migration
structure of a discipline	immigration
culture	historical bias
acculturation	power
ethnocentrism	social protest
scarcity	prejudice
region	discrimination
environmental	racism
perception	ethnic values
ethnic enclave	

Annotated Bibliography

Abrahams, Roger D. and Rudolph C. Troike, eds. *Language and Cultural Diversity in American Education.* Englewood Cliffs, N. J.: Prentice-Hall, 1972.

A useful collection of essays dealing with cross-cultural communication, with emphasis on language education in the schools.

Allport, Gordon W. *The Nature of Prejudice,* abridged ed. Garden City, N. Y.: Doubleday, 1958.

A classical and seminal study of the origin and nature of prejudice.

Banks, James A., ed. "The Imperatives of Ethnic Education." *Phi Delta Kappan,* 53, January, 1973, special issue.

A collection of evocative articles dealing with critical issues in the education of ethnic minority youths.

Daniels, Roger and Harry H.L. Kitano. *American Racism: Exploration of the Nature of Prejudice.* Englewood Cliffs, N. J.: Prentice-Hall, 1970.

A brief and lucid sociological and historical examination of racism in the United States which draws heavily on the Asian American experience for examples.

Della-Dora, Delmo and James E. House, eds. *Education for an Open Society.* Washington, D. C.: Association for Supervision and Curriculum Development, 1974.

This book consists of a hard-hitting collection of essays that will help the teacher to examine his or her racial attitudes and perceptions. The 1974 ASCD Yearbook.

Epps, Edgar G., ed. *Cultural Pluralism.* Berkeley, Calif.: McCutchan Publishing Corporation, 1974.

A stimulating collection of essays focused on the role of the school in fostering cultural pluralism.

Epps, Edgar G. *Race Relations: Current Perspectives.* Cambridge, Mass.: Winthrop Publishers, 1973.

An excellent collection of theoretical articles and studies on diverse aspects of ethnic group life in the United States.

Glock, Charles Y. and Ellen Siegelman, eds. *Prejudice: U.S.A.* New York: Praeger, 1969.

A collection of essays which explore various aspects of prejudice in American life.

Goodman, Mary Ellen. *Race Awareness in Young Children.* New York: Collier, 1952.

An important and revealing study of the racial attitudes of young children.

Henderson, George. *Human Relations: From Theory to Practice.* Norman: University of Oklahoma Press, 1974.

A perceptive and informed book which presents both the theoretical and practical aspects of human relations as a field of study.

Kitano, Harry H.L. *Race Relations.* Englewood Cliffs, N. J.: Prentice-Hall, 1974.

This book includes chapters on the theoretical aspects of race relations as well as chapters on the major ethnic minority groups in the United States.

Kurokawa, Minako, ed. *Minority Responses.* New York: Random House, 1970.

This anthology contains some excellent theoretical articles and studies on race relations in the United States, including "Ethnic Groups in America: From National Culture to Ideology" by Nathan Glazer, and "Assimilation in America: Theory and Reality," by Milton M. Gordon.

Pettigrew, Thomas F. *Racially Separate or Together.* New York: McGraw-Hill, 1971.

Although the author draws most of his examples from the Black experience, this is an insightful study of race and ethnic relations, as well as a position statement on the need for racial and ethnic integration.

Rose, Peter I., ed. *Nation of Nations: The Ethnic Experience in America.* New York: Random House, 1972.

An interesting anthology on the ethnic experience in the United States which includes literary, social commentary, and sociological readings. The noted contributors include Richard Wright, Piri Thomas, Oscar Handlin, Nathan Glazer, Vine Deloria, Jr., and James Baldwin.

Organizing and Planning the Ethnic Studies Program

4

An ethnic studies program should help students develop the ability to make reflective personal and public decisions. An ethnic studies curriculum focused on decision making must be conceptual, interdisciplinary, and based on higher levels of knowledge. Chapter 3 was designed to acquaint the reader with the nature of the disciplines so that he or she could acquire the skills needed to identify appropriate concepts and generalizations for ethnic studies.

This chapter discusses ways to organize a decision-making curriculum after the teacher is acquainted with the disciplines. It also explores other components of an effective ethnic studies program, including valuing and social action. Steps the teacher can take to master ethnic content and to select and evaluate instructional materials are also discussed.

Identifying Key Concepts and Organizing Generalizations

When planning ethnic studies curricula and units that have a comparative approach and focus, the teacher or curriculum committee should start by identifying key social science concepts that are related to ethnic content. These concepts should be higher-level ones which can encompass numerous facts and lower-level concepts and generalizations. They should have the power to organize a great deal of information and the potential to explain significant aspects of the ethnic experience. As illustrated in Chapter 3, each discipline contains concepts with these characteristics. We identified and defined some of the more powerful ones in the previous chapter and suggested ways in which they might contribute to students' understanding of ethnicity in the United States. Other important concepts were mentioned but only briefly discussed. Table 4.1 contains a list of higher-level concepts that can be used to organize ethnic studies units or to incorporate ethnic content into the regular social studies or language arts program. Most of these concepts were defined in Chapter 3. In studying this list of concepts, the reader will note that some of them such as separatism and forced assimilation are clearly interdisciplinary since the perspectives of several disciplines are needed to fully understand them.

The concepts were categorized according to which discipline has made maximum use of them. While separatism is sociological as well as political, political scientists have contributed most to our understanding of this concept. However, all social scientists use concepts from other disciplines. Rather than being a disadvantage to the teacher, the fact that many concepts that can help students to understand ethnic studies are interdisciplinary is a plus factor because the teacher should always try to help students view human events from the perspectives of several disciplines.

After a teacher or curriculum committee has selected key concepts from each of the disciplines, at least one organizing generalization related to each of the concepts chosen should be identified. Each organizing generalization should be a higher-level statement helping to explain human behavior in all cultures, times, and places. It should not contain references to any particular culture or group, and should be a universal-type statement capable of empirical verification. To illustrate how an ethnic studies program can be both interdisciplinary and incorporate the experiences of all ethnic groups, six key concepts from the various disciplines and related organizing generalizations are identified on page 95.

Table 4.1
Organizing Concepts
for Ethnic Studies Curricula

Discipline	Key Concepts	Discipline	Key Concepts
Anthropology	culture	History*	immigration
	culture diversity		migration
	acculturation		change
	forced accultura-tion	Political Science	power
			powerless
	cultural assimila-tion		separatism
			oppression
	race		social protest
	racial mixture		interest group
	subculture		legitimacy
	syncretism		authority
	melting pot		power elite
	cultural genocide		colony
	ethnocentrism		colonized
Economics	scarcity		rebellion
	poverty	Psychology	identity
	production		aggression
	consumption		repression
	capitalism		displacement
	economic exploita-tion	Sociology	discrimination
			ethnic group
Geography	ethnic enclave		ethnic minority group
	region		prejudice
	ghetto		racism
	inner city		socialization
	location		status
			values

* Identifying organizing historical concepts is especially difficult because history does not possess unique concepts but uses concepts from all social science disciplines to study human behavior in the past. For a further discussion of this point see James A. Banks, "Teaching Black History with a Focus on Decision-Making," Social Education 35 (November 1971), pp. 740–45, ff., 820–21.

KEY CONCEPTS AND ORGANIZING GENERALIZATIONS

KEY CONCEPT: Acculturation (Anthropology)

Organizing Generalization: Whenever ethnic groups have extended contact, exchange of cultural traits occurs between minority and majority groups, as well as between different ethnic minority groups.

KEY CONCEPT: Consumption-Production (Economics)

Organizing Generalization: Groups that consume large amounts of goods and services, but control few means of production, usually have little influence in determining what goods and services are produced, for whom, and how they are distributed.

KEY CONCEPT: Immigration-Migration (Geography)

Organizing Generalization: In all cultures individuals and groups have moved to seek better economic, political, and social opportunities. However, movement of individuals and groups has been both voluntary and forced.

KEY CONCEPT: Conflict (History)

Organizing Generalization: Throughout history, conflict has developed between and within racial and ethnic groups.

KEY CONCEPT: Power (Political Science)

Organizing Generalization: There is a continuous struggle both within and between various groups for power and influence. Power struggles often lead to social change.

KEY CONCEPT: Racism (Sociology)

Organizing Generalization: Groups with physical and cultural characteristics different from those of groups in power are often the victims of racist ideologies and discrimination.

Identifying Lower-Level Ideas

After a universal-type generalization is identified for each of the key concepts chosen, an intermediate-level generalization that relates to each higher order statement should be formulated. An intermediate-level generalization applies to a nation, regions within a nation, or to groups making up a particular culture. To illustrate this process of curriculum planning, we will identify subideas (intermediate-level generalizations) for the key geographical concept in our example, immigration-migration. In an actual curriculum, subideas would be identified for each organizing generalization chosen. We have limited our example to save space. Below we repeat the organizing generalization and introduce a related intermediate-level idea:

Universal-Type Generalization: In all cultures, individuals and groups have moved to different regions and within various regions in order to seek better economic, political, and social opportunities. However, movement of individuals and groups has been both voluntary and forced.

Intermediate-Level Generalization: Most individuals and groups who have immigrated to the United States and who have migrated within it were seeking better economic, political, or social opportunities. However, movement of individuals and groups to and within the United States has been both voluntary and forced.

When intermediate-level generalizations have been identified for each major concept, a lower-level generalization related to each of America's major ethnic groups should be stated. Identifying a lower-level generalization for each major ethnic group will assure that all groups will be included in the teaching units to be structured later. The ethnic groups listed below should be included in comparative ethnic studies units. Other American ethnic groups, such as Native Hawaiians, may also be included in multiethnic units (See Chapter 11).

> Native Americans
> Mexican Americans
> European Americans
> Afro-Americans
> Asian Americans
>
>> (Include Japanese Americans, Chinese Americans, and Filipino Americans. If materials can be obtained, also include information about Asian American groups such as Korean Americans and Samoan Americans)
>
> Puerto Rican Americans
> Cuban Americans

Below are lower-level generalizations related to the key concept in our example for each of the major ethnic groups:

Native Americans: Most movement of Native Americans within the United States was caused by forced migration and genocide.

Mexican Americans: Mexicans who immigrated to the United States came primarily to improve their economic condition by working as migrant laborers in the Western and Southwestern states.

European Americans: Most Southern and Eastern Europeans who immigrated to the United States came primarily to improve their economic status.

Afro-Americans: Large numbers of Blacks migrated to northern and western cities in the early 1900s to escape lynchings and economic and political oppression in the South.

Asian Americans: Most Asian immigrants who came to the United States in the 1800s expected to improve their economic conditions and to return to Asia.

During World War II, Japanese Americans were forced to move from their homes to federal concentration camps.

Puerto Rican Americans: Puerto Ricans usually come to the United States mainland seeking better jobs; they sometimes return to the island of Puerto Rico because of American racism and personal disillusionment experienced on the mainland.

Cuban Americans: Most Cuban Americans, unlike most American immigrant groups, came to the United States because of political developments in their native country.

CONCEPTS AND GENERALIZATIONS IN ETHNIC STUDIES

To help the teacher plan an ethnic studies curriculum, we have identified a number of key concepts related to ethnic groups and related intermediate-level generalizations. To save space, related universal-type generalizations are not stated. However, these can be inferred from the generalizations given. For example, our first key concept is conflict. The related key generalization, which encompasses the two statements below it, is: *Throughout history, conflict has arisen between and among groups in all cultures.* Although universal-type generalizations are not given below, they are important because they enable the teacher to incorporate content from other nations for comparative purposes and help students appreciate the power of high-level ideas. Table 4.2 shows how the students may use a data retrieval chart to study some of the following key ideas.

*CONFLICT:** Conflict exists between different generations and subgroups within ethnic minority groups. These conflicts are especially evident in values, goals, and methods of protest.

Conflict emerges both within and between ethnic groups, as subgroups or groups perceive others as attaining more social, economic, and political benefits than themselves. This kind of conflict creates tension between and within groups, and diverts attention from the real agents of oppression.

CULTURAL DIVERSITY: There is wide diversity between and within various ethnic groups. The extent of group identification by members of ethnic groups varies greatly and is influenced by many factors such as skin color, social class, and personal experiences.

The histories of ethnic minority groups in the United States are similar in many ways, but there are very significant and salient differences in their historical and present experiences.

VALUES: Many values within ethnic minority communities differ from those of the dominant group, even though their values are changing, especially as minority groups become more culturally assimilated.

Ethnic values, cultures, behavior, and means of protest are undergoing constant change.

SOCIAL PROTEST: In recent years, intense movements have emerged within ethnic minority groups to develop more pride in their groups, to shape new identities, to gain political power and

---

* *The words and phrases in italic capitals are concepts; the statements which follow them are related generalizations.*

Table 4.2

Comparative Study of American Ethnic Groups Using Selected Key Concepts

Key Concepts	American Indians	Mexican Americans	Afro-Americans	European Americans	Asian Americans	Puerto Rican Americans	Cuban Americans
CONFLICT: Within group: With other groups:							
CULTURE DIVER- SITY: Within group:							
VALUES: Unique: Shared with Others:							
SOCIAL PROTEST: Types used: Results of:							
IMMIGRATION- MIGRATION: Reasons for: When: Results of:							

control of institutions, and to shatter stereotypes. The intensity, scope, and type of movements have varied widely from group to group and have been influenced by the unique histories, values, cultures, and lifestyles of ethnic groups.

Throughout their experiences in the United States, ethnic minorities have resisted oppression in various ways. Methods of resistance have been influenced by the time, culture, and history of the group, and the attitudes of the dominant ethnic groups.

OPPRESSION: Ethnic minority groups in the United States have been and are the victims of oppression and exploitation—slavery, internment, genocide, economic exploitation, and political powerlessness.

COLOR: Color distinctions and evaluations institutionalized in the larger society are reflected and perpetuated *within* and between minority groups. Rewards and opportunities within various groups are often distributed on the basis of skin color; color is often related to social class.

PSYCHOLOGICAL CAPTIVITY: Ethnic minority individuals often accept the stereotypes of themselves that are perpetuated by the dominant society. Their acceptance of these stereotypes influences their behavior.

Ethnic minority groups tend to avoid close association with other ethnic groups that are stereotyped by the larger society and attempt to prevent the dominant group from classifying them with socially stigmatized groups.

URBANIZATION: Ethnic minority groups, like other Americans, are becoming increasingly urbanized, but at a greater rate than majority groups.

SOCIAL MOBILITY: There is a degree of social mobility within all ethnic minority groups, although most are still confined to the lower socioeconomic classes. Asian Americans are the most upward mobile racial minority in the United States.

SCIENTIFIC RACISM: Throughout American history, scientists have developed arguments and theories to justify the oppression of socially stigmatized groups, and attributed their low status to inherited inferior traits rather than the lack of opportunities and institutional racism.

ASSIMILATION: As ethnic groups become more assimilated and attain higher socioeconomic status, they tend to abandon certain elements of their traditional cultures. However, they sometimes reclaim aspects of their cultural heritage once they are secure in middle- or upper-class status. This usually occurs in the third generation.

While most White ethnic groups in the United States have become highly Anglo-Saxon in their values and culture, other White ethnic cultures are an integral part of American society.

CULTURAL PLURALISM: In recent years, most ethnic minority groups have lessened their attempts to assimilate and intensified their search for their unique culture traits and demands for cultural pluralism.

ETHNIC INSTITUTIONS: Self-help, benevolent, political, and other types of organizations have emerged within ethnic communities to respond to their unique problems and needs.

ACCULTURATION: Aspects of all ethnic cultures have become assimilated into the dominant American culture.

IMMIGRATION: Racist policies and ideologies severely restricted the immigration of non-White groups and Southern and Eastern Europeans to the United States until 1968.

TEACHING STRATEGIES AND MATERIALS

Once a teacher or curriculum committee has identified the key concepts and generalizations that can serve as a framework for an ethnic studies curriculum or unit and has stated subideas related to the experiences of ethnic groups in the United States, he or she (or the committee) can then identify the materials and teaching strategies necessary to help students derive the concepts and their related generalizations. A wide variety of teaching strategies, content, and materials can be used to teach ethnic studies. Our sample generalization about immigration-migration can be effectively taught by using content related to the forced westward migration of the Cherokee, which occurred in 1838 and 1839. This poignant migration is often called "The Trail of Tears." When teaching about Puerto Rican migrants, a group currently migrating to the United States in significant numbers, the teacher can use such excellent books as Elena Padilla's *Up From Puerto Rico* and *The Puerto Rican Experience,* edited by Francesco Cordasco and Eugene Bucchiono. Oscar Handlin's compassionate and sensitive book, *The Uprooted,* will give students a useful overview of the frustrations and problems encountered by the Southern and Eastern European immigrants to the United States. Saunders Redding, in *They Came in Chains,* poignantly describes the forced migration of Africans to

SIX KEY CONCEPTS SPIRALLED WITHIN A CONCEPTUAL CURRICULUM AT EIGHT DIFFERENT LEVELS

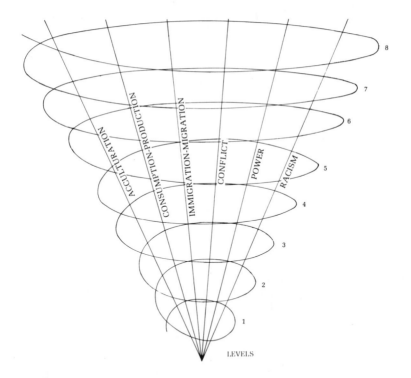

FIGURE 4.1 This diagram illustrates how information related to America's ethnic groups can be organized around key concepts and taught at successive levels at an increasing degree of complexity.

North America. Simulation, role-playing, as well as other strategies described in Chapters 5 through 11, can be used to effectively teach about immigration and other key concepts identified in this chapter.

The six key concepts and generalizations we earlier identified can be taught at every level within a spiral conceptual curriculum and developed at increasing levels of complexity with different content samples. At each level, K through 12, materials related to *each* ethnic group should be used as content samples to teach students major social science concepts and generalizations. Figure 4.1 illustrates how the six key concepts can be spiralled within a conceptual curriculum at eight different levels. This same curriculum design, of course, can be used in a K–12 program, an 8–12 curriculum, or with any levels.

Planning Lessons

To assure that every subgeneralization identified in the initial stages of planning is adequately developed within a unit, the teacher can divide a sheet of paper in half and list the key concepts, generalizations, and subgeneralizations on one side of it and the strategies and materials needed to teach the ideas on the other half as shown in Table 4.3.

THE VALUE COMPONENT OF ETHNIC STUDIES

While higher level, scientific knowledge is necessary for reflective decision making on ethnic problems, it is not sufficient. To make reflective decisions, the social actor must also identify and clarify his or her values and relate them to the knowledge he or she has derived through the process of social inquiry.*

Because many ethnic problems within our society are rooted in value confusion, the school should play a significant role in helping students identify and clarify their values, and in making

---

* *Two excellent resources for teachers that describe valuing strategies are Louise E. Raths, Merrill Harmin, and Sidney B. Simon,* Values and Teaching: Working with Values in the Classroom *(Columbus, Ohio: Charles E. Merrill, 1966); and Sidney B. Simon, Leland W. Howe, and Howard Kirschenbaum,* Values Clarification: A Handbook of Practical Strategies for Teachers and Students *(New York: Hart Publishing Co., 1972).*

Table 4.3
Key Ideas and Teaching Strategies

KEY IDEAS:	Activities
KEY CONCEPT: Immigration-Migration	1. Reading aloud selections from Takashima, *A Child in Prison Camp.*
Key Generalization: In all cultures individuals and groups have been moved to different regions in order to seek better economic, political, and social opportunities. However, movement of individuals and groups has been both voluntary and forced.	2. Discussing how Shichan, Yuki, and Mother felt when David and Father were taken away. 3. Viewing and discussing the drawings in *Child in Prison Camp.* 4. Viewing and discussing the photographs in Conrat and Conrat, *Executive Order 9066: The Internment of 110,000 Japanese Americans.*
Intermediate-Level Generalization: Most individuals and groups who have immigrated to the United States and who have migrated within it were seeking better economic, political, and social opportunities. However, movement of individuals and groups within the United States has been both voluntary and forced.	5. Reading and discussing Chapter 3, "With Malice Toward None," in Japanese American Curriculum Project, *Japanese Americans: The Untold Story.* 6. Hypothesizing about why Japanese Americans were interned. 7. Comparing textbooks accounts of "relocation" with accounts in *Executive Order 9066, Japanese Americans: The Untold Story,* Daniel's *Concentration Camps U.S.A.: Japanese Americans And World War II,* and Paul Bailey, *Concentration Camp U.S.A.*
Lower-Level Generalization: During World War II, Japanese Americans were forced to move from their homes to concentration camps.	8. Reading selections from the novel, *Journey to Topaz* by Yoshiko Uchida, and discussing the experiences of the Sakane family during internment. 9. Viewing and discussing the film, *Guilty by Reason of Race* (NBC, 1972) 10. Summarizing and generalizing about the forced migration (internment) of Japanese Americans during World War II.

value choices intelligently. While the school has a tremendous responsibility to help students make moral choices reflectively, there is abundant evidence that educators have largely failed to help students to deal with moral issues intelligently.

Some teachers treat value problems like the invisible person, i.e., they deny their existence. They assume that if students get all of the "facts" straight, they can resolve racial problems. Such teachers may be said to practice the cult of false objectivity. Other teachers use an evasion strategy; when value problems arise in the classroom, they try to change the subject to a safer topic. Probably the most frequently used approach to value education in the elementary and high school is the inculcation of values considered "right" by adults or the indoctrination of these values. Teachers who use this method assume that adults know what the "correct" values are for all times and for students from all ethnic groups. Such values as honesty, justice, truth, freedom, equality, and love (as defined by teachers) are taught with legendary heroes, stories, rituals, and patriotic songs. This approach to value education is unsound and is inconsistent with a cultural pluralistic ideology.

The goal of moral education should be to equip students with a method for deriving and clarifying their values in a reflective manner, and not to force them to accept what teachers consider the "right" values.[1] Values usually considered the right ones are those verbally endorsed by dominant groups but often contradicted in their actions. Values that are functional for ethnic minority cultures are rarely perpetuated in the school. Didactic approaches to moral education, which many teachers use, are unsound because they fail to help students to learn a process for handling value conflicts. Also, standards that guide a person's life must be freely chosen from alternatives after thoughtful consideration of their consequences.

Many teachers will find it difficult to teach for *value clarification* rather than attempt to inculcate predetermined values. Some teachers feel that the values they verbally endorse should

1. Parts of this discussion are based on James A. Banks, "Liberating the Black Ghetto: Decision-Making and Social Action," in Richard Wisniewski, ed., *Teaching About Life in the City* (Washington, D.C.: National Council for the Social Studies 42nd Yearbook, 1972), pp. 159–83. Used with permission of the National Council for the Social Studies.

be the ones students—whether White or non-White—should inculcate, and that the school should facilitate their acquisition of those values. However, values that are functional for dominant groups may be dysfunctional for oppressed ethnic minority persons. Many teachers believe that all students should respect the policeman and the fireman, and that all students should always be honest. It may be impossible for a Puerto Rican American child to respect policemen as a group when he knows that some policemen sometimes kill barrio people when they rebel against American injustice. For many Puerto Rican American children, to respect policemen would be not only impossible but abnormal.

It may also be impossible and dysfunctional for an exploited group to always value honesty as defined by the dominant group. The victims of an inhumane society, powerless groups such as Blacks often find that to act in a way the dominant group would define as honest is antithetical to their existence. The slave masters often denied the slaves food that they had produced and needed for survival. When slaves were forced to take the food they had raised from slave masters, the masters defined their behavior as dishonest. Thus the slave who valued his or her life could not at the same time behave in a way that would be regarded by the master as honest. This same kind of situation exists today. In the 1960s when Blacks burned down stores exploiting them in their neighborhoods to vent hostility and to bring their plight to the attention of policymakers, many people who had power regarded their actions as immoral.

Teachers must realize that the exploited and the exploiter often use different reference points when determining whether a particular value exists. Behavior that the oppressor regards as immoral may be seen as highly moral by the oppressed. However, one of the reasons that exploited ethnic minority groups are powerless today is that they have too often accepted the definitions of values dominant groups imposed on them. As a group, Black slaves were rather peaceful. In contrast, while slave masters were teaching Blacks to be peaceful, they were using violence against them to maintain power and to reap economic gain from slave labor.

Different values may also be functional for different cultures and social situations. One teacher told the author about an incident occurring in his inter-city classroom. A student ran to the teacher and told him that someone had stolen his money. Rather than humiliating all of the other students by searching them, the teacher told the student that one of the things he had to learn in order to survive was how to protect his property and to defend himself. In that school culture, the protection of one's property was often a higher value than honesty. I should add—for readers who might be bothered by this anecdote—that honesty is not a value endorsed by most Americans. The real American value—as opposed to the expressed one—is to appear honest and not to get caught behaving dishonestly. The story about the middle-class White father who was reprimanding his son for stealing pencils at school illustrates the point. The father told the son that he did not have to steal pencils at school because he could bring him an ample supply from the office in which he worked. The political scandals symbolized by the word *Watergate,* and public reactions to them, also revealed many basic American values.

I am not suggesting that teachers should teach students to be dishonest. However, I believe that no values are functional for all times, settings, and cultures. Raths, Harmin, and Simon write: "Because life is different through time and space, we cannot be certain what experiences any person will have. We, therefore, cannot be certain what values, what style of life, would be most suitable for any person. We do, however, have some ideas about what *processes* might be the most effective for obtaining values."[2]

The emphasis in moral education for all students should be on *process* rather than specific products. Teachers should help students develop a method for deriving and clarifying their values rather than teach them a set of unexamined, predetermined values. This is the only approach to value education that is consistent with a cultural pluralistic ideology and that is educationally sound. Serious value problems emerge in the classroom when ethnic groups are studied. Minority group students have important questions about the value of their ethnic cultures, their identities, and about effective strategies to use to bring about social change. Students who are members of dom-

2. Louis E. Raths, Merrill Harmin, and Sidney B. Simon, *Values and Teaching: Working with Values in the Classroom* (Columbus, Ohio: Charles E. Merrill, 1966), p. 28.

inant ethnic groups have many conflicting, ambivalent attitudes and negative feelings toward racial minorities.

I have developed a value inquiry model that is presented in detail in my book, *Teaching Strategies for the Social Studies,* which teachers can use when teaching students to identify, clarify, and effectively derive their values.[3] The model is reprinted below in outline form, along with sample exercises illustrating how it can be used when teaching ethnic content.

Value Inquiry Model

1. Defining and recognizing value problems: Observation-discrimination
2. Describing value-relevant behavior: Description-discrimination
3. Naming values exemplified by behavior described: Identification-description, hypothesizing
4. Determining conflicting values in behavior described: Identification-analysis
5. Hypothesizing about sources of values analyzed: Hypothesizing (citing data to support hypotheses)
6. Naming alternative values to those exemplified by behavior observed: Recalling
7. Hypothesizing about the possible consequences of the values analyzed: Predicting, comparing, contrasting
8. Declaring value preference: Choosing
9. Stating reasons, sources, and possible consequences of value choice: Justifying, hypothesizing, predicting

VALUE INQUIRY LESSONS: EXAMPLES

For value inquiry lessons, the teacher may use case studies clipped from the daily newspaper, such as incidents involving controversy between policemen and various ethnic groups or cases related to "busing" and open housing. Ethnic literature is an excellent resource for value inquiry. We will use several examples to illustrate its use. Photographs, role-playing activi-

3. James A. Banks, with Ambrose A. Clegg, Jr., *Teaching Strategies for the Social Studies: Inquiry, Valuing and Decision-Making* (Reading, Mass.: Addison-Wesley Publishing Company, 1973), p. 466.

ties, and open-ended stories related to ethnic events also can be effectively used.

Example 1: Literature

A *Child in Prison Camp* by Shizuye Takashima is a powerful and poignant autobiographical account of a young girl's experiences in a Canadian concentration camp during World War II. When the internment of the Japanese is studied, the teacher can read aloud the following section from the book about the family conflict that occurred when the family was trying to decide whether to stay in Canada or return to Japan. The teacher can then ask the questions that follow.

Spring 1944

The war with Japan is getting very bad. I can feel my parents growing anxious. There is a lot of tension in the camp; rumors of being moved again, of everyone having to return to Japan. Kazuo and his family leave for Japan. Many are angry they have left us. Some call them cowards, others call them brave! I only feel sad, for I like Kazuo so much, so very much.

Father shouts at mother, "We return to Japan!"
"But what are we going to do? You have brothers
and sisters there. I have no one. Besides, the children. . . ."
"Never mind the children," father answers.
"They'll adjust. I'm tired of being treated as a spy,
a prisoner. Do what you like: I'm returning!"

I can see Mrs. Kono looks confused.
"My husband is talking of returning to Japan, too.
I think it's the best thing. All our relatives
are still there. We have nothing here."
Yuki stares at her. "It's all right for you, Mrs. Kono,
you were born there, but we weren't.
I am not going. That's all!"
And she walks out of the house.

Mother gets very upset. I know she wants to cry.
"I don't want to go to Japan, either," I say.
"They're short of food and clothing there.
They haven't enough for their own people.
They won't want us back."[4]

4. Shizuye Takashima, *A Child in Prison Camp* (New York: Tundra Books, 1971), no pagination. Copyright © 1971 by Shizuye Takashima. Reprinted with permission of Tundra Books.

Questions

1. What problem does the family face? (Defining and recognizing value problems)
2. What does mother want to do? What does father want to do? What does Shichan want to do? (Describing value-relevant behavior)
3. What does the behavior of mother, father, and Shichan tell us about what each thinks is important? (Naming values exemplified by behavior described)
4. How are mother's, father's, and Shichan's beliefs alike? Different? (Determining conflicting values in behavior described)
5. Why do you think that mother feels the way she does? Father? Shichan? (Hypothesizing about sources of values analyzed)
6. What are some other things that the family might have been able to do? (Naming alternative values to those exemplified by behavior observed)
7. What might happen to the family if it stays in Canada? Goes to Japan? Why? (Hypothesizing about the possible consequences of the values analyzed)
8. What would you do if you were mother? Father? Shichan? Why? (Declaring value preference)
9. Why would you do what you said you would do? What might happen to you as a result of your decision? (Stating reasons, sources, and possible consequences of value choice)

Example 2: Literature

At the turn of the century, most Afro-Americans lived in the Southern states that made up the Confederacy. Later they began an exodus to Northern cities to escape the poverty, violence, and discrimination they experienced in the South. *South Town, North Town*, and *Whose Town?*, a trilogy written by Lorenz Graham, will acquaint students with the problems faced by a typical Black Southern family, and how the Williams attempted to solve them by migrating North. Each book in the trilogy contains numerous incidents which are excellent vehicles for teaching value clarification. *South Town* is a poignant, gripping, yet realistic story about the family's painful experiences with racism in a Southern community. The book is replete with examples of harsh, overt, and unrelenting incidents of bigotry. It is extremely powerful because the characters are completely believable.

In *North Town,* the Williams discover, like many other Southern Black migrants, that the North is no promised land. Their small house is in a slum, David no longer has a room of his own, and he gets into trouble with the police because he lives in a "bad" neighborhood. The family gradually discovers that prejudice "Northern style" is more covert and subtle, but no less insidious than Southern racism. In the third and most outstanding book in his trilogy, *Whose Town?,* Graham effectively and poignantly describes the Black Revolt of the 1960s as manifested in fictional North Town—which could be Newark, Detroit, Chicago or any other American city in which riots occurred. In candid detail, he relates how the racial tension in North Town results in brutal and unprovoked attacks against Blacks, killings, and finally a riot when a small Black boy is drowned by a White mob at a public pool. After reading aloud the part of the book describing the riot on pages 178–94, the teacher can ask the value clarification questions below. The description of the riot ends like this:

> Gradually the crowd fell back. The people began moving toward the east side. They left behind a block of stores and business places about half of which had been smashed open and several of which had burned. Merchandise was strewn in the street. Some of it was carried away by looters. David could not tell how many had been arrested. Some who had been hurt were carried off in ambulances and police cars. Others whose heads were bruised and whose faces were bloody were helped away by friends.[5]

Questions

1. What problem(s) is presented in this incident?
2. What does David's behavior and beliefs about Stanton Park tell you about what is important to him?

5. Lorenz Graham, *Whose Town?* (New York: Thomas Y. Crowell, 1969), p. 194.

3. How are Marybelle's and Jeanette's values and beliefs different from David's?
4. What does the behavior of the crowd that chased the Black boys at Stanton Park tell you about what is important to them?
5. What values do the statements made by the Black speakers after the boy was drowned at Stanton Park reveal?
6. What does the behavior of the Black crowd that gathered after the boy was drowned tell us about what was important to them?
7. What does the behavior of the police tell us about what was important to them?
8. The Black crowd smashed and burned a number of stores and businesses. What does this tell us about what was important to this crowd?
9. What does the behavior of the looters tell us about what was important to them?
10. What are *other* values that could have been endorsed by:
    a) Marybelle and Jeanette
    b) the crowd that chased the Black boys
    c) the Black speakers
    d) the Black crowd
    e) the police
    f) the looters
11. What may have been the possible consequences of these *different* values?
12. What would you have done if you had been: (Why?)
    a) Marybelle and Jeanette
    b) the White majority at the swimming pool
    c) the Black speakers
    d) part of the Black crowd
    e) the police
13. What might have been the consequences of your actions? Explain.
14. Could you have lived with those consequences?

Example 3: An Open-ended Story

Open-ended stories present problem situations. If carefully chosen or written, they are excellent tools for stimulating class discussions of issues related to ethnic studies and other human relations problems. After reading an open-ended story to the class, the teacher can have the students identify the problems within it, the values of the characters, the courses of action they might take to resolve the problems, and the possible consequences of the proposed solutions. The students can also act out or role play solutions to the problems.

Unfinished Stories for Use in the Classroom, an NEA publication, contains many excellent stories dealing with such problems as "Personal Shortcomings" and "Shortcomings of Others." [6] While these problems are not directly related to ethnic studies, this book is recommended because the stories can serve as models for ones the teacher and students *can write* about ethnic problems in their classroom, school, or community. The following two books include open-ended stories which deal with problems in ethnic relations: Jean D. Grambs, *Intergroup Education: Methods and Materials;* Fannie R. Shaftel and George Shaftel, *Role-Playing for Social Values: Decision-Making in the Social Studies*. The story reprinted below is from the Shaftel and Shaftel book. Questions which can be used with the story are given.

Seed of Distrust

Betty was all excited when she ran into the apartment. "Mother, will you iron my green dress tonight?"

"I was planning to do it Saturday night, honey, so you'd have it for Sunday School."

"But I'll need it!"

"What's the rush?"

"Nora's invited me to a party tomorrow after school."

"Oh, I see," her mother said slowly, as if thinking hard. "Nora's the little girl on the second floor?"

"Yes. She's real nice."

Betty's sister Lucy, who was a sophomore in high school, asked, "Does her mother know?"

"Know what?" Betty asked.

"Nora's white, isn't she?"

6. *Unfinished Stories for Use in the Classroom* (Washington, D. C.: National Education Association, 1970). Copies of this booklet are available from: NEA Publications-Sales Section, 1201 16th Street, N. W., Washington, D. C. 20036.

"Sure!"

"Does her mother know she's invited you?"

"Of course! I m-mean, I guess so."

"Does her mother know you're Negro?"   (Or Mexican, or Puerto Rican, etc.)

"Sure!"

"You mean-you think so?"

"Y-Yes," Betty stammered.

"Better make sure," Lucy said, and turned back to the math she was studying.

"I'll iron your dress, honey," Betty's mother said reassuringly. "You'll look real nice."

"Uh-huh," Betty said dully. "Thanks, Mom."

And then, next day, after lunch, the thing happened—
Nora met Betty in the hall, outside the fifth-grade room.

"Betty, I've been hunting for you," Nora said urgently. "Listen. My Aunt Dorothy phoned last night. She's arriving today for a visit. My grandma's coming over to see her, and mother's making a dinner for the whole family, cousins and all. You see? We've got to postpone my party. Until next week, maybe. I'll let you know!"

Betty looked at her, blank-faced.

"Don't bother," Betty said. "Don't bother at all." And Betty turned and walked away, her back very straight.

For an instant Nora just stood and stared. Then she ran. She caught Betty's arm and stopped her.

"Betty, what's the matter? Why're you talking like that?"[7]

Questions

1. What is the main problem in this story?
2. What do you think of these characters: Betty, Lucy, Nora? Why? What kinds of things and people do you think are important to each of them? Why?
3. Do you think that Lucy should have asked Betty if Nora's mother knew that she was Negro? Why or why not?
4. Do you think that Nora told the truth about the family dinner? Why or why not?

7. Fannie R. Shaftel and George Shaftel, *Role-Playing for Social Values: Decision-Making in the Social Studies* (Englewood Cliffs, N. J.: Prentice-Hall, 1967), pp. 383–84. Copyright © by Prentice-Hall, Inc. Reprinted with permission of the publisher.

5. What are some courses of action that Betty can take? What should Betty do? Why? What would you do if you were Betty? Why? What might be the consequences of your action? Why?

PROVIDING OPPORTUNITIES FOR SOCIAL ACTION

Racial minority groups in all regions of the United States are victims of institutionalized racism, poverty, and political powerlessness. When the teacher identifies concepts and generalizations from the social sciences, he or she should select those which will aid students in making decisions and taking actions to help eliminate these problems. This is absolutely imperative if the school is going to help bring about constructive social change. After they have mastered higher level knowledge related to these problems and analyzed and clarified their values, the teacher can ask students to list possible actions that can be taken to eradicate problems in their school and community and to predict the possible consequences of each alternative course of action. The primary purpose of such activities should be to provide students with opportunities to develop a sense of political efficacy and not necessarily to provide community services, although both goals can be attained in the most effective types of projects.

Students should be given opportunities to make some decisions about ethnic problems which they can implement through social actions projects such as setting up voter registration programs in ethnic communities, campaigning for the passage of a school levy, or implementing discussion groups to help reduce racial tension in the school. Students will be unable to *solve* the racial problems in their communities. However, they may be able to take some effective actions that can improve the racial attitudes of the students in their classroom and school, or contribute to the resolution of the racial problems in the wider community through some types of meaningful and effective social action or participation projects. Students should participate in social action projects only after they have studied the related issues from the perspectives of the social sciences and humanities, analyzed and clarified their values regarding them, identified the possible consequences of their actions, and expressed a willingness to accept them. Since the school is an institution with racial and ethnic problems mirroring those of the larger society, students can be provided practice in shaping public policy by working to eliminate ethnic conflict in their classroom, school, or school system.

GAINING THE CONTENT BACKGROUND

Most teachers, like other Americans, have large gaps in their knowledge of ethnic groups because most educational institutions have only recently begun to include ethnic content in the general school and university curricula. Ethnic studies courses are still mainly electives. Thus only a few future teachers will have studied more about ethnic groups than teachers now in the classroom. Teachers who have studied ethnic groups have rarely studied ethnicity within a comparative framework, but rather have studied one specific group.

It is absolutely essential that the teacher has a working knowledge of the role of ethnicity in American life and about the histories and the problems of the various ethnic groups before he or she can implement a sound ethnic studies program. Even for the most ambitious teacher, acquiring the minimal knowledge needed to teach comparative ethnic studies will be a challenging task. While attaining information about American ethnic groups is challenging, it is equally rewarding. Ethnic content deals with the conflicts and dilemmas that have decisively shaped American life. It sometimes evokes anger and shame, but just as often compassion, admiration, and *hope*.

The teacher should begin his or her reading program with one or two general books giving an overview of ethnicity in the United States. This type of book will provide the teacher with a conceptual framework for interpreting and comparing the experiences of the various ethnic groups, as well as serve as an excellent source for concepts and generalizations that can be taught to students. Milton G. Gordon, *Assimilation in American Life*, Peter I. Rose, *They and We: Racial and Ethnic Relations in the United States*, and James A. Banks, ed., *Teaching Ethnic Studies: Concepts and Strategies*, are highly recommended general references. These books are annotated in Chapter 1.

The teacher should read at least one general survey book

on each of the major ethnic groups. This should be a high quality book written from the perspective of the ethnic group. To become sensitive, the teacher must learn to view events from the points of view of the victims of oppression because for too long we have viewed American history primarily from an Anglo-Saxon perspective. Most teachers are quite familiar with the Anglo-Saxon point of view. They need to become aware of other ways to view American life. While many of the books recommended below were written by ethnic minorities, others were written by sensitive Whites. For example, Dee Brown and William Brandon are non-Indian, yet they have written accurate and sensitive histories of Native Americans.

Afro-Americans

Hundreds of books have been written about Afro-Americans in recent years. While many are poor, some are excellent. John Hope Franklin, *From Slavery to Freedom: A History of Negro Americans,* is the best general history of Afro-Americans. Benjamin Quarles, *The Negro in the Making of America,* and Lerone Bennett, Jr., *Before the Mayflower: A History of the Negro in America: 1619–1964,* are two popular histories that read easily. The Quarles book is a sound but conservative history of Black Americans. August Meier and Elliott Rudwick, *From Plantation to Ghetto,* rev. ed., is an insightful and well-written interpretative history of Afro-Americans that highlights the role of Black people in shaping their destiny in America. There are many excellent documentary histories of Afro-Americans, two of the best are Herbert Aptheker, *A Documentary History of the Negro People in the United States* (three volumes, covering Black history up to 1932) and *Afro-American History: Primary Sources,* edited by Thomas R. Frazier. The Frazier volume is noteworthy because it presents Black views of American history. *The Black American: A Documentary History,* edited by Leslie H. Fishel and Benjamin Quarles, is a comprehensive and scholarly documentary history. It has excellent commentaries by the editors.

Asian Americans

Asian Americans are a highly diversified group which few books treat as a whole. Rather, the teacher will need to read a book on each Asian-American group. Stanford M. Lyman, *The*

Asian in the West, is an excellent book on Chinese and Japanese Americans. Most of the chapters deal with the Chinese, and it is rather technical. Comprehensive books on Chinese Americans include *The Chinese in the United States* by Rose Hum Lee, *Chinese in American Life: Some Aspects of Their History, Status, Problems and Contributions* by S. W. Sung, Stanford M. Lyman, *Chinese Americans,* and Francis L. K. Hsu, *The Challenge of the American Dream: The Chinese in the United States.* Betty L. Sung, *The Story of the Chinese in America,* is a popular book on Chinese Americans. A useful documentary history is Cheng-Tsu Wu, ed., *"Chink!": A Documentary History of Anti-Chinese Prejudice in America.*

Many books have been written about the internment of Japanese Americans during World War II. However, there are few comprehensive treatments of the group. Harry H. L. Kitano, *Japanese Americans: The Evolution of A Subculture,* and William Petersen, *Japanese Americans: Oppression and Success,* are well-written scholarly books giving overviews of the Japanese-American experience. More recent information about Japanese Americans, as well as about other Asian Americans, are found in a special issue of the *Journal of Social Issues* (no. 2, 1973), entitled, "Asian Americans: A Success Story?" edited by Stanley Sue and Harry H.L. Kitano.

There is an appaling dearth of published sources on Filipino-Americans. However, two books about contemporary Filipino-Americans are now available. They are *The Filipinos in America* by Alfredo N. Munoz and *Makibaka: The Philpino American Struggle* by Royal S. Morales. Both books are published by Mountainview Press of Los Angeles. Bruno Lasker, *Filipino Immigration to Continental United States and Hawaii,* published in 1931, is dated but still the only source to date containing valuable information about the early immigration of Filipinos to Hawaii and the United States mainland. The most sensitive and revealing treatments of Filipino life in the United States are found in the brilliant writings of the late Filipino-American writer, Carlos Bulosan, including *America Is in the Heart,* reissued in 1973 by the University of Washington Press. This is a poignant and deeply moving book. His *Sound of Falling Light: Letters in Exile,* is perceptive and powerful. Another interesting personal account is *I Have Lived with the American People* by Manuel Buaken. *Roots: an Asian American Reader,* edited by Amy Tachiki, Eddie Wong, and Franklin Odo, contains several treatments of Filipino-Americans.

Mexican Americans

The teacher can find a number of useful books on Mexican Americans that provide a general overview of the group. Rodolfo Acuña, *Occupied America: The Chicano's Struggle Toward Liberation,* interprets the Chicano experience from a colonial perspective. Carey McWilliams, *North From Mexico: The Spanish-Speaking People of the United States,* is a good general overview of the culture and history of Mexican Americans up through World War II. *The Chicanos: A History of Mexican Americans,* by Matt S. Meier and Feliciano Rivera, is a comprehensive and extremely useful history of Mexican Americans. Joan W. Moore (with Alfredo Cuellar), *Mexican-Americans,* is a useful and readable sociological treatment of the Mexican American written from an assimilationist perspective. *A Documentary History of Mexican-Americans,* edited by Wayne Moquin with Charles Van Doren, is an excellent documentary source. Stan Steiner, *La Raza: The Mexican Americans,* is an interesting popular treatment of the group. A controversial study of the group is *Mexican Americans* by Ellwyn Stoddard.

Native Americans: Indians

There are hundreds of books about American Indians, but many of them are insensitive, racist, and justify the genocide of this group. A few sensitive, accurate books have been written in recent years. Alvin M. Josephy, Jr., *The Indian Heritage of America,* and William Brandon, *The American Heritage Book of Indians,* are extremely informative, well-written introductions to Indian cultures in all parts of the Americas. *Indians of North America,* 2nd. ed. by Harold E. Driver, is a good general source treating diverse aspects of Native American life. A brief and excellent history which includes documents is Harold E. Spicer, *A Short History of the Indians of the United States.* Two especially powerful and sensitive books are Dee Brown, *Bury My Heart at Wounded Knee* and *Touch the Earth: A Self-Portrait of Indian*

Existence, edited by T.C. McLuhan. The book by Dee Brown is written from an Indian point of view. The McLuhan volume is an outstanding collection of statements by Native Americans on a number of topics. *Great Documents in American Indian History,* edited by Wayne Moquin and Charles Van Doren, is an excellent documentary source.

Puerto Rican Americans

There are not many books dealing with Puerto Rican life on the United States mainland. However, the literature on this group is increasing. Some excellent volumes have been published in recent years. The best general treatment of the contemporary problems of Puerto Rican Americans is *Puerto Rican Americans: The Meaning of Migration to the Mainland* by Joseph J. Fitzpatrick. Elena Padilla, *Up from Puerto Rico,* is an excellent anthropological study of a Puerto Rican community in New York city. Francesco Cordasco and Eugene Bucchioni, eds., *The Puerto Rican Experience: A Sociological Sourcebook,* contains excellent selections from a wide variety of sources. Because Puerto Rican migrants on the United States mainland have a close relationship with the island, the teacher will need to read at least one book dealing with life in Puerto Rico. The best short general treatment of the island in English is *Puerto Rico: A Profile* by Kal Wagenheim. *The Puerto Ricans: A Documentary History,* edited by Wagenheim, is also useful. A "militant" view of problems on the island is presented in Juan Angel Silen, *We, the Puerto Rican People.* Gordan K. Lewis, *Puerto Rico: Freedom and Power in the Caribbean,* is a refreshing history of the island.

European Americans

There are many ethnic groups in the United States of European origin. No single book treats them comprehensively. The teacher will need to read several books about various European American ethnic groups. The works of Oscar Handlin give the best treatments of European ethnic groups collectively. The teacher will find two of his books especially helpful, *The Up-*

rooted: The Epic Story of the Great Migrations that Made the American People and *Immigration as a Factor in American Life*. *The Uprooted* is a deeply moving and compassionate story of European immigration to America. The latter book, which is an edited collection, contains some excellent documents. John F. Kennedy's *A Nation of Immigrants* is a brief but general account of the ethnic groups in the United States. Charles H. Anderson, *White Protestant Americans,* is a comprehensive treatment of our dominant ethnic group. A well written and researched source on American Jews is *Jewish Americans: Three Generations in a Jewish Community* by Sidney Goldstein and Calvin Gold-scheider. *American Immigration* by Maldwyn Allen Jones is a lucid and informed general source on American immigration. The best general treatment of nativistic movements in the United States is John Higham, *Strangers in the Land: Patterns of American Nativism 1860–1925.* An interesting, short, and readable treatment of ethnicity in modern American life is Andrew M. Greeley, *Why Can't They Be Like Us: Facts and Fallacies about Ethnic Differences and Group Conflict in America.* Marcus Lee Hansen, *The Atlantic Migration 1607–1860,* is a classic study of early European immigrants.

There are literally hundreds of books dealing with specific ethnic groups of European origin, such as *Italian Americans* by Joseph Lopreato, *White Southerners* by Lewis M. Killian, and *That Most Distressful Nation: The Taming of the American Irish* by Andrew M. Greeley. The teacher must choose the European American ethnic groups he or she wishes to include in units and locate appropriate books. The card catalog in the local public or university library is a good place to start.

SELECTING STUDENT RESOURCES

In the past the paucity of books for children and young people that dealt with ethnic groups was a great problem for the teacher. The number of books in this area has increased markedly in recent years, although there are still few excellent books. Evaluating ethnic studies books is still a major problem. We will discuss this problem later. How can the classroom teacher find out which books are published? The children's librarian in the public library and at the curriculum center of the local college or university are excellent resource people, as well as the school librarian. Children's librarians receive a number of book lists and books from a wide variety of sources. They are usually willing and able to help the teacher find books on a particular topic, such as ethnic studies.

Some of the best sources are the book lists and bibliographies published by numerous public and private organizations such as public school systems, civil rights organizations, public libraries, and professional organizations (for example, the National Council for the Social Studies and the National Council for Teachers of English.) Some organizations such as the Council on Interracial Books for Children and the Japanese American Curriculum Project provide teachers and other professionals with book lists and other resources dealing with ethnic groups, and this is their main purpose. Other organizations such as the Puerto Rican Forum and the National Association for the Advancement of Colored People publish ethnic studies book lists as a part of their public relations programs. The current addresses of these types of organizations can be found in the reference room of the local public or university library. Ask the reference librarian for help.

Magazines and newspapers such as *Ebony, The New York Times,* and *Saturday Review World,* also publish book lists periodically. The teacher should check these sources. Finally, browsing in the children's section of local bookstores in large cities can lead to the discovery of a gold mine of recent children's books. The salesperson in charge of children's books is usually willing and able to help the teacher. Below is a list of some of the better bibliographic resources the teacher will find helpful in locating books.

Bibliographic Resources

Baker, August A. *The Black Experience in Children's Books.* New York: The New York Public Library, 1971.

Banks, James A. *Teaching the Black Experience: Methods and Materials.* Belmont, Calif.: Fearon Publishers, 1971.

Books Transcend Barriers: A Bibliography of Books About Africans, Afro-Americans, Japanese, Chinese, American Indians, Eskimos, and Mexican-Americans for Elementary and Middle School Grades. Seattle: Seattle Public Schools, 1972.

Carlson, Ruth Kearney. *Emerging Humanity: Multi-Ethnic Literature for Children and Adolescents.* Dubuque, Iowa: William C. Brown, 1972.

Conwell, Mary K. and Pura Belpre. *Libros En Español: An Annotated List of Children's Books in Spanish.* New York: The New York Public Library, 1971.

Grambs, Jean D. and John C. Carr, eds. *Black Image: Education Copes with Color.* Dubuque, Iowa: William C. Brown, 1972.

Griffin, Louise, compiler. *Multi-Ethnic Books for Young Children.* Washington, D. C.: National Association for the Education of Young Children, undated.

Interracial Books for Children. Published quarterly by the Council on Interracial Books for Children. 1841 Broadway, New York, New York 10023.

Jackson, Jr., Miles M., ed. *A Bibliography of Negro History and Culture for Young Readers.* Pittsburgh: University of Pittsburgh Press, 1968.

Katz, William Loren. *Teacher's Guide to American Negro History.* Chicago: Quadrangle Books, 1971.

Keating, Charlotte M. *Building Bridges of Understanding Between Cultures.* Tucson, Ariz.: Palo Verde Pub. Co., 1971.

Koblitz, Minnie W. *The Negro in Schoolroom Literature: Resources for the Teacher of Kindergarten through Sixth Grade.* New York: Center for Urban Education, 1966.

Latimer, Bettye I. *Starting Out Right: Choosing Books about Black People for Young Children: Pre-School through Third Grade.* Bulletin no. 2314. Madison: Wisconsin Department of Public Instruction, 1972.

Reid, Virginia M., ed. *Reading Ladders for Human Relations.* 5th ed. Washington, D. C.: American Council on Education, 1972.

RIF's Guide to Book Selection: Reading is Fundamental. Washington, D. C.: Smithsonian Institution, 1970, 1971. Periodic supplements are published.

Rollins, Charlemae, ed. *We Build Together: A Reader's Guide to Negro Life and Literature for Elementary and High School Use.* Champaign, Ill.: National Council of Teachers of English, 1967.

Tanyzer, Harold and Jean Karl, eds. *Reading, Children's Books, and Our Pluralistic Society.* Newark, Delaware: International Reading Association, 1972.

GUIDELINES FOR EVALUATING AND SELECTING ETHNIC STUDIES MATERIALS

Books for Students

Finding sound ethnic studies materials has always been difficult.* When the first serious attempts were made to introduce Black Studies into the curriculum in the early 1960s, there was a tremendous paucity of resources. Currently, there is a flood of teaching materials on Afro-Americans. There are also many books on American Indians. However, there are still few resources on Mexican Americans, Asian Americans, and Puerto Rican Americans. While the quantity varies, a large number of the materials on each ethnic group are insensitive, inaccurate, and written from a White Anglo-Saxon point of view. Nevertheless, there are a few good materials on each group. Identifying them requires a great deal of time and careful evaluation and selection. The criteria and examples of books below are offered to help teachers and curriculum specialists evaluate and select ethnic studies resources for classroom use.

Books and other materials should accurately portray the perspectives, attitudes, and feelings of minority groups. There are certain values, aspirations, and points of view prevalent in American ethnic communities. Books should honestly and sensitively reflect these perspectives and feelings, both through characters and in the interpretations of events and situations. *Touch the Earth*, compiled by T.C. McLuhan, is a collection of statements and excerpts from the writing of American Indians. This book successfully conveys some of the values endemic in Indian cultures. *America Is in the Heart* by Carlos Bulosan, *House Made of Dawn* by N. Scott Momaday, and *Uptown* by John Steptoe also faithfully portray ethnic feelings and aspirations.

Fictional works should have strong ethnic characters. Many books have ethnic minority characters who are subservient, weak, and ignorant. Kristin Hunter, *The Soul Brothers and Sister Lou*,

* *This section of the chapter was first published as James A. Banks, "Evaluating and Selecting Ethnic Studies Materials,"* Educational Leadership *31 (April 1974), pp. 593–96. It is reprinted here with the permission of the Association for Supervision and Curriculum Development.*

and Thomas Fall, *Canalboat to Freedom,* have powerful and admirable characters. The strong characters and memorable incidents in *The Soul Brothers and Sister Lou* will help students to develop empathy for urban Blacks. Fierce but brilliant Fess, talented and lonesome Blind Tom, shy and sensitive Calvin, and Lou, who searches relentlessly for her Black identity, will deeply impress the reader. Children love and respect Lundius, the courageous, wise, and kind Black hero of *Canalboat to Freedom.*

Books should describe settings and experiences with which all students can identify and yet accurately reflect ethnic cultures and lifestyles. *Barrio Boy* by Ernesto Galarza, *Down These Mean Streets* by Piri Thomas, *Annie and the Old One* by Miska Miles, and *Julie of the Wolves* by Jean Craighead George faithfully portray ethnic cultures in a way that nonminority students can learn a great deal about them. A young Indian boy shares his way of life with the reader in Ann Nolan Clark's *In My Mother's House.* Non-Indian readers can learn much information about Indian life from this story. Indian children will strongly identify with the protagonist and his values.

The protagonists in some books about ethnic groups have few ethnic characteristics. Such books color Anglo-Saxons Red, Brown, and Black. *A Child in Prison Camp* by Shizuye Takashima and *Lone Heart Mountain* by Estelle Ishigo have authentic ethnic characters and faithfully portray Japanese culture. In *A Child in Prison Camp,* author-artist Takashima relates her childhood experiences in a Canadian concentration camp during World War II. This is a beautiful and poignant book. *Lone Heart Mountain* is the story of a Japanese-American family in an internment camp. The characters, events, and illustrations in this touching book reflect important aspects of Japanese-American life.

The illustrations in books should be accurate, ethnically sensitive, and technically well done. Many books have beautiful photographs or drawings that are inaccurate. Maisie and Richard Conrat, *Executive Order 9066: The Internment of 110, 000 Japanese Americans,* is a poignant and deeply moving collection of accurate photographs about the internment. The photographs in Rudy Acuña, *Cultures in Conflict: Problems of the Mexican Americans,* sensitively and accurately portray contemporary Mexican Americans in a wide variety of settings. The woodcuts by Ann Grifalconi in Mary Hays Weik, *The Jazz Man,* are movingly sad but highly effective. It is said that one picture is worth a thousand words. There is a great deal of truth in this adage. Teachers should carefully study the illustrations in books and other materials and check them for authenticity, accuracy, and sensitivity. Students can learn either stereotypes or facts from illustrations. Pictures often speak more cogently than words.

Ethnic materials should be free of racist concepts, cliches, phrases, and words. Many books contain words and statements that have negative connotations even though they might have many other strengths. Benjamin Brewster, *The First Book of Eskimos,* is very stereotypic. The author portrays Eskimos as a carefree, happy people who have no serious human problems. Ruth Murry Underhill's *Red Man's America* is a fairly good general survey of Indian cultural groups, but it is seriously flawed by the author's many insensitive references to Indian cultures. Words like *colored* (used to refer to Blacks), *savage, hostile, primitive,* and *uncivilized* can alert the teacher to a possibly insensitive book or resource, although their use in a book does not necessarily mean that it is insensitive. An author might use these words for the sake of historical accuracy, to depict the language of bigots, or for other justifiable reasons. The teacher must judge the use of words and phrases within the total context of the book or resource. Nevertheless, the teacher should watch out for these kinds of words when evaluating instructional materials.

Factual materials should be historically accurate. Books that present inaccurate information about minorities confuse students and reinforce stereotypes. They can also be the source of misconceptions about ethnic groups. Rudy Acuña, *A Mexican American Chronicle,* William Brandon, *The American Heritage Book of Indians,* Kal Wagenheim, *Puerto Rico: A Profile,* and Betty L. Sung, *The Story of the Chinese in America,* are factually accurate and sensitive books. Oliver LaFarge, *A Pictorial History of the American Indian,* is replete with inaccurate and misleading statements. The author presents the Bering Strait theory of Indian migration as a conclusive fact and portrays Native Americans as warlike and hostile savages.

Resources that purport to be multiethnic should be comprehensive both in terms of the groups included and the events discussed. Often materials that are otherwise excellent omit an entire ethnic group. Puerto Rican Americans, Asian Americans, and Mexican Americans are often neglected in these kinds of resources. Mexican Americans are not included in Joseph Gittler, ed., *Understanding Minority Groups*. *To Serve the Devil* by Paul Jacobs and Saul Landau is an extremely useful documentray history of American ethnic groups, but it totally neglects Filipino Americans, an ethnic group which numbered 343,060 in 1970. When evaluating multiethnic resources or basal textbooks for school adoption, teachers should check to see that they include these groups in a meaningful way: (1) Afro-Americans, (2) Asian Americans (including Chinese, Japanese, and Filipino Americans), (3) Mexican Americans, (4) Native Americans (Indians), (5) Puerto Rican Americans, and (6) Jewish Americans and other European American ethnic groups.

Teachers should also check to see if multiethnic resources and basal textbooks discuss major events and documents related to ethnic history. Events such as the removal of Native Americans to Indian Territory in the 1800s, and the large migrations of Puerto Ricans to the United States mainland that began in the 1920s should be included in every multiethnic and American history textbook. Key legal documents such as the Treaty of Guadalupe Hidalgo (1848) and the Chinese Exclusion Act of 1882 should be included. To be able to determine which key events and documents should be included in basic sources, the teacher will need to read at least one general book on each of the major ethnic groups as suggested earlier.

In addition to the guidelines suggested above, the teacher should determine the age level for which a particular book might be appropriate. Both interest and reading level should be considered. Some books are excellent for adult reading but are inappropriate for school use; others are fine for older readers but inappropriate for young children. The type of classroom situation should also be considered when selecting ethnic studies materials. A particular book might be appropriate for use with some classrooms but not with others. The teacher should bear in mind whether his or her class is, for example, all-Black, all American-Indian, all-Asian, all-White, or integrated. The teacher should also consider how he or she will use each resource. Some books are excellent for basic information but will not give the students a feeling for the ethnic group. Other books have excellent illustrations but poor and distorted texts. Some excellent books, like *The Jazz Man*, are not appropriate for all students, all purposes, and in all kinds of settings. The teacher must exercise sound judgment, sensitivity, integrity, and insight when selecting and evaluating ethnic studies materials for class use. In the final analysis, only the teacher can determine which materials can best help to achieve the instructional goals which he or she has identified.

SUMMARY

We have delineated the steps the teacher needs to take to structure an ethnic studies program focused on decision making. These steps include (1) the identification of key concepts and generalizations, (2) the formulation of intermediate-level generalizations, and (3) the identification of lower-level statements related to each of the major ethnic groups. Once these steps are completed, the teacher can then proceed to structure lessons and gather materials. When formulating lessons, the teacher should make sure that lessons include value inquiry exercises as well as social action activities when these are appropriate. Examples of value inquiry lessons and social participation activities were discussed.

Prior to implementing an ethnic studies program, the teacher should plan a reading program which includes (1) one or two general books on ethnicity in the United States and (2) at least one survey book on each of the major ethnic groups. Recommended books in both categories were discussed. The selection and evaluation of student materials is one of the teacher's most challenging tasks. Guidelines and resources for completing this task were given. Part I of this book deals with the goals of ethnic studies and procedures for planning and organizing instruction. Part II presents historical overviews of ethnic groups in the United States and strategies and materials for teaching about them.

Questions and Activities

Respond to the following "Ethnic Literacy Test," and discuss your responses, giving reasons for them, with your classmates or colleagues. Determine your "Ethnic Literacy Score" by comparing your responses with the answers to the test given below.

How might you use this test with your students to stimulate research and discussion? What sources might they go to to check their responses? Administer this test, in part or whole, to your class. Adapt to your students' reading and grade levels. How well did they do on the test? Why?

ETHNIC LITERACY TEST

Directions

Indicate whether each of the following statements is TRUE or FALSE by placing a "T" or "F" in the space preceding it.

1. _____Mexican Americans are the second largest "non-White" ethnic minority group in the United States.

2. _____The first Chinese immigrants who came to the United States worked on the railroads.

3. _____In 1970, there were about 10 million Afro-Americans in the United States.

4. _____Puerto Ricans on the island of Puerto Rico became United States citizens in 1920.

5. _____The forced migration of the Sioux people is known as "The Trail of Tears."

6. _____Between 1820 and 1930, 15 million immigrants came to the United States.

7. _____White Anglo-Saxon Protestants constitute the largest ethnic group in the United States.

8. _____Rosh Hashanah, which in Hebrew means "end of the year," is a Jewish holiday that comes early in the fall.

9. _____Between 1820 and 1971, Germans were the largest European group immigrating to the United States.

10. _____The first law to limit immigration to the United States was passed in 1882 to restrict the number of African immigrants.

11. _____Puerto Rican Americans in New York City tend to identify strongly with Afro-Americans in that city.

12. _____Between 1820 and 1971, more individuals from Canada and Newfoundland immigrated to the United States than from Mexico.

13. _____Most Afro-Americans came from the eastern parts of Africa.

14. _____The internment of the Japanese Americans during World War II was opposed by President Franklin D. Roosevelt.

15. _____In 1970, there were nearly a million and a half Puerto Rican Americans in the United States.

16. _____Chinese Americans constitute the single largest Asian American group in the United States.

17. _____Congress passed a Removal Act which authorized the removal of Indians from the east to the west of the Mississippi in 1830.

18. _____A Japanese settlement was established in California as early as 1869.

19. _____The United States acquired a large part of Mexico's territory under the terms of the Treaty of Guadalupe Hidalgo in 1848.

20. _____Agriculture dominates the economy of the island of Puerto Rico.

21. _____The first Blacks to arrive in North America came on a Dutch ship that landed at Jamestown, Virginia, in 1619.

22. _____The unemployment rate among American Indians was more than ten times higher than the national average in 1970.

23. _____*Paper sons* is a custom that is associated with Chinese Americans.

24. _____In 1970 there were less than one million persons in the United States who were classified as American Indians.

25. _____Some of the bloodiest riots which involved Afro-Americans and Whites took place in the early 1900s.

26. _____In the last forty years, the Mexican-American population in the United States increased by over 3 million.

27. _____The United States acquired the island of Puerto Rico from Spain in 1898.

28. _____There are only 438 Japanese surnames.

29. _____Chinese immigrants to the United States became distinguished for their outstanding work on truck farms.

30. _____The only large Puerto Rican community on the United States mainland is in New York City.

31. _____A third generation Japanese American is called a *Sansei*.

32. _____There were over one-half million Filipinos in the United States in 1970.

33. _____More than one-third of American Indians lived in urban areas in 1970.
34. _____Most Chinese immigrants to the United States came from Western China.
35. _____Eleven Italian Americans were lynched in New Orleans in 1892.
36. _____Nativism directed against Southern and Eastern European immigrants was intense when the statue of liberty was dedicated in 1886.
37. _____In 1974 there were more than a half million Cuban Americans in the United States.
38. _____Queen Liliuokalani of Hawaii was overthrown in a revolution led by Americans in 1898.

Answers to Ethnic Literacy Test

1. T   2. F   3. F   4. F   5. F   6. F   7. T   8. F   9. T
10. F   11. F   12. T   13. F   14. F   15. T   16. F   17. T   18. T
19. T   20. F   21. F   22. T   23. T   24. T   25. T   26. T   27. T
28. F   29. F   30. F   31. T   32. F   33. F   34. F   35. T   36. T
37. T   38. F

Annotated Bibliography

General

Banks, James A., ed. *Teaching Ethnic Studies: Concepts and Strategies.* Washington, D. C.: National Council for the Social Studies 43rd Yearbook, 1973.

Fourteen ethnic studies experts write about teaching the cultures of Asian Americans, Afro-Americans, American Indians, Mexican Americans, Puerto Rican Americans, White ethnic groups, and the role of women in American history. Teaching strategies and annotated bibliographies are key features of the book. Illustrated with fifty-five photographs. Available in both paperbound and clothbound editions.

Banks, James A. and William W. Joyce, eds. *Teaching Social Studies to Culturally Different Children.* Reading, Mass.: Addison-Wesley, 1971.
This anthology includes articles which discuss various aspects of the lives of ethnic minority youths and effective strategies for teaching their cultures.

Epstein, Charlotte. *Intergroup Relations for the Classroom Teacher.* New York: Houghton Mifflin, 1968.

A direct and forthright book discussing the diverse cultures of students and strategies for improving interethnic relations in the classroom.

Gordon, Milton. *Assimilation in American Life: The Role of Race, Religion, and National Origins.* New York: Oxford University Press, 1964.

An award winning book which contains a brilliant explication of the concept of ethnicity in America and a seminal theory of assimilation in American life.

Grambs, Jean D. *Intergroup Education: Methods and Materials.* Englewood Cliffs: Prentice-Hall, 1968.

Resources, methods, and open-ended stories that can be used to teach ethnic studies are included in this useful reference by a human relations veteran.

Jacobs, Paul and Saul Landau with Eve Pell. *To Serve the Devil: A Documentary Analysis of America's Racial History and Why It Has Been Kept Hidden, Two Volumes.* New York: Vintage Books, 1971.

A refreshingly honest and extremely useful history of ethnic minority groups in the United States. These books include excellent documents as well as outstanding texts by the authors.

Rose, Peter I. *They and We: Racial and Ethnic Relations in the United States.* 2nd ed. New York: Random House, 1974.

An excellent source for the definitions of key concepts in ethnic studies, such as ethnic groups, race, prejudice, and discrimination.

AFRO-AMERICANS

Banks, James A. *Teaching the Black Experience: Methods and Materials.* Belmont, Calif.: Fearon, 1970.

This handbook for classroom teachers discusses methods and materials which can be used to integrate Black Studies into the regular elementary and high school curricula.

————, and Cherry A. Banks. *March Toward Freedom: A History of Black Americans,* 2nd ed. Belmont, Calif.: Fearon, 1974.

A history of Black Americans from preslavery Africa to the present day. Can be used by teachers, junior high, and high school students.

Franklin, John Hope. *From Slavery to Freedom: A History of Black Americans.* New York: Vintage Books, 1969.

A classical history of Black Americans; it is must reading for the Black history novice.

Meier, August and Elliott Rudwich. *From Plantation to Ghetto.* Rev. ed. New York: Hill and Wang, 1970.

An extremely readable and insightful general history of Afro-Americans.

ASIAN AMERICANS

Chinese Americans

Melendy, H. Brett. *The Oriental Americans.* New York: Twayne Publishers, 1972.

A highly readable historical overview of Chinese Americans and Japanese Americans.

Sung, Betty L. *The Story of the Chinese in America.* New York: Macmillan, 1967.

The author presents the story of the Chinese in a highly interesting, empathic, and readable style.

Sung, S. W. *Chinese in American Life: Some Aspects of Their History, Status, Problems and Contributions.* Seattle: University of Washington Press, 1962.

A comprehensive and well-researched reference on the Chinese in the United States.

Japanese Americans

Daniels, Roger. *Concentration Camps U.S.A.: Japanese Americans and World War II.* New York: Holt, 1971.

An excellently written, perceptive history of Japanese during World War II.

Kitano, Harry H.L. *Japanese Americans: The Evolution of a Subculture.* Englewood Cliffs, N. J.: Prentice-Hall, 1969.

A useful sociological and historical overview of Japanese Americans by a noted expert in Asian-American studies.

Petersen, William. *Japanese Americans: Oppression and Success.* New York: Random House, 1971.

An informative but pedestrian and tedious sociological and historical treatment of Japanese Americans.

Filipino Americans

Buaken, Manuel. *I Have Lived with the American People.* Caldwell, Idaho: Caxton Printers, 1948.

An interesting personal account of the author's experiences in the United States.

Bulosan, Carlos. *America Is in the Heart.* Seattle: University of Washington Press, 1973.

A beautiful, poignant book about a young man trying to survive in a hostile, racist land. An exceedingly powerful book.

_____. *Sound of Falling Light: Letters in Exile.* Edited by Dolores S. Feria. Quezon City, Philippines: published by the editor, 1960.

A perceptive and deeply moving collection of letters and previously unpublished poems by one of the most gifted but neglected writers of this century.

Morales, Royal S. *Makibaka: The Pilipino American Struggle.* Los Angeles: Mountainview Press, 1974.

An interesting account of the contemporary problems of Filipino Americans.

MEXICAN AMERICANS: CHICANOS

Acuña, Rodolfo. *Occupied America: The Chicano's Struggle Toward Liberation.* San Francisco: Canfield Press, 1972.

A hard hitting, refreshing interpretation of the Chicano experience by a noted and prolific Mexican-American historian.

McWilliams, Carey. *North from Mexico: The Spanish-Speaking People of the United States.* New York: Greenwood Press, 1968.

A useful and highly regarded history of Mexican Americans through World War II.

Meier, Matt S. and Feliciano Rivera. *The Chicanos: A History of Mexican Americans.* New York: Hill and Wang, 1972.

A comprehensive and extremely useful history of Mexican Americans.

Moore, Joan W. with Alfredo Cuellar. *Mexican-Americans.* Englewood Cliffs: Prentice-Hall, 1970.

A useful and readable sociological treatment of the Mexican American written from an assimilationst perspective.

NATIVE AMERICANS: INDIANS

Brandon, William. *The American Heritage Book of Indians.* New York: Dell, 1961.

An extremely informative, well-written introduction to Indian cultures in all parts of the Americas. This book deserves the acclaim it has received.

Deloria Jr., Vine. *Custer Died for Your Sins*. New York: Avon, 1969.
A rhetorical and highly partisan but important articulation of the problems and future plight of modern day Indians by a noted Native American leader.

Driver, Harold E. *Indians of North America*. Rev. ed. Chicago: University of Chicago Press, 1969.
A good introductory source book on the American Indian which treats such topics as language, art, music, kinship groups, and rank and social class.

Josephy, Alvin M. *The Indian Heritage of America*. New York: Bantam, 1968.
An informed and sensitively written account of Indian cultures throughout the Americas.

Spicer, Harold E. *A Short History of the Indians of the United States*. New York: Van Nostrand Reinhold, 1969.
This excellent book includes a brief history of the American Indian and fifty-one key related documents.

PUERTO RICAN AMERICANS

Cordasco, Francesco and Eugene Bucchioni, eds. *The Puerto Rican Experience*. Totowa, N. J.: Littlefield, Adams, 1973.
An excellent collection of excerpts from books, magazines, and journal articles dealing with diverse aspects of Puerto Rican life both on the mainland and the island.

Fitzpatrick, Joseph P. *Puerto Rican Americans: The Meaning of Migration to the Mainland*. Englewood Cliffs, N. J.: Prentice-Hall, 1971.
The most up-to-date, comprehensive, and well-done general study of Puerto Ricans on the mainland that's currently available.

Padilla, Elena. *Up From Puerto Rico*. New York: Columbia University Press, 1958.
An excellent anthropological study of a Puerto Rican community in New York City by a perceptive and sensitive anthropologist.

Wagenheim, Kal. *Puerto Rico: A Profile*. New York: Praeger, 1970.
An informative book which treats diverse aspects of Puerto Rico, including its history and economy.

EUROPEAN AMERICANS

Greeley, Andrew M. *Why Can't They Be Like Us? Facts and Fallacies about Ethnic Differences and Group Conflict in America*. New York: Institute of Human Relations Press, 1969.

An interesting and informal brief book discussing various aspects of ethnicity in modern American life, including the meaning and function of ethnicity, steps in ethnic assimilation, and the future of ethnic groups in the United States.

Handlin, Oscar. *The Uprooted: The Epic Story of the Great Migrations that Made the American People.* Rev. ed. New York: Grosset and Dunlap, 1973.

In this brilliant book, the author chronicles the story of European immigrants to the United States from their peasant life in Europe to the nativistic movements in the late nineteenth and early twentieth centuries. A deeply moving and compassionate book written from the perspective of the immigrants. Recipient of the Pulitzer Prize in history in 1952.

Higham, John. *Strangers in the Land: Patterns of American Nativism 1860–1925.* New York: Atheneum, 1972.

A perceptive and pioneering study of nativistic movements in American society in the late nineteenth and early twentieth centuries. This highly readable and copiously documented book also contains a useful bibliographic essay.

Jones, Maldwyn Allen. *American Immigration.* Chicago: University of Chicago Press, 1960.

An excellent, well-written, and comprehensive history of the immigration of European nationality groups to the United States up through the 1950s. A good introductory source.

PART II

Teaching Ethnic Cultures: Concepts, Strategies, and Materials

Introduction to Part II

Part I of this book deals with the goals of ethnic studies and ways to organize and plan the ethnic studies program. Part II is designed to help the teacher acquire the content needed to teach about ethnic groups, to acquaint the teacher with exemplary strategies for teaching key concepts and generalizations with ethnic content, and to help the teacher identify the materials and resources needed by the students and the teachers.

Chapters 5 to 11 consist of: (1) chronologies of key events, (2) historical overviews of the various ethnic groups, (3) illustrative key concepts and teaching strategies, (4) annotated bibliographies for teachers, and (5) annotated bibliographies for

students. Recommended grade levels are given for each student reference. These designations are used to indicate the suggested grade levels: **primary, intermediate, upper,** and **high school**. Some of the books are recommended for use with *all levels*. These books are so designated. While the bibliographies are selective, few of the books are appropriate for all purposes and settings. The teacher should carefully examine each book before assigning it to his or her students. However, the annotations will help teachers to identify books appropriate for their students.

Chapter 12 highlights and summarizes the major points discussed in the book and illustrates how the teacher can use the information and strategies described in earlier chapters to implement and evaluate multiethnic units which focus on more than one ethnic group. The major components of a sample multiethnic unit are presented to illustrate the steps in unit construction.

Native Americans: Concepts, Strategies, and Materials **5**

They made us many promises, more than I can remember, but they never kept but one; they promised to take our land, and they took it.

Introduction

Unlike other ethnic groups discussed in this book, school children often study about American Indians and Eskimos. However, they most often learn myths and stereotypes rather than accurate information about this nation's first inhabitants. Textbooks often depict Native Americans as hostile savages who scalped the colonists and practiced exotic customs and strange religions.

We must teach students more accurate information about Native Americans and help them to view American history from an Indian point of view. Only in this way will they be able to understand America's social and political institutions. Students need to study the diverse and complex Native cultures which had developed in the Western Hemisphere when Europeans arrived in the fifteenth century. These cultures must be viewed from a humane perspective, which respects differences and regards all human cultures as valid. To evaluate them by imposing a foreign conceptual framework—such as an Anglo-Saxon norm—will violate their integrity and do more harm than good.

The full truth needs to be told about so-called Indian hostility and warring. Indians were friendly to the first European settlers in the Americas. However, when the Europeans promoted divide-and-conquer tactics among the Indian tribes and aggressively invaded Indian lands, the Natives responded defensively. In the final analysis, White violence was more decisive than Indian hostility because the Indian was conquered and enchained. The making and breaking of treaties and the forced removal of Indians to the West is one of the most poignant chapters in our history. To be unaware of these atrocities is to be ignorant of American history.

Pre-Columbian cultures and oppression are not the total of the Indian experience. Native Americans are a growing social force in American life. There were nearly 800,000 Indians in the United States in 1970, and their count jumps upward at every census. Indians are making demands for redress of old grievances, shaping new identities, and fighting for the right to determine their own destinies. Without knowledge of their past and present, students will be ignorant of the very foundations upon which this nation is built.

Native Americans: Historical Perspective

Important Dates

1513	Juan Ponce de León landed on the Florida peninsula while on route from Puerto Rico. The relationship between Europeans and North American Indians began.
1565	The Spaniards established the St. Augustine colony in Florida, the first settlement organized by Europeans in present-day United States.
1637	Connecticut colonists murdered more than 500 Native Americans when the Pequot tribe tried to stop the colonists from invading their territory. This massacre is known as the Pequot War.

Important Dates cont.

1675–76 King Philip, a Wampanoag chief, led a coalition of Indian troops which nearly defeated the English colonists. However, his forces were eventually beaten and his body dismembered by the colonists.

1680 The Pueblos rebelled against the Spaniards and drove them from Pueblo territory. Many Spaniards were killed during the uprising.

1754–63 The French and Indian War took place. It was one of a series of wars in which the French and the British struggled for control of the eastern part of North America. Each nation vied for Indian support.

1794 A group of Indians suffered a crushing defeat at Fallen Timbers in Ohio on August 20. In 1795, they were forced to sign a treaty that ceded large segments of their lands in the Northwest Territory to Whites.

1812 The War of 1812, a war between the United States and Britain, caused deep factions among the Indian tribes because of their different allegiances. The Indian allies of the British were severely punished by the United States when the war ended.

1824 The Bureau of Indian Affairs was established in the War Department.

1830 Congress passed a Removal Act which authoried the removal of Indians from the east to west of the Mississippi and stated conditions under which removal could be legally undertaken.

1831 The Supreme Court recognized Indian tribes as "domestic dependent nations" within the United States. In an 1832 decision, the Court declared that such nations had a right to self-government.

1838–39 The Cherokee were forcefully removed from Georgia to Indian Territory in present-day

Important Dates cont.

	Oklahoma. Their poignant journey westward is recalled as the "Trail of Tears."
1864	The Colorado militia killed nearly 300 Cheyennes in a surprise attack at Sand Creek after the Cheyenne leaders had negotiated an armistice. This incident is known as the Sand Creek Massacre.
1871	A congressional act prohibited the making of further treaties with Native tribes.
1876	Sioux tribes, under the leadership of Sitting Bull, wiped out Custer's Seventh Cavalry at Little Big Horn. This was one of the last victories for Native tribes.
1885	Helen Hunt Jackson's *A Century of Dishonor* was published. It was the first influential book to dramatize the poignant plight of Indian people in the United States.
1886	The brave Apache warrior, Geronimo, surrendered to American forces in September 1886. His surrender marked the defeat of the Southwest tribes.
1887	Congress passed the Dawes Severalty Act which was designed to partially terminate the Indian's special relationship with the United States government. It proved to be disastrous for Native Americans.
1890	Three hundred Sioux were killed in a massacre at Wounded Knee Creek in South Dakota.
1924	The Snyder Act made Native Americans citizens of the United States.
1928	The Meriam Survey recommended major changes in federal policy related to Indian affairs; many of its recommendations were implemented in subsequent years.
1934	The Wheeler-Howard Act made it possible for Native Americans to reestablish aspects of their traditional cultures, including tribal lands and governments.

Important Dates cont.

1944	The National Congress of American Indians was organized by Native Americans.
1946	The Indian Claims Commission was established to hear cases related to possible compensations due Indians for loss of land and property.
1948	Indians were granted the right to vote in New Mexico and Arizona.
1953	A congressional act enabled nonreservation Indians to purchase alcohol. Reservations were authorized to determine local policy with regard to the sale of alcohol.
1954	Congressional acts terminated the relationship between the federal government and several Indian tribes, including the Klamath tribe in Oregon, the Menominee of Wisconsin, and the California Indians.
1961	The National Indian Youth Council was organized.
1970	President Richard M. Nixon made a statement advocating Indian self-determination.
1972	Congress restored the Menominee tribe of Wisconsin to federal-trust status.
1973	Members of the American Indian Movement and other Indians occupied Wounded Knee, South Dakota, to dramatize the Indian's condition in the United States.
1974	Indians in Washington state won major fishing rights victories in the state's courts.

Early Life in the Americas

When the European explorers arrived in the Western Hemisphere in 1492, it was populated by many different cultures and groups that became collectively known as "Indians" to Europeans. Columbus thought that he had reached India when he landed in San Salvador in 1492. This misnaming of the aboriginal peoples of the Americas by the Europeans foreshadowed the misunderstanding, distrust, and hostility which later developed between the two groups.

The early history of Native Americans is still somewhat of a mystery to scientists. Archaeologists are trying hard to unravel their early history by digging up fossils that give clues to early human life in the Americas. Occasionally, landmark archaeological discoveries are made, enabling scientists to learn more about early people in the Western Hemisphere. In 1927, near Folsom, New Mexico, scientists found a point embedded between the ribs of a Pleistocene bison that early Americans used to kill. This finding proved that men and women were in the Americas when Ice Age animals were roaming freely on this continent. Similar points were found at a dig near Clovis, New Mexico in 1932. Scientists were able to date the points to 9200 B. C. by using Carbon 14.[1]

The Origins of Native Americans

We do not know exactly when people first came to the Americas. However, archaeologists have ruled out the possibility that men and women evolved in the Western Hemisphere because no fossils of pre–Homo sapiens have been found on this continent.[2] No remains of the closest cousins of human beings, the great apes, have been found in the Americas either. Despite these theories, however, many Native American groups believe that they evolved in the Americas. These beliefs must be respected until archaeological findings are more conclusive. Archaeologists believe that the ancestors of Native Americans originally came from Asia. Estimates of when they came to this continent vary greatly. However, some archaeologists believe that people may have been in the Western Hemisphere as long as 35,000 years.[3]

Most archaeologists use the Bering Strait theory to explain how the first people reached the Western Hemisphere. The body of water separating Siberia and Alaska today is called the Bering Strait. Archaeologists believe that at various points in prehistory this water receded and a land mass bridged present-

1. C. W. Ceram, *The First American: A Story of North American Archaeology* (New York: Mentor Books, 1971). p. 304.
2. Alvin M. Josephy, Jr., *The Indian Heritage of America* (New York: Bantam Books, 1969), p. 36.
3. Wendell H. Oswalt, *This Land Was Theirs,* 2nd ed. (New York: John Wiley, 1973), p. 16.

day Siberia and Alaska. The early ancestors of Native Americans crossed this stretch of land while hunting animals and plants to eat. Archaeologists do not believe that these immigrants looked like present-day Asian peoples. They came to the Americas before Asians had acquired their modern physical traits. If we accept this theory, we can think of the ancestors of Native Americans as physically "pre-Asian."

The Diversity of Native Cultures

Although the word *Indian* connotes a stereotypic image in the popular mind, Native American peoples were quite diverse, both physically and culturally. Their skin colors ranged from dark brown to white. Their height, hair texture, and facial features also varied greatly. Native Americans spoke 2,200 different languages, which anthropologists have tried, with great difficulty, to categorize into six major language families. The ways in which they made their living also varied widely. Some groups, like the tribes of the Subarctic, did not practice agriculture, but obtained food by fishing and hunting. Agriculture was the basis of the sedentary communities and complex cultures of the Southwest Indians.

Political institutions in Native cultures were also quite diverse. Highly sophisticated confederations were common among the Northeast tribes, such as the Creek Confederacy and the League of the Iroquois. These confederations contrasted strikingly with political life within the California tribes. These tribes usually had no formal political institutions, but were organized into small family units that were headed by men who had group responsibilities but little authority over others. Warring and raiding were important aspects of the Apache culture. However, the Hopi, who called themselves "the peaceful ones," were one of the most tranquil people on earth. Social class had little meaning among the Southwest tribes, but was extremely important in the Northwest Pacific Coast cultures. Food, hunting methods, house types, clothing, tools, and religious ceremonies also varied greatly between and within various Native American cultural groups.[4]

4. See Ruth M. Underhill, *Red Man's America*, rev. ed. (Chicago: University of Chicago Press, 1971).

Similarities in Native Cultures

Although Native American cultures were highly diverse, they were similar in many ways. Some of their similar traits, especially those related to core values, make up "Indianness" or what is uniquely "Indian" or Native. Most Native Americans were deeply religious and spiritual peoples. Religon greatly influenced all aspects of their lives. Because Indians saw people existing within a spiritual world which included all other living things, animal spirits often played major roles in their religions. They viewed the universe as a harmonious whole, with every object and being having a sacred life; to separate human beings from nature was antithetical to the Great Spirit, for to the Great Spirit all was life.

The tribes of the Northwest Pacific Coast believed in many spirits, such as those of the eagle, beaver, and whale. They sought the protection of these spirits through various ceremonies and rituals. The shaman, who played a key role in many Native religions, helped them to gain contact with the spiritual world.

The Southwest tribes had a rich and elaborate year-round sequence of ceremonials including songs, dances, and poetry. Native Americans often called upon the help of the spirits in their daily lives. The Hopi performed dances to bring rain; the Apaches engaged in special dances and ceremonies to gain the support of the spirits before undertaking raids or going into war. Tribes in the Plains and the Northwest Coast often sought contact with the spirits by going on a vision quest. Religious beliefs and rituals permeated every aspect of Native life.

Native Americans had a deep respect and reverance for the earth and all other living things. They believed that people must not harm the earth and should regard it as sacred. Many Native religious leaders were often shocked by the ways in which the White people's agriculture defiled the Mother Earth. Forbes has summarized these beliefs: "the Earth our Mother is holy and should be treated as such . . . all forms of life are our brothers and sisters and have to be respected. . . . Life itself is a holy, sacred experience . . . we must live our lives as a *religion*, that is, with constant concern for spiritual relationships and values . . . we must live lives that bring forth both physical and spiritual 'beauty.' All life has the potentiality of bringing forth Beauty and Harmony, but man in particular has also the ability to bring forth ugliness and disharmony."[5]

In their literature and speeches, Native Americans often bemoaned the ways in which the Whites destroyed and defiled the earth, as in this passage by an old Winto woman: "the White people plow up the ground, pull down the trees, kill everything. The tree says, 'Don't. I am sore. Don't hurt me.' But they chop it down and cut it up. The spirit of the land hates them. They blast our trees and stir it up to its depths. . . . How can the spirit of the earth like the White man? . . . Everywhere the White man has touched it, it is sore."[6]

The Native American's conception of the earth and his relationship to the land differed greatly from the European's and was a source of conflict between the two cultures. The Native believed that people could use the earth as long as they treated it with respect, but they could not sell it anymore than they could sell the air or the sea. When, in exchange for gifts, Native Americans gave Europeans permission to use their lands, many did not realize that from a European point of view they were also giving up their rights to use the lands. The European regarded the earth as a commodity which could be broken into parts and owned by individuals. To the Native American, the earth was sacred and consequently could never be owned by human beings.

The Native American also had a deep respect for the rights and dignity of the individual. Decisions in Native councils and confederacies were usually based on group consensus. Deliberations were often long and decisions of governing bodies slow because consensus had to be attained. The Creek Confederacy reached all of its decisions by consensus. However, each nation within the confederacy maintained its autonomy and was not bound to a decision with which it did not agree. The Europeans learned a great deal from the Native Americans about repre-

5. Jack D. Forbes, "Teaching Native American Values and Cultures," in James A. Banks, ed., *Teaching Ethnic Studies: Concepts and Strategies* (Washington, D. C.: National Council for the Social Studies, 1973), pp. 208–209. Reprinted with the publisher's permission.

6. T. C. McLuhan, ed., *Touch the Earth: A Self-Portrait of Indian Existence* (New York: Pocket Book, 1971), p. 15. Reprinted with the publisher's permission.

sentative government and the rights and dignity of the individual, which they incorporated into the major constitutional documents upon which American democracy is based.

Leaders of groups within the Subartic tribes had little authority over their followers. This was characteristic of Native American societies. Leaders were rarely deified as they were in Europe and other parts of the Old World. There were few hierarchical political organizations in the Americas. Leaders often had to earn the respect of others by becoming outstanding warriors, acquiring a special ability to communicate with the spirits, or learning to perform some other service the community needed and valued. Communities were usually democratic, with no kings or other kinds of rulers. However, there were exceptions to these generalizations. The Inca Empire of Peru was one of the most totalitarian states that ever existed in human history. However, the Inca Empire was the exception, not the rule.

Because of their feudalistic background, the Europeans looked for kings among the Native Americans and assumed that Indian chiefs had absolute authority over their tribes. The European settlers created tremendous problems by imposing their conceptions of the nation-state on Native societies. They made treaties with chiefs and assumed that they were binding to their tribes. They did not understand that the chief's authority was usually limited by the tribal council. He had little power which the tribe did not grant him. This was one of the cultural conflicts between the Europeans and the Americans that haunted their relationships for centuries.

Early Contact With Europeans

The Native American's earliest contacts with the Europeans were usually friendly. Their relationships usually involved trade. The French, the English, and the Dutch exchanged European goods and tools for Native American furs. This exchange of goods was initially beneficial for both groups. The furs greatly increased the Europeans' wealth; the European goods and tools made life easier for the Indians. Eventually, the Native Americans began to consider the European goods necessities rather than luxuries. What had begun as a mutually beneficial trade relationship was destined to cause disaster for the Indians.

Native Americans acquired rum, guns, gunpowder, horses, and other goods from the Europeans. Tribes that wanted European goods but had depleted the supply of fur producing animals on their lands began to invade the territories of other tribes to get furs for trade. These invasions led to skirmishes and eventually to wars. European goods made intertribal warring more likely and possible. It was rather easy for the tribes that had European guns and gunpowder to defeat tribes lacking these supplies. Thus the Europeans, through trade and other schemes (discussed later), initiated divide-and-conquer tactics among the Indian tribes in New England. Native American wars, raids, and attacks were greatly intensified by the presence of the Europeans.

The League of the Iroquois began an aggressive campaign to gain a monopoly of the European trade and to wipe out competing tribes. The league had eliminated hundreds of Hurons and forced those remaining into captivity by 1649. The Iroquois were feared by tribes throughout New England. They eventually dominated the Delawares, the Nanticokes, and other groups of Algonkian-speaking tribes by 1680. The league became so powerful that the British regarded it as a power to be reckoned with.

The Native American and European Wars

From about 1540 to the 1790s, no one power was dominant in the Indian territory that had been invaded by the Europeans in the Northeast. The Swedes and the Dutch had been driven from the area before 1700. However, the Frenchmen, Spaniards, and Englishmen struggled for control of the region. The Indians also tried to maintain their power. The power struggle became more intricate and intense when the British colonies entered the contest. Until the American Revolution, the Native Americans were unable to tell which of the warlike European nations, if any, would become the dominant power. The Indians probably thought that a balance of power would eventually be established in the region, in which they would be a major participant.

The European wars and struggles for power deeply influenced Native American policy and political institutions. In each of the White people's wars, the Indians had to decide which

group, if any, they would support. Each of the powers competed for Native American alliance and support. Although the
Indians often tried to maintain a policy of neutrality, this became increasingly difficult as the European nations aggressively
vied for their support. The Creeks and the Cherokees fought on
the side of the French, against the British, in the French and
Indian War. The French were defeated and their Indian allies
were severely punished by the British for helping the enemy.
The Indians were also weakened by their severe losses during
the war.

The European wars caused deep factionalism within the Indian tribes and confederations. In the War of 1812, the various
tribes became deeply divided over whether they should support
the colonies or the British. The treaties ending the War of 1812
and the American Revolution stunned and angered Britain's
Indian allies. Neither treaty acknowledged the decisive roles
the Indians played in these wars. After the American Revolution, the British granted the colonists lands which were occupied
by her Indian allies. The British had pitted Indian tribes against
each other and ignored her allies' self-interests when the fighting
stopped. In time, the Indians began to see the futility of becoming involved in the European wars. They became increasingly committed to a policy of neutrality. Alexander McGilliv-
ray, the Creek diplomat, used the White people's tactics and
pitted the colonists against the Spaniards by astutely negotiating.

The Decline of the League of the Iroquois

The League of the Iroquois was deeply affected by the European wars and was eventually destroyed by the factionalism
caused by the wars. The league, the French, and the British
were the three major powers in the Northeast in the first decades
of the 1700s. Factionalism developed within the league over
the positions it should take in the European wars. One of
the nations, the Senecas, fought on the side of the French in the
French and Indian War. The other nations supported the British.
Even greater disunity developed within the league when the
American Revolution began. Some of the nations supported the
British; others were sympathetic to the colonists. Internal splits
developed within several of the nations over the issue. The colo-

nists looted and burned Iroquois villages after the Revolution and flaunted their newly gained power.

The fate of the Iroquois was later experienced by other tribes. The Iroquois had warred against other Indian tribes to obtain furs to trade and fought as allies in the White people's wars. Their confederation was later destroyed because of splits caused by the European wars. The Indian nations did not realize that they had a common fate in the Northeast, and that the future of one Indian nation was intricately tied to the future of all Indian tribes. Culturally and politically, Native Americans were separate and distinct peoples. However, the Whites saw them as a group that had to be pushed west of the Mississippi and ultimately conquered or destroyed.

Treaties and Indian Removal

The relationship between Native Americans and European settlers had developed into a pattern by the time of the American Revolution. The initial contact usually involved trade, whereby Indians acquired tools and firearms and the Europeans obtained furs. These initial events usually pitted Indian tribes against each other as they competed for the European trade and for the lands containing fur-producing animals. When the furs had been depleted, the Europeans began an aggressive drive to obtain the lands the Indians occupied. The Indians often formed confederations and alliances to fight back the European invaders or extended the functions of existing confederations. Ironically, however, the Indian's involvement in the White people's wars usually disrupted these confederations. Native Americans adamantly resisted the attempts by the Whites to displace them. They fought defensive wars, such as the King Philip's War in 1675 and the Black Hawk War in 1832. Indian uprisings also occurred, like the Sioux uprising in 1862 and the Little Crow uprising in 1863.

Despite their aggressive and bold resistance, the Europeans were destined to win the struggle. The Whites retaliated with shocking massacres, like Sand Creek in 1864, biological warfare, and massive wars in which men, women, and children were brutally murdered and often dismembered and scalped. After Indian resistance was crushed, Whites legitimized the taking of

Indian lands by getting their leaders to sign treaties. They often used force, bribery, or other tactics to get the treaties signed. Indian chiefs were frequently offered gifts or other bribes to sign treaties. Once an Indian group had signed a treaty, the Whites schemed to remove them from their land. Often the Indians were forced to go west of the Mississippi into Indian Territory (present-day Oklahoma), land which the Whites considered uninhabitable. If only a few Indians remained after the conquest, they were often absorbed by local tribes or forced onto reservations.

This cycle was repeated many times as the White settlers pushed westward. When Whites went further west, Native Americans were forced to sign new treaties granting Whites the lands earlier treaties had assured them. Some Indian groups, like the Winnebagos, were forced to move as many as six times. The Winnebagos were shifted from location to location for thirty years. No aspect of American history is more poignant than the accounts of the making and breaking of Indian treaties by Whites and the forced removal of Native Americans across the United States. This prediction by a Cherokee newspaper regarding how Whites would go about getting Indian land in Texas highlights the way in which treaties were often made: "a Commissioner will be sent down to negotiate, with a pocket full of money and his mouth full of lies. Some chiefs he will bribe, some he will flatter and some he will make drunk; and the result will be . . . something that will be called a treaty."[7]

The Westward Journeys

Some Native American tribes, realizing the futility of resistance, accepted their fate and moved westward without force. Others, however, bitterly resisted removal and were removed by troops. Generally, the tribes that had to be removed at gun point suffered the most. However, they all suffered greatly. The Winnebagos, who offered little resistance, were shifted from place to place between 1829 and 1866. About half of them perished during the perpetual sojourn. The Seminoles, who signed a removal treaty in 1832, violently resisted removal. Hostilities

7. William T. Hagan, *American Indians* (Chicago: University of Chicago Press, 1961), p. 99.

broke out in 1835 and continued for seven years. The United States lost nearly 1,500 men and spent over $50 million in its attempts to crush the Seminoles' resistance. Most of the Seminoles were eventually forced to Indian Territory. However, several hundred remained in the Florida Everglades, where their descendants live today.

The Georgians began an aggressive drive to remove the Cherokees from their homeland when gold was discovered on Cherokee land in 1829. The Cherokees initiated a court battle against removal. In 1831, the Supreme Court ruled that the Cherokee had a right to remain on their land. However, this ruling by the high court did not halt the determined efforts of the Georgians and President Andrew Jackson to remove the Cherokees. Harassed and pressured, part of the tribe finally signed a removal treaty in 1835. Even though only a minority of the tribe's leaders signed the treaty, the Cherokee were forced to move to Indian Territory in 1832. During the long march from Georgia to Oklahoma in 1838 and 1839, almost a fourth of the Cherokees died from starvation, diseases, and the perils of the journey. Their long westward journey is recalled as the "Trail of Tears." The Creeks were forced to sign a treaty in 1832, which gave the Whites rights to their lands east of the Mississippi. Nearly half of the Creeks perished during the migration and their early years in the West.

Like the White people's wars, removal caused deep factions within the various Native American tribes and nations. Some of the leaders felt that it was in their best interests to cooperate with the White authorities; others believed that removal should be resisted until the bitter end. These splits within the tribes intensified when the Indians arrived in the West and hastened the disintegration of their institutions that had begun before removal.

In retrospect, it is clear that the fate of the Indians was doomed and that they either had to relocate or be exterminated. The federal government legitimized Indian removal with the Removal Act of 1830. This act legalized Indian removal and specified the conditions under which Indians could be removed legally. The act provided funds for removal and authorized an exchange of lands for displaced Indians. The act stipulated that the tribe's consent must be obtained. It made little difference in the actual removal of Native Americans. Local officials continued to use any possible tactics to get Indians to sign treaties and to go westward.

Native Americans in the West

Much tension developed in the West when the eastern tribes reached their destinations. Many of the eastern tribes were forced to settle in territories occupied by the plains Indians. The plains tribes had acquired the White people's guns and horses and were tough fighters when the eastern tribes began to settle in their territories. When competition for the buffalo became acute, they fought and raided the eastern tribes. The United States government failed to provide the eastern tribes military protection as it had promised when they were forced to settle in the West.

The conquering and displacement of tribes that took place in the East later occurred west of the Mississippi. However, the conquest of the plains tribes and other western tribes took place in a shorter period of time. The powerful Sioux nation of the northern plains was defeated and forced onto reservations within twenty-seven years. The Comanche of the southern plains had been conquered by the White settlers by 1873. Notes Spicer, "The other plains tribes presented about the same picture as the Comanche or the Sioux: a twenty or twenty-five year period of intensive warfare both with other tribes and the Americans, a period of unsettled and sometimes desperate conditions as they were forced on reservations and finally unhappy acceptance of the new way."[8]

When the United States acquired most of the territory that now makes up the Southwest from Mexico in 1848 (see page 291), the fate of the Indians living in that area was doomed. The southwestern tribes quickly learned that their new conquerors were enemies, not friends. The Spaniards had never completely conquered the southwestern tribes; they had retained a great deal of their culture and many Native institutions. Indians such as the Pueblos and the Pimas had hoped that the United States would protect them from the Navahos and the Apaches. How-

8. Edward H. Spicer, *A Short History of the Indians in the United States* (New York: Van Nostrand Reinhold, 1969), p. 87.

ever, the new government's goal was to conquer all of the tribes and to place them on reservations. The California gold rush of 1849 hastened the defeat of the western tribes. A congressional act in 1871 that prohibited further treaties with the Indian tribes indicated that the Native American's resistance had been broken and that they were now a conquered and defeated people. The act declared that in the future, "no Indian nation or tribe within . . . the United States shall be acknowledged or recognized as an independent nation, tribe or power."[9] This act represented a major change in federal policy in Indian affairs and reversed the policy declared by the Supreme Court in 1831. The Court ruled in 1831 that the "Cherokees and other Indians were dependent domestic nations . . . definable political entities within the United States."[10] The 1871 congressional act closed an important chapter in Native American history. When he surrendered in 1877 Chief Joseph of the Nez Perces said, "Hear me, my chiefs, I am tired; my heart is sick and sad. From where the sun now stands, I will fight no more forever."

Messianic Movements: The Utopian Quests

Indians had been conquered by the late 1880s and vigorous efforts to eradicate their cultures, values, and ways of life were already underway. Many were forced to live on reservations that were operated by superintendents and government agents who ruled the Indians with an iron hand and stifled all their efforts for self-initiative. Confined to reservations (some of which were fenced in), many of the proud Indian warriors were forced to farm, which they considered women's work. In their desperation, Indians turned to religious prophets who promised a return to the traditional ways and the extermination of Whites and their lifestyles. Messianic leaders who heralded the end of White domination emerged within many of the eastern and western tribes.

A prophet arose among the Delawares in the 1760s. He urged his followers to reject European goods and to return to their old way of life. Tenskwatawa, a Shawnee, experienced a revelation in 1805 which told him that White Americans would

9. Josephy, *Indian Heritage,* pp. 339–40.

10. Spicer, *Short History,* p. 66.

be destroyed by a natural catastrophe. Tenskwatawa and his brother, Tecumseh, taught the Shawnees to hold firm to their lands and refuse to relinquish them to the Whites. Handsome Lake began preaching among the Senecas around 1800 after the League of the Iroquis had been broken up. He urged the Senecas to remain neutral in the White people's wars, not to indulge in the White vices, and to live by his moral code. Handsome Lake became very important to those Senecas who were trying to resist cultural domination by the Whites.

As Whites began to conquer Indian tribes in the West, prophets who envisioned a utopian future emerged among the western tribes. In 1855 a prophet called Smohalla began preaching among the Wanapum Indians in the Oregon Territory. Like the eastern prophets, Smohalla preached that the White people would be eliminated and that their way of life was detrimental. He believed that the way the White people farmed harmed Mother Earth.

A Paiute prophet named Wovoka started having visions in 1885. He preached that a natural catastrophe would destroy White people and that the Indians' ancestors would return. The White authorities became very alarmed about Wovoka's religion and its ritualistic dance. The religion became known to Whites as the "Ghost Dance." It spread rapidly among the Indians and eventually reached the Sioux on the Pine Ridge Reservation in South Dakota. A frightened Indian agent called soldiers to the reservation in 1890. When a misunderstanding arose between the soldiers and the worshipers, the soldiers massacred 300 Sioux at Wounded Knee Creek. This incident shocked the nation and wiped out the Ghost Dance among most Indian tribes. The Wounded Knee "episode marked the completion of the White man's conquest of the Indian in the United States."[11]

Native Americans and Federal Policy

When the Indians had been thoroughly conquered and placed on reservations, White authorities began efforts to "civilize" them; *civilize* meant to make them as much like Whites as possible. The goal of federal policy was to quickly assimilate the Indian into the dominant society. No attempt was made to give Native Americans a choice or to encourage them to retain

11. Josephy, *Indian Heritage*, p. 343.

elements of their cultures. Efforts were made to make Native Americans farmers and to give their children the White people's education. Native children were sent to boarding schools far away from the reservations so that the authority of their parents would be undermined. The schools were a dismal failure. When Indian children left them, they were unable to function well in either their ethnic communities or within the dominant society. What the schools tried to teach had almost no relevance to life on the reservations. The schools also failed to teach Indian children the White people's culture. The quality of the teachers and the curricula were exceedingly poor.

Policymakers felt that they had to break up the Indians' tribal lands and make individual allotments to family heads to make Indians independent and successful farmers. That this would violate Native culture and traditions was not a major concern. In 1887 Congress passed the Dawes Severalty Act. It was designed to make Indians independent and to terminate their special relationship with the federal government. It was destined to have the opposite effect. The act authorized the president to break up tribal lands and to make individual allotments to family heads. Each family head was to receive 160 acres, minors 80 acres each. "Surplus" land was to be sold on the open market. The government was to hold the land in trust for twenty-five years. Citizenship was to be granted to family heads when they received their allotments. Many tribes adamantly opposed the act from the beginning.

The results of the act were disastrous for Native Americans. Many Whites bought or leased lands from Indians at outrageously low prices or obtained land from them in extralegal ways. Some Whites persuaded their Native American friends to will them their lands. Indians who made such wills often turned up mysteriously dead shortly after finalizing the will. A 1906 congressional act gave the federal government more authority to supervise the administration of the Dawes Act. However, schemes for getting the Indians' lands developed more rapidly than government policies to safeguard it. Many Native Americans became poverty stricken during the period in which the act was in effect. They lost about 90 million out of a total of 138 million acres of land between 1887 and 1932.

It was clear by the late 1920s that the Dawes Act had failed. It had not only resulted in the loss of millions of acres of tribal land but had increased rather than decreased the role of the federal government in Indian affairs. The Meriam Report was published in 1928. It recommended major reforms in federal Indian policy, including the abandoning of the allotment plan and the consolidation of Indian land for use by the tribes. John Collier, who became commissioner of Indian affairs in 1933, believed that tribal land should be reestablished, as well as Indian government and other aspects of Native culture. In 1934 Congress passed an act sanctioning the new federal policy. Termination had failed; the government would not take a more active role in Indian affairs and urge Indians to reestablish aspects of their cultures. The Wheeler-Howard Act of 1934 brought a halt to the allotment of Indian lands, made it possible for tribes to acquire additional lands, and granted Native Americans the right to local government based on their traditional cultures.

By the 1950s, advocates for the termination of the federal government's role in Indian affairs were again dominant in the nation's capital. During the 1950s, Congress passed several laws which gave the states additional responsibilities for Indian affairs. A 1954 termination bill ended the relationship between the federal government and the Klamath tribe in Oregon. The tribe and their reservation were legally abolished. However, termination was disastrous for the Klamaths because they had not achieved economic independence when it began.

Although the cries for termination of the federal government's role in Native American affairs has waned since the 1950s, they have by no means dissipated. Some feel that termination is ultimately inevitable, even though it might have adverse consequences. Many people who are concerned about the future of Native Americans believe that the federal government should fulfill its treaty and other legal obligations to Indian tribes and make every effort to insure that those whose lives will be affected will be the major policymakers. Tribes should be able to shape their own destinies, and federal policy should make this possible. Local tribes should decide for themselves when, if ever, they want to terminate their relationship with the federal government. Native history dictates that this be done.

Pan-Indianism

Indians of many different tribes have participated in common religious movements and ceremonies since the 1800s. The

Native American Church may be regarded as one of the earliest Pan-Indian organizations. This church combined Native American and Christian beliefs and became quite popular among many different Indian groups, even though it was vigorously opposed by established White churches. Because the participants in the church used Peyote, White authorities tried unsuccessfully to abolish the church legally.

In recent years, the Pan-Indian movement has been primarily a social protest rather than a religious force. Native Americans, like other oppressed ethnic minorities, understand that they have a common destiny in the United States and have become aggressive in demanding their rights. Although Indians still value their tribal allegiances and identities, they often join with other tribes to make common demands from the White establishment. Members of various tribes formed the National Congress of American Indians in 1944. Membership was restricted to American Indians. The formation of this organization indicated that the Native Americans wanted to be their own spokespersons and lead the fight for their rights. Earlier civil rights organizations promoting Indian rights were run by Whites. In 1961 younger Native Americans formed the National Indian Youth Council to articulate their grievances and to promote social change. Native Americans are rapidly growing, and not vanishing, Americans. It is clear that they are a cogent social force with which the White establishment must reckon. Old promises are going to require new answers; old answers are not going to suffice.

Teaching Strategies

To illustrate how content related to Native Americans can be used to integrate the curriculum, exemplary strategies are identified for teaching these concepts at the grade levels indicated: *family relationships* (primary grades), *cultural diversity and similarity* (intermediate and upper grades), and *federal policy* (high school grades).

PRIMARY GRADES

CONCEPT: Family Relationships

Generalization: Sometimes we must learn to live without family members with whom we have strong positive relationships.

1. Ask the children, "Has one of your parents ever gone away for a long or short trip?" "Did you miss your parent?" "How do we feel when someone we like very much goes away?" "Why do we feel that way?" Record the children's responses on the board or butcher paper. Through further questioning and discussion, bring out that we often feel lonely and sad when certain family members are away because we have strong positive feelings toward them.

2. Ask the pupils, "What do you think life would be like for you if mother went away forever?" "If father went away forever?" "How would you feel?" "Why?" "How do you think you would feel if your sister or brother went away forever?" "Why would you feel that way?" "How do you think that members of your family would feel if you went away forever?" "Why would they feel that way?" Through further questioning and discussion, help the students to understand how emotionally difficult it might be if they no longer had one of their family members.

3. Say to the class, "Today we are going to read a story about an Indian girl named Annie and her grandmother, the Old One." Show the students the picture of Annie and her grandmother on page 7 of *Annie and the Old One* by Miska Miles. This is a beautiful and cogent story of a young Navajo girl who tries to halt time to delay her beloved grandmother's death. Her grandmother teaches her how to face life and to accept death. Say, "Grandmother lives with Annie and her parents. She is a member of Annie's family." Ask, "Do grandmothers live with any of you?" "Do any relatives beside your father, mother and brothers and sisters live with any of you?" Discuss the pupils' responses. Say, "There are many different types of families in the United States. Many families have only mother, father, and brothers and sisters. However, other families have other members like Annie's family, such as grandmother, grandfather, and cousins. Other families have a mother and no father. Some have a father and no mother." Ask, "Why do you think there are different kinds of families?" Discuss the children's responses. Help them to understand why there are many different types of families in our society.

4. Focus the students' attention on the picture of Annie and her grandmother again. Ask, "What do you think this story is about?" List the students' responses on the board or butcher paper. Read the book to the class, stopping at various points to discuss these questions:

   a) How did Annie know that her grandmother was going to die?

   b) How did Annie feel when she learned that her grandmother was going to Mother Earth? Have you ever felt that way? When? Why?

   c) What did Annie do to try to stop time to delay her grandmother's death? Was she able to stop time? Why or why not?

   d) How did Annie learn to accept her grandmother's death? How did what her grandmother told her help? How did her grandmother's actions help her? What did Annie learn from grandmother about life? About death?

Summarize the lesson by helping the children to understand how we sometimes have to learn to live without family members with whom we have very strong, positive relationships. Personalize the lesson by giving an example from your own life. Tell the children how you faced the problem and eventually dealt with it successfully, like Annie in the story.

INTERMEDIATE AND UPPER GRADES

CONCEPT: Cultural Diversity and Similarity

Generalization: Native American cultures used both different and similar means to satisfy common human needs and wants.

1. Ask the students to name some things they think all human beings need in order to survive and satisfy unique human wants. Their responses will probably include "food," "a place to live in," and "clothing." Probing questions might be necessary to bring out that people also have such needs as the need to explain unknown phenomena in the universe, for government, and for self-esteem.

2. List the student responses on the board and, with the class,

group them into specific categories, such as food, shelter, clothing, government, family, religion, and economy.

3. Ask the students to name some institutions and means used in our society to meet the needs they have identified and categorized. Write their responses, in abbreviated form, on the board. Tell the class that in this unit they will be studying about ways in which four earlier cultures in North America satisfied these same human needs in very different ways than we usually satisfy them today.

4. Before introducing the four cultures, develop, with the class, key questions related to each of the categories. The students will use the questions as guides when studying the four cultures. Examples are:

   a) Food
      1) What kinds of foods did the people eat?
      2) Were they primarily hunters and gatherers or farmers?
      3) How was the food usually prepared? By whom?
   b) Government
      1) Who or what group made major decisions and laws?
      2) How were major decisionmakers chosen?
      3) How were rules and laws enforced?
   c) Economy
      1) What goods and services were produced?
      2) How were they produced? By whom? For whom?
      3) How were goods and services exchanged? Was some form of money used? Barter?

5. The students should record the key questions in their notebooks. They will use them as guides when examining the four cultures.

6. Introduce the four cultures the class will study. When selecting four Indian cultures for the unit, try to select cultures which (1) have both similarities and differences that the students will be able to see rather clearly and (2) cultures for which you have adequate and high-quality student books and resources. To assure cultural diversity, select the four groups from four different geographical areas, such

as the Southeast, the Northwest, the Southwest, and California. This unit could be taught with as few as two groups. However, generalizations are more powerful when they are developed from a larger content sample. On the other hand, it is difficult for elementary students to study more than four cultures in one unit. In our example, we have chosen the Iroquois (a Southeast Indian group), the Haida (Northwest), the Hopi (Southwest), and the Pomo (California). These four groups clearly illustrate both the similarities and diversity that existed within Indian cultures. Two good books for this unit are: Marion E. Gridley, *Indians of Yesterday* and Daniel Jacobson, *Great Indian Tribes*.

7. Ask the students to construct a data retrieval chart (like the one illustrated in Table 5.1) which includes: (1) the categories and key questions they identified earlier and (2) the names of the four groups. As they read and discuss each group, they should complete the blank spaces in the chart. When the chart is completed, ask the students key questions which will enable them to formulate this generalization: "Native cultures used both different and similiar means to satisfy common human needs and wants."

8. This activity is designed to test the student's ability to apply the generalization which they have learned in this unit. *The American Indian Speaks* is a film which presents case studies of the Muskogee, Creek, Rosebud Sioux, and the Nisqually. Before showing the film, ask the students to focus on ways in which these groups are alike and different. Show the film. After the students have viewed it, discuss ways in which the groups portrayed in the film are alike and different.

Valuing Activity

Questions and problems related to the use of drugs can evoke lively value discussions in the classroom. Exposing students to materials that relate to the use of drugs within various subcultures in American society can be a springboard for value discussion and analysis. The last part of the book, *Tinker and the Medicine Men* by Bernard Wolf, deals with the use of peyote, a hallucinogenic drug, in a Navajo spiritual ceremony. The book is a story about a six-year-old Navajo boy named Tinker Yazzie.

Tinker wants to become a medicine man like his father and grandfather. Medicine men are very important and respected people in Navajo society. They help to maintain their people's physical and mental health. They also foster the Navajo's religious beliefs and values. Medicine men are sometimes peyote chiefs. Peyote chiefs use peyote during special ceremonies. Tinker's father, Tony Yazzie, is a Peyote chief. When the time comes, he allows Tinker to take peyote during a religious rite. Read the section of the book dealing with the use of peyote and ask your students the following questions.

Questions

1. Do you think that Tinker's father should use peyote? Why or why not? (Explain to the students that peyote is a hallucinogenic drug; describe how it effects its users.)
2. Do you think that Tinker's father should have allowed him to use peyote? Why or why not?
3. If you were Tinker, would you have wanted to take peyote? Why or why not?
4. Should drugs ever be used other than for medical purposes? Why or why not?
5. Do you think that it was illegal for Tinker's father to give him peyote? Why or why not? Do you think that the use of peyote should be legal? Why or why not?
6. What do you think happened to Tinker? Why?

HIGH SCHOOL GRADES

CONCEPT: Federal Policy

Generalization: Most federal policy on Indian affairs was made without Indian input and usually sought Indian assimilation and termination of federal-tribal relationships.

1. To gain an understanding of the legal relationship Indian tribes have with the federal government, the students should examine some of the Indian treaties made between the United States government and Indian tribes. These treaties were usually made when Indian tribes were forced to cede their territories and to relocate on reservations. They were granted reservation land in exchange for their land. Several such

Table 5.1

Data Retrieval Chart for Comparing and Contrasting Four Cultures

Categories and Related Questions	Iroquois	Haida	Hopi	Pomo
Food (Questions)				
Shelter (Questions)				
Clothing (Questions)				
Government (Questions)				
Family (Questions)				
Religion (Questions)				
Economy (Questions)				

treaties are reprinted in Chapter 2 of Vine Deloria, Jr., ed., *Of Utmost Good Faith.*

2. Shortly after Indians had been conquered and forced onto reservations in the late 1800s, efforts were begun by the federal government to terminate its special relationship with the tribes, to force them to give up most aspects of their cultures, and to force assimilation into the dominant culture. These goals of federal policy were implemented in the Dawes Severalty Act of 1887. Ask the students to research the arguments, both pro and con, which preceded the passage of the act.

   a) Although many White liberals favored the passage of the act, most Indian tribes opposed it. When the bill was being debated in Congress, representatives of the Five Civilized Tribes sent a strong message to Congress opposing its passage. Ask the class to read and discuss this statement, which is reprinted on pages 307–309 of Deloria, *Of Utmost Good Faith.*

   b) White allies of Indians strongly supported the passage of a bill, such as Dawes, that would break up tribal lands and allot them to individual household heads. They felt that such a bill would enable Indians to assimilate into the dominant culture. In 1884, the Indian Rights Association of Philadelphia, whose members were White friends of the Indian, issued a pamphlet strongly advocating the passage of an allotment bill. Ask the students to read and discuss excerpts from this pamphlet, reprinted on pages 386–91 of Washburn, ed., *The Indian and the White Man.* The class should then compare the statement sent to Congress by the Five Civilized Tribes and the excerpt from the pamphlet. They should discuss the merits and weaknesses of the two positions.

3. Ask several students to role play a debate between those who favored the Dawes bill and those who opposed it.

4. Ask the students to research these questions: "What effects did the Dawes Severalty Act have on Indian people?" "On White Society?" "How do you think Indian life might be different today if the bill had failed in Congress?" "Why?" Alvin M. Josephy, Jr., *The Indian Heritage of America* and

Edward H. Spicer, *A Short History of the Indian in the United States,* contain good discussions of the disastrous effects of the act on Indian tribes.

5. Because of the loss of millions of acres of tribal lands and the severe poverty of Indians, it was clear by the 1920s that the Dawes Act had been a colossal failure. John Collier, who became commissioner of Indian affairs in 1933, outlined a new federal policy for Indians. Ask the students to read and discuss his statement, "A New Deal for the Red Men," in Washburn, pages 393–96, and the new federal act of 1934 that embodied the new federal policy, the Wheeler-Howard Act, in Deloria, pages 99–106.

6. Ask the class to research the effects the Wheeler-Howard Act has had on Indian life and on the larger society. They can share their research findings by using role-playing, debates, or group discussion techniques.

7. Heated arguments for the termination of federal-tribal relationship surfaced again in the 1950s. Ask the class to prepare research reports on these topics:

   a) The House Concurrent Resolution 108, 83rd Congress, 1st session, passed on August 1, 1953, which called for the termination of the federal role in Indian affairs.

   b) How termination policy affected these tribes and the conditions of the termination policy in each case:

      1) the Klamaths of Oregon
      2) the Menominees of Wisconsin
      3) the Alabamas and Coushattas in the South

8. Ask the class to study the various debates on termination that have taken place in the 1960s and 1970s among Indians and federal officials. An interesting argument against termination by an Indian is Earl Old Person (Blackfoot), "Testimony against Proposed Congressional Legislation, 1966," reprinted in Moquin with Van Doren, eds. *Great Documents in American Indian History,* pp. 351–54.

9. To terminate this unit, ask the students to divide into three groups and pretend that they are three different reservation tribes that have legal relationships with the federal government. Each tribe must unanimously decide, in the Indian tradition, whether they will terminate or maintain their legal

relationship with the federal government. When the role-playing is over, the class should reassemble and discuss the decisions of each "tribe" and the process and arguments they experienced in reaching them.

Materials and Resources

REFERENCES FOR THE TEACHER

Especially Recommended

Brandon, William. *The American Heritage Book of Indians.* New York: Dell, 1961.

An extremely informative, well-written introduction to Indian cultures in all parts of the Americas. This book, which can be used in high school courses, deserves the acclaim it has received.

Brown, Dee. *Bury My Heart at Wounded Knee: An Indian History of the American West.* New York: Holt, 1971.

This is a compassionate, poignant, and powerful history of Native Americans written from an Indian point of view.

Deloria, Vine, Jr. *Custer Died for Your Sins.* New York: Avon, 1969.

A rhetorical and highly partisan but important articulation of the problems and future plight of modern day Indians by a noted Native American leader.

Josephy, Alvin M., Jr. *The Indian Heritage of America.* New York: Bantam Books, 1968.

This is an extremely informative, detailed, and sensitive history of North, South, and Central American Indians. The book also contains a comprehensive treatment of recent archaeological findings and an extensive bibliography.

McLuhan, T. C., ed. *Touch the Earth: A Self-Portrait of Indian Existence.* New York: Pocket Books, 1971.

An outstanding and powerful collection of statements by Native Americans on a number of topics. Highly recommended for use with students.

Spicer, Edward H. *A Short History of the Indians of the United States.* New York: Van Nostrand Reinhold, 1969.

This excellent book includes a brief history of the American Indian and fifty-one key related documents. The book is sympathetically and perceptively written. A very good introductory source.

Other References

Bahr, Howard M., Bruce A. Chadwick and Robert C. Day, eds. *Native*

Americans Today: Sociological Perspectives. New York: Harper and Row, 1972.

Indian education, acculturation, and identity, the urban Indian, and Red power are some of the topics discussed in this comprehensive anthology.

Ceran, W. W. *The First American: A Story of North American Archaeology.* New York: Mentor Books, 1971.

An informative and strikingly illustrated introduction to the archaeology of North America.

Costo, Rupert and Jeanette Henry, *Textbooks and the American Indian.* San Francisco: Indian Historian Press, 1970.

An important study of the treatment of Native Americans in school books that is extremely useful to teachers and textbook selection committees.

Council on Interracial Books for Children, ed. *Chronicles of American Indian Protest.* New York: Fawcett, 1971.

A sensitive collection of documents with useful commentaries by the editors.

Deloria, Vine, Jr. *Behind the Trail of Broken Treaties: An Indian Declaration of Independence.* New York: Dell, 1974.

The author sets forth a plan for congressional relationships with the Indian tribes and reviews past injustices.

———. *God is Red.* New York: Grosset and Dunlap, 1973.

A widely acclaimed study of Native American religious beliefs.

———, ed. *Of Utmost Good Faith.* New York: Bantam Books, 1971.

This valuable anthology contains key documents related to the Indian's legal status in the United States. A good source for studying about the major Indian treaties and other legal statutes.

Debo, Angie. *A History of the Indians of the United States.* Norman: University of Oklahoma Press, 1970.

An informative and readable general history of the Native American.

Driver, Harold E. *Indians of North America,* 2nd ed. Chicago: University of Chicago Press, 1961.

A good introductory book on the American Indian which covers a wide range of topics, including language, clothing, marriage and the family, and kinship groups.

Fey, Harold E. and D'Arcy McNickle. *Indians and Other Americans.* New York: Harper and Row, 1959.

An important book focusing on the struggles and conflicts the Native American has experienced in American life.

Forbes, Jack D., ed. *The Indian in America's Past.* Englewood Cliffs, N. J.: Prentice-Hall, 1964.

An outstanding documentary history of Native Americans by a distinguished scholar of Native cultures. The book is perceptive and written from an Indian point of view.

Grosvenor, Gilbert M. "Indians of North America." Published and distributed by the National Geographic Society, Washington, D. C. 20036. Available on regular paper, heavy chart paper, or plastic.

A detailed and striking color wall map showing Indian tribes in the Americas. Measures 32½ inches by 37 inches.

Hagan, William T. *American Indians.* Chicago: University of Chicago Press, 1961.

This is a lucidly written historical overview of Indian-White relationships in the United States up through the 1950s. It is flawed in parts by White ethnocentrism and insensitive statements but is overall a useful introductory source.

Jacobs, Wilbur R. *Dispossessing the American Indian.* New York: Charles Scribner's Sons, 1972.

An extremely readable and sympathetic treatment of the relationship between Indians and Whites in colonial times.

Marriott, Alice and Carol Rachlin. *American Epic: The Story of the American Indian.* New York: Mentor Books, 1969.

A well-written general history of American Indians by two veteran anthropologists that is a good "first" book for the novice.

————. *American Indian Mythology.* New York: Mentor Books, 1968.

This book contains a collection of American Indian myths, legends, and contemporary folklore.

Moquin, Wayne and Charles Van Doren, eds. *Great Documents in American Indian History.* New York: Praeger, 1973.

Native Americans tell their own history in this valuable and comprehensive documentary source.

Rothenberg, Jerome, ed. *Shaking the Pumpkin: Traditional Poetry of the Indian North American.* Garden City, N.Y.: Doubleday, 1972.

A comprehensive and valuable collection of Native American literature. An excellent book for use with students.

Steiner, Stan. *The New Indians.* New York: Dell, 1968.

A sensitively written popular book focusing on recent Indian protest movements.

Stoutenburgh, John, Jr. *Dictionary of the American Indian.* New York: Crown, 1960.

A useful reference book containing definitions of thousands of words and terms.

Swanton, John R. *The Indian Tribes of North America.* Washington, D. C.: U. S. Government Printing Office, 1952.

A valuable reference book that includes basic information on each Indian tribe arranged by the states in which they are located. An excellent guide for studying local tribes.

Underhill, Ruth M. *Red Man's America.* Rev. ed. Chicago: University of Chicago Press, 1971.

A fairly good anthropological survey of the general characteristics of the major Indian cultural groups. However, this book is written from an Anglo-Saxon point of view and contains some disturbing and insensitive arguments.

Vlahos, Olivia. *New World Beginnings: Indian Cultures in the Americas.* Illustrated by George Ford. Greenwich, Conn.: Fawcett, 1970.

A good introduction to the archaeology of Native Americans intended for juvenile readers. However, it is also an informative teacher source.

Vogel, Virgil J. *This Country Was Ours: A Documentary History of the American Indian.* New York: Harper Torchbooks, 1974.

A comprehensive and thoughtful documentary history with an outstanding bibliography of works on the American Indian.

Walker, Deward E., Jr., ed. *The Emergent Native Americans.* Boston: Little, Brown, 1972.

A scholarly and comprehensive collection of essays focusing on diverse aspects of Native American life.

Washburn, Wilcombe, ed. *The Indian and the White Man.* Garden City: Doubleday, 1964.

This inclusive collection of documents focuses on the White man's views of the Native American.

Wax, Murry L. *Indian Americans: Unity and Diversity.* Englewood Cliffs, N. J.: Prentice-Hall, 1971.

A fair general overview of contemporary Native Americans written from an assimilationist point of view.

BOOKS FOR STUDENTS*

Amon, Aline. *Talking Hands: Indian Sign Language.* Garden City, N. Y.: Doubleday, 1968.

Children will find this book, which shows how to speak in sign language, fascinating. (All Levels)

* *"Books for Students," in Chapters 5 through 10, was prepared by Cherry A. Banks.*

Anderson, LaVere. *Black Hawk: Indian Patriot.* Champaign, Ill.: Garrard Publishing Co., 1972.

An interesting biography of the great Indian leader. The biography centers around Black Hawk's encounters with Whites in an effort to save his land. (Intermediate)

————. *Sitting Bull: Great Sioux Chief.* Champaign, Ill.: Garrard Publishing Co., 1970.

A good biography of a noted Native Americán leader. Sitting Bull's life from age fourteen to death is covered in the book. Fictional episodes add interest to the text. (Intermediate)

Armer, Laura. *Waterless Mountain.* New York: David McKay, 1930.

The story of a Navajo boy who is destined to become a medicine man. Winner of the Newbery Medal. (Intermediate)

Bales, Carol Ann. *Kevin Cloud: Chippewa In the City.* Chicago: Reilly and Lee Books, 1972.

This book is about a contemporary urban Indian. It shows how he bridges the gap between two cultures. Excellent illustrations. (Intermediate)

Baylor, Byrd. *Before You Came This Way.* New York: E. P. Dutton, 1969.

An informative poem inspired by drawings left on rocks by the early inhabitants of the Southwest. Interesting illustrations. (All Levels)

————. *When Clay Sings.* New York: Charles Scribner's Sons, 1972.

The author uses broken Indian pottery to poetically describe the Native American past. This is a good book to introduce young children to archaeology. Illustrated. (All Levels)

Bealer, Alex W. *Only the Names Remain: The Cherokees and the Trail of Tears.* Boston: Little, Brown, 1972.

The poignant story of the Cherokee removal is retold in this book. (Intermediate)

Benchley, Nathaniel. *Only Earth and Sky Last Forever.* New York: Harper and Row, 1972.

This book shows how events leading up to the Battle of the Little Big Horn and the battle itself affected the life of a young Indian. (Upper)

Buckmaster, Henrietta. *The Seminole Wars.* New York: Collier, 1966.

A story about the relationship between the Seminole Indians and Black slaves and how they joined together in the Seminole wars. (Upper)

Clark, Ann Nolan. *In My Mother's House.* New York: Viking, 1941.

The story of a Native American child, his way of life, the land he lives in, and the things important to him. This book gives the reader a feeling for the essence of Indian life. (Primary)

Collier, Peter. *When Shall They Rest? The Cherokees' Long Struggle with America.* New York: Holt, 1973.

The story of the Cherokee and the tragedies they suffered. (Upper)

Coy, Harold. *Man Comes to America.* Boston: Little, Brown, 1973.

This informative book discusses a number of theories that try to explain how people came to the Americas. (High School)

Crary, Margaret. *Susette La Flesche: Voice of the Omaha Indians.* New York: Hawthorn Books, 1973.

An interesting account of the life of a courageous Indian woman who fought for her people's rights. The book should inspire all students. (Upper)

Custis, Edward S. *Portraits from North American Indian Life.* New York: Promontory Press, 1972.

A fantastic collection of photographs about Native American life and culture. (All Levels)

Every, Dale Van. *Disinherited: The Lost Birthright of the American Indian.* New York: William Morrow, 1966.

A detailed history of the Indian Removal Act and the events preceding it. The author focuses on the Cherokee. (High School)

Field, Edward. *Eskimo Songs and Stories.* New York: Delacorte Press, 1973.

An interesting collection of poems about the daily life of the Netsilik Eskimos. (High School)

Fish, Byron. *Eskimo Boy Today.* Anchorage, Alaska: Alaska Northwest Publishing Co., 1971.

The story about a young Eskimo boy who bridges two cultures: his own and Anglo-American life. (Intermediate)

Fleischmann, Glen. *The Cherokee Removal, 1838.* New York: Franklin Watts, 1971.

A detailed account of the events which led to the Cherokee removal. This book is easy to read and contains a lot of information on the removal. (Intermediate)

Forman, James. *People of the Dream.* New York: Farrar, Straus & Giroux, 1972.

A fair story of Chief Joseph and the Nez Perces. (Upper)

George, Jean Craighead. *Julie of the Wolves.* New York: Harper and Row, 1972.

A powerful story about a young Eskimo girl's courage. Julie realizes the beauty and meaning of her Eskimo heritage and wants to make it part of her life. Some teachers may think that some of the events treated in this book are too mature for their students. Winner of the Newbery Medal. (Upper)

Glubok, Shirley. *The Art of the North American Indian.* New York: Harper and Row, 1964.

The author reviews a wide variety of art forms, such as masks, wood carvings, dolls, pottery, and drawings. The use, material used to make the object, and the Indian tribe associated with the art form are also discussed. Illustrated. (All Levels)

Goble, Paul and Dorothy Goble. *The Fetterman Fight.* New York: Pantheon Books, 1972.

A good account of an important victory in Native American history. The story is told through the eyes of Brave Eagle. It focuses on a major battle in which Red Cloud and his people fought for, and held onto, their land. The illustrations are especially noteworthy. (Intermediate)

———. *Custer's Last Battle.* New York: Pantheon Books, 1969.

A very interesting account of the battle of the Little Big Horn. This account is told by a fifteen-year-old Oglala Sioux. It adds a new perspective to one of the best known battles of the 1800s. The color illustrations complement the text. (Intermediate)

Gridley, Marion E. *Contemporary American Indian Leaders.* New York: Dodd, Mead and Co., 1972.

A collection of twenty-six biographies of contemporary Native American leaders. People in government, the arts, sciences, and community action are represented. (High School)

———. *Indians of Yesterday.* New York: M. A. Donohue and Co., 1940.

An informative and sensitive book about Native American cultures. A good general introductory book for students. (Upper)

———. *The Story of Haida.* New York: Putnam, 1972.

The story of a proud group of Northwest Indians. The Haida's traditions, family life, and customs are discussed. Colorful illustrations. (Intermediate)

Hertzberg, Hazel W. *The Great Tree and the Longhouse: The Culture of the Iroquois.* New York: Macmillan, 1966.

A description of the culture of the Iroquois. The author looks at family relationships, religion, roles, and contemporary life. (Upper)

Hofsinde, Robert. *Indian Music Makers.* New York: William Morrow, 1967.

The author tells how musical instruments were made, provides historical information on their use and traditions, and tells how they differed from tribe to tribe. (All Levels)

Hoyt, Olga. *American Indians Today.* New York: Abelard-Schuman, 1972.

The similarities and differences among many different Indian tribes are discussed. The needs of Indians, their cultures, and their efforts to establish self-help organizations are treated. (High School)

Jones, Jayne Clark. *The American Indian in America.* Minneapolis: Lerner Publications, 1973, two vols.

Volume 1 of this comprehensive history of American Indians is entitled, *Prehistory to the end of the 18th Century.* Volume 2 is the *Early 19th Century to the Present.* Although this book is not without flaws, it is good general history of Native Americans for young readers. (Upper)

Kimball, Yeffe and Jean Anderson. *The Art of American Indian Cooking.* Garden City, N. Y.: Doubleday, 1965.

Recipes for making a variety of Indian dishes, such as salads, desserts, and appetizers, are included in this interesting book. (All Levels)

Kroeber, Theodora. *Ishi: Last of His Tribe.* Berkeley, Calif.: Parnassus Press, 1964.

A moving account of a young Indian boy who is the last survivor of his tribe, which has been destroyed by Anglo-Americans. (Upper)

Levenson, Dorothy. *Homesteaders and Indians.* New York: Franklin Watts, 1971.

An excellent history of the settling of the West. The author tries to present the story from both the Indian and White points of view. The book includes a chapter on Blacks in the West. (Intermediate)

Lewis, Richard, ed. *I Breathe A New Song: Poems of the Eskimo.* New York: Simon and Schuster, 1971.

A collection of poems written by Eskimos which reveals who they are and what they are about. The introduction is a good overview of the Eskimo experience. Illustrated. (Upper)

Lisitzky, Gene. *Four Ways of Being Human.* New York: Viking, 1956.

An excellent introduction to anthropology that includes chapters on polar Eskimos and the Hopis. (High School)

Macfarlan, Allan A. *Book of American Indian Games.* New York: Association Press, 1958.

A collection of 150 games played by Native Americans long ago. The author names the tribe that originated each game, describes the setting, and gives the number and age of players appropriate for the game. Detailed illustrations show how each game is played. (All Levels)

McDermott, Gerald. *Arrow to the Sun: A Pueblo Indian Tale.* New York: Viking Press, 1974.

A beautifully illustrated folk tale about a boy who searches for his father. (Primary)

McKeown, Martha Ferguson. *Come to Our Salmon Feast.* Portland, Oregon: Binfords and Mort, 1959.

An informative and interesting book about the customs and rituals that surround the salmon feast. (Intermediate)

Miles, Miska. *Annie and the Old One.* Illustrated by Peter Parnall. Boston: Little, Brown, 1971.

A beautiful and touching story about a young Navajo girl's attempt to stop time to delay her beloved grandmother's impending death. The excellent drawings greatly enhance the text. A Caldecott Honor book. (Primary)

Momaday, Natachee Scott, ed. *American Indian Authors.* Boston: Houghton Mifflin, 1972.

A collection of interesting writings by historic as well as contemporary Native Americans. Short stories, legends, speeches, and poems are included. Discussion questions are included at the end of each selection. (High School)

Momaday, N. Scott. *House Made of Dawn.* New York: Signet, 1966.

A novel about a Native American's relationship with the Indian and non-Indian worlds. A Pulitzer Prize winner. (High School)

O'Dell, Scott. *Island of the Blue Dolphins.* Boston: Houghton Mifflin, 1960.

A powerful and touching story about an Indian girl's eighteen-year survival on an island with a pack of wild dogs. The book is based on actual events and was the winner of the Newbery Medal in 1961. (Upper)

————. *Sing Down the Moon.* Boston: Houghton Mifflin, 1970.

The story of a young Navajo girl and her people who were forced from their homes to Fort Sumner in the "Long Walk," their removal journey. (Upper)

Pearson, Keith L., *The Indian in American History.* New York: Harcourt, 1973.

This general history of American Indians, which is designed to be used as a text, uses the experiences of several Indian groups to tell the story of the Native Americans. Some of the author's interpretations and points of view are not acceptable to Indians. However, the book is useful and is one of the few general textbooks on American Indians. (High School)

Perrine, Mary. *Salt Boy.* Boston: Houghton Mifflin, 1968.

A beautiful story about an Indian father and son. (Intermediate)

Pollack, Dean. *Joseph, Chief of the Nez Perce.* Metropolitan Press, 1950.

The story of a young boy who grows up and becomes a great leader of his tribe. The book includes much historical information about the Nez Perce. (Intermediate)

Reit, Seymour. *Child of the Navajos.* New York: Dodd, Mead and Co., 1971.

The story of a young Navajo boy who lives on an Arizona reservation. (Primary)

Rousseliere, Guy Mary, photographer. *Beyond the High Hills: A Book of Eskimo Poems.* New York: World Publishing, 1961.

Beautiful color photographs illustrate this collection of Eskimo poems. (Upper)

Scott, Ann Herbert. *On Mother's Lap.* New York: McGraw-Hill, 1972.

A sensitively told story about sibling rivalry when a new baby arrives. Illustrated with dramatic black and white drawings. (Primary)

Shor, Pekay. *When the Corn is Red.* New York: Abingdon, 1973.

The author retells the legend of the Tuscaroran Indians which tells the significance of red corn to the tribe and why the tribe lost its land. The Tuscaroran awaits the return of red corn. (Primary)

Showers, Paul. *Indian Festivals.* New York: Crowell, 1969.

The author reviews several Native American and Eskimo festivals. He describes the reasons for the festivals and the details of how they are celebrated. This book is well-written and a good source for discussion of holidays in all cultures. (All Levels)

Sneve, Virgina Driving Hawk. *High Elk's Treasure.* New York: Holiday House, 1972.

An adventure story about a modern Indian family and their link with their famous ancestors. The story is interesting and readable. (Upper)

―――. *Jimmy Yellow Hawk.* New York: Holiday House, 1972.

Jimmy is a young boy who wants a new name. His story is one of adventure and suspense. The book reveals some of the problems of reservation life. A Council on Interracial Books for Children Award winner. (Upper)

Steiner, Stan. *The Tiguas: The Lost Tribe of City Indians.* New York: Collier, 1972.

An interesting account of a modern group of urban Indians who are trying to maintain their traditional customs and values. The book is marred by the author's insensitivity. He sometimes presents the group as strange and different. (Intermediate)

Terrell, John Upton. *Apache Chronicle: The Story of the People.* New York: World Publishing, 1972.

A refreshing and novel interpretation of the Apache and their interactions with the peoples who invaded their land. A sensitive and significant book. (High School)

Tolboom, Wanda Neill. *Little Eskimo Hunter.* New York: Sterling Publishing Co., 1956.

The story of a young Eskimo boy who becomes a hunter. Many facets of Eskimo life, such as food, transportation, and housing are described in the story. The story is weak, but the information about Eskimo culture is useful. (Intermediate)

Wilde, Arthur L. *Apache Boy.* New York: Grosset and Dunlap, 1969.

An interesting photographic essay about a ten-year old Apache child who lives on an Arizona reservation. (Upper)

Wilson, Edmund. *Apologies to the Iroquois.* New York: Vintage, 1950.

An extremely well-written journalistic account of the Iroquois' fight for their rights in modern times. (High School)

Wolf, Bernard. *Tinker and the Medicine Men: The Story of a Navajo Boy of Monument Valley.* New York: Random House, 1973.

A strikingly illustrated true story of a young Navajo boy who wants to become a medicine man like his father and grandfather. The author treats many aspects of his young hero's life. Although this book is extremely well written and interesting, the treatment of the use of peyote in Navajo spiritual ceremonies might make its use controversial in some schools. (Upper)

Wood, Nancy. *Hollering Sun.* New York: Simon and Schuster, 1972.

A collection of poetic statements about the beliefs and philosophy of the Taos Indians. This book reveals how the Taos feel about themselves and their environment. The photographs are excellent. (Upper)

European Americans:
Concepts, Strategies, and Materials

6

Give me your tired, your poor,
Your huddled masses yearning to breathe free,
The wretched refuse of your teeming shore,
Send these, the homeless, tempest-tossed, to me:
I lift my lamp beside the golden door.

> Emma Lazarus
> Inscription on the Statute of Liberty
> New York Harbor

Introduction

Between 1820 and 1970, over 45 million immigrants entered the United States. Most of them were Europeans and belonged to many different religious, political, and cultural groups. The making of a coherent society from so many different ethnic and

179

nationality groups is one of the most amazing chapters in human history. Yet social scientists, and therefore classroom teachers, have largely ignored the role of ethnicity in American history and in modern society. American social scientists have been preoccupied with the "melting pot" concept. They predicted that ethnicity would vanish in the United States by the third generation. Their prophecy was wrong. Although most White ethnic groups have attained high levels of assimilation into the dominant ethnic group,* many maintain a sense of ethnic identity, important elements of their ethnic cultures, and are political, economic, and social interest groups. Most of their primary relationships also occur within their ethnic groups. Thus, while our society has a high degree of cultural assimilation, it contains many ethnic subgroups and institutions. Ethnic factors also influence political behavior in America.

European Americans should be included in a sound ethnic studies program because the processes of acculturation and assimilation which they experienced, and which many groups are still experiencing, must be taken into account when students formulate high-level concepts and generalizations about ethnicity in American society. The virulent anti-Chinese agitation which arose on the West Coast in the late 1800s was related to the nativistic movements directed against Catholics, foreign "radicals," and Southern and Eastern European immigrants. Nativism culminated in the notorious Immigration Act of 1924. Most European immigrants, like many upward mobile non-Whites, denied their ethnic heritages to gain admission into the dominant ethnic group. However, while assimilated White ethnics were able to enter the larger society, culturally assimilated non-Whites continue to be excluded because of their skin color.

The contemporary theories of Jensen and Schokley about the inferiority of non-Whites are reminiscent of those popularized by Ripley and Grant in the late nineteenth and early twentieth centuries about the genetic inferiority of Southern and Eastern Europeans. While the experiences of European Americans and non-White ethnic groups are similar in some ways, they are also different. However, valid generalizations about ethnicity in the United States must reflect the experiences of all groups.

---

*White Anglo-Saxon Protestants are the dominant ethnic group in the United States.

European Americans: Historical Perspective

Important Dates

1565	Pedro Menéndez Avilés founded St. Augustine, Florida on the site of an Indian village.
1607	English immigrants established their first permanent American colony at Jamestown, Virginia.
1620	The Pilgrims came to America from England on the *Mayflower* and established a settlement at Plymouth, Massachusetts.
1623	The Dutch West India Company settled New Netherland as a trading post.
1654	The first Jewish immigrants to North America settled in New Amsterdam to escape persecution in Brazil.
1683	The first German immigrants to North America settled in Pennsylvania.
1718	The Scotch-Irish began immigrating to the American colonies in large numbers.
1729	The Pennsylvania Colony increased the head taxes charged to entering immigrants to discourage further foreign settlement.
1798	A Federalist-dominated Congress enacted the Alien and Sedition Acts to crush the Republican party and harass aliens.
1803	The British Passenger Act was enacted to discourage immigration.
1825	Great Britain repealed laws which prohibited immigration. The first group of Norwegian immigrants arrived in the United States.
1845–49	A series of potato blights in Ireland caused thousands of its citizens to immigrate to the United States.
1855	The antiforeign Know-Nothing movement reached its zenith and had a number of political successes in the 1855 elections.

Important Dates cont.

	The movement rapidly declined after 1855. Castel Garden immigrant depot opened in New York.
1863	The Irish working classes expressed discontent with the Civil War and hostility toward urban Blacks in the New York draft riots which lasted for four days.
1882	A congressional immigration act established a head tax of fifty cents and excluded lunatics, convicts, idiots, and those likely to become public charges.
1883–85	An economic depression escalated nativistic feelings in the United States.
1885	The Foran Act outlawed the immigration of contract laborers.
1886	The Haymarket Affair in Chicago greatly increased fear of foreign "radicals" and stimulated the growth of nativistic sentiments in the United States.
	The Statue of Liberty was dedicated as nativism soared in the United States.
1891	Eleven Italian Americans were lynched in New Orleans during the height of American nativism, after being accused of murdering a police superintendent.
1892	Ellis Island opened and replaced Castle Garden as the main port of entry for European immigrants.
1894	The Immigration Restriction League was organized in Boston by intellectuals to promote the passage of a bill that would require entering immigrants to pass a literacy test. The passage of the bill was urged to restrict immigration from Southern and Eastern Europe.
1899	William Z. Ripley's *The Races of Europe* was published. Ripley divided European peoples into three major racial groups, thus giving the nativists intellectual justifications for their movement.

Important Dates cont.

1901–10	Almost 9 million immigrants entered the United States, most of whom came from Southern and Eastern Europe. This mass immigration greatly intensified the activities of nativistic groups.
1907	A congressional act extended the classes of immigrants excluded from the United States. Victims of tuberculosis and persons who had committed certain kinds of crimes were added to the list.
1911	The Dillingham Commission, formed in 1907, issued its forty-one volume report in which it strongly recommended a literacy test for entering immigrants and made a marked distinction between the "old" and "new" immigrants.
1916	Madison Grant, a well-known anthropologist, published *The Passing of the Great Race in America.* This popular book gave the nativists more ammunition.
1916–19	The movement to Americanize aliens was widespread and intense.
1917	A comprehensive immigration bill was enacted which established the literacy test for entering immigrants, added to the classes of those excluded, and increased the head tax from $4 to $8. This act was a major victory for the nativists.
1919–20	During the height of antiradical attitudes in America, hundreds of alien radicals were captured and deported in a movement led by A. Mitchell Palmer.
1921	The Johnson Act signaled a turning point in American history. It set up a nationality quota system and imposed the first numerical limits on European immigration to the United States.
1924	The Johnson-Reed Act established extreme quotas on immigration and blatantly discrim-

Important Dates cont.

	inated against Southern and Eastern European and non-White nations.
1927	Two Italian radicals, Nicola Sacco and Bartolomeo Vanzetti, were executed during a period of extreme antiracial sentiment in America. Their execution kicked off a wave of reactions throughout the Western world.
1952	The McCarran-Walter Act, which allegedly removed racial barriers to immigration, essentially continued the policy established in 1924 and was in some ways more restrictive.
1954	The closing of Ellis Island marked the end of mass immigration to the United States.
1965	A new immigration act, which became effective in 1968, abolished the national origins quota system and greatly liberalized American immigration policy.
1971	Less than 400,000 aliens entered the United States, one of the smallest numbers to enter in any year in the twentieth century.

Spaniards in the Americas

Spain was the first European nation to establish permanent settlements in the Americas. Spanish ships arrived in the Americas in 1492 under the leadership of Christopher Columbus. In 1496 Columbus and his brother Bartholomew founded the city of Santo Domingo on the island of Hispaniola. Santo Domingo was the first permanent continuing European settlement in the Americas. A number of Spanish explorers, including Coronado, Cortez, Cabeza de Vaca, and Ponce de León followed Columbus. These and other Spaniards explored and settled in the Americas. In 1526, San Miguel de Gualdape, a Spanish colony in South Carolina, was established by Lucas Vasquez de Ayllon. Another Spaniard named Pedro Ménendez de Avilés founded the oldest permanent city in the United States, St. Augustine, Florida in 1565. These early Spaniards heavily influenced the language, religion, and other cultural aspects of the Americas.

Even though their influence in the Americas was great, very few Spaniards came to the Americas. It has been estimated that no more than 300,000 Spaniards came to the Americas during the entire three colonial centuries. Many of these people only stayed a short time. Many of the Spaniards that remained in America fathered children with Indian women. These unions produced a new ethnic group in the Americas, the Mexicans (see Chapter 8).

Today the number of Spanish-born Americans is still small. Between 1820 and 1971, only 229,235 Spaniards immigrated to the United States. It has been estimated that between 1820 and 1968 not more than 50,000 Spanish-born persons were living in the United States at any given time.

More Europeans Come to America

Europeans started settling in America in significant numbers in the 1600s. The economic, social, and political conditions existing in Europe caused many of its inhabitants to cross the Atlantic searching for a new home. The main causes of the waves of immigrations were the drastic economic and social changes taking place in Europe. Serfdom had been the basis of European society for centuries. Most of the people were peasants who earned their living by farming. Throughout Europe the old relationships between peasants and the land were changed and the peasants suffered severely. The land owned by the village was divided into individual plots. With each succeeding generation, the land was further divided. Eventually, the plots of land became so small that younger sons were unable to make a living. Some peasants suffered when land holdings were consolidated by the landlords.

The peasant became landless and thus lost his place in the social order. He was attached to the land. Without it, he was unable to make a living or maintain a sense of being. The tremendous population growth Europe experienced in the seventeenth and eighteenth centuries increased the peasants' problems. Famine and crop failures also caused many to immigrate.

The early settlers were a diverse group, although most of them were peasants. Many were unable to pay for their passage and became indentured servants in order to make the journey. However, merchants, artisans, professionals, and laborers made up a small but significant part of the immigrants during the entire colonial period. Vagrants and convicts, who were unwanted by European nations, were also with the first settlers. However, there were never as many criminals and paupers among the colonists as is often believed.

While the bulk of the first European immigrants came to North America primarily for economic reasons, some came for religious and political reasons. Most European nations had established churches associated with the state. Religious dissenters who wanted to practice other religions sometimes immigrated to America. The Separatists who arrived in the colonies in 1620 on the *Mayflower* were seeking a place where they could freely practice their religion. The Jewish immigrants who settled in North America during the colonial period were also seeking religious and political freedom.

Once the European immigrations were underway, the movement itself produced forces that stimulated it. The letters settlers sent back to friends and relatives in Europe extolling the wonders of America were a cogent factor that pulled more Europeans to America. Guidebooks about wages and living conditions in America were distributed in Europe by travel and shipping agents. These books helped to motivate thousands of Europeans to immigrate.

The rise of the industrial revolution and scientific farming in the nineteenth century also stimulated European immigration to America. The development of industry put many artisans out of work. Modern farming methods displaced many farmers. These displaced workers tried to solve their problems by immigrating to America. Ship companies eager to get passengers and American states and railroad companies that wanted to settle sparsely populated areas in the United States recruited European immigrants. European governments either discouraged or legally prohibited immigration in the 1600s and 1700s. However, these obstacles to immigration were largely removed in the nineteenth century. This too encouraged Europeans to immigrate. The development of more efficient and inexpensive ocean transportation also stimulated European immigration in the nineteenth century.

Although all of these factors contributed to European immigration to America, it was the search for a chance to earn a better living which caused most European immigrants to come to the United States. The tide of immigration rose and fell with economic conditions in the United States. When times were good the immigrants came in great numbers. When depression set in, immigration dropped significantly. During some brief periods, the number of immigrants returning to Europe actually exceeded the number that arrived. The key role that economic factors played in the European immigrations to North America make them very similar to other mass movements to the United States from such nations as Canada, Mexico, the Philippines, China, and Japan.

Although some religious and political dissenters came to America so that they could freely practice their beliefs, this aspect of European immigration has been greatly exaggerated and over-simplified in textbooks and in the popular mind. Most came mainly for economic reasons. Most who were religious and political dissenters also hoped to improve their economic lot. The widespread belief that most of the first European settlers in America loved freedom and liberty has also been grossly exaggerated. The Puritans and other religious dissenters who settled in North America were not liberty-loving people, but were provincial groups who believed that their religions were the only true and valid ones. They were as intolerant of religious differences as those who protected the official churches in Europe.[1] Their aim was to find a place where they could practice *their* religions freely, and not to build a nation in which all religions would be tolerated.

Religious freedom and toleration developed in North America not because of the goals and wishes of the early colonists, but because the motley collection of religious groups that came to America competed for and won the right to practice their beliefs. The same is true about American democracy and the colonists. The colonists were Europeans in mind and spirit. They tried hard to establish European institutions and beliefs on American soil. They were not liberty-loving citizens who had a deep belief in democracy. Quite the contrary was true. They were the products of a hierarchial and class structured society and had internalized these beliefs.[2] That they failed to establish a highly stratified society in America was not due to the fact that

1. Maldwyn Allen Jones, *American Immigration* (Chicago: University of Chicago Press, 1960), pp. 6–38.

2. Ibid., pp. 141–42.

they did not try. Rather, a form of democracy emerged in the United States because the social and economic conditions that developed in North America made it impossible to establish a new Europe and fostered the development of a more open society. Thus American democracy did not stem primarily from the vision the colonists brought from Europe but resulted mainly from the social and economic forces which evolved in North America.

The Passage to America

Especially in the seventeenth century, the journey from the peasants' European homes to the American port cities was hard and hazardous.[3] The peasant made the decision to come to America only after much thought. Often, only the threat of starvation or the loss of status compelled him to attempt the difficult journey. The trip was also expensive, especially during the first immigrations. Thus, even after he made the decision to come to America, he often had to save money for a long time before he could begin the trip.

The peasant's first step in the journey to America was taking a long trip, usually by foot, to a European city that had a seaport from which ships sailed to America. Not everyone who started out was able to complete this stage of the journey. Many of those who made it to the European port cities were tired and battered. Once they arrived in the port city, the peasants had to wait for weeks and sometimes months before the ship departed for America. The ship captains waited until the ships were full of goods and human cargo before they sailed for North America because the fuller ship was more profitable. During the long wait, the peasants became restless and tired. Some were not able to board the ship when it was finally ready to depart. As each day went by during the long wait for the American departure, the food the peasants had stored for the journey steadily dwindled. Renting a room at the European port city also took a large part of the meager funds they had saved up for the trip.

Finally the day came when the ship headed for America. The peasants' joy at the departure was to be short-lived. The

3. Oscar Handlin, *The Uprooted: The Epic Story of the Great Migrations that Made the American People* (New York: Grosset and Dunlap, 1951), pp. 37–62.

conditions on the ships were depressing and harsh. To maximize his profits, the ship captain packed the vessels like sardines. Each family was assigned an extremely small space on the ship. The family spent most of its time in these dark, crowded compartments. Diseases were rampant on the vessels and took many lives. Dysentery, cholera, yellow fever, and smallpox were some of the more common ship diseases. The journey was long, often over a month. Many families barely had enough food to last throughout the journey. Eventually, European nations passed laws requiring peasants to take a certain amount of food for the trip. However, ship captains, who wanted to profit from selling food on the ships, thought of many ingenious ways to evade these weakly enforced laws.

The Atlantic journey, especially before the time of the steamship, was a tremendous shock to the peasants. The family disruption that continued when they reached America began on the ship. Almost wholly dependent on the ship's crew, the father was unable to exercise his traditional role as leader and master of the family. The mother could not function in her traditional role either. When food was getting scarce, she had to try to keep the family fed. These transatlantic conditions severely strained family relationships.

The peasants who survived the journey eventually landed at an American port city. The landing was eagerly awaited and celebrated. However, the peasants still had some hurdles to overcome. They had to be checked and questioned by American immigration officials before they could roam freely in America. Wrong answers to questions or poor health could mean further questioning by officials and boards, a stay in a hospital, or even a trip back to Europe. In the earliest years, the inspection focused on physical health and ability to work. Gradually, questions related to the immigrant's morals and political beliefs were added. In 1917 Congress enacted a law requiring immigrants to demonstrate literacy in some language before they could enter the United States.

Most of the immigrants were broken, both financially and physically when they arrived at American seaport cities. Some were the sole survivors in their families. Broken and lonely, some found asylum in poorhouses. Many immigrants who had planned to settle elsewhere never left the port cities in which their vessels landed. Thousands who had planned to settle elsewhere stayed in cities like Milwaukee, Chicago, and St. Louis. Some of the first settlers found work on construction projects in cities. Later, railroad construction provided work for immigrants. When the industrial revolution got underway, factory work became available. In all of these lines of work, the immigrants were paid low wages and were outrageously exploited by their employers. Few immigrants became successful farmers or settled in the West. Farming required resources and capital most of the peasants did not have. American farming was also different from agriculture in the European village. Few of the immigrants were able to settle on the frontier. They lacked both the resources and the ability to push the Indians off their land like many of their American-born contemporaries.

The Urban Ghetto

Most of the European immigrants settled in cities, like most migrants from rural areas today. They had neither the means nor the desire to settle in rural areas. Like his or her today's counterpart, the new immigrant settled in blighted and dilapidated areas that became ethnic ghettos. Irishtowns, Germantowns, and Little Italys developed in most of the cities in the Northeast and Middle West. Ethnic organizations, like schools, newspapers, and churches, emerged within these communities. The immigrants, especially the more recent arrivals, usually lived in run-down housing near the business and manufacturing districts that had been vacated by suburban-bound upward mobile residents when the manufacturing district sprawled outward into their communities.

When the upward-mobile left the inner city, their old mansions were converted into multiple family dwellings for the immigrants. The multiple dwelling units became a source of quick profit for the owners. Little was done to make these dwellings comfortable. Profit, not comfort, was what the slum landlord sought. When these neighborhoods were deserted by the old residents, they were also forsaken by the street cleaners and sanitary crews. The smells from the garbage were pungent. The immigrants' habit of throwing garbage out of the window and keeping animals in their backyards made these communities even more unpleasant. High-rise apartments went up in some of the ethnic communities. Most of these buildings were crowded and uncomfortable. Many did not have interior plumbing or central heating. Some of the earliest ones had no toilets. There were only two toilets on each floor in some later apartments. To help pay the rent, some families took in lodgers.

The usual pathologies associated with oppressed urban communities existed in these ethnic ghettos. Diseases such as cholera, tuberculosis, and smallpox thrived. Many of the men used alcohol to escape their daily problems, and alcoholism became a major problem in ethnic urban communities. Gambling was also one of the immigrants' favorite pastimes. Gambling halls, dance halls, saloons, and houses of prostitution were not uncommon sights in the ghetto. Immigrants became involved in crimes, but usually petty ones. Irish immigrants in New York represented more than 50 percent of those arrested for crimes in 1859. European immigrants were also overrepresented on the welfare rolls in American cities. Nearly 90 percent of the persons who were on welfare in New York City in 1860 were immigrants.[4]

The immigrants looked forward to the day when their income would permit them to leave the ghetto and join the exodus to the suburbs. For most ethnic groups, this day eventually came. However, as one ethnic group vacated the ghetto, another group replaced it. In New York City, Italians took over old Irish communities. Jews from Russia and Poland occupied districts where the Germans had lived. After World War II, many of the urban communities that had been occupied by European ethnic groups received a large number of Afro-Americans from the South, Mexican Americans from the Southwest, and migrants from Puerto Rico.

Immigrants and the Urban Political Machine

When European immigrants arrived in the United States, their experiences, visions, hopes, and aspirations were decidedly European. They encountered many events and attitudes in American life which they regarded as foreign and strange. Many of these new ideas and phenomena they found unsettling and alarming; others they simply found baffling. No idea in America was more foreign to the European peasants than the notion of American democracy, which suggested that all men were created

---

4. Jones, *American Immigration*, p. 133.

equal and deserved certain inalienable rights. The rigid social structure they had learned to accept in Europe was too dominant in their minds for them to grasp the meaning of American democracy. They could appreciate these high-sounding ideals even less. The European peasants believed that there was a pecking order in the natural scheme of things and that everyone should know his or her correct social status. It was wrong and shameful for people to try to act like they belonged to a different social class. This was not only the way things were in Europe, but it was the way that they should be everywhere, even in America.

Most immigrants who settled in urban areas became pawns of political bosses in cities like Chicago, New York, and Boston. There were few agencies to help the immigrants find jobs, lend them money, and provide them with social services. In the beginning, only the mutual aid societies provided some of these services. In exchange for votes, the political bosses and their workers provided the immigrants with jobs, loans, and rent money, helped them when they got into trouble with legal authorities, and gave them friendship and sympathy. All of these services helped the urban immigrant to endure the shock of immigration and settlement in America. The immigrants were more than willing, even anxious, to exchange their votes, which they neither valued nor understood, for the things they really needed to survive in American cities. The political bosses gave jobs to foremen on public work labor gangs. These foremen earned their positions by delivering votes to the political bosses.

The political corruption and bribery which grew up around the urban political machines were scandalous and outraged urban reformers and progressives. Some bosses gathered up hordes of recently arrived immigrants and had them naturalized en masse before they had been in America long enough to become legal citizens. They had to become naturalized in order to vote. These mass naturalizations usually took place immediately before elections. Progressives took steps to reform political life in the cities. However, the immigrants, who were staunchly conservative, strongly defended their bosses and regarded the reformers as troublemakers who wanted to upset the status quo. The immigrant knew what it meant to be given a job by a political boss or to have him get his son out of trouble with the police. However, the concept of the "reform of the democratic process," which was urged by the progressives, was both meaningless and useless to him. Most immigrants remained indifferent, if not hostile, to the most noble ideas of the reformers.

The urban political machines were dealt a fatal blow by the New Deal programs of social security, welfare benefits, and social services. The immigrant could now depend upon other agencies to meet his or her practical needs for jobs and public assistance. He or she was less dependent upon the political boss and his machine. Although the development of public social agencies contributed largely to the decline of the political machine, the drastic halt in the number of immigrants entering the United States that took place in the 1920s took away most of the machine's chief beneficiaries, the newly arrived immigrants. With other agencies taking over its benevolent functions, and the number of its adherents drastically reduced, the days of the political machine became increasingly numbered. However, remnants of these machines existed in cities like Chicago and New York in the 1970s.

Immigrant Political Action

The immigrant's participation in the urban political machines, though significant, was not the total of his or her importance in the American political process. Early in American political history, when the number of immigrants in American cities became substantial, and their votes had the power to sway or determine election outcomes, politicians became increasingly sensitive to the concerns and wishes of immigrant groups. Even politicians like Theodore Roosevelt and Woodrow Wilson, who felt rather negatively about the "new" immigrants, were forced on occasions to say positive things about them publicly. However, it was difficult for Wilson to convince the Southern and Eastern European immigrants that he had had a change of heart.

Nevertheless, the major American political parties began to aggressively vie for immigrant support and to include references to immigrants in their political platforms which reflected the specialized concerns of America's ethnic groups. These groups had many special concerns and aspirations, usually related to American foreign policy and the ways in which the United States was treating their "Mother" countries. Although many European immigrants did not have much of a sense of nationality when they arrived in America, intense nationalist movements developed

among them. Writes Jones: "there was a tendency among Irish
political refugees as well as German Forty-eighters, to look upon
themselves as exiles and to use the United States simply as a base
for promoting European causes. . . . [These movements] af-
forded a means of group identification and self-assertion." [5]

While the actions of these political refugees were probably
extreme, most European immigrant groups did continue to see
themselves as Europeans. Many groups were formed among the
immigrants to aggressively campaign for European causes and
to sway American foreign policy. In World War I, German
Americans criticized Wilson's actions toward Germany and the
Irish Americans became bitter because of Wilson's pro-British
actions. The Irish voted strongly against Wilson in the subsequent election. The militant actions by some of the European
American groups, especially German Americans, caused many
Americans to seriously question their loyalties to the United States.
However, while some of these movements were very radical and
aggressively nationalistic, the most radical ones were unable to
attract mass support because of the deep conservatism of most
immigrants.

Anglo-Saxon Cultural Dominance

The early European settlements in America were highly
ethnically mixed. English, Scotch-Irish, Germans, French Huguenots, Africans, and Jews were among the earlier colonists.
These groups were widely dispersed throughout the colonies,
although ethnic enclaves developed. Ethnic conflict also developed early in the colonies. Englishmen were dominant during
the first years of colonial settlement. Consequently, they shaped
the basic social and political institutions in colonial America.
The English cultural dominance of the colonies was challenged
by subsequent groups, but it remained the dominant social force
in American life. Because of English social and cultural dominance, Anglo-Saxon culture became the ideal by which all subsequent ethnic groups were judged and by which levels of assimilation and acculturation were judged. To become "acculturated"
became synonymous with acquiring Anglo-Saxon Protestant lifestyles, values, and language. The English language was dominant in almost every American colony by 1775.

5. Ibid., p. 145.

Early in American colonial life, non-English groups began to be evaluated negatively. The New England colonies, which were predominantly English, took steps to bar the settlements of Roman Catholics. The French Huguenots became the focal point of English hostility. Later, the Scotch-Irish and the German immigrants were the victims of English antagonism. An English mob prevented a group of Irish immigrants from landing in Boston in 1729. Several years later another mob destroyed a new Scotch-Irish Presbyterian church in Worcester. The attitude that English culture and institutions were superior to all others profoundly shaped American life and was extremely significant in the nativistic movements which emerged after the Civil War. However, when the Southern and Eastern European immigrants began their mass exodus to America in the late 1800s, public opinion leaders extended the "superior" traits of the English to all Northern and Western European "races."* This was necessary to enable the "old" immigrants to band together to condemn the "new" immigrants. However, race assumed a new meaning when the Southern and Eastern European groups attained "acceptable" levels of assimilation in the twentieth century. All White races became one. Racial hostilities could now focus on non-White ethnic groups, such as Afro-Americans, Asian Americans, Mexican Americans, and American Indians. Whites of Southern and Eastern European descent joined former adverse White ethnic groups to damn and exclude non-White groups from full participation in American life.

The Southern and Eastern European Immigrants

Before 1812, most of the European immigrants who came to America were from Northern and Western European nations, such as England, Germany, France, and Scandinavia. Northern and Western Europeans exceeded the number of immigrants from other parts of Europe up to the last decades of the nineteenth century. However, by 1896, a major change had taken place in the source of European immigrants to the United States. Most of the European immigrants to America now came from South-

---

* *In the eighteenth century, Europeans were considered to belong to several races, such as the Teutonic, the Alpine, and the Mediterranean. The races of Northern and Western Europe were considered superior to the races in Southern, Central, and Eastern Europe.*

ern, Eastern, and Central Europe. Austria-Hungary, Italy, and Russia sent the largest number of new immigrants. However, substantial numbers also came from countries such as Greece, Rumania, Bulgaria, Armenia, and Finland. Fifteen million European immigrants arrived in the United States between 1890 and 1914. Most of them came from Southern and Eastern Europe.

When immigrants from Southern and Eastern Europe started coming to the United States in significant numbers, a number of arguments evolved which were designed to distinguish them from immigrants who had come earlier from the Northern and Western parts of Europe. The Southern and Eastern immigrants became known as the "new" immigrants; the earlier immigrants were referred to as the "old" immigrants. The mass media, intellectuals, and politicians perpetuated the myth that the new immigrants were inferior to the older ones, that they caused major problems in the cities, and that steamship companies and American industries eager for unskilled labor were the main cause of the new traffic. The Dillingham Commission, which was formed to investigate immigration in 1907, concluded that there was a fundamental difference in both the character and the causes of the new and old immigrations.

Repetition of this myth became evidence of its validity. It was eagerly embraced by writers, historians, and policymakers and significantly influenced the racist immigration legislation enacted in the 1920s. The nativistic movements reached their zenith in the 1920s and chose the Southern and Eastern European immigrants as their chief targets. Only the Asian immigrants in California were more damned. The distinctions made between the old and the new immigrants were artificial and based on inaccurate information and false assumptions. The Southern and Eastern European immigrants came to the United States for the same reasons that the earlier immigrants had come: to improve their economic conditions and to seek religious and political freedom. Steamship lines and American industries played no greater role in stimulating immigration from Southern and Eastern Europe than they played in stimulating immigration from other parts of Europe. In both cases, their influence was rather meager and has been grossly exaggerated.

The types of immigrants that came from Southern and Eastern Europe, like the older immigrants, were highly diverse. Some Southern and Eastern Europeans came to the United States for temporary work not because of something unique about them, but because the new steamship lines had so greatly reduced the length of the Atlantic trip that it was practical and possible to come to the United States for seasonal work.

Southern and Eastern European immigrants were judged innately inferior to older Americans partly because they started coming to the United States when the notion that the United States should be an asylum for the oppressed peoples of Europe was beginning to wane. When the Statue of Liberty was dedicated in New York City in 1886, many Americans had lost faith in the poetic words penned by Emma Lazarus about Europe's "huddled masses." They had also begun to question the melting pot theory and to raise serious questions about whether Europeans could be as readily assimilated as they had originally believed. The doubts about the new immigrants were not caused by their inability to be assimilated, but by the conditions and conceptions of foreigners emerging within American life. Thus the rush of Southern and Eastern European immigrants to the United States was poorly timed. The internal conditions in America were giving birth to distinctly antiforeign attitudes. A scapegoat was needed to blame for urban blight, political corruption in the cities, and economic recession. The new immigrants were vulnerable and convenient targets. Consequently, they were judged intellectually and culturally inferior to the old immigrants and declared unassimilable. That they were an inferior "race" became widely accepted both in the intellectual community and in the popular mind.

Nativistic Movements

As early as 1727, nativistic* feelings toward the Germans in Pennsylvania ran high. To discourage further foreign settlement in the colony, Pennsylvania passed a statute in 1729 increasing the head tax on foreigners, allegedly to prevent persons likely to become public charges from entering the colony. Other antiforeign legislation emerged in the eighteenth century. In 1798 Congress, dominated by the Federalists, passed the Alien and Sedition Acts to crush the Republican party by destroying its

---

* *Nativism was a movement designed to restrict immigration to America and to protect the interests of the native-born. It was an extreme form of nationalism and ethnocentrism.*

large base of immigrant support. These acts were also designed to silence criticism of the Federalists and to harass European immigrants. The Alien and Sedition Acts lengthened the time required to become an American citizen from five to fourteen years and gave the president almost unlimited control over the behavior of immigrants. They virtually nullified the freedoms of speech and the press.

Nativistic sentiments continued to ebb and flow during the eighteenth and nineteenth centuries, although their most violent expressions did not arise until the late nineteenth and early twentieth centuries. Nativism reached its zenith in the 1920s, culminating with the passage of the Johnson-Reed Act in 1924. The Know-Nothing movement, which emerged in the 1840s and reached its climax in 1855, was one of the most successful nativistic movements in the nineteenth century. The various secret organizations constituting this movement, such as the Order of United Americans and the Order of the Star-Spangled Banner, were strongly anti-Catholic and agitated for an extension of the period required for an immigrant to become an American citizen and for the election of only "Americans" to political office. The movement, which became less secretive in 1855 and openly called itself the American party, enjoyed tremendous political successes in a number of states in the 1855 elections. However, the Know-Nothing movement died as quickly as it emerged. Conflict over slavery within the American party severely strained and weakened it. Nativistic sentiments in America in the 1850s were not strong enough to sustain the Know-Nothing movement.

By the late 1800s, anti-Chinese agitation on the West Coast was vicious and virulent and race ideologies emerged to justify it. The concept of the inferiority and superiority of various races became rampant in the West. In 1882 Congress passed the Chinese Exclusion Act, the first immigration bill specifically designed to exclude a particular race. Although many Americans viewed the case of the Chinese as separate from European immigration, the anti-Chinese act gave impetus to antiforeign attitudes throughout American society. Three months after the anti-Chinese bill was passed, Congress enacted a bill further restricting the classes of Europeans who could enter the United States. Convicts, idiots, and lunatics, as well as those who might become public charges, were excluded.

Nativism grew more and more intense as the fear of a Catholic take-over of the federal government and of foreign radicals soared. The big jump in the number of Southern and Eastern European immigrants entering the United States in the 1880s added fuel to the fire. Cries of "100% Americanism" and "America for Americans" became salient. Agitations for antiforeign legislation became intense, especially legislation that would exclude foreign "radicals" and require immigrants to pass a literacy test.

Congress, responding to pressure in 1885, passed the Foran Act which prohibited the importation of contract labor from Europe. Violence also erupted during these turbulent times. Italians and Jews were frequently the victims of violent and outrageous acts. Eleven Italians were murdered in a mass lynching in New Orleans in 1891 when they were accused of killing a police superintendent. Riots directed at Jews took place in a number of American cities. In 1886 the Haymarket Riot in Chicago increased public paranoia about foreign "radicals." Congress further extended the classes of immigrants excluded from the United States in 1907. Imbeciles and victims of tuberculosis were now added to the list.

Nativistic movements, which were directed against most foreign-born groups in the 1850s, began to focus increasingly on Southern and Eastern European immigrants, as masses of them arrived in American cities. The intellectual community legitimized the racist myths about the innate inferiority of Southern and Eastern Europeans. William Z. Ripley was one of the leading intellectual nativists. His book, *The Races of Europe*, published in 1899, divided Whites into three major races: the Teutonic, the Northern blondes; the Alpine, the central race of stocky roundheads; and the Mediterranean, dark and slender longheads.[6] The Teutonic was the superior race. Ripley warned against racial mixture that would pollute the superior race with Southern and Eastern European racial groups.

Madison Grant, a well-known anthropologist, also argued for racial purity in his popular book, *The Passing of the Great Race in America*, published in 1916. Ripley and Grant, as well as other intellectuals and writers in the early twentieth century, provided the nativists with the scientific and intellectual justifi-

6. John Higham, *Strangers in the Land: Patterns of American Nativism 1860–1925* (New York: Atheneum, 1972), p. 154.

cations for their movements and issued a ringing plea for restrictive legislation.[7] As in other periods of mass hysteria in America, social and physical scientists justified and legitimized prevailing social attitudes and myths.

When the twentieth century opened, nativistic sentiments and attitudes had gained tremendous momentum in American life. They did not subside until they culminated in the extreme restrictive legislation enacted in the 1920s. The Dillingham Commission, which issued its report in 1911, noted that the new European immigrants were essentially different from the old, and strongly recommended the passage of a bill that would require immigrants to pass a literacy test. Agitation for a literacy test bill became intense, but the advocates of the bill faced repeated opposition in Congress and from President Wilson. As the United States prepared to enter World War I, nativism—directed especially at German Americans—became intense. Patriotic groups demanded that all aspects of German culture, including music and the names of streets and schools, be eradicated in the United States. Although most German Americans were loyal citizens during this period, they were often the victims of harassment. However, the abuses they endured were mild compared with those suffered by Japanese Americans during World War II (see Chapter 9).

Just before the United States entered the war, the literacy bill advocates finally mustered enough congressional votes to override a second Wilson veto, and the literacy bill was passed on February 5, 1917. Adult immigrants now had to be able to read a passage in some language before they could enter the United States. The bill was very comprehensive. It codified existing legislation and added vagrants, chronic alcoholics, and psychopaths to the list of excluded aliens. The head tax was increased from $4 to $8.[8] Although nativists celebrated their victory, they began immediately to plan strategies to further restrict immigration to the United States.

Although America's entry into World War I diverted attention from nativistic concerns, campaigns to "Americanize" aliens already in the United States became a national passion during the war. When the war ended, pressure was again put on Con-

7. Ibid., pp. 155–56.

8. Ibid., pp. 203–204.

gress to enact restrictive legislation. The law requiring immigrants to pass a literacy test did not halt immigration as the nativists had thought. In fact, it reduced it very little. Consequently, nativists pushed for a quota system to restrict immigration. Antiforeign groups and organizations experienced tremendous growth in memberships. The Ku Klux Klan grew enormously in the South and Middle West. It had over two and a half million members by 1923. The phenomenal growth of the Klan was symptomatic of pervasive antiforeign attitudes in American life.

Eventually, the nativistic forces gained congressional victories. The Johnson Act was enacted in 1921. It marked a turning point in the history of American immigration. The Johnson Act set up a nationality quota system and imposed the first numerical limits on immigration from European nations. The quota system was based on the various nationality groups in the United States. The most important immigration bill of this period was enacted in 1924—the Johnson-Reed Act. The quotas this act set were severe and blatantly discriminated against Southern and Eastern European and non-White nations. It halted Japanese immigration completely. After 1927, the act allowed only 150,000 Europeans to enter the United States each year, which were "parceled out in ratio to the distribution of national origins in the white population of the United States in 1920."[9] Since Europeans from the North and West represented the largest percentages of Whites in the United States in 1920, the authors of the Johnson-Reed Act had thought of an ingenious way to severely limit the number of immigrants from Southern and Eastern Europe, while at the same time assuring that a significant number were allowed to enter from the North and West. Nativism had triumphed and an important chapter in American history had been closed.

Subsequent Immigration Acts

There was little change in American immigration policy from 1924 until the outbreak of World War II. A number of Europeans were displaced by the events of World War II and sought asylum as refugees in the United States. After much

9. Ibid., p. 324.

debate, a Displaced Persons Act was passed in 1948, which permitted about 400,000 refugees to enter the United States over a four-year period. The McCarran-Walter Act, passed in 1952, allegedly to remove racial barriers to immigration, essentially continued the policy established in 1924 and was in some ways more restrictive. In 1953 Congress passed a temporary measure, the Refugee Relief Act, to enable refugees from Communist nations to settle in the United States. However, major reform in American immigration policy was not made until 1965. President John F. Kennedy strongly urged Congress to pass an enlightened immigration act. After much discussion and vigorous debate, the bill finally became a reality during the Johnson administration on July 1, 1968. This act abolished the national origins quota system and allowed 170,000 persons to enter the United States each year from the Eastern Hemisphere and 120,000 from the Western Hemisphere.[10] Technical skill and kinship, rather than country or origin, became the major criteria for admitting immigrants to the United States. This bill was a major victory for liberal thinking Americans and is a tribute to the ideals which Americans profess.

Ethnic Politics in Contemporary American Society

In recent years researchers have investigated the relationship between ethnicity and political behavior.[11] The relationship between political behavior and ethnic group membership is highly complex. However, political scientists have found that much of the political behavior of ethnic groups cannot be explained by factors other than ethnicity. However, almost all generalizations made about ethnic factors in modern political life are highly tentative and must admit many exceptions.

Since the 1930s and 1940s, urban ethnic groups such as Slavic Americans, Italian Americans, and Jewish Americans have voted overwhelmingly Democratic and have identified themselves with the Democratic party. Catholics have also voted heavily for Democratic candidates. While Democratic candi-

10. Luman H. Long, ed., *The World Almanac and Book of Facts,* 1970 ed. (New York: Newspaper Enterprise Association, 1969), p. 449.

11. For a summary of this research, see Edgar Litt, *Ethnic Politics in America* (Glenview, Ill.: Scott, Foresman and Company, 1970).

dates most often obtain pluralities in urban ethnic communities, the Democratic hold on ethnic groups is not nearly so complete or certain as it was in the past.

As ethnic groups become more assimilated into the dominant society and attain higher social class status, they tend to move to the suburbs and to vote more like their suburban neighbors than their old neighbors in the city. The Irish, who formerly dominated the big city Democratic political machines, but who are now one of America's most assimilated ethnic groups, are moving to the suburbs in record numbers. While most Irish still vote for Democrats in presidential elections, the Democrats are steadily losing their hold on the Irish vote, especially in the suburbs. Irish suburbanites in New York and Chicago supported their favorite son, John F. Kennedy, much less strongly than the Irish in the heart of the cities in the 1960 presidential election. Suburban Jews, like their Irish counterparts, also supported Kennedy less strongly than did city Jews. Increasingly, urban-suburban splits are developing within ethnic groups that have historically been Democrats. The more upward mobile members of these ethnic groups are voting increasingly for Republican candidates; their urban counterparts usually remain faithful to the Democratic party. Despite these changes, most Jews, Italians, Irish, and Catholics, regardless of their social class, still vote for Democrats, especially in presidential elections.[12]

All members of these ethnic groups, however, have by no means always voted for Democratic candidates or considered themselves Democrats. Ethnic voting is also influenced by other factors, such as whether the name on the ticket is ethnic. Choosing ethnic candidates with obvious ethnic names is one way of gaining ethnic votes that the major parties have used since they recognized the value of the ethnic vote. One of the most striking illustrations of the power of the ethnic candidate is provided by a case study of ethnic politics in New Haven, Connecticut.[13] In 1939, when the Republican party was in deep trouble in New

12. Mark R. Levy and Michael S. Kramer, *The Ethnic Factor: How America's Minorities Decide Elections* (New York: Simon and Schuster, 1972), pp. 12–22.

13. Raymond E. Wolfinger, "The Development and Persistence of Ethnic Politics," in Lawrence H. Fuchs, ed., *American Ethnic Politics* (New York: Harper and Row, 1968), 163–93.

Haven (the Irish Democrats controlled city hall), it successfully ran an Italian, William C. Celentano, for mayor. The Italians, because of their foreign-birth and poverty, would have been expected to support the Democratic candidate. However, they overwhelmingly supported Celentano and became staunch Republicans. Writes Wolfinger, "Since 1947 the Italian wards have been the most Republican ones in the city. . . . Most Italians not only vote for Republican candidates, but consider themselves Republicans. Their party identification was changed and fixed by Celentano's several campaigns."[14]

While Celentano was able to pull the Italians to the Republican party in New Haven in the 1930s, ethnic names often do not have this kind of power to draw votes. Other factors become involved. This has been especially true in recent years. Slavic Americans voted for John Kennedy in the presidential election of 1960 in greater numbers than Irish Catholics. Slavs are considerably more working class than Irish Catholics and consequently more inclined to vote for a Democratic presidential candidate than are Irish Catholics, who have attained high levels of economic and social mobility. Slavs also strongly supported Kennedy because he shared their religion, although the Irish are also predominantly Catholic.

Jews, who have a strong sense of ethnic identity and are the most liberal American White ethnic group, do not always support Jewish candidates, even liberal ones. When Arthur Goldberg ran against Nelson Rockefeller in the race for governor in New York State in 1970, his showing in Jewish precincts was unimpressive. Goldberg refused to emphasize his ethnicity in the race. Rockefeller hinted that he might have Jewish ancestors. Rockefeller also ran a much better campaign than Goldberg. In the 1971 race for mayor in Chicago, Mayor Richard Daley was opposed by Richard Friedman, a young Jewish lawyer. The Chicago Jews voted for Daley and forsook their Jewish brother.

Ethnic factors still play a major role in American politics and no astute political candidate will ignore this fact. However, the relationship between ethnicity and politics is complex and often unpredictable. The 1972 presidential election is a case in point. Richard M. Nixon beat George McGovern by a landslide and ethnic groups, which had historically supported Demo-

14. Ibid., pp. 177–80.

cratic presidential candidates, deserted McGovern and supported Nixon in record numbers. Groups such as Italian Americans, Slavic Americans, and Irish Americans tend to be predominantly Democrats. However, they are also conservative. These groups saw McGovern as too radical and were afraid that he was too sensitive to Black demands and civil rights.

Voter behavior in the 1972 presidential election was, in some ways, a cogent statement by White ethnic groups that they were fed up with integration, busing, and social legislation they perceived as too pro-Black. The crushing defeat of McGovern was to some extent a revolt by the White ethnics and the dominant middle-class groups against the War on Poverty and other reforms of the 1960s envisioned by Kennedy and implemented by Johnson. This election demonstrated how traditional ethnic allegiances to the Democratic party can be dramatically changed when major issues related to Black-White problems surface. White ethnic groups tend to vote as a bloc when they perceive civil rights for Blacks to be against their collective interests. The significant margin of support George Wallace received from Slavic and Italian Americans during the 1968 presidential election illustrates how White ethnic groups will form coalitions to oppose civil rights for non-White ethnic groups.

European Ethnic Groups in American Society

The mass settlement of Europeans in North America was one of the most unique phenomena in human history. Over 45 million immigrants entered the United States between 1820 and 1970. Most came from Europe. The European immigrants represented many religious, political, and cultural groups. Yet the United States, by forcing the immigrants to acquire the culture of the dominant ethnic group, was able to prevent the Balkanization of America and establish a unified society. The immigrants paid a heavy price for cultural assimilation and acculturation. Nevertheless, a rather culturally homogeneous society emerged, although ethnicity is still a viable force in American life.

When European immigrants arrived on America's shores, their thoughts, feelings, aspirations, and attitudes were decidedly European. The immigrants aggressively tried to structure European institutions in America. They tried to maintain their religious life by building churches similar to those in Europe. They established parochial schools, ethnic newspapers, ethnic theaters, and self-help organizations in their futile attempts to hold onto the old order. Some groups such as the German Americans tried to create ethnic colonies where their European cultures and ethnic kinships could flourish. Despite the concerted efforts by the immigrants to establish European institutions in the United States, these attempts were by and large destined to fail. Forces within American life worked against them and eventually eroded or greatly modified most European cultures in the United States. The public schools, the American press, and American political institutions played key roles in mitigating the attempts to establish and maintain European institutions on American soil. By the beginning of the nineteenth century, the English dominated most American institutions, such as the schools, the courts, and the popular press. The immigrants and their children often found it necessary to acquire Anglo-Saxon cultural traits before they were allowed to fully participate in American society. School teachers demeaned foreign languages; employers often preferred to hire assimilated immigrants. European Americans, especially the second generation, often responded to these cogent forces by becoming ashamed of their ethnic cultures, deliberately denying them, such as by Anglicizing or changing their surnames, and actively seeking to assimilate. No genuine cultural synthesis took place in America. Rather, English culture dominated. Many second and third genneration immigrants became—in mores, values, and outlook—thoroughly Anglo-Saxon. The psychological price the immigrants paid for abandoning their ethnic cultures, and consequently their identities, was incalculable.

Many of the European American ethnic groups that abandoned their cultures and became culturally Anglo-Saxons are now members of the comfortable middle and upper classes. Some of them, now that they have made it, are suffering from an acute identity crisis. Ethnicity provides people with a sense of being, purpose, and belonging. The Anglo-Saxon culture in America, which has become very diffuse, is too nebulous to provide its converts with a strong sense of ethnic kinship. The problems of White ethnic groups are compounded by the fact that Anglo-Saxon culture, especially in recent years, has been harshly damned by non-White ethnics and blamed for the major ills in American life, such as racism, pollution, and immorality. Also, having a strong sense of ethnicity, which these groups lack, came into vogue in the 1960s and 1970s. Schrag argues that the prestige of WASP culture has begun to decline.[15] The identity crisis suffered by Americans of European descent, caused partly by a lack of a "sense of peoplehood," results in dysfunctional behavior, such as widespread drug use, alcoholism, and a lack of strong moral commitment. In recent years, European Americans have begun to search for ethnic ties and have emphasized their Irish, Slavic, Italian, and Swedish heritages. Some have even found or invented ancestors who belong to non-White ethnic groups such as Indians. The scope of these quests for ethnic identification and their possible outcomes are very problematical at this writing.

While most European ethnic groups succumbed to the forces of assimilation, some stubbornly clung to important aspects of their ethnic heritages. Others, for a variety of social and economic reasons, have not attained high levels of assimilation. Jewish Americans have been able to maintain a strong sense of ethnic identity and kinship within an Anglo-Saxon dominated society. Large segments of Slavic Americans and Italian Americans remain distinctly ethnic, perhaps because they have not yet had ample opportunities to assimilate. However, if the prestige of the WASP culture is declining, as Schrag argues, ethnic groups might strive for acculturation less aggressively in the future than they did in the past. There are signs that this might be the case. Many White ethnic groups in cities like Chicago and New York have organized or breathed new life into ethnic organizations that promote ethnic interests and cultures.

Despite the enormous acculturation that has taken place in American society, many European American ethnic groups, such as Poles, Italians, and Jews, still restrict most of their primary relationships to their ethnic group.[16] Thus a significant amount of what Gordon calls *structural pluralism** exists in American

15. Peter Schrag, *The Decline of the WASP* (New York: Simon and Schuster, 1970).

16. Milton Gordon, *Assimilation in American Life: The Role of Race, Religion and National Origins* (New York: Oxford University Press, 1964).

* See Chapter 1, p 43–45, for a further discussion of structural pluralism.

life. There are indications that ethnicity might be more important in the lives of European American ethnic groups in the future than it is today. It is extremely risky to forecast the future of ethnicity in a society with an ethnic history as complex and diverse as ours. Only the future itself can speak with certainty.

Teaching Strategies

To illustrate how content related to European Americans can be used to integrate the curriculum, exemplary strategies are identified for teaching these concepts at the grade levels indicated: cultural contributions (primary grades), immigration (intermediate and upper grades), and nativism (high school grades).

PRIMARY GRADES

CONCEPT: Cultural Contributions

Generalization: Our ancestors came from many different nations and belonged to many ethnic groups. All of these groups made outstanding contributions to American life.

1. To collect the information needed for this unit, duplicate the following letter and give each child one to take home. Tell the pupils to ask their parents to complete the form and return it to you the next day.

> Dear Parents:
>
> To help our students understand and appreciate the contributions all ethnic groups have made to American life, we are studying about ethnic groups and their role in America. I want to make sure that we study the ethnic heritages of all of my students. To do this, I need your help. Would you please study the list below and place an "X" by the group indicating your child's ethnic heritage. If your child has a mixed heritage, such as "English" and "Russian," please check both of these. However, please try to limit your checks to three by checking only the *main* strains in your child's ethnic heritage. The list below is based on the categories used by the United States Bureau of the Census. They represent the largest ethnic groups in America. However, many American ethnic groups are not included. If your child's ethnic heritage is not listed, please check "Other" and fill in the name(s) of your child's ethnic group(s), such as "Spanish" or "French."

Name of Child _____

Ethnic Groups

English _____

Scottish _____

Welsh _____

German _____

Irish _____

Italian _____

Polish _____

Russian _____

Jewish _____
  (Specify nation)

Afro-American _____

American Indian _____

Mexican American _____

Asian American _____
  (Specify group)

Puerto Rican American _____

Other(s) (Please specify) _____

Please send this form back to me tomorrow morning. Thank you very much for your cooperation. I am sure that your response will help us to have a much better unit.

> Sincerely,
> Mrs. Mildred Jones
> Third Grade Teacher

2. When you have received the forms back from the parents, make a table showing the ethnic groups represented in your class. Put the table on butcher paper and list the children's names under the appropriate ethnic categories. Your table might look like this:

Table 6.1
Our Ethnic Heritages

English	Irish	Italian	German	Afro-American	Polish
Susie John	Cathy *Pete	Roy Pat	*Pete Ray	Jack Sam	Linda Terry

* Pete has both Irish and German ancestors. Some of the children might be listed under several categories.

3. Discuss the table with the students, bringing out that our ancestors came from many different nations. Using a primary globe, locate and write the names of some of the nations from which the children's ancestors came, such as England, Africa, and Germany. Discuss these nations with the students.

4. Using the photographs in a book such as *Strangers at the Door* by Ann Novotny or *A Nation of Immigrants* by John F. Kennedy, tell the children the story of the great immigrations from Europe. Point out some of the reasons why the immigrants came, how they came, and how they settled in America. The special case of Afro-Americans, as well as immigrants from non-European nations, should also be discussed.

5. Make another table on butcher paper listing the major ethnic groups represented in your class and other major American ethnic groups. Under each major group, list some famous Americans and the fields in which they have made outstanding contributions to American life. Your table might look like table 6.2.

There are many books containing information about the ethnic backgrounds of famous Americans (see Materials and Resources in this chapter and in other chapters in Part II of this book). The "In America Series," published by Lerner Publications Company in Minneapolis, Minnesota is a comprehensive series that includes twenty-six books on various American ethnic groups, such as Germans, Greeks, and Hungarians. The ethnic series published by Franklin Watts,

Table 6.2

Famous Ethnic Americans

English	Italian	Afro-American	Polish
George Washington President	Joe DiMaggio Baseball player	Benjamin Banneker Scientist	Helena Modjeska Actress
Benjamin Franklin Scientist	Frank Sinatra Singer	Martin L. King Civil rights leader	Edmund S. Muskie U. S. Senator

Inc. in New York City, and edited by William Loren Katz is also comprehensive and well researched and written.

6. After you have completed the Famous Ethnic Americans table, making sure that all of the children's ethnic heritages are represented, discuss the table with the students and help them to formulate, in their own words, the following generalization: Our ancestors came from many different lands and groups, and all of these groups made many outstanding contributions to American life. Make sure that each child knows at least one famous person who belongs to his or her ethnic group. This exercise must be modified in classrooms in which there is only one ethnic group. Use some famous Americans from the students' own ethnic group, but also select heroes from at least five or six other ethnic groups not represented in your classroom.

INTERMEDIATE AND UPPER GRADES

CONCEPT: Immigration

Generalization: Europeans immigrated to the United States for various economic, political, and social reasons. Their experiences in the United States were both similar and different.

1. To help the students gain the needed content background to study American immigration, assign appropriate readings in the books listed below (or similar books), which will enable them to answer these questions about the first or old immigrants to America:

   a) What European nations did the first immigrants to America come from during the colonial period?
   b) Why did they come?
   c) Was America like they expected? If so, in what ways? If not, why not? Explain.

   The readings are:
   Thomas J. Fleming, *The Golden Door: The Story of American Immigration,* pp. 1–87.
   Alberta Eiseman, *From Many Lands,* pp. 3–108.

2. After the students have completed their reading assignments, discuss the three questions above with the class.

These readings deal with the immigration of the English, Germans, Irish, French, Norwegians, Swedes, Jews, and other nationality groups represented among the early settlers in the American colonies. During the discussion, list the reasons on the board why the various groups immigrated to the United States. When the reasons have been listed on the board, group them, with the class, into three or four categories, such as "economic," "political," and "social" reasons.

3. Ask the students to read about the new immigrants who came to the United States from Europe in the late 1800s and early 1900s in the Fleming and Eiseman books or other appropriate books, such as *American Fever: The Story of American Immigration* by Barbara Kaye Greenleaf. (See Materials and Resources, pp. 224–28.) These immigrants came primarily from Southern and Eastern Europe and included Ukrainians, Russians, Poles, Italians, Greeks, and many other groups from Southern and Eastern Europe. The students should discuss the same three questions about these immigrants which they discussed after reading about the old immigrants.

4. After the students have read about and discussed the old and new immigrants, they should compare and contrast these groups. These questions can be used to guide discussion:

   a) Did the old and new immigrants come to the United States for similar or different reasons? Explain.

   b) How did the new immigrants differ from the old? Why?

   c) How did American life differ at the times that the old and new immigrants came to America? How did this difference affect the adjustment of the newly arrived immigrants?

   d) Both the old and the new immigrants experienced problems on the trip across the Atlantic. How were these problems similar and different?

   e) How were the problems of settlement and finding jobs in America similar and different for the two groups of immigrants?

   f) Ethnic conflict developed early during the settlement

of European nationality groups in America. What problems of prejudice and discrimination were experienced by the various groups? Which groups of immigrants were discriminated against the most? The least? Why?

The students can summarize this phase of the unit by making a data retrieval chart to summarize and compare information about major ethnic groups representing old and new immigrants, similar to Table 6.3

5. To help the students gain a feeling for the harshness of the journey across the Atlantic that the immigrants experienced, read Chapter 2, "The Crossing," in Oscar Handlin, *The Uprooted*, aloud to them. The class can develop a dramatization of the passage as described in Handlin and present it in a school assembly. The entire class should be involved in the writing and presentation of the dramatization.

6. European immigrants in the United States often wrote to their friends and relatives in Europe describing the wonders of America and occasionally their problems. Three such letters are reprinted in *America's Immigrants: Adventures in Eyewitness History* by Rhoda Hoff. "A Letter to His Wife in England" by John Downe and "A Letter to a Friend at Home" by a Norwegian immigrant tells about the greatness of America. "A Letter to Her Mother and Daughter in Norway" by Guri Endresen talks about tragic encounters her family had with American Indians. Read and discuss these letters (or similar ones) with the class. Ask the students to pretend that they are new European immigrants in America in the 1800s. They should write a letter to a friend or relative back in Europe telling about their experiences. This activity can be correlated with the language arts.

7. Have the students role-play the situation below, which involves a poor Italian farmer and an agent of a steamship company who tries to persuade the farmer to immigrate to the United States. After the role-playing situation, ask the students the questions which follow:

Mr. Pareto, A Poor Italian Farmer in Southern Italy in the 1800s

Mr. Pareto is in his thirties. He is a very hard worker and is very close to his family, which includes his wife,

Table 6.3
Generalizing About the Old and New European Immigrants

	old immigrants			new immigrants		
	English	Irish	Germans	Italians	Southern & Eastern Jews	Poles
Reasons for immigrating						
Kinds of people in group						
Problems on Atlantic journey						
Problems of settlement						

Table 6.3 (Cont.)
Generalizing About the Old and New European Immigrants

| | old immigrants | | | new immigrants | | |
	English	Irish	Germans	Italians	Southern & Eastern Jews	Poles
Prejudice and discrimination experienced						
Immigration laws in European country of origin						
Relationships *within* the nationality group						

eight children, and both of his parents. For the past three years, Mr. Pareto has been unable to feed and clothe his family well because of severe crop failures. He has heard about the greatness of America and has often thought about going there. However, he knows that his father feels he should stay in Italy so that he can depend on him in his old age. He also realizes that if he goes to America he will have to leave his wife and children in Italy.

Mr. Rossi, An Agent for a Steamship Company that Makes Trips to America

Mr. Rossi tries to persuade Italian men to immigrate to America. The more men that he can persuade to go to America on his company's steamship line, the more money he makes. He goes up to Mr. Pareto at the village market and tells him about the wonders of America and why he should go there. He tells him that he can get a job quickly in America and become a wealthy man. He knows that if Mr. Pareto goes to America he will not be able to carry his family. However, Mr. Rossi tells Mr. Pareto that he will be able to send for his family within two or three months after he gets to America.

Questions

a) Did Mr. Rossi persuade Mr. Pareto to go to America? Why or why not?

b) If Mr. Pareto goes to America, what do you think will happen to his family?

c) If Mr. Pareto stays in Italy, how do you think he will take care of his family?

d) How do you think his wife, parents, and children will react if Mr. Pareto goes to America? Why?

e) What else can Mr. Pareto do besides stay in his Italian village or immigrate to America?

f) If you were Mr. Pareto would you immigrate to America? Why or why not? Explain.

8. Conclude this unit by viewing and discussing several of the filmstrips in the series *Immigration: The Dream and the Reality*. Titles in the series include *The Dream, The Reality, No Irish Need Apply,* and *Little Italy.* See Appendix B for complete citations for films and filmstrips.

Valuing Activity

Read the following story to the class and ask the questions which follow.

WHAT SHOULD MARSHA DO?

Marsha and her parents, Dr. and Mrs. Henry Goldstein, live in one of New York's wealthiest communities. Marsha is an only child. She has always been very close to her parents. Although Marsha does not brag about it, she gets almost everything she wants. Last Christmas, her parents bought her a Mustang for her twentieth birthday. Marsha is now a junior at a private college in New York City. Almost everyone admits that she is good looking and very intelligent. She is very popular with males and envied by females at the predominantly Jewish college she attends.

Marsha had told her parents about Stan but she had not told them that he was a Catholic. Stan is a handsome junior at Stanford that Marsha met last summer in Europe. They spent a lot of time together in Europe but have not seen each other very much since then. However, they have been talking to each other on the phone frequently and writing all year. Recently, Stan asked Marsha if she would marry him. Marsha feels that she loves Stan very much and wants to marry him. However, when she told her parents that she wanted to marry Stan they became very upset. Dr. and Mrs. Goldstein, who are Orthodox Jews, feels very strongly that Marsha should marry a Jew. They have very negative feelings about Catholics. They told Marsha that if she loved them she would not hurt and shame them by marrying a Catholic. Dr. Goldstein became so upset when Marsha asked them about marrying Stan that he told her that if she married Stan she and Stan would not be welcomed at their house. Next weekend, Stan is coming to New York city. Marsha has to decide what she will do.

Questions

1. What do you think Marsha will do?
2. What do you think Marsha *should* do?

3. What would you do if you were Marsha?
4. Do you think that it would be unfair to Marsha's parents if she married Stan? Why or why not?
5. Do you think Dr. and Mrs. Goldstein are being unfair to Marsha? Why or why not?

HIGH SCHOOL GRADES

CONCEPT: Nativism

Generalization: Negative feelings toward immigrant groups emerged early in colonial America. However, American nativism did not become widespread until the late nineteenth and early twentieth centuries. It eventually led to a virtual halt to European immigration.

1. Ask the students to read the chapters listed below and be able to discuss these questions when they have finished reading them:

   a) Antiforeign attitudes were present in the early American colonies. What groups were the main victims of these negative feelings?

   b) What forms did nativism take in colonial America? What acts and laws were passed in colonial America that reflected antiforeign attitudes?

   The readings are:

   Chapter 2, "Ethnic Discord and the Growth of American Nationality," in Maldwyn Allen Jones, *American Immigration.*

   Chapter 1, "The Age of Confidence," in John Higham, *Strangers in the Land: Patterns of American Nativism 1860–1925.*

   When the students have completed these readings, discuss the above questions with the class. They will discover that the Irish, French Huguenots, Catholics, and Germans were the main targets of early antiforeign attitudes in America. Record their responses to the questions above, in summary form, on the board.

2. Ask individual students or groups of students to prepare reports on the following topics and present them to the class.

The Know-Nothing movement in the 1850s

The Chinese Exclusion Act of 1882

The Immigration Act of 1882, which excluded certain classes of European immigrants

The Immigration Restriction League, formed in 1884

The Foran Act of 1885

The Haymarket Affair, 1886

The lynching of eleven Italians in New Orleans, 1891

William Z. Ripley's *The Races of Europe*, published in 1899

The Dillingham Commission, which issued its report in 1911

The 1917 Immigration Act

Madison Grant, *The Passing of the Great Race in America*, published in 1916

The Johnson Act of 1921

The Johnson-Reed Act of 1924

The McCarran-Walter Act of 1952

The Immigration Act of 1965

The books by Jones and Higham, cited above, are two excellent sources for information about the above topics. When the students are sharing their reports, help them to identify some of the causes of nativistic movements. These causes should be noted on the board and in the students' notebooks. They include: anti-Catholic attitudes, fear of foreign "radicals," domestic recession and depression, the mass of new immigrants that arrived in the United States in the late 1800s and early 1900s, the belief that aliens were taking jobs away from American citizens, and the popularity of beliefs about the innate inferiority of Southern and Eastern European immigrants perpetuated by such writers as William Z. Ripley and the well-known anthropologist, Madison Grant.

3. Heated debates took place in Congress as well as in other public forums about the passage of a bill which would require immigrants to pass a reading test before they could enter the United States. Two opposing views of the literacy test are found in Chapter 8 of Oscar Handlin, ed., *Immigration as a Factor in American History*. Samuel Gompers defends the test and President Woodrow Wilson opposes it.

Read these two accounts to the class. Ask the students to role-play a session of Congress in 1917 in which the bill is discussed. Different students should argue for and against the bill. After the speeches on the floor, the students should vote for or against the bill. After the voting, they should discuss why their final vote was similar to or different from the congressional vote in 1917.

4. Anthropologists and physical scientists divided Whites into various "races" in the 1800s. William Z. Ripley and Madison Grant popularized these views and argued that Southern and Eastern European immigrants were innately inferior to immigrants from the Northern and Western parts of Europe. Ask the class to compare the views of these writers with the racial views of contemporary scientists such as Arthur R. Jensen and William Shockley.

5. Social and physical scientists blamed the new immigrants for political corruption, urban blight, crime, and large welfare rolls. Ask the students to study writings about the immigrants during the 1800s and to compare these writings with writings today about ethnic minorities such as Afro-Americans, Mexican Americans, and Puerto Rican Americans. The class can discuss the ways in which the old and new criticisms are alike and different, and why they are alike and different. Oscar Handlin, *The Uprooted*, Maldwyn A. Jones, *American Immigration*, and John Higham, *Strangers in the Land*, contain information and references that will help students to carry out this activity.

6. The Johnson-Reed Act of 1924 marked the end of an era in the history of American immigration since it put a virtual end to immigration and discriminated blatantly against Southern and Eastern European immigrants and non-White nations. Duplicate a copy of this act for the class and ask them to discuss its legal, moral, and political implications. The students can then compare the Johnson-Reed Act with the McCarran-Walter Act of 1952 and the Immigration Act of 1965. They should also discuss the legal, political, and moral implications of the 1965 act. You can conclude this unit by asking the students to write a five to ten-page paper on "Nativism as a Factor in American History." This activity can be correlated with English or the language arts.

Materials and Resources

REFERENCES FOR THE TEACHER

Especially Recommended

Gordon, Milton. *Assimilation in American Life: The Role of Race, Religion and National Origins.* New York: Oxford University Press, 1964.

This award-winning book contains a brilliant explication of the concept of ethnicity in America and sets forth a seminal theory of assimilation and acculturation in American society. Must reading.

Handlin, Oscar. *The Uprooted: The Epic Story of the Great Migrations that Made the American People.* Rev. ed. New York: Grosset and Dunlap, 1973.

In this brilliant book, the author chronicles the story of European immigrants to the United States from their peasant life in Europe to the nativistic movements in the late nineteenth and early twentieth centuries. This deeply compassionate book is written from the perspective of the immigrants and is a pioneering portrait of their problems, frustrations, and triumphs in North America. Recipient of the Pulitzer Prize in history in 1952.

Higham, John. *Strangers in the Land: Patterns of American Nativism 1860–1925.* New York: Atheneum, 1972.

A perceptive and pioneering study of nativistic movements in American society in the late nineteenth and early twentieth centuries. In this interpretative work, the author views economic events as major determinants of nativistic forces. This highly readable and copiously documented book contains a useful bibliographic essay.

Jones, Maldwyn Allen. *American Immigration.* Chicago: University of Chicago Press, 1960.

An excellent, well-written, and comprehensive history of the immigration of European nationality groups to the United States up through the 1950s. A good introductory source.

Other References

Bailey, Harry A., Jr. and Ellis Katz, eds. *Ethnic Group Politics.* Columbus, Ohio: Charles E. Merrill, 1969.

This anthology contains a number of essays that treat a wide range of topics related to ethnic politics. Oscar Handlin, John Hope Franklin, James Q. Wilson, and Nathan Glazer are among the contributors.

Bowers, David F., ed. *Foreign Influences in American Life.* Princeton: Princeton University Press, 1944.

The influence of European culture on various aspects of American life is treated in the eight essays in this book.

Dinnerstein, Leonard and Frederic Cople Jaher, eds. *The Aliens: A History of Ethnic Minorities in America.* New York: Appleton-Century-Crofts, 1970.

This collection of readings contains a series of historical essays on various ethnic groups such as Blacks, Germans, Scotch-Irish, Scandinavians, and the Irish. The essays are rather specialized. This is not a good source for a general historical overview of ethnic groups, as the subtitle implies.

Divine, Robert A. *American Immigration Policy 1924–1952.* New Haven: Yale University Press, 1957.

Although this history of American immigration policy is useful, it lacks essential detail.

Friedman, Murray, ed. *Overcoming Middleclass Rage.* Philadelphia: The Westminster Press, 1971.

This collection of readings focuses on the alienation and problems of working and lower middle-class White ethnic Americans. An appeal is made by the editor to include these groups in social change programs.

Fuchs, Lawrence, ed. *American Ethnic Politics.* New York: Harper and Row, 1968.

This anthology includes articles that discuss various aspects of ethnic politics. Each selection is preceded by a useful commentary by the editor.

Gambino, Richard. *Blood of My Blood: The Dilemma of the Italian-Americans.* New York, Doubleday, 1974.

A sensitive and thought-provoking study of Italian Americans which highlights the cultural conflicts and dilemmas of contemporary Italian-Americans.

Glazer, Nathan and Daniel P. Moynihan, *Beyond the Melting Pot.* 2nd ed. Cambridge, Mass.: The M. I. T. Press, 1970.

This study, which has been well-received, conceptualizes ethnic groups as political interest groups and includes chapters on the Jews, Italians, and Irish of New York City. A very partisan but thought-provoking book.

Goldstein, Sidney and Calvin Goldscheider. *Jewish Americans: Three Generations in a Jewish Community.* Englewood Cliffs, N. J.: Prentice-Hall, 1968.

A scholarly and comprehensive, yet highly readable, treatment of one of America's most interesting ethnic minorities. Marriage and family, religion, and the problems of being Jewish in American society are some of the major topics discussed.

Greeley, Andrew M. *That Most Distressful Nation: The Taming of the American Irish.* Chicago: Quadrangle Books, 1972.

An interesting and witty sociological examination of the historical and contemporary experiences of the Irish in the United States.

———. *Why Can't They Be Like Us? Facts and Fallacies about Ethnic Differences and Group Conflict in America.* New York: Institute of Human Relations Press, 1969.

An interesting and informal brief book discussing various aspects of ethnicity in modern American society, including the meaning and function of ethnicity, steps in ethnic assimilation, and the future of ethnic groups in the United States.

Handlin, Oscar. *The American People in the Twentieth Century.* Cambridge: Harvard University Press, 1954.

Chapter 3 of this book is an interesting discussion of the Southern and Eastern European immigrants that settled in the United States in the late 1800s and early 1900s.

———, ed. *Immigration as a Factor in American History.* Englewood Cliffs, N. J.: Prentice-Hall, 1959.

A carefully edited documentary history, with commentaries, which depicts the immigrant's role in American history and traces the forces which brought immigration to an abrupt halt in the 1920s.

———. *Race and Nationality in American Life.* Garden City: Doubleday Anchor Books, 1957.

Drawing upon the experiences of both Black and White ethnic groups, the author analyzes the various ways in which racism has influenced American social and political institutions. A thoughtful and important book.

Hansen, Marcus Lee. *The Atlantic Migration, 1607–1860.* Edited by Arthur M. Schlesinger. Cambridge, Mass.: Harvard University Press, 1940.

In this important study, Hansen describes the European social and political conditions that motivated thousands of Europeans to immigrate to the United States. This book is well written and is especially important because it focuses on the European factors that stimulated the great immigrations to the United States. Winner of the 1941 Pulitzer Prize in history.

———. *The Immigrant in American History.* Cambridge: Harvard University Press, 1940.

A seminal interpretative study of immigration in American history. An essential reference for the serious student of American immigration.

Hawkins, Brett W. and Robert A. Lorinskas, eds. *The Ethnic Factor in American Politics.* Columbus, Ohio: Charles E. Merrill, 1970.

This anthology contains a number of papers discussing the relationship between ethnicity and political behavior.

Kennedy, John F. *A Nation of Immigrants.* Rev. ed. New York: Harper and Row, 1964.

A brief overview of immigrants to the United States with emphasis on the contributions of each group. The book includes a useful chronology, a comprehensive bibliography, and a revealing pictorial essay. A good source for high school students.

Levy, Mark R. and Michael S. Kramer. *The Ethnic Factor: How America's Minorities Decide Elections.* New York: Simon and Schuster, 1972.

This book includes an analysis of the voting behavior of Jews, Irish, Slavs, and Italians in presidential elections in the 1960s. The authors argue that ethnic factors play a major role in American voting.

Litt, Edgar. *Ethnic Politics in America.* Glenview, Ill.: Scott, Foresman and Company, 1970.

A carefully reasoned study that presents broad generalizations about ethnic politics within a theoretical framework. Although this book is technical, it is a good source of generalizations about ethnic factors in American political behavior.

Lopreato, Joseph. *Italian Americans.* New York: Random House, 1970.

A medium quality book which describes the reasons why Italians immigrated to the United States, their patterns of settlement, and problems of adjustment and assimilation in the United States. A useful source for understanding the problems of the "new" immigrants that came to the United States in the late 1800s and early 1900s.

Moquin, Wayne, with Charles Van Doren, eds. *A Documentary History of the Italian Americans.* New York: Praeger Publishers, 1974.

A useful documentary history which contains more than 100 selections divided into 6 major parts.

Novak, Michael. *The Rise of the Unmeltable Ethnics.* New York: Macmillan, 1971.

A highly rhetorical and ringing plea for justice toward lower middle-class White ethnic groups such as Poles, Italians, Greeks, and Slavs. This book is demagogic, simplistic, and anti-Black. However, the author does attempt to convey the frustrations and aspirations of working class White ethnic groups.

Schrag, Peter. *The Decline of the WASP.* New York: Simon and Schuster, 1971.

Schrag traces the rise of the dominant culture in America and argues that the WASP cultural group is declining in power and prestige and becoming an American minority.

Sklare, Marshall. *America's Jews.* New York: Random House, 1971.

A readable and worthwhile introductory book on contemporary Jewish life in America. Family and identity, community and identity, and Jewish education and identity are some of the topics discussed.

Stephenson, George M. *A History of Immigration 1820–1924.* Boston: Ginn and Company, 1926.

This earlier history of American immigration includes chapters on specific nationality groups as well as on key issues and problems related to American immigration.

Wheeler, Thomas C. *The Immigrant Experience: The Anguish of Becoming American.* New York: Dial Press, 1971.

In this compassionately written book, a group of American ethnic writers (novelists, poets, etc.) share their personal rage and anguish experienced in becoming Americans.

Wigginton, Eliot. *The Foxfire Book.* Garden City, N. Y.: Doubleday, 1972.

An outstanding book of folk culture of Appalachian Whites compiled by a teacher and his students. This book has a sequel, *Foxfire Book II* (also Doubleday).

Wittke, Carl. *We Who Built America: The Saga of the Immigrant.* Englewood Cliffs, N. J.: Prentice-Hall, 1939.

An important early study that includes useful information about European immigrants in the United States.

Ziegler, Benjamin Munn, ed. *Immigration: An American Dilemma.* Boston: D.C. Heath and Company, 1953.

A valuable collection of essays that discuss various issues related to American immigration up to 1952.

BOOKS FOR STUDENTS

Barash, Ashler. *A Golden Treasury of Jewish Tales.* Translated by Murray Roston. New York: Dodd, Mead and Company, 1966.

An interesting collection of didactic folktales that entertain. These tales reveal important aspects of Jewish culture. (High School)

Beard, Annie E. S. *Our Foreign-Born Citizens.* New York: Thomas Y. Crowell, 1968.

These twenty-three biographies of distinguished foreign-born Americans chronicle their lives from their birthplaces to their achievements in America. (Upper)

DeAngeli, Marguerite. *Up the Hill.* Garden City, N. Y.: Doubleday, 1942.

This story about a Polish American family reveals interesting facts about Polish songs, holidays, foods, and family relationships. (Intermediate)

Eiseman, Alberta. *From Many Lands.* New York: Athenum, 1970.

A brief history of several immigrant groups in the United States. The author highlights both similarities and differences in the groups. Illustrated. (High School)

Eubank, Nancy. *The Russians in America.* Minneapolis: Lerner Publications, 1973.

A general historical overview of Russian-Americans. The book provides information on the different groups of Russian immigrants and describes contributions Russians have made to American life. (Upper)

Fleming, Thomas J. *The Golden Door: The Story of American Immigration.* New York: Grosset and Dunlap, 1970.

The author discusses the problems and successes experienced by various groups of immigrants to the United States. He focuses on European ethnic groups but also discusses Asians, Puerto Ricans, Mexicans, and Afro-Americans. Although the book gives the reader a feeling for the immigrant experience, the book contains some implied as well as stated errors. Illustrated. (High School)

Gay, Kathlyn. *The Germans Helped Build America.* New York: Julian Messner, 1971.

The author discusses the conditions in Germany leading to German immigration to the United States and describes the German-American's reactions to a variety of events in the United States, including the two world wars. The contributions German-Americans have made to American life are also highlighted. (Upper)

Gracza, Rezsoe and Margaret Gracza. *The Hungarians in America.* Minneapolis: Lerner Publications, 1969.

This historical overview of Hungarian-Americans describes the reasons why they immigrated to the United States, their role in American life, and contributions they have made to our society. Biographies are stressed in the book. Illustrated. (Upper)

Greenleaf, Barbara Kaye. *America Fever: The Story of American Immigration.* New York: Four Winds Press, 1970.

This book is a good history of American immigration from colonial times up to the early 1900s. While the book concentrates on European immigration, other American ethnic groups are discussed. (High School)

Handlin, Oscar and the editors of the Newsweek Book Division. *Statue of Liberty.* New York: Newsweek, 1971.

A beautifully illustrated and well-written story of the Statue of Liberty interspersed with the history of the great European immigrations. Handlin writes about the immigrants with his usual insight and sensitivity. (Upper)

Heaps, Willard A. *The Story of Ellis Island.* New York: Seabury Press, 1967.

An interesting account of the experiences of immigrants who landed at Ellis Island. Some of the incidents are told through the eyes of the immigrants. (High School)

Hoff, Rhoda. *America's Immigrants: Adventures in Eyewitness History.* New York: Henry Z. Walck, 1967.

An excellent collection of documents about immigrant life in the United States. Some of the letters, poems, and other documents in this book are excellent for teaching inquiry lessons. Each document is preceded by a helpful introduction by the editor. (High School)

Hutchmacher, Joseph J. *A Nation of Newcomers: Ethnic Groups in American History.* New York: Dell, 1967.

This book contains brief historical overviews of selected immigrant groups in the United States and a good multiethnic chronology. (Upper)

Iorizzo, Luciano J. and Salvatore Mondello. *The Italian-Americans.* New York: Twayne Publishers, 1971.

This study of the Italian Americans focus on the period between 1880 and 1920. (High School)

Judson, Clara Ingram. *Sod-House Winter.* Chicago: Follett, 1957.

A fictional account of a Swedish American family in the mid-1800s. The story reveals how early Swedish immigrants lived. (Intermediate)

———— . *They Came From France.* Boston: Houghton Mifflin, 1943.

A fictional account of a young Frenchman's journey across the Atlantic and his life in America. (Intermediate)

———— . *They Came from Scotland.* Boston: Houghton Mifflin, 1944.

A story of a Scottish American family in the 1800s. The story does not reveal much about the Scots in America but is a fair adventure story. (Intermediate)

Kuropas, Myron B. *The Ukranians in America.* Minneapolis: Lerner, 1972.

A historical overview of the Ukraine and an account of Ukrainian immigration to the United States are presented in this book. Ukranian-American culture and their contributions to the United States are also highlighted. (Upper)

LaGumina, Salvatore J. *An Album of the Italian-American,* New York: Franklin Watts, 1972.

An excellent book about the immigration of Italians to the United States and their life in America. The book is well illustrated with black and white photographs. (Upper)

Novotny, Ann. *Strangers at the Door*. Riverside, Conn.: Chatham Press, 1971.

This book provides a good account of European immigration to America but fails in its attempt to discuss the immigration of non-European groups. The text is profusely illustrated with black and white photographs, which alone tell an interesting story of American immigration. (All Levels)

Pilarski, Laura. *They Came from Poland: The Stories of Famous Polish-Americans*. New York: Dodd, Mead and Co., 1969.

The contributions and life stories of famous Polish Americans are stressed in this historical overview of the Polish in the United States. (Upper)

Sekorová, Dagmar. *European Fairy Tales*. New York: Lothrop, Lee and Shepard, 1971.

A collection of nineteen fairy tales representing eight European nations. Both unfamiliar and old favorite tales, like Cinderella, are included. (All Levels)

Sheehan, Ethna. *Folk and Fairy Tales from Around the World*. New York: Dodd, Mead and Co., 1970.

A delightful collection of native tales from a variety of nations, but mostly from Europe. The tales range from serious to frivolous. (All Levels)

Suhl, Yuri. *An Album of the Jews in America*. New York: Franklin Watts, 1972.

A good historical overview of Jewish immigration to the United States, Jewish life in America, and the contributions Jews have made to American life. Illustrated. (Upper)

Thompson, Stith. *One Hundred Favorite Folktales*. Bloomington: Indiana University Press, 1968.

A comprehensive collection of European tales from many European nations such as France, Russia, Hungary, Italy, and Portugal. (All Levels)

Wytrwal, Joseph A. *The Poles in America*. Minneapolis: Lerner, 1969.

Drawing largely on the biographies of famous Polish Americans, the author tells the story of Polish immigration to the United States, the experiences of Polish immigrants in America, and the contributions the Poles have made to American life and culture. (Upper)

Afro-Americans: Concepts, Strategies, and Materials

7

Blacks have been, and are, the victims of a system whose only fuel is greed, whose only god is profit . . . for the perpetuation of this system, we have all been mercilessly brutalized, and have been told nothing but lies . . . about love, life and death, so that both soul and body have been bound in hell.

James Baldwin

Introduction

Africans have had a unique experience in the Americas. They came with the earliest European explorers and settlers and were gradually enslaved in the North American colonies in the 1600s. When the eighteenth century began, slavery was flourishing in North America. The Black experience in the United States has strikingly revealed the gross discrepancies between American ideals and reality more than any other events in American life. Throughout their history in America, Blacks have called upon America to make its dream a reality. Their cries have usually fallen on deaf ears. Afro-American history and culture must be studied to enable students to fully understand and appreciate the great conflicts and dilemmas in American society and to develop a commitment to help make America's great ideals a reality.

Afro-Americans: Historical Perspective

Important Dates

1565	Blacks helped to establish a colony in St. Augustine, Florida.
1619	The first Blacks arrived in the English North American colonies.
1808	The slave trade was legally ended, but illegal slave trading began.
1829	David Walker published his *Appeal*, in which he harshly denounced slavery and urged slaves to take up arms and rebel.
1831	Nat Turner led a slave revolt in which nearly sixty Whites were killed.
1850	The Fugitive Slave Act, which authorized the federal government to help capture runaway slaves, was enacted. It helped pave the way to the Civil War.
1857	The Supreme Court ruled that slaves did not become free when they moved to free territory in the *Dred Scott Decision*. It also held that Afro-Americans were not and could not be citizens.
1861–62	Congress enacted several Confiscation Acts designed to prevent the Confederacy from using slaves in its war effort.
1863	Many Afro-Americans in New York City were attacked and killed by largely Irish mobs that were protesting the draft laws and expressing anti-Black feelings. On January 1, 1863, President Lincoln issued the Emancipation Proclamation which freed slaves in those states fighting the Union.
1865	Slavery was legally abolished throughout the United States by the enactment of the Thirteenth Amendment to the Constitution.
1866	The Fourteenth Amendment, which made Afro-Americans United States citizens, was enacted. The Civil Rights Act of 1866 was enacted. It

Important Dates cont.

extended the Afro-American's civil liberties in several areas.

1870   The Fifteenth Amendment was enacted. It enabled many Afro-Americans to vote.

1876   In the disputed Hayes-Tilden election, Hayes' supporters promised that he would remove the remaining federal troops from the South. This bargain symbolized the extent to which Northern Whites had abandoned the Southern Black man.

1896   In a historic decision, *Plessy* vs. *Ferguson,* the Supreme Court ruled that "separate but equal" facilities were constitutional.

1905   W. E. B. DuBois and a group of Black intellectuals organized the Niagra Movement to promote civil rights for Afro-Americans.

1910   The National Association for the Advancement of Colored People (NAACP) was organized. It successfully fought for Black legal rights.

1911   The National Urban League was founded to help the Black urban migrant adjust to city life and to find jobs.

1914   Marcus Garvey organized the Universal Negro Improvement Association. Garvey urged Afro-Americans to return to Africa.

1917   One of the worst riots in American history took place in East St. Louis, Illinois. Thirty-nine Blacks were killed.

1919   A series of riots occurred in a number of cities during the "Red Summer" of 1919. One of the most serious took place in Chicago, in which thirty-eight people lost their lives.

1943   White violence directed at Afro-Americans led to a serious riot in Detroit, in which thirty-four people were killed.

1954   In a landmark decision, *Brown* vs. *Board of Education,* the Supreme Court ruled that

Important Dates cont.

	school segregation was inherently unequal.
1955	Afro-Americans in Montgomery, Alabama, began a boycott of the city's buses which ended bus segregation there in 1956.
1957	Martin Luther King, Jr. and a group of Baptist ministers organized the Southern Christian Leadership Conference (SCLC).
	National guardsmen were required to integrate Central High School in Little Rock, Arkansas.
1960	On February 1, 1960, the sit-in movement, which desegregated public accommodation facilities throughout the South, began in Greensboro, North Carolina.
1961	The Congress of Racial Equality (CORE) led "Freedom Rides" through the South to desegregate interstate transportation.
1963	Over 2,000 people participated in a "March on Washington for Freedom and Jobs."
	In a Birmingham demonstration, led by Martin Luther King, Jr., civil rights demonstrators were violently attacked by the police.
1964	The Civil Rights Act of 1964, the most comprehensive civil rights bill in American history, was enacted and signed by President Lyndon B. Johnson.
	An antipoverty act launched the War on Poverty.
1965	Partly in response to civil rights demonstrations, the Voting Rights Act of 1965 was enacted.
1965–68	A racial rebellion in the Watts district of Los Angeles in 1965 launched one of the most serious series of racial disturbances in American history. Some of the most tragic riots took place in Newark and Detroit in 1968. A new wave followed the assassination of Martin Luther King, Jr. in 1968.
1966	Stokely Carmichael issued a call for "Black

Important Dates cont.

	Power" during a civil rights demonstration in Greenwood, Mississippi. The Black Panther party was organized in Oakland, California.
1968	Martin Luther King, Jr. was assassinated in Memphis, Tennessee, while there to help striking garbage workers. A Poor People's Campaign was staged in Washington, D. C. to dramatize the plight of the American poor. The Kerner Commission, appointed by President Lyndon B. Johnson, issued an influential report stating that White racism was the major cause of the city rebellions.
1969	The Chicago police raided the home of a Black Panther leader and killed him and another Panther activist.
1971	People United to Save Humanity (PUSH) was organized by Rev. Jesse L. Jackson.
1972	More than 8,000 delegates attended the first National Black Political Convention in Gary, Indiana. President Richard M. Nixon signed a bill that was designed to end busing for racial integration of the schools.
1973	Afro-Americans were elected mayors in Detroit, Atlanta, Los Angeles, and other cities.

Black Explorers in America

Africans have been in America for many centuries. Inconclusive evidence suggests that they established a colony in Mexico long before Columbus's voyage in 1492. Blacks were with the first Europeans who explored America. Africans had been living in Europe for many years when European explorations to America began. The Moors, a North African people, invaded Europe in 711. They eventually conquered and ruled Spain. Other Africans were brought to Europe as slaves beginning in the 1400s. These Africans worked in private homes as servants, in banks, shipyards, and in "mercantile establishments."

Diego el Negro was with Columbus on his last voyage to America in 1502. When Balboa arrived at the Pacific Ocean in 1513, his crew included a Black man, Nuflo de Olano. Blacks explored present-day Kansas in 1541 with Coronado. Africans were also with many of the other early Spanish expeditions to the Americas. Estevanico, a Moor, is one of the most famous early Black explorers. Arriving in America in 1529, he explored present-day New Mexico and Arizona and paved the way for later Spanish explorations of the Southwest.

In addition to exploring America, Blacks were among its first non-Indian settlers. Some of the settlers of the ill-fated South Carolina colony in 1526, San Miguel de Gualdape, were Black. Blacks helped to establish St. Augustine, Florida in 1565, which is the oldest non-Indian settlement in the United States. A number of colonies were established by Blacks and Frenchmen. These groups settled in the Mississippi Valley in the seventeenth century.

The Slave Trade

The Moslems invaded Africa and enslaved Blacks long before Europeans arrived on the continent. The European nations became involved in the African slave trade when they started trading with Africa in the 1400s. In the mid-fifteenth century, European monarchs sent explorers to Africa to obtain goods such as skins and oils. Many of these explorers took back these wares as well as African slaves and gold as gifts for their rulers. These gifts greatly pleased the European monarchs. As more and more Europeans explored Africa and took Africans back to Europe, the slave trade gradually gained momentum. However, Black slavery never became widespread in Europe, but grew by leaps and bounds when Europeans started settling in America in the 1600s. Europeans developed large plantations in the West Indies which grew crops such as sugar, indigo, cotton, and tobacco. Sugar production reigned supreme over all other crops. To produce increasing amounts of sugar, the Europeans brought thousands of slaves to the West Indies from Africa.

The slave trade became highly lucrative. European nations competed aggressively to monopolize it. At first, the Portugese dominated the slave trade. Portugal was eventually challenged by the Dutch. Gradually, more and more nations gained a toehold in Africa. However, England was dominating the slave trade when it peaked in 1700. The European nations greatly benefited from the slave trade. They got many raw materials from Africa which helped them to attain high levels of industrial growth. The ships that left Europe carried small items to use for exchange with the Africans. While in Africa, they picked up wares such as gold, ivory, and dyewood as well as slaves. The ships usually traveled from Africa to the West Indies, where the slaves were sold and exchange goods acquired. The goods were taken back to Europe. The journey from the West Coast of Africa to the West Indies was known as the "Middle Passage" because it was only part of a route which eventually led back to Europe.

When the slave trade in the West Indies began, European nations granted monopolies to a few favorite companies, such as the Dutch West India Company and the Royal African Company of England. Later, when these nations realized that they could make more money by allowing companies to compete, the monopoly system was abandoned. Before the monopolies ended in the late 1600s, the European colonists in North America were not able to get nearly as many slaves as they wanted. The major companies sold most of their slaves on the more profitable markets on the West Indian sugar plantations. However, the North American colonists were able to buy as many slaves as they wished when monopolies ended. The smaller companies were anxious to trade with them.

While the slave trade was very profitable for European nations and contributed to their industrial growth and development, it was disastrous for the West African nations. When the trade first began, African rulers sold captives and criminals. Most of the captives had been taken from other tribes during warfare. However, as the Europeans sought more and more slaves, these sources became inadequate. The African rulers were so fascinated with the trinkets, rum, firearms, and other items they received in exchange for slaves that they started warring to get slaves, using the firearms they got from Europeans. Warring became increasingly frequent and destructive as the Europeans' desire for slaves soared. As warring increased, some groups had to sell slaves to acquire the firearms they needed to protect themselves. These wars adversely affected African political stability. The slave trade also drained off many of Africa's strongest and most productive young men and women. The slave traders wanted only healthy captives who could survive the horrible middle passage and the back-breaking work on the plantations in America.

The Beginning of Bondage

The captive's life was terrifying, brutal, and shocking. Slave catchers, who were usually Africans, raided the interior of the West African coast looking for captives. When Blacks were caught, they were chained together and marched long distances, often hundreds of miles, to the European forts near the ocean coast. Here they waited, sometimes for months, to be forced onto ships headed for America. The captives adamantly resisted bondage. Some of them escaped on the long march to the forts. Others jumped overboard once the ships were at sea. Mutinies occurred, both on the African shore and in mid-ocean. In 1753 a group of captives seized a ship bound for America, killed the White crew, and forced the ship back to Africa.

Conditions on the slave ships were degrading and dehumanizing. The bondsmen were packed into the ships like sardines. The men were chained together with iron ankle fetters. The space for each slave was so small that they were forced to lie down in the ship. Because of the crowded and filthy conditions on the ships, diseases were rampant and took many lives. Many slaves died from scurvy, dysentery, and smallpox. Sometimes everyone on a ship was blinded by ophthalmia. Slaves who got very sick were dumped into the ocean since dead slaves were worthless on the American slave market. More than half of the slaves sometimes died during the journey. Some historians estimate that one out of every eight captives died on the middle passage and never reached the Americas. This painful trip usually took from forty to sixty days.

Slavery in North America

The first Africans to arrive in the English North American colonies came in 1619 on a Dutch ship. These twenty Africans were not slaves but, like most of the Whites who came to the colonies during this period, were indentured servants. To pay for his passage to America, an indentured servant agreed to work for his sponsor for a specified period of time. When he had completed his period of service, he became free. At first, the English colonists met their labor needs with indentured servants.

Increasingly the colonists began to feel that they were not getting enough workers with this system and that slavery had many advantages over it. For one thing, indentured servitude was much more expensive than slavery. The servants had to be provided certain goods and services. Eventually, they became free. With slavery, the worker received few benefits and remained a servant for life. Also, the slaves' children would also be slaves. Clearly, slavery was a much more profitable system than indentured servitude. The colonists deliberately decided to replace indentured servitude with Black slavery for economic reasons.

Slavery existed in practice in most of the colonies long before it acquired legal status. The legal institutionalization of slavery was a gradual process. By 1630 in Virginia, laws and legal cases were beginning to evolve which would culminate in the legalization of slavery. In that year, a court sentenced a White man to a whipping for having sex with a Black woman. The Virginia House of Burgesses passed a law in 1643 limiting the years for White indentured servants but not for Black servants. The House enacted a law in 1662 which declared that children would inherit their mother's status. This law reversed English common law which held that children inherited their father's status. A 1667 law enacted by the House enabled Christians to be slaves. A law passed in Maryland in 1664 openly declared that Blacks and their children would be slaves in that colony. By the end of the seventeenth century, slavery existed in fact as well as in law in colonial America.

American slavery was a unique institution in human history that was designed to totally dehumanize Blacks and to convince them that they were inferior and deserved the treatment they received. It was also designed to enable Whites to make maximum profits from Black labor and to reinforce ideas of White supremacy. All of the laws, customs, and norms that developed around slavery reflected and reinforced its major goals. The slave was regarded as a piece of property who should cater to the whims and wishes of his or her master. A number of arguments and traditions emerged to justify slavery and to insure its continuation. Because of their treatment of Blacks, and because of constant attempts by the captives to resist bondage, Whites developed a chronic fear of slave rebellions and retaliation. Sometimes, especially after a slave rebellion or when one was rumored, White fears of slave insurrections and uprisings became chronic, paranoid, and widespread. Consequently, the slave codes were made more severe and the institutions and norms supporting bondage were revitalized.

Attempts by Whites to deny the Black captives humanity and to oppress them are reflected in the numerous slave codes enacted in colonies from New York to Georgia. These codes varied from colony to colony and tended to be most severe in the Southern colonies and mildest in New England. However, all of them were degrading and designed to reinforce bondage. In some colonies, slaves could not form groups without the presence of a White; they could not carry or own firearms, testify in court against a White person, or be taught to read or write. Some colonies prevented them from owning property or drinking liquor and did not recognize their marriages as legal. They were forbidden from leaving the plantation unless they had a special pass. Punishment for crimes was severe, although some planters did not welcome the death penalty because it deprived them of profitable workers. Slaves were subject to the death penalty for such crimes as rape, arson, and robbery.

Slaves worked in a wide variety of occupations, especially in the Northern colonies. They worked as laborers and house servants in New England, but also as skilled artisans. Many skilled slaves in the North hired themselves out and saved enough money to buy their freedom. Few skilled slaves in the South were allowed to keep the money they earned hiring themselves out. Although slaves in the South worked in many different fields, especially in the cities where many were skilled artisans, most worked on the large plantations owned by a few rich members of the Southern aristocracy. Life on these large plantations, which specialized in such crops as tobacco and cotton, was arduous and poignant. Driven by a merciless overseer and a driver, the slaves worked from sunup to sundown. They usually lived in mud-floor shacks on the plantation that were cold in the winter and hot in the summer. Their food consisted mostly of hominy and fatback. Their clothing was very limited. Men usually had little more than two shirts and two pairs of trousers.

Even though Whites tried to deny the slaves a human existence, Blacks succeeded in developing a sense of community and a social life quite apart from the world of Whites. Slaves had stable marriages, even though they were not legally recognized by White society. These marriages usually took place after long courtships. The slave family was very important to the slaves. Family members taught the child how to survive the harsh White environment, as well as how never to submit totally to the whims of the master. Black fathers openly disapproved of the way Whites treated their families. However, these men usually obeyed the master so that they could avoid severe punishment or death. Many slave families that had developed strong bonds of love and kinship were broken up when their master sold family members to different buyers or sold only some members of the family. Some slaves escaped to search for members of their families when they were sold.

Most Black captives never totally submitted to slavery or accepted it. They resisted it in both covert and blatant ways. To avoid work, slaves would sometimes feign illness. They sometimes destroyed farm equipment deliberately or cut up the plants when they were hoeing crops. A few slaves maimed themselves to avoid work. Some domestic slaves put poison into their master's foods and killed them. Other slaves escaped. The number of runaways increased greatly when the Civil War began and when the Emancipation Proclamation was issued in 1863. Many slaves were helped to the North and Canada by a loosely organized system known as the Underground Railroad. Free Blacks, many of whom were escaped slaves, made numerous trips to the South to help Blacks escape. Blacks such as Harriet Tubman and Josiah Henson helped hundreds of slaves follow the North Star to freedom. The slaves traveled by night, and were helped by "conductors" of the Underground Railroad. While some slaves were helped by Underground Railroad conductors, many of them escaped alone. These lone and brave captives were determined to escape bondage at any cost.

Bondsmen also resisted slavery by rebellion. While most slave uprisings were unsuccessful, partly because of slave informers, historical records indicate that at least 250 took place.[1]

1. Herbert Aptheker, *American Negro Slave Revolts*. (New York: International Publishers, Inc., 1963).

One of the most ambitious slave uprisings was planned by Gabriel Prosser in 1800. Prosser and a group of about 1,000 slaves armed themselves and headed for Richmond, Virginia. A heavy rainstorm stopped the rebels and the authorities in Richmond, who had been alerted, were armed and waiting for them. Gabriel Prosser and thirty of the other captives died at the end of a rope. Denmark Vesey, a free Black in Charleston, South Carolina, planned an insurrection in 1882. The group he led armed themselves and were prepared to take Charleston's two arsenals. The revolt was crushed before it got started and the participants were hanged. The most successful slave revolt of the antebellum period was led by Nat Turner in 1831. Turner was a highly imaginative slave preacher who felt that he was destined by God to free his people from bondage. Turner organized and armed a crew that killed about sixty Whites, including his master and family. The Turner rebels caught their victims by surprise. Whites crushed the rebellion after it had raged for forty-eight hours. When they were seized, Turner and nineteen other rebels were hanged.

The Abolitionists

The first societies organized to agitate for the abolition of slavery were formed during and after the American Revolution. The earliest was founded in Philadelphia in 1775. The Quakers were the leading figures in this society. Other abolitionary societies were formed during this period. Most of the members of these early societies were propertied men who were very sympathetic to the South. They spoke kindly of the South, were soft spoken, and felt that slave owners who freed their slaves should be compensated. They advocated a gradual abolition of slavery. Because of the tactics they used, many Southerners supported these societies. These abolitionists did not believe in or practice social equality. Women and Afro-Americans were excluded from their organizations.

The abolitionary societies organized in the 1800s were much more militant and aggressive than the earlier ones. They harshly denounced slavery and slave owners and demanded an immediate end to slavery. These groups were very unpopular in both the North and the South. They became known as militants and extremists. Both Whites and Blacks participated in these societies, although the Whites, who did not believe in racial equality, tried to keep the Blacks in the background. Frederick Douglass, Robert Purvis, and Henry Highland Garnet were some of the leading Black abolitionists.

One of the most militant societies was the American Anti-Slavery Society, organized in 1833. Although this society vigorously denounced slavery, it kept Blacks in the shadow. In its early years, it had no Black lecturers. Most of the policy was made by Whites. Members of the society discouraged Blacks when they started editing their own newspapers and lecturing. They wanted only a few Blacks to be visible in the organization for symbolic purposes. The Afro-American abolitionists harshly condemned the White abolitionists, accusing them of discriminating against Blacks in their businesses and their daily lives.

The Black abolitionists often went their separate ways. They edited newspapers and gave moving speeches giving Black views of abolition. Despite objections from White abolitionists such as William Lloyd Garrison, Frederick Douglass edited and published a paper, the *North Star*. Black abolitionists also expressed their views in the series of conventions they held in the antebellum period. At the National Negro Convention in 1843, Henry Highland Garnet gave a controversial speech in which he urged slaves to rise up and fight for their freedom. He later worked with William G. Allen to edit a newspaper, *The National Watchman*. As was to be the case in later years, Black and White participants in Black liberation movements in the 1800s often had different goals and aims, and they used different approaches. These divergent goals and methods inevitably led to conflict and hostility between these groups.

The Colonization Movement

In the early nineteenth century, an intense movement developed among Whites to deport Afro-Americans to another country. The motives of the advocates of colonization varied. Some saw themselves as humanitarians and felt that because of White racism, Blacks would never be able to achieve equality in America. They believed that Blacks would have a much better chance in another nation. Other advocates of colonization were supporters of slavery and wanted to deport *free* Blacks because they felt that nonslave Blacks were a threat to the "peculiar" institution. Many Southern Whites eagerly supported the American Colonization Society, organized in 1816 by a group of eminent White Americans.

Many influential Whites, such as Francis Scott Key and Henry Clay, supported colonization. A region in West Africa, named Liberia, was acquired by American colonizationists in 1822. Despite the enthusiastic support for the movement, it did not succeed. Less than 8,000 Blacks had immigrated to Liberia by 1852. Many of these were slaves who had been granted their freedom on the condition that they immigrate to Africa. The colonization movement failed primarily because most Blacks were adamantly against it. The American Colonization Society made its plans and solicited support from eminent White Americans but ignored the feelings of Afro-Americans. Black leaders denounced the society, which often condoned racist practices, in loud terms and argued that they would not leave the United States because their fathers had helped to build this country and because they had a right to live in America by birthright. The free Blacks who strongly opposed colonization saw it as an attempt by slaveowners to get rid of them and thus make slavery more safe and secure. These leaders argued that their fate rested with the fate of their enchained brothers and sisters.

A few Afro-Americans who became very disillusioned with the United States began to advocate colonization. However, some of these leaders, such as Martin Delany, strongly criticized the American Colonization Society. Delany felt that the society's members were "arrogant hypocrites." Delany correctly perceived the White colonizationists' motives as quite different from his. Black colonizationists wanted to leave the United States because they had become disillusioned and frustrated. Most White colonizationists hoped to deport Blacks so that they could get rid of a race they did not want in the United States.

From time to time, small groups of despairing Afro-Americans thought seriously about colonization and sometimes took concrete actions to actualize their aspirations. Paul Cuffe took thirty-eight Blacks to Sierre Leone in 1815. In 1859 Martin R. Delany obtained a piece of land in Africa for an African American settlement. A Black colonization group, the African Civilization Society, was organized by a group of eminent Blacks in 1858. Despite these attempts, Black colonizationists had no more success than White colonizationists because most Afro-Americans were determined to remain in the United States. Back-to-Africa advocates emerged later in the nineteenth and twentieth centuries, but their cries continued to fall on deaf ears. Marcus Garvey was a strong advocate of African colonization in the 1930s.

Nonslave Blacks

Not all Blacks were slaves, either in the North or South, during the antebellum period. Many Afro-Americans in the North hired themselves out and earned their freedom. Some in New England sued for their freedom in courts and won it. Some bondsmen were awarded their freedom after service in the Revolutionary War. A few Blacks were descendants of Black indentured servants and thus were never slaves. In the South, some slave masters left wills freeing their slaves upon their deaths. Often these slaves were their blood relatives. Some Southern slaves were given their freedom after meritorious service to their communities. Others obtained their freedom by escaping. In both the North and the South, the nonslave Black was harassed and demeaned and was often treated like he was a slave. When Whites saw Blacks, they assumed that they were slaves. The nonslave Black had to prove that he or she was free. Free Blacks had to carry papers, which they usually had to purchase, that certified their freedom. However, they were often captured and enslaved whether they carried "free" papers or not.

Many of the legal limitations imposed upon the slave also governed the nonslave Black. In many parts of the South, nonslave Blacks were forbidden from forming groups without the presence of a White, were prohibited from testifying against a White, and were not allowed to own a gun or a dog. In the North, they were denied the franchise and prohibited by law from migrating to such states as Illinois, Indiana, and Oregon. The free Black could settle in other old Northwest states only after paying bonds up to a thousand dollars. Southerners regarded free Blacks as a nuisance and a threat to slavery. They blamed them for most of the slave rebellions and for encouraging slaves to escape. For these reasons, many Southern Whites eagerly supported the move to deport free Blacks to Africa.

Nonslave Northern Blacks played an extremely important

role in Afro-American life. They strongly protested the racism and discrimination Blacks experienced. The Negro Convention Movement served as an important protest forum. Black conventions were held from 1830 up to the beginning of the twentieth century. At most of them, the delegates issued cogent statements demanding an end to racism in various areas of American life. The colonization movement, discrimination in Northern schools, and segregation in the church were targets of Black protest.

Free Blacks also organized significant institutions, including the numerous self-help and mutual-aid societies from which most of today's Black insurance companies grew. One of the earliest mutual-benefit societies, the African Union Society, was organized in Newport, Rhode Island in 1780. Like many similar societies organized later, it helped its members when they were out of work, gave them decent burials, and set up an apprenticed program that trained young Blacks to be skilled artisans. Other mutual-aid societies included the Masonic Order organized by Prince Hall in 1787 and the Grand United Order of Odd Fellows, established in 1843. These organizations were extremely important within the Black community.

Afro-Americans also organized their own churches. Blacks were forced to sit in separate pews in White churches and were sometimes interrupted in the middle of prayers if they were seated in the "wrong" sections. These kinds of indignities led Blacks such as Richard Allen and Absolam Jones to organize independent Black churches. In 1794 two Black Methodist churches were founded in Philadelphia, St. Thomas Protestant Episcopal Church and the Bethel African Methodist Episcopal Church. Black Methodist churches soon spread to many other cities. Black Baptists also established independent churches. The Black church became an extremely important institution in Afro-American life. It trained most Black protest leaders, opened schools for Black children, and gave Blacks practice in self-governance and increased their self-respect. The church and the fraternal orders, which were affiliated with the church, were the key institutions within Black America. Today the Black church still performs many of its historic functions and remains an important Black organization.

The Civil War and Reconstruction

Afro-Americans viewed the Civil War as the god-sent conflict that would emancipate them from bondage. However, they were virtually alone in this view. Most White Americans, including President Lincoln and the U.S. Congress, viewed the war as a conflict to preserve the Union. When news of the war spread, Northern Blacks rushed to recruiting stations and tried to enlist in the armed forces. Their services were rejected. Leaders thought that the war would last only ninety days. The war dragged on for four long years. When it became evident that the war would last much longer than was originally thought, the Union, and later the Confederacy, reluctantly allowed Blacks to take up arms.

Congress and President Lincoln took a number of steps to weaken the Confederacy. They realized that the slaves were being used to help the Confederate forces to maintain their strength. Consequently, Congress enacted a number of laws that undermined the Confederacy. In 1861 Congress enacted legislation enabling it to free slaves who were used to help the Confederate forces. In the summer of 1862, Congress passed a bill that freed slaves who had escaped and authorized the president to use Black troops. President Lincoln also used his authority to weaken the Confederacy. On September 22, 1862, he announced that slaves in rebel states would be freed on January 1, 1863. Lincoln kept his promise and issued the Emancipation Proclamation freeing those slaves in rebel states on January 1, 1863. Although Afro-Americans and abolitionists rejoiced when the Emancipation Proclamation was issued, legally it did no more than the act that was passed by Congress in 1862. The thousands of slaves in states not fighting the Union were not freed. However, the proclamation did give Blacks a moral uplift and motivated more slaves to escape. However, captives had been escaping in large numbers ever since Northern soldiers started coming to the South.

After four bitter years and the bloodiest war in American history up to that time, Lee surrendered at Appomattox on April 9, 1865 and the Civil War ended. On April 14, 1865 Lincoln was assassinated by John Wilkes Booth. Andrew Johnson became president. President Johnson, like Lincoln, favored a lenient plan for readmitting the Southern states back into the Union. However, the Republican Congress wanted to gain a toehold in the South so that the Republican party could win future presidential elections. To obtain their objective, they franchised the newly freed Blacks so that they would develop an allegiance to the Republican party. In a series of acts, Congress gave Blacks the right to vote, extended their civil rights, and endeared them to the Republicans. In 1865 it enacted the Thirteenth Amendment, which abolished slavery throughout the United States. Congress passed a Civil Rights Act in 1866 which made Afro-Americans citizens and granted them certain legal rights. The Fourteenth Amendment, enacted in 1866, also recognized Blacks as citizens. The Reconstruction Act of 1867 divided the South into five military districts and required the Confederate states to enact constitutions that would be approved by Congress and to ratify the Fourteenth Amendment before they could be readmitted into the Union. The South considered the Reconstruction Act especially galling.

Because they could now vote and run for public office, a number of Blacks held elected offices for brief periods during Reconstruction. Most of them held minor local offices. However, twenty-two served in the United States Congress. Two of these were U.S. Senators. Black elected officials were too few in number and their tenure too brief for them to play a leading role in shaping policy. However, the South obtained its most enlightened state constitutions during Reconstruction and enacted some of its most humane social legislation. For years after Reconstruction, Southern apologists justified Southern violence by arguing that the South was reacting to the former Black control of the Southern states. However, Afro-Americans never controlled any of the states' legal bodies and none were elected governors.

The Rise of White Supremacy

The Republicans' plan to grab the Black man's vote was successful. Blacks in large numbers voted for the Republican presidential candidate in the election of 1868. However, by 1876, the Republicans, who were dominated by Northern industrial interests, had new interests and no longer needed the Black man to attain them. In fact, Afro-Americans stood in their way. Northern industrialists were now interested in extending their trade in the South, and consequently wanted to court the Southern Whites. To appease Southern Whites, Northern Whites decided to leave the question of the Black person's fate up to the South. The handling of the Hayes-Tilden election in 1876 indicated the extent to which Northern Whites had abandoned Blacks. In that disputed election, an Electoral Commission named the Republican candidate, Hayes, president. To placate the South, Hayes supporters promised White Southerners that when he became president, Hayes would remove all of the remaining federal troops from the South.

Hayes kept this promise when he became president. By the time that the last federal troops were removed from the South, Southern Whites were reestablishing their control of state governments throughout the South and had aggressively begun their campaigns to make Blacks chattels even though slavery had been legally abolished. One of the first acts of the state legislatures was to disenfranchise Afro-Americans. A motley collection of ingenious methods were used to keep Blacks from voting. The Democratic primary, the grandfather clause, literacy tests, and the poll tax were among the many ways in which Afro-Americans, and inadvertently some poor Whites, were prevented from voting.

Determined to "put Blacks in their place," violence against Blacks became rampant. The goal of this violence was to intimidate Blacks, to keep them from voting, and to reestablish the caste system that existed before the Civil War. Afro-Americans became victims of a rash of riots which swept throughout the South between 1866 and 1898. When Afro-Americans tried to obtain the right to vote in New Orleans in 1866, a riot erupted in which forty-eight Blacks were killed. A riot broke out in Savanna, Georgia in 1872 when Blacks tried to end segregation on the city's streetcars. Thirty Afro-Americans were killed in a riot that erupted in Meridian, Mississippi in 1871. Forty-six died in a Memphis riot in 1866. While Blacks were usually innocent victims in these riots, they struck back at Whites in the Charleston Riot of 1876. The Ku Klux Klan was reorganized in 1915. It became a prime leader of anti-Black violence. The lynching of Blacks also became widespread. About 100 Blacks met their death each year at the end of a rope during these trying years.

Southern state legislatures also enacted most of their Jim Crow laws during this period. Laws were passed requiring segregation in schools, parks, restaurants, theaters, and in almost all other public accommodation facilities. Tennessee passed a Jim Crow railroad car act in 1881. Most of the other Southern and Border states soon followed Tennessee's lead. In a series of cases, the Supreme Court upheld and legitimized the South's Jim Crow laws. In 1883 it ruled that the Civil Rights Act of 1875 was unconstitutional. In the *Plessy* vs. *Ferguson* case of 1896, it upheld a Louisiana law that required segregation in railroad cars. The Court ruled that literacy tests and poll taxes required for voting were constitutional. It stripped the Fourteenth and Fifteenth Amendments of all their meaning as far as Blacks were concerned and encouraged White Southerners to enact more racist laws.

Many Afro-Americans expected forty acres and a mule after the Civil War. However, most of the land confiscated from Southern plantation owners was either given back to them or to other members of the Southern aristocracy. Few Blacks were able to obtain land. Most of them became bound to the land and to White landowners in the sharecropping system. The sharecropper's life was very much like that of a slave. In theory, a sharecropper received a share of the crop. However, Black sharecroppers, who had to buy their merchandise from their boss's store, were severely cheated. Each year when the crops were harvested, they found themselves further and further in debt and required to stay on the land until they paid their bills. The sharecropper's status was little better than that of a slave and in some ways worse.

To make the system even more like slavery, Southern state legislatures enacted a series of laws between 1865 and 1866 that became known as the *Black Codes*. These laws were very similar to the old slave codes. In some states, Blacks could not testify in court against Whites, carry guns, or buy some types of property. Blacks who were unemployed could be arrested. Those who were unable to pay their fines were hired out. In some places, Black workers could not leave the farm without permission. By the beginning of the twentieth century, White Southerners had totally succeeded in reestablishing White supremacy and reducing the Afro-American to the status of a peon. Black hopes that were born during the Civil War had been completely shattered. When the twentieth century opened, Afro-Americans were completely disillusioned and saw little hope for the future. They attempted to solve their problems by migrating North, still in search of the American Dream.

Migration and City Life

After the Civil War, large numbers of Afro-Americans began to migrate to urban areas in the South and to settle in the Southwest. Because of the widespread discrimination they faced in America, some Afro-Americans established all-Black towns. Nearly thirty such towns were established near the turn of the century, including Mound Bayou, Mississippi in 1887 and Langston, Oklahoma in 1891. Many Afro-Americans also wanted to make Oklahoma an all-Black state but this idea never materialized.

While many Afro-Americans settled in the South and Southwest, most who migrated near the turn of the century settled in large cities in the Midwest and East. New York City's Black population doubled between 1900 and 1910. During the same period, Chicago's increased over 30 percent. Afro-Americans migrated to Northern cities in large numbers in the early 1900s because of the severe economic, political, and social conditions in the South. Southern states had stripped Afro-Americans of most of their legal rights. Disatrous floods, the boll weevil, and the sharecropping system combined to make life on the Southern plantations nearly intolerable. The beginning of World War I had nearly stopped immigration from Southern and Eastern Europe. Consequently, Northern manufactures badly needed laborers. Some of them sent agents to the South to lure Blacks to the North. Black newspapers such as the *Chicago Defender* described the North as a land of milk and honey and urged Afro-Americans to leave the South. These forces caused nearly a half million Southern Blacks to head for the North during and immediately after World War I. This mass migration to the North greatly disturbed Southern Whites because it deprived them of a cheap source of labor. They tried to stop Blacks from going North but their efforts were useless.

When the Afro-Americans arrived in midwestern and eastern cities, they had a rude awakening. Life in these cities was extremely difficult. Afro-Americans were the victims of White violence and experienced gross discrimination in housing and employment. Many Blacks who moved into White communities were beaten and their homes were bombed. Because of a variety of techniques used by real estate agents, Blacks were excluded from many neighborhoods. Consequently, the Black urban community grew by leaps and bounds because Afro-Americans were forced to live in areas that were predominantly Black. Also, many Blacks preferred to live in communities that had established Black churches, clubs, and fraternal orders.

As Afro-Americans competed with Whites for housing and jobs, conflict and tension developed between them. Whites were determined to keep Blacks from their jobs and out of their communities. White aggression and violence in the early 1900s led to some of the bloodiest riots that the United States had experienced. One of the worst riots took place in East St. Louis in 1917. The riot was started when a group of Whites fired into a Black neighborhood and Blacks retaliated. Thirty-nine Afro-Americans and nine Whites were killed. During the same year, riots also occurred in Philadelphia and Chester, Pennsylvania. Over twenty riots occurred in cities throughout the United States in 1919. The gifted writer James Weldon Johnson called that summer the "Red Summer" because of the blood that ran in city streets. The most tragic riot that summer occurred in Chicago. The riot started when a Black youth was drowned after being chased by a group of Whites at a segregated beach on Lake Michigan. The riot lasted for almost two weeks. When it ended thirty-eight people had been killed, twenty-three of them Black. More than 1,000 homes were destroyed and 537 people were injured. In 1919 riots also occurred in cities such as Washington, D. C. and Longview, Texas.

World War I

As with other wars, Blacks enthusiastically supported World War I and were impressed with President Wilson's high-sounding rhetoric about fighting the war to "make the world safe for democracy." Afro-Americans took Wilson seriously and joined the armed forces in massive numbers. However, it was not long before they realized that White Americans intended for Blacks to be second-class citizens in the military. The discrimination which Black soldiers experienced during the war was blatant. When the United States first entered the war, no training camps were established for Afro-American soldiers. Many Black professionals, like doctors, were made privates in the army. Most Black soldiers were given noncombatant assignments, although some fought on the battlefield. A tragic incident which took place in Houston, Texas in 1917 symbolized to Afro-Americans more than anything else the status of the Black soldier. When a group of Black soldiers tried to board a segregated street car, a fight took place in which twelve civilians died. Thirteen of the soldiers were sentenced to die and fourteen were sent to prison for life. The fate of these soldiers shocked and dismayed the Afro-American community.

Black Organizations

During these trying times, a number of Black institutions and organizations emerged to help Afro-Americans adjust to city life and to fight racism and discrimination in the courts. W. E. B. DuBois, a militant spokesman for Black rights, and a group of Black intellectuals founded the Niagara Movement in 1905. The men in this movement issued a strong statement denouncing American racism. The Niagara movement was short-lived. However, the National Association for the Advancement of Colored People (NAACP), organized in 1910, was an outgrowth of it. Although most of the officers of the NAACP were White, Black people strongly supported it. The NAACP concentrated on improving the Afro-American's legal status. Under its leadership, the legal status of Blacks greatly improved. A group of social workers founded the National Urban League in 1911 to help Black migrants adjust to city life and to find employment. The Urban League worked against enormous odds because of job discrimination. However, it experienced some gains.

While the NAACP and the National Urban League appealed greatly to middle class and upward mobile Afro-Americans, Marcus Garvey's Universal Negro Improvement Association (UNIA), organized in 1914, was a movement which strongly attracted the

Black poor. Garvey preached Black pride and urged Afro-Americans to return to Africa since they would never have equality in the United States. He also urged Blacks to establish businesses and to improve their own communities. The UNIA operated a number of businesses, including restaurants, grocery stores, and a hotel. Garvey was contemptuous of light-skinned and middle-class Afro-Americans and felt that they wanted to associate with Whites instead of other Blacks. The leading Black spokesmen and organizations were very threatened by Garvey. Partly as a result of their efforts, he was jailed for irregularities in the handling of his Black Star Line. More than any other leader during this period, Garvey helped the lower class Afro-American to feel proud of being Black.

The Harlem Renaissance

During the 1920s and 1930s Afro-American artists, writers, and musicians produced some of their best works. Like their counterparts in the 1960s, they deliberately tried to reflect the Afro-American cultural heritage in their works. They emphasized Black pride and strongly protested against racism and discrimination. Gifted poets such as Claude McKay and Countee Cullen penned angry poems that reflected Black aspirations and frustrations. Other Afro-American writers during this period such as Langston Hughes, Jean Toomer, and James Weldon Johnson wrote outstanding novels. Afro-American musicians further developed blues and jazz. These two types of music became recognized throughout the world.

World War II and Riots

Afro-Americans did not expect World War II to bring them any great gains. Their memories of World War I were still too vivid and poignant. However, the war created additional jobs in the large cities and masses of Southern Blacks migrated during and after the war years. Many Blacks migrated to the West Coast as well as to the North. More than 150,000 Afro-Americans left the South each year between 1940 and 1950.

Black city migrants encountered problems similar to those

experienced by Afro-Americans who had migrated in earlier decades. Segregation in housing was still increasing. Many manufacturers with government contracts to make war-related materials refused to hire Blacks or hired them only for the lowest paying jobs. President Roosevelt refused to take action to stop job discrimination until A. Philip Randolph threatened a massive march on Washington of 100,000 Afro-Americans. To prevent the march, Roosevelt issued an executive order which outlawed discrimination in defense-related jobs and set up a federal committee on fair employment.

Violence and riots also erupted in the cities. The most serious one during this period occurred in Detroit in the summer of 1943. The riot lasted for more than thirty hours. When it was over, thirty-four persons were dead, twenty-five of them Black. During the same summer, riots also took place in Los Angeles and the Harlem district of New York City. These riots, especially the one in Detroit, greatly alarmed American politicians. Mayors in many cities formulated commissions to study the causes of the racial outbreaks and to recommend ways to eliminate their causes.

President Truman

President Harry S. Truman, who won the presidential election in 1948 with heavy Black support, took a number of steps to improve race relations and helped to pave the way for the Black Revolt that reached its height in the 1960s. With the use of executive orders, he desegregated the armed forces and created a Committee on Civil Rights which investigated the condition of the Afro-American. The committee's publication, *To Secure These Rights*, recommended total integration in American society. Truman also ordered industries doing business with the federal government to end discrimination. These measures were mainly symbolic and did not greatly affect the Afro-American's status in the United States. However, they contributed greatly to setting an atmosphere of racial tolerance and to the rising expectations of Afro-Americans.

The Supreme Court

More important than Truman's action in improving race relations during the 1940s and 1950s were the actions of the United

States Supreme Court. During the decades after the Civil War, the Supreme Court had consistently made decisions which denied Afro-Americans civil liberties and legitimized and legalized racist practices. It now began to rule in favor of civil rights. In a series of cases, most of which were led or supported by the NAACP, the Court ruled for greater civil liberties for Afro-Americans, thus reversing its racist tradition. In 1946 the Court ruled against segregation in interstate commerce. It made a negative ruling regarding the restrictive covenants in 1948. In a number of cases related to Afro-Americans attending segregated White universities in the Southern and Border states, it consistently ruled that Black Americans should be provided a higher education equal to that of Whites in their home states. These rulings forced many states to integrate their state universities. However, many of them created "instant" professional schools for Afro-Americans. The landmark decision of this period was the Brown Decision of 1954, which ruled that school segregation is inherently unequal. Perhaps more than any other single event, this decision helped to pave the way for the Black Revolt.

THE BLACK REVOLT

In the 1960s Afro-Americans began a fight for their rights which was unprecedented in our nation's history. However, the Black Revolt of the 1960s was intimately related to the heritage of Black protest in America, marked by the slave rebellions and uprisings. Black Americans have always been angry with White America and have protested in ways that were consistent with the times in which they lived. David Walker, Henry Highland Garnet, and W. E. B. DuBois are a few of the many eminent Afro-Americans who strongly protested against American racism through the years. Men like Martin Luther King, Jr., Stokely Carmichael, and Bobby Seale joined this long family of protest leaders in the 1960s. The Black Protest in the 1960s was unique in our history because the times were different. Black protest tends to reflect the times in which it occurs.

During the late 1940s and 1950s, a number of events occurred which elevated Black people's hopes for a better life in America. These included the actions of President Truman, the Brown Decision of 1954, and the Civil Rights Act of 1957. As Afro-

Americans saw more and more signs indicating that things were getting better, they became increasingly impatient with their caste status. Signs of the Afro-American's second-class status were rampant throughout the South when the Montgomery bus boycott began in 1955. The boycott started when a tired Black seamstress was jailed for taking a seat in the "White" section of a city bus. Montgomery Blacks decided that they had taken enough and that they were going to fight the city's bus company until it eliminated segregation. They began a boycott of the busline that did not end until a federal court outlawed racial segregation on Montgomery buses a year later. Martin Luther King, Jr., the young Black preacher who led the boycott, became America's most influential civil rights leader and remained so until he was assassinated in 1968. Under his leadership and influence, the civil rights movement used direct-action and non-violent tactics to protest racism and discrimination in housing, education, politics, and in other areas.

The Black Revolt actually got underway when four Afro-American students sat down at a segregated lunch counter at a Woolworth's store in Greensboro, North Carolina on February 1, 1960 and refused to leave when they were not served. They had launched the "sit-in" movement. Within a short time the sit-in movement had spread throughout the South and Black college students were desegregating lunch counters and other public accommodation facilities in many cities below the Mason-Dixon line. Black Student activists formed the Student Nonviolent Coordinating Committee (SNCC) in 1960 to coordinate their protest activities.

The student protests stimulated other civil rights groups to become more active. The Congress of Racial Equality (CORE), which had been organized since 1942, sponsored a number of freedom rides to Alabama and Mississippi in 1961 to test interstate transportation laws. The CORE riders were the victims of much hostility and violence. Many of them were beaten and jailed and some of the buses in which they rode were burned. In 1957 King and a group of Black ministers organized the Southern Christian Leadership Conference (SCLC). SCLC trained its volunteers to use civil disobedience tactics and led numerous mass demonstrations. In 1963 King led a demonstration in Birmingham to protest racism and discrimination. The demonstrators were the victims of blatant police violence which was viewed throughout the United States and the world on television. Mass demonstrations culminated in the summer of 1963 when over 200,000 people participated in the March on Washington for Freedom and Jobs.

These demonstrations resulted in some small but significant legal gains for Afro-Americans. The historic March on Washington helped to rally public opinion for support of the Civil Rights Act, which finally passed in 1964 after much filibustering in Congress. A voting rights act was enacted in 1965 after King led demonstrations in Selma, Alabama. As a result of this act, which authorized federal workers to oversee elections in the South, the number of Afro-American voters increased sharply in some Southern states and counties. However, the mass of Afro-Americans remained poor and without political power. By 1965 many young Black leaders, such as Stokely Carmichael and H. Rap Brown, who had been staunch supporters of nonviolent resistance, began to raise serious questions about this approach and to urge for more militant action and different goals.

During a civil rights demonstration in 1966 Carmichael issued a call for "Black Power," and both the phrase and the ideas it signified spread throughout Black America like wildfire. Carmichael had coined a term that described a mood already pervasive within Black America. The concept of Black Power emerged during a time when the Civil Rights movement was losing momentum and when Blacks were becoming increasingly frustrated with the gains they had acquired using civil disobedience tactics. Black Power had different meanings for Whites and Afro-Americans. It meant political power, pride in Blackness, Black control of schools and communities, and Black self-help organizations to most Blacks. To most Whites the concept meant retaliatory violence and "Black racism." Malcolm X candidly articulated the concept to the Black masses. Black organizations such as the Black Panther party, which was organized in Oakland, California in 1966, tried to implement the concept. The Panthers attempted to protect the Black community and organized free lunch programs for Afro-American children. The Nation of Islam (Black Muslims) also reflected the concept in its businesses, farms, schools, and weekly newspaper.

Black frustrations, which reached new highs in the mid- and late 1960s, were manifested in a series of tragic racial rebellions in American cities. Unlike the earlier riots in which Whites attacked Blacks, these rebellions were different in that they involved little contact between White and Black people. Rather, urban Blacks directed their attacks toward the symbols of White society within their communities. They burned buildings owned by absentee landlords and looted stores run by merchants who they believed cheated them. The prestigious Kerner Commission, which was appointed by President Johnson, concluded in 1968 that the riots were caused by the White racism that was endemic in American life. Rebellions occurred in cities from New York to Los Angeles. Two of the most serious took place during the summer of 1967 in Newark and Detroit. Twenty-three people lost their lives in the Newark rebellion; forty-three died in the Detroit outbreak. As in all of the rebellions during the 1960s, most of the victims were Afro-Americans killed by White law officials. The Kerner Commission concluded in its massive report on the rebellions, "Our nation is moving toward two societies, one white, one black—separate and unequal. . . ."[2] Little has been done since the report was issued in 1968 to halt the trends the commission described.

When the 1970s opened, Afro-Americans discovered that the hopes that were born during the 1960s were beginning to fade. The legal gains of the 1960s abruptly ended. A strong reaction against Black demands for civil rights was triggered within the White community. A call for law and order arose. To many White Americans, *law and order* meant an end to Black demands and campus rebellions. Most political leaders, unlike those of the 1960s, did not include civil rights as major parts of their platforms. Candidates who championed law and order were elected mayors of several major American cities. Many White communities in the North strongly resisted efforts to integrate their schools. Anti-Black feelings and attitudes were expressed as opposition to busing. Several congressional anti-busing bills were enacted during the Nixon administration. In some communities violence erupted.

Despite this ominous sociopolitical climate, Afro-Americans continued their historic struggle for liberation in the seventies. Their emphasis shifted from pushing for integration to saving Black institutions, building self-help programs, and improving

2. *Report of the National Advisory Commission on Civil Disorders.* (New York: Bantam Books, 1968), p. 1.

the Black community. As the larger society turned its back on the plight of Blacks in the early seventies, Afro-Americans thought deeply and acted reflectively about their future in America.

Teaching Strategies

To illustrate how content related to Afro-Americans can be used to integrate the curriculum, exemplary strategies are identified for teaching these concepts at the grade levels indicated: tradition (primary grades), Black protest (intermediate and upper grades), and separatism (high school grades).

PRIMARY GRADES

CONCEPT: Tradition

Generalization: Afro-American and African folktales, like all ethnic folktales, reflect the cultural traditions of the people and explain how things in the world began.

1. There are many excellent collections of ethnic folktales that can be used to teach children about the fantasies, hopes, and fears of Third World cultures. One such collection is *Black Folktales* by Julius Lester. Some of the tales in this book are still heard by African children. "The Girl with the Large Eyes," reprinted below from *Black Folktales,* can be used to teach students how some early Africans explained the origin of water lillies. Tell the students what folk tales are and why they are a part of the cultural traditions of ethnic groups. Tell the class the story of "The Girl with the Large Eyes." For best effect, memorize the events in the story and recreate them in your own words.

THE GIRL WITH THE LARGE EYES

Many years ago in a village in Africa, there lived a girl with large eyes. She had the most beautiful eyes of any girl in the village, and whenever one of the young men looked at her as she passed through the marketplace, her gaze was almost more than he could bear.

The summer she was to marry, a drought came upon the region. No rain had fallen for months, and the crops died, the earth changed to dust, and the wells and rivers turned to mudholes. The people grew hungry, and when a man's mind can see nothing except his hunger, he cannot think of marriage, not even to such a one as the girl with the large eyes.

She had little time to think of the wedding that would have been had there been no drought. She had little time to daydream of the hours of happiness she would have been sharing with her new husband. Indeed, she had little time at all, for it was her job each day to find water for her family. That was not easy. She spent the morning going up and down the river bank, scooping what little water she could from the mudholes until she had a pitcher full.

One morning, she walked back and forth along the river bank for a long while, but could find no water. Suddenly, a fish surfaced from the mud and said to her, "Give me your pitcher and I will fill it with water."

She was surprised to hear the fish talk, and a little frightened. But she had found no water that morning, so she handed him the pitcher, and he filled it with cold, clear water. Everyone was surprised when she brought home a pitcher of such clear water, and they wanted to know where she had found it. She smiled with her large eyes, but she said nothing.

The next day she returned to the same place, called the fish, and again he filled her pitcher with cold, clear water. Each day thereafter she returned, and soon she found herself becoming fond of the fish. His skin was the colors of the rainbow and as smooth as the sky on a clear day. His voice was soft and gentle like the cool, clear water he put in her pitcher. And on the seventh day, she let the fish embrace her, and she became his wife.

Her family was quite happy to get the water each day, but they were still very curious to know from where she was getting it. Each day they asked her many questions, but she only smiled at them with her large eyes and said nothing.

The girl's father was a witch doctor, and he feared that the girl had taken up with evil spirits. One day he changed the girl's brother into a fly and told him to sit in the pitcher and find out from where she was getting the water. When she got to the secret place, the brother listened to the girl and the fish and watched them embrace, and he flew quickly home to tell his father what he had heard and seen. When the parents learned that their daughter had married a fish, they were greatly embarrassed and ashamed. If the young men of the village found out, none of them would ever marry her. And if the village found out, the family would be forced to leave in disgrace.

The next morning, the father ordered the girl to stay at home, and the brother took him to the secret place beside the river. They called to the fish, and, when he came up, they killed him and took him home. They flung the fish at the girl's feet and said, "We have brought your husband to you."

The girl looked at them and then at the fish beside her feet, his skin growing dull and cloudy, his colors fading. And her eyes filled with tears.

She picked up the fish and walked to the river, wondering what was to become of the child she was carrying inside her. If her parents had killed her husband, would they not kill her child when it was born?

She walked for many miles, carrying her husband in her arms, until she came to a place where the waters were flowing. She knew that suffering could only be cured by medicine or patience. If neither of those relieved it, suffering would always yield to death.

Calling her husband's name, she waded into the water until it flowed above her head. But as she died, she gave birth to many children, and they still float on the rivers to this day as water lillies.[3]

2. When you have finished telling the story, ask the students these questions:

    a) What happened in the village when the girl with large eyes was to marry?
    b) What was her job each day?
    c) Who filled her pitcher with cold, clear water each day?
    d) How did the girl feel when she first met the fish?
    e) What did the fish look like?

3. From Julius Lester, *Black Folktales* (New York: Grove Press, 1969), pp. 57–61. Reprinted by permission of *Grove Press, Inc.* Copyright © by Julius Lester.

f) Why did the girl marry the fish?
g) How did her family feel about the marriage?
h) What happened to the fish? Why?
i) What happened to the girl? Why?
j) According to this story, why do we have water lillies?
k) Why do you think stories like these were made up and told?

Summarize the lesson by helping the students to understand the purposes of folktales in all cultures.

3. Help the pupils to prepare a dramatization of "The Girl With the Large Eyes." Make sure that each child has a role in the pageant. Most of the students can play village people who have heard that the girl has married a fish. The students might want to invite another class or their parents to see their pageant. Other tales in *Black Folktales*, as well as in other books, can be used to extend this lesson.

INTERMEDIATE AND UPPER GRADES

CONCEPT: Black Protest

Generalization: Afro-Americans have protested against racism and discrimination throughout their history in America. The forms of protest reflected the times in which they occurred.

1. Begin this unit by showing and discussing with the students the film (or a similar one), *Martin Luther King: Montgomery to Memphis*. In the discussion, focus on the reasons why Black protest emerged and the forms which it took during the years covered in the film.

2. Tell the students the story of the slave mutinies that occurred both on the West African coast and in mid-ocean. Herbert Aptheker, *American Negro Slave Revolts*, is a well-researched and highly regarded source of information on slave rebellions. Ask the students to act out, in role-playing situations, the stories they have heard. After the role-playing situations, ask them to hypothesize by responding to the questions below. Write their responses on the board.

a) Why do you think the slaves were captured?
b) Why do you think they started mutinies?
c) Why didn't the mutinies end the slave trade?

Ask these valuing questions:

- a) Do you think that it was right for slaves to be captured? Why or why not?
- b) Do you think that it was right for slaves to rebel? Why or why not?

After the students have responded to these questions, read to them, or ask them to read, selections on the slave trade so that they can test their hypotheses. Two helpful sources are: James A. Banks and Cherry A. Banks, *March Toward Freedom: A History of Black Americans*, 2nd ed., and Edgar A. Toppin, *The Black American in United States History*.

3. Ask three different groups of students to research these three topics:

- a) The Gabriel Prosser revolt of 1800
- b) The Denmark Vesey revolt of 1822
- c) The Nat Turner revolt of 1831

To help them guide their research, ask the groups to focus on these questions:

- a) Where did the revolt occur?
- b) Why did the revolt occur?
- c) Who led the revolt?
- d) Was the revolt successful? Why or why not?
- e) How were the rebels punished? Why were they punished?

Discuss the questions above with the entire class when the groups have presented their research. List the students' responses on the board. Through questioning, help the students to see how the slave insurrections were both alike and different and why, of the three rebellions, only the Turner revolt was successful. After the class discussion, ask each of the groups to plan and present to the class a dramatization showing the sequence of events in the rebellion they studied.

4. Afro-Americans were active in the abolitionary movement and in the Underground Railroad, a loosely organized system which helped many slaves escape to the North and to Canada. Ask individual students to research the lives of and to "become" in a dramatization, the following people:

- a) David Walker

b) Henry Highland Garnet
c) Robert Purvis
d) Samuel Cornish
e) James Forten
f) Frederick Douglass
g) Harriet Tubman

These sources will be especially helpful with this activity:

Russell L. Adams, *Great Negroes Past and Present*, 3rd ed.
Arna Bontemps, *Frederick Douglass*
Ann Petry, *Harriet Tubman: Conductor on the Underground Railroad*
Wilhelmena S. Robinson, *Historical Negro Biographies*
Philip Sterling and Rayford Logan, *Four Took Freedom*

When the dramatizations are presented, discuss these questions with the class:

a) Why did Black Abolitionists oppose slavery? How did their views differ from those of White abolitionists? Why did White abolitionists discriminate against Black abolitionists?

b) What was the Underground Railroad? How did it help slaves escape? Who were some of the outstanding "conductors" on the railroad? What risks did bondsmen take when they escaped? Why did they take them? If you had been a slave, would you have tried to escape? Why or why not?

5. Ask individual students or groups of students to research the following organizations and movements and to describe ways in which they protested racism and discrimination.

a) The Negro Convention movement (1800s)
b) The Niagara Movement (1905)
c) The National Association for the Advancement of Colored People (1910)
d) The National Urban League (1911)
e) The Universal Negro Improvement Association (1914)
f) The Black church in the 1800s

When their research is complete, the students should share it with the class. The class should discuss how these organizations and movements expressed discontent with the Afro-

American's plight, the actions they took to improve it, and the successes and failures they experienced and why.

6. Have the class role-play a civil rights conference in 1966 in which leaders of the organizations listed below debate the future directions of the movement. Each organizational representative should be thoroughly familiar with his organization's philosophical position in 1966. By that year, the Civil Rights movement was becoming increasingly radicalized and deep factions had developed between the various organizations.

   a) Southern Christian Leadership Conference (SCLC)
   b) National Association for the Advancement of Colored People (NAACP)
   c) National Urban League
   d) Congress of Racial Equality (CORE)
   e) Student Nonviolent Coordinating Committee (SNCC)
   f) Black Panther party
   g) Revolutionary Action Movement (RAM)

7. Have the students role-play a meeting of the following people after a serious racial rebellion in a major city in 1967. These people have met to decide what can be done to eliminate the causes of city riots. Ask individual students to play specific roles. To structure this activity more tightly, write a role description for each character on a 3 x 5-inch index card and give the cards to the student role-players.
   Roles:

   a) the mayor of the city
   b) an SCLC spokesperson
   c) an NAACP spokesperson
   d) a National Urban League spokesperson
   e) a CORE spokesperson
   f) a SNCC spokesperson
   g) a Black Panther party spokesperson
   h) a RAM spokesperson
   i) a young man who has participated in a riot

8. To enable the students to summarize this unit and to derive the key generalizations stated above, have them complete the data retrieval chart in Table 7.1.

Valuing Activity

Read the following story to the class and ask the questions that follow.

TRYING TO BUY A HOME IN LAKEWOOD ISLAND

About a year ago, Joan and Henry Green, a young Black couple, moved from the West Coast to a large city in the Midwest. They moved because Henry finished his Ph.D. in chemistry and took a job at a big university in Midwestern City. Since they have been in Midwestern City, the Greens have rented an apartment in the central area of the city. However, they have decided that they want to buy a house. Their apartment has gotten too small for the many books and other things they have accumulated during the year. In addition to wanting more space, they also want a house so that they can get breaks on their income tax which they do not get living in an apartment. The Greens also think that a house will be a good financial investment.

The Greens have decided to move into a suburban community. They want a new house and most of the houses within the city limits are rather old. They also feel that they can get a larger house for their money in the suburbs than in the city. They have looked at several suburban communities and have decided that they like Lakewood Island better than any of the others. Lakewood Island is an all White community, which is made up primarily of lower-middle-class and middle-class residents. There are a few wealthy families in Lakewood Island, but they are the exceptions rather than the rule.

Joan and Henry Green have become very frustrated because of the problems they have experienced trying to buy a home in Lakewood Island. Before they go out to look at a house, they carefully study the newspaper ads. When they arrived at the first house in which they were interested, the owner told them that his house had just been sold. A week later they decided to work with a realtor. When they tried to close the deal on the next house they wanted, the realtor told them that the owner had raised the price three thousand dollars because he had had

Table 7.1
Black Protest: Data Retrieval Chart

Form of Protest, Organization or Movement	Goal of Protests	Ways of Protests	Results of Protests
Slave mutinies			
Slave rebellions (in USA)			
Black abolitionary movement			
Underground Railroad			
Niagara Movement			
NAACP			
National Urban League			
SCLC			

Table 7.1 (Cont.)

CORE					
SNCC					
Black Panther party					
RAM					

the house appraised since he put it on the market and discovered that his selling price was much too low. When the Greens tried to buy a third house in Lakewood Island, the owner told them that he had decided not to sell because he had not gotten the job in another city which he was almost sure that he would get when he put his house up for sale. He explained that the realtor had not removed the ad about his house from the newspaper even though he had told him that he had decided not to sell a week earlier. The realtor the owner had been working with had left the real estate company a few days ago. Henry is very bitter and feels that he and his wife are the victims of racism and discrimination. Joan believes that Henry is paranoid and that they have been the victims of a series of events that could have happened to anyone, regardless of their race.

Questions

1. Do you think that the Greens were discriminated against in Lakewood Island? Why or why not?
2. What should the Greens do? Why?
3. If you were the Greens what would you do? Why?
4. What can the Greens do to determine whether they are victims of discrimination?

HIGH SCHOOL GRADES

CONCEPT: Separatism

Generalization: Black separatist movements emerge when Afro-Americans experience acute discrimination and a heightened sense of racial pride.

1. Either through choice or force, Black separatism has always existed in America. Most of the slave's social life was confined to his or her community. One of the earliest manifestations of Black separatism was the colonization movement led by Afro-Americans. To begin this unit, ask several students to prepare and present research reports on the following topics:

    a) Martin R. Delany
    b) Paul Cuffe

c) The African Civilization Society

When the reports are presented to the class, these questions should be discussed:

a) Why did colonization movements emerge among Afro-Americans?
b) Were these movements popular and successful? Why or why not?
c) Why did back-to-Africa movements fail to appeal to most Afro-Americans?
d) If early Black-led colonization attempts had succeeded, how do you think the subsequent history of Afro-Americans would have differed?

2. Because of discrimination and the need for group solidarity, a number of Black organizations emerged in the 1800s. Ask a group of students to prepare short papers on the following topics and present them to the class in a panel discussion on separate Black institutions in the 1800s.

a) The Black church
b) Black fraternal and self-help organizations
c) Black businesses
d) Black schools and colleges
e) The Negro Convention Movement

Role play a Negro Convention in the 1800s in which the participants draft a position statement stating their major grievances about the plight of Afro-Americans and a plan of action for social change. All of the delegates to the simulated convention must reach agreement on the position statement they prepare. The student roleplayers will need to be thoroughly familiar with the Negro Convention Movement and the various points of view that were presented in the series of Negro Conventions held in the 1800s.

3. The Niagara Movement was a Black protest organization organized in 1905 by W. E. B. DuBois and a group of Black intellectuals. Ask a group of students to prepare a research report on this movement and present it to the class.

Most of the national civil rights organizations in the early 1900s were interracial. Ask the students to do required readings on the history and development of the NAACP and the National

Urban League. When they have completed the readings, they should compare and contrast these two organizations with the Niagara Movement and earlier Black protest movements and organizations such as the Negro Convention Movement. Particular attention should be paid to: (1) reasons why the organizations emerged, (2) who made major policy and held key positions within them, (3) types of problems that arose within the organizations, (4) the major goals of the organizations, and (5) ways in which the organizations succeeded or failed and why. While studying these organizations, the students should compare and contrast the ideas and actions of Booker T. Washington and W. E. B. DuBois. To conclude this activity, ask two students to role-play a debate between Washington and DuBois on the kind of education needed by Afro-Americans. Two excellent references for this last exercise are: Booker T. Washington, *Up from Slavery* and Walter Wilson, ed., *The Selected Writings of W. E. B. DuBois.*

4. Ask a group of students to prepare a panel discussion on the ideas and actions of Marcus Garvey and the Universal Negro Improvement Association. Ask them to focus on these questions:

   a) What social, economic, and political conditions made Garvey's movement particularly appealing to poor Afro-Americans?
   b) How did Garvey's ideas help to improve the poor Blacks' feelings about themselves?
   c) Why was Garvey's back-to-Africa movement unsuccessful?
   d) Why did conflict develop between Garvey and other Black leaders?
   e) Why was Garvey ultimately crushed as a leader?
   f) What was the main significance of Garvey's movement?

   The classic biography of Garvey is E. D. Cronon, *Black Moses.* Another excellent book for this activity is John Henrik Clarke, ed. *Marcus Garvey and the Vision of Africa.*

5. When the Black Revolt emerged in 1960, its major goal was to desegregate public accommodation facilities and other institutions. Action tactics and court battles achieved much de-

segregation. However, by 1965, many Afro-Americans, especially young Black activists, were very disillusioned with the attainments of the movement and realized that integration alone would not eliminate the Afro-American's major social, economic, and political problems. These young activists felt that both the goals and tactics of the movement should be changed. They issued a call for Black Power.

Ask the entire class to read, *Black Power: The Politics of Liberation in America,* by Stokely Carmichael and Charles V. Hamilton. Discuss each of the chapters with the class. These questions and exercises can help to guide class discussion and student research:

a) What does the concept Black Power mean? Does it mean the same things to Afro-Americans and White Americans?

b) Compare and contrast the goals of the Black Power movement and the goals of civil rights organizations like SCLC and the NAACP in the early 1960s.

c) What kinds of economic, political, and social institutions are implied by the concept of Black Power?

d) Compare and contrast the views of these men:

    1) David Walker
    2) Martin R. Delany
    3) Richard Allen
    4) Prentice Hall
    5) Paul Cuffe
    6) Marcus Garvey
    7) W. E. B. DuBois
    8) Stokely Carmichael
    9) Malcolm X
    10) Adam Clayton Powell
    11) Jesse Jackson

6. To conclude this unit, role play a Black Power political convention in the late 1960s in which the delegates formulate a major platform for the improvement of the Afro-American's social, economic, and political conditions. Each student in the class should be a delegate representing a particular group such as the Afro-American Educators Association and the Black Panther party. An alternative plan would be to ask

each student to represent a well-known Afro-American in the 1960s, such as Stokely Carmichael, H. Rap Brown, Angela Davis, and Adam Clayton Powell. Each student role-player should be thoroughly aquainted with the views and philosophy of the organization or groups he or she represents. The convention delegates must approve by three-fourths majority vote the platform that it adopts. The platform should be written up and duplicated.

Materials and Resources

REFERENCES FOR THE TEACHER
Especially Recommended

Banks, James A. and Jean D. Grambs, eds. *Black Self-Concept: Implications for Education and Social Science.* New York: McGraw-Hill, 1972.

This book includes a collection of original papers that explore various aspects of the development of Black children and youths.

Banks, James A. *Teaching the Black Experience: Methods and Materials.* Belmont, Calif.: Fearon, 1970.

This book deals with ways to teach Black studies units and how to integrate ethnic content into the regular curriculum. It includes teaching strategies and an annotated bibliography.

Blassingame, John W. *The Slave Community.* New York: Oxford University Press, 1972.

A pioneering and lucidly written study focusing on the way in which slavery was viewed by the slaves. This book is destined to become an American history classic.

Clark, John Henrik, ed. (with the assistance of Amy Jacques Garvey) *Marcus Garvey and the Vision of Africa.* New York: Vintage Books, 1974.

A comprehensive and thought provoking collection of essays and writings, reprinted from many sources, by and about Garvey.

Fishel, Leslie H. and Benjamin Quarles, eds. *The Black American:* A *Documentary History.* Rev. ed. Glenview, Ill.: Scott, Foresman, 1970.

An extremely comprehensive collection of documents with informed and extensive essays by the editors.

Franklin, John Hope. *From Slavery to Freedom: A History of Negro Americans.* New York: Vintage Books, 1969.

The best general history of Afro-Americans. It is well-researched and clearly written.

Frazier, Thomas R., ed. *Afro-American History: Primary Sources.* New York: Harcourt, Brace and World, 1970.

An excellent documentary history containing Black views of American history and helpful commentaries by the editor.

Meier, August and Elliott Rudwick. *From Plantation to Ghetto.* Rev. ed. New York: Hill and Wang, 1970.

An insightful and well-written interpretative history of Afro-Americans that highlights the role of the Blacks in shaping their destiny in America. A good introductory source.

Other References

Baker, Augusta. *The Black Experience in Children's Books.* New York The Public Library, 1971.

A useful and comprehensive guide to books for young readers.

Baldwin, James. *The Fire Next Time.* New York: Dell, 1963.

This book contains a collection of perceptive, courageous, and widely acclaimed essays by one of the most distinguished writers of this century.

Bennett, Lerone, Jr. *Before the Mayflower: A History of the Negro in America 1619–1964.* Baltimore: Penguin Books, 1964.

A popular and highly readable book presenting novel interpretations of the role of Blacks in America.

Bontemps, Arna, ed. *American Negro Poetry.* New York: Hill and Wang, 1963.

Many immortal poems by Langston Hughes and other gifted poets are in this immensely popular book. The newer Black poets, however, are not represented.

Bracey, John H., August Meier, and Elliott Rudwick, eds. *The Afro-Americans: Selected Documents.* Boston: Allyn and Bacon, 1972.

A useful and comprehensive collection of documents.

Carmichael, Stokely and Charles V. Hamilton. *Black Power: The Politics of Liberation in America.* New York: Vintage Books, 1967.

This book is imperative for readers who want a candid and brilliant explication of the concept of Black Power.

Clark, Kenneth B. *Dark Ghetto: Dilemmas of Social Power.* New York: Harper and Row, 1965.

In one of the most widely acclaimed books of recent times, Clark poignantly and sensitively describes the devastating effects the Black inner-city has on its victims.

Drimmer, Melvin, ed. *Black History: A Reappraisal.* Garden City, N. Y.: Doubleday, 1969.

This deservedly popular documentary history of Afro-Americans contains excellent and informative commentaries by the editor.

Fanon, Frantz. *The Wretched of the Earth.* New York: Grove Press, 1963.

A brilliant and courageous book by a late Black psychiatrist that will help teachers understand the cry among many Black liberation leaders for a Third World Revolution.

Grambs, Jean D. and John C. Carr, eds. *Black Image: Education Copes with Color.* Dubuque, Iowa: Wm. C. Brown, 1972.

This book includes essays on the treatment of Afro-Americans in teaching materials as well as an excellent bibliography of books for young people.

Jackson, George. *Soledad Brother: The Prison Letters of George Jackson.* New York: Bantam Books, 1970.

These brilliant and cogent letters reveal a young imprisoned Black man's attempt to understand an oppressive and dehumanized world. This is a courageous and poignant book.

Katz, William Loren. *Teachers' Guide to American Negro History.* Rev. ed. Chicago: Quadrangle Books, 1971.

This book contains outlines of Black history, chronologies, and many bibliographies.

King, Woodie and Ron Milner, eds. *Black Drama Anthology.* New York: Signet, 1961.

This anthology contains twenty-three plays by some of America's most gifted dramatists.

Litwack, Leon F. *North of Slavery: The Negro in the Free States, 1790–1860.* Chicago: University of Chicago Press, 1961.

An informed and well-researched study of nonslave Northern Blacks in the late eighteenth and nineteenth centuries. This book is well-written and copiously documented.

The Autobiography of Malcolm X, with the assistance of Alex Haley. New York: Grove, 1964.

A brilliant and powerful book about the emergence of a leader and a social movement.

Miller, Elizabeth W., compiler. *The Negro in America: A Bibliography.* Cambridge, Mass: Harvard University Press, 1968.

An excellent guide to books about Afro-Americans arranged by topics. Revised periodically.

Pinkney, Alphonso. *Black Americans.* Englewood Cliffs, N. J.: Prentice-Hall, 1969.

A valuable and readable sociological and historical overview of the Afro-American.

Ploski, Harry A. and Ernest Kaiser, eds. *Afro-USA: A Reference Work on the Black Experience.* New York: Bellweather Publishing Co., 1971.

This "almanac" on the Black experience contains much useful information. However, despite its 1110 pages, it has serious informational gaps.

Quarles, Benjamin. *The Negro in the Making of America.* Rev. ed. New York: Collier, 1969.

A comprehensive and readable but conservative general history of Afro-Americans. A useful introductory book.

Randall, Dudley, ed. *The Black Poets.* New York: Bantam Books, 1971.

An excellent anthology which includes the best of the classics and a rich collection of poems written during the 1960s.

Redding, Saunders. *They Came in Chains.* Rev. ed. Philadelphia: Lippincott, 1973.

An interesting history of Afro-Americans written in a literary, popular style. Unfortunately, the book contains some insensitive statements and interpretations about American Indians.

Robinson, Wilhelmena S. *Historical Negro Biographies.* International Library of Negro Life and History, edited by Charles H. Wesley. New York: Publishers Company, 1967.

An extremely useful source for biographical information that can be profitably read by upper grade students and used as a resource by teachers.

Stone, Chuck. *Black Political Power in America.* Rev. ed. New York: Delta, 1970.

A useful book discussing various aspects of Black politics and the future of Black political power.

Williams, John A. *The Man Who Cried I Am.* New York: New American Library, 1967.

The author unfolds a frightening but credible tale of a master plot designed to eliminate Blacks in America. The story focuses on the protagonist's discovery of the plot and his attempt to disclose it.

Wilson, Walter, ed. *The Selected Writings of W. E. B. DuBois.* New York: New American Library, 1970.

This careful anthology of the selected writings of DuBois contains examples of all the types of work written by this Olympian American. The book includes a selected bibliography of DuBois's writings and a chronology of the most significant events in his amazing life.

Woodson, Carter G. and Charles H. Wesley. *The Negro in Our History.* 10th ed. Washington, D. C.: Associated Publishers, 1962.

A pioneering work by two eminent Afro-American historians.

Yette, Samuel F. *The Choice: The Issue of Black Survival.* New York: Berkeley Medallion Books, 1971.

In this alarming and disturbing book, Yette argues that the extermination of the Blacks in America is a genuine possibility. His argument is cogent and thought-provoking.

BOOKS FOR STUDENTS

Adams, Russell L. *Great Negroes Past and Present.* 3rd ed. Chicago: Afro-Am Publishing Co., 1969.

A rich collection of biographies for teacher reference and for students in the middle and upper grades. Marketed with companion wall photographs. (Upper)

Adoff, Arnold. *Black Is Brown Is Tan.* New York: Harper and Row, 1973.

A delightful story about the life of two children in an interracial family. (Primary)

―――, ed. *The Poetry of Black America: Anthology of the 20th Century.* New York: Harper and Row, 1973.

A comprehensive collection of poems written by noted Black authors. (All Levels)

Angelou, Maya. *I Know Why the Caged Bird Sings.* New York: Random House, 1970.

A powerful and beautiful account of the author's early years. The teacher should read this book before assigning it to students. The sequel to this book is *Gather Together in My Name.* New York: Random House, 1974. (High School)

Bambara, Toni Cade, ed. *Tales and Stories for Black Folks.* Garden City, N. Y.: Doubleday, 1971.

A good collection of short stories dealing with many subjects. (Upper)

Banks, James A. and Cherry A. Banks. *March Toward Freedom: A History of Black Americans.* 2nd ed. Belmont, Calif.: Fearon, 1974.

An illustrated history of Black Americans written especially for teenagers. (Intermediate)

Bontemps, Arna. *Frederick Douglass.* New York: Alfred A. Knopf, 1959.

A well-written and sensitive account of the life of the great abolitionist. (Primary)

―――― . *Story of the Negro.* New York: Alfred A. Knopf, 1948.

A very readable and interesting interpretative history of Black Americans. (Intermediate)

Brooks, Gwendolyn. *Bronzeville Boy and Girls.* New York: Harper and Row, 1956.

An excellent collection of poems about children in the inner-city. This book includes happy, sad, as well as thoughful reflections by urban children revealing their feelings and emotions. (Primary)

Bryan, Ashley. *The Ox of the Wonderful Horns and Other African Folktales.* New York: Antheneum, 1971.

A collection of five African folktales that are beautifully illustrated. (All Levels)

Chittenden, Elizabeth F. *Profiles in Black and White: Stories of Men and Women Who Fought Against Slavery.* New York: Charles Scribner's Sons, 1973.

An excellent collection of ten biographies of men and women who took courageous stands against slavery. The accounts are interesting and well written. (Upper)

Clifton, Lucille. *All Us Cross the Water.* New York: Holt, 1973.

A thought-provoking book about the origin of Afro-Americans. Young Ujamaa's search for the homeland of his ancestors raises many questions that can stimulate class discussion. This book, illustrated by John Steptoe, is written in Black English. (Primary)

―――― . *Good Says Jerome.* New York: Dutton, 1973.

A delightful story about a young boy who is always asking questions. Beautifully illustrated. (Primary)

―――― . *The Black BC's.* New York: Dutton, 1970.

With prose and poetry, the author uses the alphabet to tell how Afro-Americans have contributed to American life. Illustrated. (Intermediate)

―――― . *The Boy Who Didn't Believe in Spring.* New York: Dutton, 1973.

A delightfully interesting book about two boys and their search for spring. Excellent illustrations. (Primary)

Cronon, E. D. *Black Moses.* Madison: University of Wisconsin Press, 1955.

The pioneering study of Garvey. (High School)

Davidson, Basil. *A Guide to African History.* Garden City, N. Y.: Doubleday, 1965.

An excellent general history of Africa from its beginnings to modern times. (Intermediate)

Dietz, Betty Warner and Michael Babatunde Olatunji. *Musical Instruments of Africa*. New York: John Day, 1965.

A well-illustrated book discussing some musical instruments from Africa south of the Sahara. (All Levels)

Drisko, Carol F. and Edgar A. Toppin. *The Unfinished March*. Garden City, N. Y.: Doubleday, 1967.

An interesting and well-written account of the period from Reconstruction to World War I. (Intermediate)

Editors of Ebony. *The Ebony Handbook*. Chicago: Johnson Publishing Co., 1971.

A useful reference which includes statistics and information on diverse aspects of Afro-American life. (High Schcool)

————. *Ebony Pictorial History of Black America*, 4 vols. Chicago: Johnson Publishing Co., 1973.

A useful general survey of the Black experience that is profusely illustrated with photographs and drawings. Titles in the series are: *African Past to Civil War; Reconstruction to Supreme Court Decision 1954; Civil Rights Movement to Black Revolution; The 1973 Year Book*. (Upper)

Fall, Thomas. *Canalboat to Freedom*. New York: Dial, 1966.

An exciting tale of the Underground Railroad and those who made it work. (Upper)

Feelings, Tom. *Black Pilgrimage*. New York: Lothrup, Lee and Shepard, 1972.

A moving autobiography told with words and beautiful drawings. (Primary)

Folsom, Franklin. *The Life and Legend of George McJunkin: Black Cowboy*. New York: Thomas Nelson, 1973.

An interesting biography of a man whose curiosity led to the discovery of the Folsom point, an important archeological find. (Intermediate)

Fox, Paula. *The Slave Dancer*. Scarsdale, N. Y.: Bradbury Press, 1973.

Jessie Bollier is kidnapped from his home in New Orleans, taken aboard a slave ship, and forced to play his fife. This story describes his experiences and the horrors he encountered on the ship. Winner of the Newbery Medal. (Intermediate)

Gaines, Ernest J. *The Autobiography of Miss Jane Pittman*. New York: Bantam Books, 1971.

An excellent and moving novel about strength and dignity in the face of terror and tragedy. The life of Miss Jane Pittman is traced from slavery to the Civil Rights era. (High School)

Giovanni, Nikki. *Ego-Tripping and Other Poems for Young People.* New York: Lawrence Hill, 1973.

A beautiful collection of poems that capture the spirit of being Black in today's world. The poems deal with a variety of emotions and people. Well illustrated. (Upper)

————. *Spin A Soft Black Song: Poems for Children.* New York: Hill and Wang, 1971.

A beautiful collection of poems about Black life for young readers by the gifted Black poet. (Primary)

Glasser, Barbara and Ellen Blustein. *Bongo Bradley.* New York: Hawthorn Books, 1973.

Bradley Clark goes to the South to visit his father's family. He learns about life in the South and discovers how little he knows about the farm. (Intermediate)

Graham, Lorenz. *Hongry Catch the Foolish Boy.* New York: Crowell, 1946.

An African folktale about a foolish boy who leaves home, loses all of his money, and then returns. Written in Black English. (Intermediate)

————. *Whose Town?* New York: Thomas Y. Crowell, 1969.

The third and best story in a trilogy about a Southern Black family that migrates to the North. The Williams family confront many problems in Northtown which they did not expect. The other books in the trilogy are *Southtown* (Follett, 1958), and *Northtown* (Crowell, 1965). (Intermediate)

Green, Robert L. *Daring Black Leaders.* Milwaukee: Franklin Publishers, 1973.

An exciting and informative package of materials. It contains thirty biographies of contemporary Black leaders and sixteen cassettes that provide direct readings of the biographies. This set is well researched and is stimulating reading for students. (Upper)

Greene, Robert Ewell, *Black Defenders of America 1775–1973: A Reference and Pictorial History* (Chicago: Johnson Publishing Co., 1974)

An excellent reference on Blacks who have served in the military. (High School)

Greenfield, Eloise. *Rosa Parks.* New York: Crowell, 1973.

A short biography of the "Mother of the Civil Rights Movement." The story is well written and depicts a strong, committed woman who is dedicated to human justice. Recipient of the first Carter G. Woodson Book Award (1974). (Primary)

Harrison, Deloris, ed. *We Shall Live in Peace: The Teachings of Martin Luther King, Jr.* New York: Hawthorn Books, 1968.

Many of King's most important writings are reprinted in this anthology, which is edited for young readers. (Intermediate)

Hunter, Kristin. *Guests in the Promised Land.* New York: Scribner's, 1968.

A powerful collection of short stories about life in the inner-city. The characters are convincing and will evoke strong emotions in the reader. A prize-winning book. (Upper)

————. *The Soul Brothers and Sister Lou.* New York: Scribner's, 1969.

A powerful story about life in the inner-city. The book has strong, memorable characters. It can be used to teach about family life in Black urban communities. (Intermediate)

Jackson, Florence. *The Black Man in America: 1877–1905.* New York: Franklin Watts, 1973.

An excellent history of Black Americans from the Reconstruction era to the turn of the century. A number of eminent men and women are discussed. (Intermediate)

Jackson, Jesse and Elaine Landau. *Black in America: A Fight for Freedom.* New York: Julian Messner, 1973.

A general history of Afro-Americans that is written from a Black perspective. (Intermediate)

Johnston, Johanna. *Paul Cuffe: America's First Black Captain.* New York: Dodd, Mead, 1970.

A good biography of a free Black living in the Massachusetts Bay Colony. (Intermediate)

Jordan, June. *Dry Victories.* New York: Holt, 1972.

Two Afro-American children discuss the empty victories Blacks experienced during Reconstruction and the Black Revolt of the 1960s. Beautifully illustrated. An excellent book. (Upper)

———— . *Fannie Lou Hammer.* New York: Crowell, 1972.

An inspirational and well-written story of a courageous Black woman. (Intermediate)

Katz, William Loren. *The Black West: A Documentary and Pictorial History.* Rev. ed. Garden City: Doubleday, 1971.

A well-researched account of Blacks in the West. This illustrated book contains much information which is generally unknown. (Upper)

Kromer, Helen. *The Amistad Revolt: The Slave Uprising Aboard the Spanish Schooner.* New York: Franklin Watts, 1973.

The author recounts the exciting story of one of the most well-known slave revolts. (Upper)

Latham, Frank B. *The Dred Scott Decision: March 6, 1857.* New York: Franklin Watts, 1968.

The major events which led up to the Dred Scott Decision, as well as those which took place after it, are discussed in this carefully researched book. (Upper)

Lester, Julius. *Black Folktales.* New York: Grove Press, 1969.

An outstanding and excellently written collection of African and Afro-American tales. Highly recommended. (All Levels)

————. *To Be a Slave.* New York: Dial, 1969.

A distinguished collection of documents dictated by former slaves with helpful commentaries by the author. A Newbery Honor book. Highly recommended. (Upper)

McGovern, Ann. *Black is Beautiful.* New York: Scholastic, 1969.

A beautiful collection of black and white photographs and the text show the beauty of Blackness. (Primary)

Mathis, Sharon Bell. *Listen for the Fig Tree.* New York: Viking Press, 1974.

A good story about a young girl's struggles after the death of her father. (Upper)

Mead, Margaret and James Baldwin. *A Rap On Race.* New York: Dell, 1971.

In this unusual and insightful book, Baldwin rises to his usual brilliance. He speaks from deep personal experiences, and expresses pain, despair, and rage about being Black in America. Mead epitomizes the White liberal and envisions a humane America. (High School)

Meltzer, Milton, ed. *In Their Own Words: A History of the American Negro, 1619–1865.* New York: Crowell, 1964.

A useful documentary history of Afro-Americans. This book is one in a series of three. The volumes cover various historical periods. (Upper)

Meltzer, Milton and August Meier. *Time of Trial, Time of Hope: The Negro in America: 1919 to 1941.* Garden City: Doubleday, 1966.

Black migrations to the North and the problems Afro-Americans faced are highlighted in this useful period history. (Intermediate)

Meriwether, Louise. *Don't Ride the Bus on Monday: The Rosa Parks Story.* Englewood Cliffs, N. J.: Prentice-Hall, 1973.

A fairly good account of one of the stars in the civil rights drama. (Intermediate)

Mitchison, Naomi. *African Heroes.* New York: Farrar, Straus and Giroux, 1968.

Eleven African heroes south of the Sahara are discussed. These stories originated in the African oral tradition. (High School)

Petry, Ann. *Harriet Tubman: Conductor on the Underground Railroad.* New York: Crowell, 1955.

An extremely well done life story. (Intermediate)

Radford, Ruby L. *Mary McLeod Bethune.* New York: Putnam's, 1973.

A touching and well-written biography of the great Afro-American educator and leader. (Intermediate)

Shearer, John. *I Wish I had An Afro.* New York: Cowles Books Co., 1970.

An intriguing story of a young man who is becoming aware of his Blackness and wants an Afro to symbolize his awareness. (Upper)

Steptoe, John. *Birthday.* New York: Holt, 1972.

A thought-provoking book about a young boy who celebrates his birthday in an all-Black town called Yoruba. The book emphasizes the positiveness of Blackness. (Primary)

———. *My Special Best Words.* New York: Viking Press, 1974.

This book about the affection of a father and his two children deals honestly with life and natural functions, such as toilet training and runny noses. Dramatically and unusually illustrated. Because of its candor and unusual illustrations, this book will most likely evoke controversy. (Intermediate)

Sterling, Philip and Rayford Logan. *Four Took Freedom.* Garden City, N. Y.: Doubleday, 1967.

Lucid accounts of the lives of Harriet Tubman, Frederick Douglass, Robert Smalls, and Blanche K. Bruce. (Intermediate)

Stevenson, Janet. *The Montgomery Bus Boycott: December, 1955.* New York: Franklin Watts, 1971.

A good account of the events that surrounded this historic boycott. (Intermediate)

Toppin, Edgar A. *The Black American in United States History.* Boston: Allyn and Bacon, 1973.

An excellent illustrated history for high school students. (High School)

Weik, Mary Hays. *The Jazz Man.* New York: Atheneum, 1968.

A deeply moving and poignant story about a lonely and lamed boy in the inner-city. Illustrated. (Intermediate)

White, Ann Terry. *North to Liberty: The Story of the Underground Railroad.* Champaign, Ill.: Garrard, 1972.

An interesting narrative about the Underground Railroad. (Intermediate)

Udry, Janice May. *What Mary Jo Shared.* New York: Scholastic, 1966.

A delightful story about a shy young girl who has a hard time deciding what she will share with her classmates. Her final decision delights and surprises the reader. Illustrated. (Intermediate)

Washington, Booker T. *Up from Slavery.* Garden City, N. Y.: Doubleday, 1963.

A pioneering, inspiring, and well-written autobiography by the eminent Afro-American leader and educator. (High School)

8

Mexican Americans:
Concepts, Strategies,
and Materials

*The current revolt of Chicanos against the Anglo system of life
and thought is essentially a prophetic statement of purpose. We
Chicanos are convinced that it is our destiny to carry out a major
role in the coming decades . . . Los Chicanos hope to participate
in the creation of a new world. . . . .*

Armando B. Rendon

Introduction

Mexican Americans are the second largest ethnic minority group
in the United States. The census indicated that there were
5,073,000 Mexican Americans in the United States in 1970. Some
writers believe that this figure is inaccurate and that there were
probably 10 to 12 million Chicanos in the United States in 1970.
Mexican Americans are similar in many ways to the other ethnic
groups discussed in this book. However, their history and current plight are in some ways unique. Mexican Americans are
highly concentrated in the five Southwestern states. Nearly 80
percent of them lived in California, Texas, New Mexico, Arizona,
and Colorado in 1970. California had the largest number

(2,200,000), followed by Texas (1,630,000). Significant numbers also lived in midwestern industrial cities such as Chicago; Gary, Indiana; and Milwaukee, Wisconsin. However, Mexican-American communities existed throughout the United States, including in the East and in the Northern Pacific Rockies.

Mexican Americans were in the land that is now the United States before all other American groups except the American Indian. Their ancestors had settled in the region which is now the Southwestern United States before Jamestown was settled by the English colonists in 1607. They became an ethnic minority when their territory was conquered by Anglo-Americans during the Mexican-American War, which lasted from 1846 to 1848. Their civic and cultural rights were guaranteed by the Treaty of Guadalupe Hidalgo, the treaty ending the war in 1848. In the decades after 1848, the treaty was blatantly disregarded and Mexican Americans were made second-class citizens by Anglo-Americans who migrated and settled in the Southwest. There were about 80,000 Mexicans living in the territory Mexico ceded to the United States in 1848. Most modern Mexican-American communities were formed by Mexican immigrants who came to the United States after 1910. The study of the conquest and subjugation of Mexican Americans and their resistance, which has intensified since the 1960s, is necessary to understand the nature of American society and the genesis of the ethnic conflict endemic in American life.

Mexican Americans: Historical Perspective

Important Dates

1519	Hernán Cortés, the Spanish conquistador, and a group of Spaniards arrived in the region which is now Mexico.
1521	Cortés, with the support of thousands of Indian allies, seized the Aztec capital city, Tenochtitlán, and the empire fell.
1810	On September 16, 1810 Father Miguel Hidalgo sounded a battle cry known as the *El Grito de Dolores*, which signaled the begin-

Important Dates cont.

	ning of the Mexican revolutionary era that eventually resulted in Mexican independence from Spain in 1821.
1836	Mexico's President Santa Anna and his troops defeated the rebelling Texans at the Alamo. Six weeks later Santa Anna was defeated by Sam Houston and his Texan troops at San Jacinto. Texas declared itself independent and formed the Lone Star Republic.
1845	The United States annexed Texas, which had declared itself independent from Mexico in 1836. This was one of the key events leading to the Mexican-American War.
1846	On May 13, 1846, the United States declared war on Mexico and the Mexican-American War began. The United States invaded New Mexico and California.
1848	The United States and Mexico signed the Treaty of Guadalupe Hidalgo which ended the Mexican-American War. Mexico lost nearly one-third of its territory, and the United States acquired most of the territory that makes up the Southwestern states.
1853	James Gadsden, representing the United States, obtained from Mexico, through purchase, 45,532 square miles of additional land which was rich in copper and opened a railroad route.
1859	Juan N. Cortina, who became a United States citizen under the privisions of the Treaty of Guadalupe Hidalgo, led a series of rebellions against Anglo-Americans in the Lower Rio Grande Valley of South Texas.
1862	On May 5, 1862, French forces that had invaded Mexico were defeated at Pueblo by Mexican forces led by Ignacio Zaragosa, a Texas Chicano. May 5 (*Cinco de Mayo*) is an important Mexican holiday also observed by Mexican Americans.

Important Dates cont.

1878　　　The El Paso Salt War took place, in which Mexicans organized and rebelled against Anglos because of a dispute over rights to salt beds.

1910　　　A revolution starting in Mexico caused many Mexican peasants to immigrate to the United States looking for jobs. Other immigrants came to escape political turmoil and persecution.

1924　　　Congress established the Border Patrol to monitor traffic across the Mexican-United States border. This border had previously been primarily "free."

1928　　　The League of United Latin American Citizens was formed in Harlingen, Texas. Like other earlier Mexican-American civil rights organizations, the League stressed United States citizenship and assimilation.

1929–35　Thousands of Mexican immigrants were repatriated to Mexico, most without legal proceedings.

1942　　　The United States and Mexico made an agreement that authorized Mexican immigrants to work temporarily in the United States. This project is known as the *bracero* program.

1943　　　The anti-Mexican "zoot-suit" riots took place in Los Angeles during the summer of 1943.

1951　　　The United States and Mexico made a Migratory Labor Agreement (Public Law 78), which established a new *bracero* program.

1954　　　The United States Immigration and Naturalization Service began "Operation Wetback," a massive program to deport illegal Mexican immigrants to Mexico.

1965　　　A grape strike led by Cesar Chavez and the National Farm Workers Association began in Delano, California, a town in the San Joaquin Valley.

　　　　　Rodolfo "Corky" Gonzales formed the Crusade for Justice in Denver. This important

Important Dates cont.

civil rights organiation epitomized the Chicano movement that emerged in the 1960s.
The United States Congress passed an immigration act limiting the number of Mexican immigrants to the United States to 20,000 annually.

1970   La Raza Unida was organized by Jose Angel Gutierrez in Crystal City, Texas.

The Spanish Conquest

Nearly 25 million Indians were living in the Western Hemisphere when the Spanish Conquistadores arrived there in 1517. There were a wide variety of Indian cultures and groups in the region which is now Mexico. The Mayas and the Aztecs developed some of the most complex societies in the region. The Mayas' domestication and cultivation of corn greatly influenced agriculture in the Americas. A powerful military state and the most impressive contemporary cities were built by the Aztecs. Tenochtitlán, their capital city, has been called "the most modern city in the world" at the time of the Spanish conquest.[1]

Hernán Cortés, a Spanish explorer, led an expedition into Mexico in 1519. Before he reached the Aztec capital, he gained military help from other Indian civilizations by negotiating and conquering. After a two-year intermittent struggle with the Aztecs, Cortés finally seized Tenochtitlán on August 13, 1521, and the Aztec empire fell. Despite the Aztecs' military strength, the Spaniards were able to defeat them because they were helped by other Indian nations and had superior firearms and horses. Although the Spaniards were eventually successful in their conquest of much of the land stretching from Southern South America to most of what is today the United States Southwest, this task was not easily accomplished. The Indians living in these areas fought hard to maintain their power and started many rebellions after the Spanish conquest. The Spaniards defeated most Indian groups only gradually and with the loss of many of their men.

1. Jack D. Forbes, *Mexican-Americans: A Handbook for Educators* (Washington, D.C.: U.S. Government Printing Office, no date), p. 3.

The Spanish settlements in Mexico and the Southwestern United States differed in several significant ways from the English colonies in the Eastern parts of North America. Most of the English colonists considered themselves permanent settlers in North America. Consequently, they usually brought their families. Most of the Spanish settlers in the Americas were adventurous men who came to the Americas hoping to find gold and other treasures. They rarely brought their wives. Many more settlers came from England than Spain. It is estimated that about 300,000 Spaniards came to the Americas during three centuries of settlement.[2]

These unique characteristics of the Spanish settlers significantly influenced the physical and cultural development of the new "race" that was formed in the Americas. Because the Spaniards brought few women with them, most had Indian concubines or wives. The offsprings of these ethnically mixed unions were known as *mestizos*. The biological and cultural heritage of the Mexican American includes African strains although it is primarily Spanish-Indian. When they came to the Americas, the Spaniards had had long contact with a group of Africans called the Moors. Moors came with the Conquistadores to the Americas. Estevan is perhaps the most famous. Nearly 200,000 African slaves were also brought to Mexico. They were so thoroughly mixed with the Spaniards and Indians by 1900 that they were no longer distinguishable as a separate racial group.[3] The Mexican's biological heritage is much more Indian than Spanish. Although the Spaniards imposed their culture and religion on the Indian nations, many Indian culture elements survived and highly influenced the development of Mexican culture. Thus both the physical traits and culture of the Mexican Americans are primarily blends of Spanish and Indian influences. "To attempt to unravel any single strand from this pattern and label it 'Spanish' is to do a serious injustice to the Mexican and Indians . . . through whom . . . Spanish cultural influences survived. . . ."[4]

2. Carey McWilliams, *North from Mexico: The Spanish-Speaking People of the United States* (New York: Greenwood Press, 1968), p. 20.

3. John Hope Franklin, *From Slavery to Freedom: A History of Negro Americans,* 3rd Edition (New York: Vintage, 1967), pp. 113–14.

4. McWilliams, *North from Mexico,* p. 34.

The Texas Revolt

At the begining of the nineteenth century, Mexico was in a perpetual state of political turmoil. Greatly concerned about the waning population in Texas, the Spanish and later the Mexican government encouraged Anglo-Americans to settle there by making *empresario* land grants. The Spanish government gave an *empresario* grant to Moses Austin in 1821. His son Stephen received a reconfirmation of the original grant from the Mexican government in 1823. Because Texas was geographically close to the United States, it attracted a large number of Anglo immigrants. They were interested in Texas's rich resources and open territory. Most of the Anglo settlers in Texas failed to keep the terms of their land-grant agreements with the Mexican government, such as becoming loyal citizens and Catholics. They were not interested in Mexican culture but wanted to establish Anglo institutions in the Mexican province and to control it.

Texas Mexicans were angry about President Santa Anna's attempts to centralize his power over the northern Mexican territories. The Anglo immigrants in Texas added fuel to the fire because of their disdain for the Mexican government. By permitting and encouraging United States citizens to settle in sparsely inhabited Texas, Mexico had inadvertently set the stage for revolt in the province and its eventual loss to the United States.

By the time that Mexico realized that Anglo-Mexicans were gaining control in Texas and took steps to undermine their power, antigovernment forces in Texas had already been firmly established. The Mexican government attempted to undermine Anglo power in Texas by abolishing slavery there in 1829, by restricting Anglo immigration into Texas, and by enforcing custom regulations at the Texas-United States border. These actions greatly angered the Texas Mexicans and evoked attacks against the central government. Mexican federal troops arrived in Texas in 1835 after Texas proclaimed itself "conditionally independent." These troops were badly defeated. In 1836, President Santa Anna led several thousand Mexican troops into Texas. His army killed 187 Texans at a Franciscan mission in San Antonio called the Alamo. The Mexican army had another victory at Goliad, but experienced a crushing defeat by Sam Houston and his "Remember the Alamo!" shouting Texas troops at San Jacinto on April 21. After this victory, Texas sought world recognition of its independence and started the chain of events which eventually led to its annexation to the United States in 1845.

The Mexican-American War

When the Mexican government took serious steps to halt Anglo immigration to the Southwest, the United States had begun, in the name of Manifest Destiny, an aggressive campaign to annex all of Mexico's northern territories. She began a military conquest when negotiations failed. The United States angered Mexico by annexing Texas in 1845. She declared war on Mexico in 1846 when a boundary dispute developed between the two nations. The United States defeated Mexico within two years and occupied subdued California and New Mexico by the end of 1846. Mexico's northern provinces had little allegiance to the nation's capital. Anglo settlers who had a strong toehold in Mexican provinces such as California and New Mexico actively sought Mexico's defeat. Mexico was also greatly weakened by internal strife and her inability to rally internal support for the war.

The Treaty of Guadalupe Hidalgo

After Mexico was defeated by the United States, representatives of the two nations signed a treaty on February 2, 1848, in the Mexican village of Guadalupe Hidalgo. The United States forced Mexico to surrender its claim to Texas, which the United States had annexed in 1845, and to cede about one-third of its territory to the United States. This chunk of land included most of the territory now making up the states of the United States Southwest, including Arizona, California, New Mexico, Utah, Nevada, and a section of Colorado. The United States paid Mexico $15 million for this large piece of land.

All Mexicans who remained in this newly acquired territory received the right to become United States citizens. Only about 2,000 of the nearly 80,000 persons living in the area chose to move to the Mexican side of the border. The treaty guaranteed Mexican Americans "all the rights of citizens of the United States . . . [and] the free enjoyment of . . . liberty and property." [5] "By this

5. "The Treaty of Guadalupe Hidalgo," in Wayne Moquin with Charles Van Doren, eds., *A Documentary History of Mexican Americans* (New York: Bantam Books, 1971), p. 247.

treaty the United States gained not only an immense new territory but also a large group of new citizens. Although they were left in their same geographic and cultural setting, these new citizens were now exposed to unfamiliar legal, political, and social institutions. . . . Guaranteed full protection of property rights, they soon became enmeshed in a web of confusing Anglo laws which required proof of ownership unfamiliar to them." [6]

After the Conquest: Oppression and Conflict

After 1848, forces were set in motion which were destined to make the Mexicans in the United States a conquered, powerless, and alienated ethnic minority. Although they were guaranteed property and citizenship rights by the Treaty of Guadalupe Hidalgo, it was only a matter of time before Anglo-Americans, through a series of legal and financial maneuvers, had obtained control in all of the Southwest territories and reduced the native Mexicans to the status of second-class citizens.

The pattern of conquest differed somewhat in the various Southwest territories. Before the Anglos came to New Mexico, a rigid class structure existed which sharply divided the rich and the poor. The Anglos in New Mexico pitted the rich against the poor in order to gain control of the territory. Anglo dominance emerged more gradually in New Mexico than in California and Texas. A mass of Anglos immigrated to California during the gold rush of 1849 and in subsequent years. Mexicans were completely outnumbered. They thoroughly dominated northern California by 1851. Anglo domination of southern California was somewhat delayed because most Anglo immigrants first settled in the northern part of the territory. However, eventually they settled in the south and within a few years expanded their dominance over the entire state. Anglos had begun, to exercise considerable power in Texas prior to 1848. There were over 30,000 Anglos and only 5,000 native Mexicans in Texas as early as 1834. After 1848, the Texan Anglos extended and institutionalized their dominance in that territory.

The Anglo-Americans were able to obtain most of the land

6. Matt S. Meier and Feliciano Rivera, *The Chicanos: A History of Mexican Americans* (New York: Hill and Wang, 1972), p. 71.

owned by the Mexicans by imposing a series of legal and financial restraints. Land boundaries in Mexico had been rather loosely and casually defined. Many Mexicans had to appear in Anglo courts to defend their rights to the land they owned. Often they did not have the legal papers proving their ownership of their land. In many cases they had to sell their land to pay taxes imposed by the new government or exorbitant fees to Anglo lawyers to argue their cases in court. Legal battles over land titles often dragged out in the courts for years and became very expensive. Tactics such as these and the Congressional Land Act of 1851, which required United States recognized proof of land-ownership, had the ultimate effect of making the Mexican largely landless and poverty stricken.

Rioting, lynchings, burnings, vigilante action, and other forms of violence were directed at America's "newest aliens" during this period of turmoil and Hispano defeat in the Southwest. Moore contends that "No other part of the United States saw such prolonged intergroup violence as did the Border States from 1848 to 1925."[7] Many Anglo outlaws and social misfits settled in the Southwest during this period. They declared "open season" on Mexicans and often attacked them "just for fun." There was little or no law enforcement in many parts of the Southwest during this period. In 1850, California passed a Foreign Miner's Tax that was designed to drive Mexicans out of the mines.

The Mexican Revolution of 1910 contributed to this atmosphere of hostility and violence. Banditry and filibustering* took place on both sides of the border. Mexican-Anglo hostility reached new highs. Mexicans considered Anglo-Americans "gringos" and Anglos called Mexicans "greasers." By the turn of the century, the Mexicans had been conquered and made foreigners within their homeland. Culturally, politically, and economically they were second-class citizens. Mexican Americans faced the beginning of the twentieth century suffering from a crushing second defeat in the Southwest.

7. Joan W. Moore with Alfredo Cuellar, *Mexican-Americans* (Englewood Cliffs, N. J.: Prentice-Hall, 1970), p. 36.

* Filibustering *is pursuing military activity in a foreign nation for adventure.*

NORTH FROM MEXICO

Early Immigrants

During the early development of agriculture in the South-west, agribusinessmen depended upon a large and cheap labor supply. This labor need was met in the late 1800s by the Chinese immigrants and later by immigrants from Japan and the Philippines. (See Chapter 9.) The expansion of irrigated farming in the Southwest at the turn of the century coincided with the Mexican Revolution of 1910. Many Mexicans were displaced by the Revolution. They came north to the United States Southwest seeking job opportunities. They found jobs in truck farming, cotton and sugar beets fields, in mines, in industry, and on the railroads. Hundreds of Mexican immigrants worked on the construction of railroad lines that crossed the west. Many Mexican-American communities in the Southwest grew up around railroad camp sites.

There was no legal agreement between Mexico and the United States which protected the rights of these immigrants. Consequently, they were often outrageously exploited by their employers. They were paid the lowest wages, given the worst jobs, and were forced to live in the crudest shacks. Many became migrant workers who followed the crops. The mass of Mexican immigrants to the Southwest depressed wages so drastically that many native Mexican Americans migrated to midwestern cities such as Detroit, Gary, and Chicago to get higher wages. The large number of Mexican immigrants who came to the Southwest between 1920 and 1930 laid the foundations for most modern Mexican communities.

Many Anglo groups in the Southwest became alarmed with the large number of Mexicans that were entering the United States in the 1920s. Vigorous efforts were made to halt their immigration. Although the legal attempts to stop their immigration failed because of the powerful opposition from agribusinessmen who wanted them for cheap labor, other efforts were successful. The United States-Mexican border had historically been a "free" border, with Mexicans and United States citizens crossing it at will. The Border Patrol was established in 1924 by Congress to control traffic across the border.

When the Great Depression hit in 1929, and many Mexicans, like other Americans, lost their jobs and found it necessary to get on welfare in order to survive, loud cries were heard against the Mexicans. Mexicans were regarded as "foreigners" who did not deserve welfare benefits. As with other non-White immigrants who came before them, attempts were made to deport the Mexicans when their labor was no longer needed. Jobs became increasingly scarce as the "dust bowl" White immigrants fled to the Southwest to compete for the few available jobs. The United States Immigration Service began an aggressive drive to repatriate immigrants.

In the eagerness to rid the United States of Mexicans in order to cut back on welfare rolls, many Mexican-American citizens were "encouraged" or forced to go to Mexico. The civil rights of American citizens of Mexican descent were blatantly violated in this outrageous repatriation movement. More than 64,000 Mexican aliens were returned to Mexico between 1930 and 1934 without the benefits of legal proceedings. The Mexican population in the United States declined from 639,000 to 377,000 from 1930 to 1940.[8]

The Bracero Program

When World War II began, a new demand for unskilled labor developed in the United States. Agribusiness leaders spoke vigorously about their desperate need for Mexican labor. Partly as a gesture to help with the war effort, Mexico agreed to a seasonal work program with the United States. The two nations signed an agreement in July 1942, which enabled Mexican citizens to work in the United States during work seasons. They were to return to Mexico when the work season ended. Unlike the earlier Mexican immigrants, these workers came under an agreement which guaranteed them specific conditions relating to such problems as wages, working conditions, transportation, and worker rights.

Although these contract stipulations helped to reduce some of the extreme conditions experienced by earlier Mexican immigrants, their wages and living conditions were often depressing. The bracero program formally ended in December 1947. When

8. Ibid., p. 42.

it terminated, the number of illegal immigrants crossing the United States-Mexican border soared. Smuggling illegal immigrants across the border became a highly profitable business in which many "men snatchers" engaged and profited.[9]

In 1954 the United States Immigration and Naturalization Service began a massive drive known as "Operation Wetback" to deport illegal immigrants to Mexico. Operation Wetback grossly violated the civil rights of many Mexicans as did the repatriation project in the 1930s. Hundreds of Mexican-American citizens were arrested and harassed. They were threatened and forced to produce "proof" of their citizenship. Only a few of the thousands of Mexicans deported had formal hearings. Operation Wetback successfully attained its goal but alienated and outraged many Mexican-American citizens. When the project ended, more than a million persons had been deported to Mexico.

In 1951 the United States and Mexico jointly accepted a Migratory Labor Agreement known as Public Law 78. This agreement set forth conditions for a new bracero program. It contained conditions similar to the earlier bracero agreement. Public Law 78 was extended for various periods until it ended in December 1964. In 1965 the United States Congress passed a new immigration act that became effective in 1968, which limited the annual immigration from Western Hemisphere nations to 120,000. Each nation, including Mexico, was given an annual quota of 20,000. This new act solved, at least for the time, problems concerning the number of Mexican nationals that could legally enter the United Sates. However, by 1974, large numbers of illegal immigrants were entering the United States from Mexico.

VIOLENCE AND RACE RIOTS

In the 1940s anti-Mexican feelings and sterotypes were rampant in the Southwest. The stereotypes, which depicted the Mexican American as criminal and violent, were perpetuated by the established Anglo press, especially the Hearst newspapers. The anti-Mexican press propaganda enflamed racial feelings and

9. McWilliams, *North from Mexico*, pp. 178–79.

antagonisms toward the Mexican Americans. Anti-Mexican racism was the basic cause of the case of the Sleepy Lagoon and the zoot suit riots which took place in Los Angeles in the summer of 1943.

The Sleepy Lagoon Case

A young Mexican American, José Díaz, died mysteriously on August 2, 1942, apparently from a fractured skull. Without· seriously seeking the facts of the case, the Los Angeles police immediately arrested twenty-four young men who were thought to be members of a Mexican "gang" accused of killing Diaz. All of them were charged with murder. When seventeen of the twenty-four youths were convicted, the Sleepy Lagoon Defense Committee* was organized. The committee, headed by journalist Carey McWilliams, successfully appealed the case. The case was dismissed because of insufficient evidence when the district court of appeals reversed the convictions on October 4, 1944.

The Zoot-Suit Riots

On June 3, 1943, eleven sailors were allegedly attacked by a group of boys in a predominantly Mexican neighborhood in Los Angeles. After this incident, the Los Angeles police conducted a "raid" which enflamed the community but failed to find the attackers. This incident kicked off a chain reaction resulting in one of the most serious series of race riots that has occurred in the United States. Encouraged by the actions of the police and the pervasive anti-Mexican attitudes in Los Angeles, about 200 sailors began to violently attack Mexican American youths on the night of June 4.

The police responded by arresting the victims of the attacks and keeping their hands off the sailors. The Los Angeles press played its usual role in the conflict; it warned that the dangerous "zoot-suiters"** would retaliate the next night. The press suc-

* *A gravel pit, which became a central focus in the case, was dubbed "The Sleepy Lagoon" by a Los Angeles reporter.*

** *Some Mexican-American youths were referred to as "zoot-suiters" because of the style of dress they wore during the 1940s.*

ceeded in alarming the public and in stirring up anti-Mexican feelings. On the night of June 7, hundreds of Anglos went into the streets and began a massive attack on Mexican-American youths. Many "zoot-suiters" were beaten and stripped naked in the streets. This ruckus continued until military authorities intervened late on the night of June 7. Other riots took place in cities as far away as Philadelphia, Chicago, and Detroit in the summer of 1943.

THE CHICANO MOVEMENT

The Chicano movement that emerged in the 1960s called for self-determination, a cultural renaissance, and political power for Mexican Americans. It was both a political and cultural movement. Its leaders, who often differed on tactics, had a variety of goals. They believed that Chicanos would be able to overcome oppression in the United States only when they had political power and control over those institutions, such as schools and courts, which influenced their lives and destinies. It is inaccurate to interpret the Chicano movement as a protest force which suddenly arose in the 1960s, or to refer to Chicanos as the "awakening minority." Often this is done. To fully understand the Chicano movement, we must view it as an important link in the long chain of resistance activities in which Chicanos have been involved since 1848. The movement cannot be viewed in isolation. As historian Rodolfo Acuña points out, "Men like Juan Patron and J. J. Jerrerra were the precursors of today's breed of rebels or insurrectionists. In understanding them . . . and others of their kind, we shall better understand the present, and the words of Reies Lopez Tijerina will take on more significant meaning." [10]

Early Resistance to Anglo Dominance

Mexican Americans have resisted Anglo oppression and colonialization since Anglo-Americans conquered and occupied the Southwest. Chicanos such as Juan N. Cortina, Juan Jose Herrerra, and Juan Patron led organized resistance efforts in the

10. Rodolfo Acuña, *Occupied America: The Chicano's Struggle Toward Liberation* (San Francisco: Canfield Press, 1972), p. 77.

1800s. Cortina isued a "declaration of grievances" and urged Mexican Americans to "exterminate" their oppressors. Many Mexicans responded to the revolutionary calls issued by Cortina, Herrerra, and Patron.[11] Mexican-American organizations such as Las Gorras Blancas fought Anglo leaders who were illegally taking land owned by Mexican Americans in New Mexico.

Unions and Strikes

In the first decades of the twentieth century, most Mexican Americans worked in agriculture, although many worked in mines, industry, and on the railroads. Farm workers were highly exploited by rich and powerful agribusinessmen. Mexican-American workers aggressively opposed their conditions and organized unions and strikes, thus shattering the myth that they were docile workers. The period from 1900 to 1940 was characterized by active Chicano involvement in strikes and union organization. In 1927 the Confederacion de Uniones Obreras Mexicanas was organized in California. This union organized a strike in 1928 in the Imperial Valley. Farm owners and law officials, which formed coalitions, responded violently to the strike. They broke it up by deporting some strikers to Mexico and assaulting and intimidating others.

This pattern was used extensively by farm owners to crush strikes by Mexican Americans. However, strikes and union activities continued in the midst of these oppressive tactics. Meier and Rivera summarize this period, "Although Mexican Americans gained much labor union experience from 1900 to 1940, their organizations achieved only limited success. Some gains were made in wages and working conditions; however, the hopes and aspirations of Mexican American workers continued to be frustrated by repression and discrimination."[12]

Civil Rights Organizations

A number of civic, service, and political organizations have been organized since the late nineteenth century to promote the

11. See Acuña for a detailed and perceptive discussion of these early revolutionary leaders.

12. Meier and Rivera, *Chicanos*, p. 184.

civil rights and interests of Mexican Americans. One of the first
was a mutual aid organization formed in Arizona in 1894, the
Alianza Hispano-Americana. These early societies restricted
membership to individuals of Mexican descent who were citizens
of the United States. They were made up primarily of the middle and upper classes and promoted assimilation by urging
their members to become loyal American citizens. Cuellar
argues that these organizations pusued a "politics of adaptation,"
rather than aggressively pushing for their political rights.[13] They
included the Order of the Sons of America, organized in San
Antonio in 1921, and the League of United Latin-American Citizens, formed in Corpus Christi, Texas in 1929.

Mexican Americans became much more politicized in the
post–World War II period. The organizations emerging during
these years reflected acute political awareness and skill. The
Community Service Organization, which was formed in Los
Angeles in 1947, stressed political involvement and broad political participation. It organized a number of successful voter
registration drives. The American G. I. Forum, founded in 1948,
the Mexican American Political Association, organized in 1959,
and the Political Association of Spanish-Speaking Organizations,
formed in 1960, stressed political involvement. These organizations were direct predecessors to the Chicano movement that
emerged in the 1960s.

The Militant Movement in the 1960s

Mexican Americans' protest acitvities, which had been going
on historically, were intensified in the 1960s and became collectively known as the "Chicano movement." In addition to being more intense than earlier Mexican-American movements,
the Chicano movement had other unique characteristics. It was
much more militant and often used forms of direct confrontation.
It included a large range of individuals among its ranks, such as
intellectuals, students, and community activists. Its goals were
much more radical than the goals of traditional Mexican-American civil rights groups. It demanded Chicano control of institutions within the Mexican-American community. Its leaders

13. Moore with Cuellar, *Mexican-Americans*, p. 142.

frequently argued that Chicanos in the United States were a colonized people who had been culturally and politically oppressed. They demanded redress of these grievances.

Chicano leaders also gave much more attention to their mixed Mexican heritage than earlier leaders. Their unique heritage, they argued, was to be celebrated and not denied, as was often done in the past by Mexican Americans who insisted on being viewed as "Spanish" instead of "Mexican." Much emphasis was placed on Mexican culture, values, foods, and especially the speaking of Spanish. They demanded the right to speak Spanish in all American institutions such as the school and church. Chicano leaders argued that "revolution" was necessary to liberate them.

Although there were many local Chicano leaders in 1973, four young men epitomized the movement in the public vision. They were Cesar Chavez, Reies Lopez Tijerina, Rodolfo "Corkey" Gonzales, and Jose Angel Gutierrez. Chavez headed the United Farm Workers Organizing Committee and successfully led the famous Delano grape strike in 1965. Tijerina demanded that Anglos in New Mexico return the lands they had taken from Mexican Americans in the 1800s. He formed the Federal Alliance of Free Cities in 1963 to push for the return of New Mexican lands to Chicanos. An important and militant civil rights group, the Crusade for Justice, was organized in Denver in 1965 by Gonzales. The crusade initiated successful projects related to improved education, better housing, and the eliminating of police brutality in the Mexican-American community. As a result of the political activities of the political party, La Raza Unida, which was organized in 1970 by Gutierrez, Chicanos exercised unprecedented political power in Crystal City, Texas in the 1970s, which spread throughout the lower Rio Grande valley.

These four charismatic leaders embodied the hopes and aspirations of millions of Chicanos and proved unequivocally that Mexican Americans can and will shape their destiny in a nation which made them captives in their homeland. Writes Acuña, an important Chicano spokesman: "the movement is toward separatism, with the goal of increasing awareness in a small but unified Chicano community that is inner-directed instead of being directed from without. . . . The Chincano people seek self-determination in what were formerly and rightfully their lands. . . ." [14]

Teaching Strategies

To illustrate how content related to Mexican Americans can be used to integrate the social studies, language arts, and humanities program, three key social science concepts have been identified and exemplary strategies are given for teaching them. Strategies are presented for teaching *role, immigration,* and *social protest* for the primary, intermediate and upper, and high school grades, respectively.

PRIMARY GRADES

CONCEPT: Role

Generalization: Members of Mexican-American families, like members of other American families, function in many different roles and help one another.

1. Ask the children, "What are some of the jobs you do around the house?" Their responses might include:
   "I help mother clean the house." "I help father wash the car." "I help mother shop."
   List their responses on the board or butcher paper.
2. Ask the pupils, "Do the things you do around the house help other members of the family?" "If so, how? If not, why not?" Record their responses on the board or butcher paper.
3. Ask the pupils to name some of the things these members of their families do to help each other: (a) father, (b) mother (c) brothers(s), (d) sister(s). Ask, "Are these things similar or different from the ones you do?"
4. Ask the pupils, "What do you think would happen in your family if (a) father was no longer in the family, (b) mother was no longer in the family, (c) brother or sister was no longer in the family?" Record their responses on the board or butcher paper.

14. Acuña, *Occupied America,* p. 277.

5. Show the pupils the picture of Graciela on page 2 of *Graciela: A Mexican-American Child Tells Her Story* by Joe Molnar. Ask the students, "How old do you think this girl is? Who do you think she lives with? Why?" Read the text on page 1. Ask the pupils, "What do you think Graciela does to help her family? What do you think Graciela's seven brothers and two sisters do to help the family? What do you think Graciela's mother and father do to help the family?

   Read the related text and discuss with the class the pictures in the book which show Graciela taking care of the baby Noe and helping mother in the kitchen. Ask the pupils, "Do you or your brothers and sisters ever do the kinds of things Graciela is doing?" "Why or why not?"

   Read the section of the book to the class that tells how Graciela's family moves from Texas to Michigan each year to work in the fields. Explain why the family goes to Michigan each year to work. Ask the class, "Why does Graciela work in the fields?" "Why does mother work in the fields?" "How is what Graciela does to help the family similar to what you do to help your family?" "How is what Graciela does to help her family different from what you do to help yours? Why?"

6. Show the pupils the pictures of Lupie's family in *Soy Chicano: I am Mexican American* by Bob and Lynne Fitch. Ask the pupils: "What do you think that each of these family members do to help the family: (a) father, (b) mother, (c) Lupie?" Record their responses on the board or butcher paper. Read the parts of the book that tell the kinds of things these family members do. Father works in the vineyards as an irrigator. Mother goes shopping, works around the house, and does work for the union. Lupie baby-sits and cuts grass to earn money.

7. To conclude the lesson on role, review with the class: (a) the things their family members do, (b) the things Graciela's family members do, and (c) the things Lupie's family members do to help one another. Ask questions which will enable the pupils to compare and contrast the roles in the various families and to illustrate, in all of the families, how family members function in many different roles and help one another.

MIDDLE AND UPPER GRADES

CONCEPT: Immigration

Generalization: Social, economic, and political conditions have influenced Mexican immigration to the United States. Mexican immigrants in the United States have been the victims of racism, deportation, and labor exploitation.

1. Tell the students that about a million Mexican immigrants came to the United States between 1910 and 1930. Ask them to state hypotheses to explain why so many Mexicans immigrated to the United States during this period. List their responses on the board. When the students have finished stating their hypotheses, ask them to group their hypotheses into several categories, using symbols such as "×" and "+" to indicate statements which should be grouped together. When the statements have been grouped, ask the students to label the groups. The hypotheses might be grouped into such broad categories as "social reasons," "political reasons," and "economic reasons." These categories need not be mutually exclusive. In this initial exercise, you will be teaching your students how to hypothesize and conceptualize, which involves three major steps: listing, grouping, and labeling.*

2. When the first exercise is completed, the students should record their hypotheses and categories in their notebooks. They will need to refer to them later in this exercise when they are tested. The students should now collect and study data to test their hypotheses. Their readings should include information on the Mexican Revolution of 1910 and the tremendous need for agricultural labor that had developed in the Southwest by the turn of the century. The Mexican Revolution caused many displaced Mexican peasants to come to the United States looking for jobs after 1910. The wealthy farmers in the Southwest wanted a large and cheap labor supply. A good account of the Mexican Revolution is in Rudy Acuña, *A Mexican American Chronicle*, pages 57–72. The reasons for the large number of Mexican immi-

---

* See James A. Banks with Ambrose A. Clegg, Jr., *Teaching Strategies for the Social Studies: Inquiry, Valuing and Decision-Making* (Reading, Mass.; Addison-Wesley, 1973), pp. 91–93.

grants during this period are discussed in this same book on
pages 108–111.

3. Students should investigate the conditions of the early Mexican immigrants to the United States. Most became migrant
workers who followed the seasonal crops. Many of their
dreams were shattered in the United States. Their problems
are vividly and poignantly revealed in Manuel Gamio, *The
Life Story of the Mexican Immigrant*. Ask five students to
read and dramatize to the class the accounts by these migratory laborers: Gumersindo Valdéz, Juan Berzunzolo, Elías
Garza, and Nivardo del Río. Accounts by these writers are
found on pages 141–59 of the Gamio book.

4. When the Great Depression struck in 1929, a movement
began to deport Mexican immigrants to Mexico. Ask a student to prepare a class presentation giving the views of the
United States Immigration Service and another to prepare a
report revealing how different segments of the Mexican-
American community felt about this massive repatriation
movement. The class should discuss the problem after these
two presentations have been given.

5. Beginning in 1942, Mexican immigrants entered the United
States under the terms of an agreement between the United
States and Mexico. Ask the students to pretend that it is
January 1942, and that the *bracero* bill is being debated in
the United States Congress. Ask different members of the
class to play the roles of various kinds of people in the Mexican-American community (such as old settlers, new immigrants, etc.), Southwest agribusinessmen, and representatives
of major unions in the United States. Ask the students play-
ing the assigned roles to argue for or against the bill before
the simulated Congress. The class should vote to decide the
fate of the *bracero* bill of 1942 after they have heard the
arguments. The class should then compare the results of
their vote with the bill passed by Congress in 1942.

6. To help the students get a feeling for some of the problems
of Mexican-American migrant workers today, read the class
some of the poignant and revealing profiles in *Small Hands,
Big Hands: Seven Profiles of Chicano Migrant Workers and
Their Families* by Sandra Weiner. Relate this exercise to a
writing activity by asking the students to write a creative

essay on "My Life as a Migrant Worker." The powerful photographs in *La Causa: The California Grape Strike* by Paul Fusco and George D. Horowitz will also give the students deep insights into the plight of migrant workers.

7. Ask several students in the class to make reports on Public Law 78, the Migratory Labor Agreement, and Operation Wetback, which began in 1951. Conduct a class discussion on the legal, social, and moral implications of these two activities that were implemented by the United States government. Particular attention should be given to how they affected American citizens of Mexican descent.

8. Summarize the unit by asking the students to take out the hypotheses they formulated at the beginning of this unit and evaluate them, using the information they have collected and evaluated. They should determine which hypotheses can remain as they were originally stated, which ones must be modified, and which ones must be totally rejected on the basis of the evidence collected.

9. Culminate the unit by showing and discussing a film such as *Chicano* or *I am Joaquin.* See Appendix B for descriptions and annotations of these films. In the discussion, focus on the social, economic, and political conditions that have influenced Mexican immigration to the United States.

Valuing Activity

Read the following story to the class and ask the questions which follow.

THE SÁNCHEZ FAMILY AND THE GRAPE STRIKE

Mr. and Mrs. Sánchez and their seven children came from Mexico to live in California one year ago. Mr. Sánchez had been told by relatives who had been to the United States that he could make a lot of money very quickly if he came to California. When Mr. Sánchez arrived in California, he found that it was very hard to make a living working in the fields. Since the Sánchez family has been living in California, it has had to move many times in order to follow the crops and find work.

The family has traveled as far as Texas and Michigan to work in the fields.

The work in the fields is very hard. Everyone in the family, except little Carlos, works in the fields so that the family can make enough money to get by with. Even Mrs. Sánchez, who used to stay at home and take care of the home when they lived in Mexico, now must work in the fields. The pay for the work is very low. Mr. and Mrs. Sánchez find that they get further and further into debt each year.

The Sánchez family is now living in the San Joaquin Valley in California. The family went to live there to work in the grape fields. For a while everything there was okay. Recently, a lot of things have been happening in the valley that Mr. and Mrs. Sánchez do not fully understand. Most of the field workers have said that they will not go to work next week because the Mexican American Union, lead by Juan Gonzalez, who is very popular with the workers, has called a strike. The union is demanding that the owners of the grape fields pay the workers more money and give them better worker benefits. The workers who belong to the Union are threatening to attack any worker who tries to go to work while the strike is on.

Mr. Sánchez is not a member of the union. He wants very much to go to work next week. He has a lot of bills to pay and needs money for food and clothing. The family simply cannot get by with the small amount of money that the union has promised to give Mr. Sánchez if he joins it and refuses to work next week. Mr. Sánchez also realizes that if the grapes are not picked within the next two weeks, they will rot. He has heard that these strikes sometime last for months. His boss told him that if he wants to go to work next Monday morning—the day the strike is to begin—he will give him protection from the unionized workers. Mrs. Sánchez thinks that Mr. Sánchez should support the strike so that he can make higher wages in the future.

Questions

1. Do you think that Mr. Sánchez and his family will go to work in the fields next Monday? Why or why not?
2. If Mr. Sánchez does go to work, what do you think will happen to him and his family?

3. If Mr. Sánchez does not go to work in the grape fields next Monday, what do you think he might do to earn money?
4. What do you think that Mr. Sánchez should do? Why?
5. What would you do if you were (a) Mr. Sánchez (b) Mrs. Sánchez (c) the children? Why?
6. Tell whether you agree or disagree with this statement and why: "The head of a family should never let his or her spouse and children do without the food and clothing they need."

HIGH SCHOOL GRADES

CONCEPT: Social Protest

Generalization: Since the Anglo-American conquest of the Southwest, Mexican Americans have used a variety of means to resist oppression and discrimination. This resistance has intensified and assumed new characteristics in recent years.

1. The teacher can begin this unit by having the students read and dramatize the epic poem of the Chicano movement, *I Am Joaquin*, by Rodolfo Gonzales (available in Bantam paperback). This poem is a powerful statement of the history and culture of Chicanos, with emphasis on their oppression and struggle for freedom. The author draws on nearly 2,000 years of Mexican and United States history. Among the many references made in the poem related to social protest are Father Miguel Hidalgo and *El Grito de Dolores of* 1810, Cinco de Mayo, the Treaty of Guadalupe Hidalgo, and the Anglo conquest of the Southwest in the 1800s. This poem will stimulate many questions students can pursue during their study of Chicano resistance to oppression. The teacher may also want to show the film based on the poem, *I Am Joaquin.*
2. References are frequently made to the Treaty of Guadalupe Hidalgo by Chicano spokesmen. After students have studied the events that led to the treaty, have them examine the treaty in detail and give their interpretations of it. They should compare their interpretations of the treaty with interpretations given by contemporary Chicano leaders. The complete text of the treaty is found in Moquin with Van

Doren, eds., *A Documentary History of Mexican Americans*, pp. 240–49. A useful annotated copy of the treaty appears in Bill Tate, *Guadalupe Hidalgo Treaty of Peace 1848 and and The Gadsden Treaty With Mexico 1853*, 5 ed., published by the Tate Gallery, P. O. Box 428, Truchas, New Mexico 87578, no date.

3. Ask a group of students to prepare and present to the class a dramatization portraying the positions and statements of early Mexican-American militant leaders such as Juan Patron, J. J. Herrerra, and Juan N. Cortina.

4. Some of the earliest Chicano resistance activities were unionization and strikes. Ask a group of students to prepare short reports on the various strikes and union activities during the period from 1900 to 1940. The strike in the California Imperial Valley in 1928 should be highlighted. Chapter 10 in Meier and Rivera, *The Chicanos: A History of Mexican Americans*, is one of the most complete, succinct accounts of these activities that is currently available.

5. The earliest Mexican-American civil rights organizations pursued what Cuellar has called a "politics of adaptation." Mexican-American civil rights organizations became more politicized in the post–World War II period. Militant Chicano organizations emerged in the 1960s. Ask the students to research the goals, tactics, and strategies used by the following Mexican-American civil rights groups. They will discover the trends delineated above.

    a) Order of the Sons of America (formed in 1921)
    b) League of United Latin-American Citizens (1929)
    c) The Community Service Organization (1947)
    d) The American G.I. Forum (1948)
    e) Federal Alliance of Free Cities (1963)
    f) Crusade for Justice (1965)

6. Ask the class to research these questions: How is the Chicano movement similar to other Mexican-American protest movements? How are its goals and strategies different? When did the movement emerge? What problems has it solved? What problems has it created within the Mexican-American community? How might these problems be resolved? In what ways is the Chicano movement similar

to, and different from, civil rights movements which emerged within other ethnic minority communities in the 1960s? What future directions do you think the movement will take? What long-term effects do you think the movement will have on the Anglo-American community? Why? A number of excellent readings are now available in inexpensive paperback form which will help students to answer these questions. The following sources are especially recommended:

"The Chicano Movement," by Ysidro Ramon Macias in Moquin with Van Doren, eds., A *Documentary History of Mexican Americans,* pp. 498–506. This is an excellent introductory essay on the movement. The other essays in Part V of this book are also valuable.

Part X, "La Causa: The Chicanos," in Valdez and Steiner, eds., *Aztlan: An Anthology of Mexican American Literature,* pp. 281–344.

Stan Steiner, "Chicano Power: Militance among Mexican Americans," in Edward Simmen, ed., *Pain and Promise: The Chicano Today,* pp. 130–36.

After the students have read and discussed accounts and interpretations of the Chicano movement, ask them to write an essay on "The Chicano Movement: Its Past, Present, and Future."

7. The Union activity led by Cesar Chavez during the 1960s and 1970s was an integral part of the Chicano movement. You may begin a study of these events by reading to the class the brilliant and poignant letter that Chavez wrote to E. L. Barr, Jr., president of the California Grape and Tree Fruit League, reprinted on pages 14–15 of Fusco and Horwitz, *La Causa: The California Grape Strike.* The moving photographs in this book will evoke many questions and comments about the strike. The students can also read the excellently written book on the strike by John Gregory Dunne, *Delano: The Story of the California Grape Strike.*

8. After the students have read and discussed accounts and interpretations of Mexican-American resistance and the Chicano movement, ask them to write and present a dramatization on "Mexican American Resistance to Oppression in the United States, 1848 to the present day."

Materials and Resources

REFERENCES FOR THE TEACHER

Must Reading

Acuña, Rodolfo. *Occupied America: The Chicano's Struggle Toward Liberation.* San Francisco: Canfield Press, 1972.

An angry and provocative history of the Chicano written from a colonialist perspective. A highly partisan but important book that will provide the teacher with new interpretations of old events such as the Alamo and the "winning of the West."

McWilliams, Carey. *North from Mexico: The Spanish-Speaking People of the United States.* New York: Greenwood Press, 1949, updated edition, 1968.

A good general overview of the culture and history of Mexican Americans through World War II. Too little attention is given to the Chicano's Indian and African heritages. At times, the book seems anti-Indian. Nevertheless, it is a valuable book that shatters many cherished myths and insidious stereotypes.

Meier, Matt S. and Feliciano Rivera. *The Chicanos: A History of Mexican Americans.* New York: Hill and Wang, 1972.

This essential teacher reference is a comprehensive history of the Chicano. It is the most useful general history of the Mexican American to appear to date. The book includes an excellent bibliographic essay.

Moore, Joan W., with Alfredo Cuellar. *Mexican-Americans.* Englewood Cliffs, N. J.: Prentice-Hall, 1970.

This introductory study is primarily sociological but includes a useful historical overview. Written from an assimilationist perspective, the author focuses on change, conflict, and cultural diversity. The final chapter by Cuellar on politics is especially useful.

Other References

Burma, John H., ed. *Mexican-Americans in the United States: A Reader.* Cambridge: Schenkman, 1970.

This anthology contains a collection of specialized studies on selected topics such as prejudice, education, and social and political behavior.

Cortés, Carlos E. "Teaching the Chicano Experience." In James A. Banks, ed. *Teaching Ethnic Studies: Concepts and Strategies.* Washington, D. C.: National Council for the Social Studies 43rd Yearbook, 1973, pp. 180–199.

A perceptive and informative essay presenting five alternative frames of reference that can be effectively used to study and teach about Mexican Americans.

Dunne, John Gregory. *Delano: The Story of the California Grape Strike.* New York: Farrar, Straus and Giroux, 1967.

A well-written journalistic and dispassionate account of the famous strike. Easy to read, this book can be used by students and teachers.

Galarza, Ernesto. *Merchants of Labor: The Mexican Bracero Story.* Charlotte: McNally and Loftin, 1964.

A useful and careful study of the immigration of Mexican farm workers to the United States from 1942 to 1960.

Gamio, Manuel. *The Life Story of the Mexican Immigrant.* New York: Dover Publications, 1971.

An important collection of statements by early Mexican immigrants to the United States. These accounts can be successfully used to teach inquiry lessons.

————. *Mexican Immigration to the United States: A Study of Human Migration and Adjustment.* Chicago: University of Chicago Press, 1930.

This book contains useful information on the first waves of Mexican immigrants to the United States.

Grebler, Leo, Joan W. Moore, Ralph C. Guzman, et al. *The Mexican-American: The Nation's Second Largest Minority.* New York: Free Press, 1970.

An exhaustive interdisciplinary study (777 pages) which treats diverse aspects of the Mexican American. Divided into seven major parts, this book is meant for the reader who wants specialized information.

Forbes, Jack D. *Aztecas Del Norte: The Chicanos of Aztlan.* Greenwich, Conn.: Fawcett, 1973.

The author focuses on the Indian heritage of Mexican Americans. Forbes provides novel interpretations of the Chicano experience which are somewhat controversial.

Fusco, Paul and George D. Horwitz. *La Causa: The California Grape Strike.* New York: Collier Books, 1970.

The poignant photographs and text of this book are deeply moving and powerful. The photographs are good "teaching" pictures.

Ludwig, Ed and James Santibanez, eds. *The Chicanos: Mexican American Voices.* Baltimore: Penguin Books, 1971.

This anthology includes articles, poetry, and fiction which present a variety of views of Chicano life.

Moquin, Wayne with Charles Van Doren, eds. *A Documentary History of Mexican Americans.* New York: Bantam Books, 1971.

This anthology includes sixty-five selections divided into five major historical periods. A wide range of documents are included in this excellent book.

Nava, Julian. *Mexican Americans: A Brief Look at Their History.* New York: Anti-Defamation League of B'nai B'rith, 1970.

A succinct but useful general overview of the Mexican American.

Ortego, Philip D., ed. *We Are Chicanos: An Anthology of Mexican-American Literature.* New York: Pocket Books, 1973.

This anthology includes folklore, poetry, drama, and fiction as well as essays of social commentary.

Pitt, Leonard. *The Decline of the Californios: A Social History of the Spanish-Speaking Californians, 1846–1890.* Berkeley: University of California Press, 1970.

A scholarly study of the conquest of the Mexican settlers in early California.

Rendon, Armando B. *Chicano Manifesto: The History of the Second Largest Minority in America.* New York: Collier Books, 1971.

A highly partisan, journalistic, and rhetorical history of the Chicano. However, the book provides important insights on the Chicano movement.

Robinson, Cecil. *With the Ears of Strangers: The Mexican in American Literature.* Tucson: University of Arizona Press, 1963.

A comprehensive and well-researched study.

Romano–V, Octavio I., ed. *El Espejo-The Mirror: Selected Mexican-American Literature.* Berkeley: Quinto Sol Publications, 1969.

A useful collection of literature by Mexican American writers.

Samora, Julian, ed. *La Raza: Forgotten Americans.* Notre Dame: University of Notre Dame Press, 1966.

This collection of essays treats different aspects of Chicano life and culture.

Servin, Manuel P., ed. *The Mexican-Americans: An Awakening Minority.* Beverly Hills: Glencoe Press, 1970.

This anthology contains specialized historical essays on the Mexican American. Six of the papers are published for the first time. The subtitle of the book is misleading and inaccurate. This book has been severely criticized by some Chicano activists.

Simmen, Edward, ed. *The Chicano: From Caricature to Self-Portrait.* New York: Mentor Books, 1971.

The short stories in this anthology illustrate how the Mexican American was portrayed in literature from the mid-nineteenth century through the 1960s. The stories are divided into three major literary periods.

────── . *Pain and Promise: The Chicano Today.* New York: Mentor Books, 1972.

The thirty-two essays reprinted in this anthology are intended primarily for the popular reader. High school students will be able to profitably read this book.

Spicer, Edward H. *Cycles of Conquest: The Impact of Spain, Mexico and the United States on the Indians of the Southwest, 1533–1960.* Tucson: University of Arizona Press, 1962.

The author discusses ways in which Native American cultures reponded to contact with the various groups which occupied the Southwest.

Steiner, Stan. *La Raza: The Mexican Americans.* New York: Harper Colophon Books, 1969.

An interesting and readable popular treatment of Mexican Americans.

Steiner, Stan and Luis Valdez, eds. *Aztlan: An Anthology of Mexican American Literature.* New York: Vintage Books, 1972.

This valuable and comprehensive anthology contains a rich collection of historical essays, social commentaries, and literary selections that cannot be easily found elsewhere.

Wagner, Nathaniel N. and Marsha J. Haug, eds. *Chicanos: Social and Psychological Perspectives.* Saint Louis: C. V. Mosby Company, 1971.

This reader contains theoretical and research articles on the psychological aspects of the Mexican-American experience.

Weber, David, ed. *Foreigners in Their Native Land: Historical Roots of the Mexican American.* Albuquerque: University of New Mexico Press, 1973.

This book contains a valuable collection of historical documents about Mexican Americans.

BOOKS FOR STUDENTS

Acuña, Rudy. *Cultures in Conflict: Problems of the Mexican American.* New York: Charter School Books, 1970.

An excellent book which uses a problem-oriented case study approach. The photographs are an integral part of the text. (Intermediate)

────── . *A Mexican American Chronicle.* New York: American Book Company, 1971.

A highly readable and interesting history which uses a topical rather than a straight chronological approach. A unit on the Chicano movement is included. (Upper)

────── . *The Story of the Mexican Americans: The Men and the Land.* New York: American Book Company, 1969.

A good history concentrating on the period prior to 1910. Well-illustrated. (Intermediate)

Brown, Gertrude S., with the advice of Dr. Manuel Guerra. *Our Mexican Heritage.* Lexington, Mass.: Ginn and Co., 1972.

A comprehensive history of early Mexico and Spain. A worthwhile background source for the heritage of the Mexican American. The book contains almost no information on the Mexican American. (Intermediate)

Chandler, David. *¡Huelga!* New York: Simon & Schuster, 1970.

A well-written and interesting fictional account of the Chicano's fight for the rights of migrant workers. (High School)

de Garza, Patricia. *Chicanos: The Story of Mexican Americans.* New York: Julian Messner, 1973.

A well-written and interesting history of Mexican Americans. The author discusses the contributions Mexican Americans have made to the United States and the problems they have encountered. (Intermediate)

Dobrin, Arnold. *The New Life-La Vida Nueva.* New York: Dodd, Mead and Co., 1971.

This book presents a panoramic view of the Mexican American today. The author looks at their hopes, aspirations, and problems. Illustrated. (Intermediate)

Eiseman, Alberta. *Mañana Is Now: The Spanish-Speaking in the United States.* New York: Atheneum, 1973.

A good general history of Puerto Rican Americans, Mexican Americans and Cuban Americans. This book is well written and is a good introduction to the experiences of Spanish-speaking groups in the United States. (High School)

Fitch, Bob and Lynne Fitch. *Soy Chicano: I Am Mexican American.* Mankato, Minn.: Creative Educational Society, 1970.

An autobiographical account of selected events in the life of a perceptive young Mexican American girl. An effective book which is well illustrated with black and white photographs. (Intermediate)

Franchere, Ruth. *Cesar Chavez.* New York: Crowell, 1970.

A good biography of the famed Chicano leader. The reader gets a feeling for the life of the migrant worker and of a man struggling to help his people. (Primary)

Galarza, Ernesto. *Barrio Boy.* Notre Dame, Ind.: University of Notre Dame Press, 1971.

A well-written, interesting autobiography of a noted Mexican-American scholar. A good book to use to teach the concept of acculturation. (Upper)

Gee, Maurine H. *Chicano, Amigo.* New York: William Morrow, 1972.

An unfortunate book about a young Mexican-American boy who wants to become a boy scout. Kiki, the protagonist, is portrayed as a dull child who is a pest. The book could add to children's negative images of the Chicano. (Intermediate)

Gonzales, Rodolfo. *I Am Joaquin.* New York: Bantam Books, 1967.

An important epic poem of the Chicano people. The book includes a useful chronology of Mexican-American history. (Upper)

Haddox, John. *Los Chicanos: An Awakening People.* El Paso, Texas: Western Press, 1970.

The author discusses self-concept, culture, and values of Chicanos and looks to the future. He writes with deep feeling. (High School)

Krumgold, Joseph. *And Now Miguel.* New York: Thomas Y. Crowell, 1953.

Miguel struggles to become a man in this powerful and beautifully written Newbery Medal book. The reader experiences his conflicts and identity crisis. (Upper)

Lampman, Evelyn Sibley. *Go Up the Road.* New York: Atheneum, 1972.

A stereotypic and poorly done book about Mexican-American migrant workers. Not recommended. (Intermediate)

McWilliams, Carey. *The Mexicans in America: A Students' Guide to Localized History.* New York: Teachers College Press, 1969.

The author provides a short and valuable historical overview of Mexican Americans. (Upper)

Madsen, William. *Mexican-Americans of South Texas.* New York: Holt. Rinehart and Winston, 1964.

An ethnocentric interpretation of Chicanos. This book epitomizes what the Chicano movement is fighting to eradicate. Not recommended. (High School)

Martin, Patricia Miles. *Chicanos: Mexicans in the United States.* New York: Parents' Magazine Press, 1971.

A sympathetic history of Mexican Americans for the youngest readers. The author emphasizes the positive aspects of life for the migrant worker and the barrio dweller. (Intermediate)

Martinez, Gilbert T. and Jane Edwards. *The Mexican American.* Boston: Houghton Mifflin, 1973.

A comprehensive history of Mexican Americans. The authors include information on the early Indian civilizations in Mexico but concentrate on the period after 1810. This book is well-written and researched. (Upper)

Madison, Winifred. *Maria Luisa.* New York: J. B. Lippincott, 1971.

A touching story about a young Mexican-American girl who leaves the familiar surroundings of a small town and her mother to go to San Francisco to live with relatives whom she does not know. The family seems more Anglo than Chicano. (Intermediate)

Molnar, Joe. *Graciela: A Mexican American Child Tells Her Story.* New York: Franklin Watts, 1972.

A young girl gives a sensitive and moving account of her family's efforts to survive in a hostile environment. Illustrated. (Intermediate)

Nava, Julian. *Mexican Americans: Past, Present and Future.* New York: American Book Company, 1969.

This book deals primarily with Spain and Mexico. One chapter is devoted to the Mexican American today. This book provides a brief view of the heritage of the Mexican American. (Intermediate)

Newlon, Clarke. *Famous Mexican Americans.* New York: Dodd, Mead and Co., 1972.

A collection of twenty well-written biographies of eminent Mexican Americans. (Upper)

Paredes, Américo and Raymund Paredes, eds. *Mexican-American Authors.* Boston: Houghton Mifflin, 1972.

This is an anthology of contemporary Mexican-American literature. A variety of literary forms and discussion exercises are included. (High School)

Pinchot, Jane. *The Mexicans in America.* Minneapolis: Lerner Publications, 1973.

A good general history of Mexican Americans including biographical sketches of eminent Mexican Americans. (Intermediate)

Polito, Leo. *Pedro, The Angel of Olvera Street.* New York: Charles Scribners Sons, 1946.

This book is somewhat stereotypic and dated. However, it includes an interesting account of the Christmas procession called La Posada and two Christmas songs. (Primary)

———. *Song of the Swallows.* New York: Charles Scribners Sons, 1949.

The drawings and the text date this book. It should not be used to illustrate the life of a modern Mexican-American child. (Primary)

Sanchez, Ricardo. *Canto y Grito Mi Liberación.* Garden City, N. Y.: Doubleday, 1971.

An interesting collection of poetry written by Chicano poets. Most of the selections are in English but some are in Spanish. (High School)

Sonnichsen, C. L. *Pass of the North.* El Paso, Texas: Western Press, 1968.

This extensive history of El Paso, Texas, covers the period from 1541 to 1919. The author discusses the roles played by the Spaniards, Indians, Mexicans, and Anglos in the town's history. The interactions between these ethnic groups is highlighted. (High School)

Tebbel, John and Ramón Eduardo Ruiz. *South by Southwest.* Garden City, N. Y.: Zenith Books, 1969.

A sensitive and informative book on the Chicano's Mexican heritage. Most of the book is devoted to the Spanish invasion of Mexico. (Intermediate)

Terzian, James P. and Kathryn Cramer. *Mighty Hard Road: The Story of Cesar Chavez.* Garden City, N. Y.: Doubleday, 1970.

An interesting biography of the famous union leader. This book concentrates on Chavez the activist although other periods of his life are discussed. Illustrated with photographs. (Intermediate)

Weiner, Sandra. *Small Hands, Big Hands: Seven Profiles of Chicano Migrant Workers and Their Families.* New York: Pantheon Books, 1970.

These accounts are poignant and deeply moving. Illustrated with black and white photographs. (Intermediate)

Asian Americans: Concepts, Strategies, and Materials

9

Asia Americans can no longer afford to watch the black-and-white struggle from the sidelines. They have their own cause to fight, since they are also victims—with less visible scars—of . . . white institutionalized racism. A yellow movement has been set into motion by the black power movement. Addressing itself to the unique problems of Asian Americans, this "yellow power" movement is relevant to the black power movement in that both are part of the Third World struggle to liberate all colored people.

Amy Uyematsu

Introduction

Asian Americans, one of America's most diverse and interesting ethnic groups, are rarely studied in the elementary and high school grades. When discussed in textbooks, they are most often used to illustrate how a non-White ethnic group can succeed in the United States. Because of their economic and educational success, Japanese Americans have been called the "model minority" in the United States. Serious problems, of which the teacher should be aware, arise when the "success" of Asian Americans is emphasized in teaching materials. Despite the fact that Japanese Americans and Chinese Americans have achieved high educational and economic mobility, such traditional measures of success are misleading and divert attention from the serious psychological and social problems that Asian Americans still experience in American life and from their cultural characteristics. The "success" argument also implies that non-White people can succeed in the United States only if they work hard, and that if they do not it is because of their own shortcomings. Thus, when carried to its extreme, the success thesis can be used to make invidious comparisons among ethnic minority groups and become a justification for institutional racism.

The economic mobility of Asian Americans, and the factors which can explain it, should be studied in ethnic studies. However, when Asian Americans are studied, the focus should be on their values, identity, ethnic institutions, histories, and cultures, and not on their economic success. Focusing on the economic and educational attainments of any ethnic group is much too narrow and will fail to help students fully understand and appreciate the complex nature of an ethnic group's experience and culture. Chun-Hoon, in commenting on aspects of the Asian-American experience that should be included in the school curriculum writes,

> There needs . . . to be a recognition of Asian-American personalities in the teaching of the Asian-American experience so that there can be some discovery of the common human dimension shared by Asians and Americans alike.[1]

In 1970 there were about 1.5 million Asian Americans in the United States, out of a total national population of 204 million people. The largest Asian-American groups were the Japanese Americans (591,290), Chinese Americans (435,062) and Filipino Americans (343,060). Other Asian-American groups are Korean Americans and Samoan Americans. This chapter only discusses the three largest Asian-American groups because of the paucity of data available on the other groups.

Asian Americans are one of the most highly diversified

1. Lowell K. Y. Chun-Hoon, "Teaching the Asian-American Experience," in James A. Banks, ed., *Teaching Ethnic Studies: Concepts and Strategies* (Washington, D. C.: National Council for the Social Studies 43rd Yearbook, 1973), p. 136.

ethnic groups in the United States. The attitudes, values, and ethnic institutions often differ within Japanese-American, Chinese-American, and Filipino-American communities. However, Asian Americans have had some parallel experiences in the United States. Each successive wave of Asian immigrants shared this sequence of events: their immigration was begun when there was a need for cheap labor; they were harassed and demeaned; and immigration laws were passed to exclude them. After the Chinese Exclusion Act was passed in 1882, there was still a desire for cheap laborers in Hawaii and California. Consequently, Japanese immigrants began arriving in California in significant numbers in the 1890s. When the Gentlemen's Agreement of 1908 and the Immigration Act of 1924 halted Japanese immigration, California farmers imported Filipinos from Hawaii and the Philippines to work in the fields. Anti-Filipino forces emerged on the West Coast and culminated when Congress limited Filipino immigration to fifty persons per year in 1934. This quota constituted, in effect, the virtual exclusion of Filipino immigrants.

Because of their tremendous diversity, similarities, and unique experiences in the United States, the study of Asian Americans can greatly help students to increase their ethnic literacy and develop a respect for cultural differences.

Chinese Americans: Historical Perspective

Important Dates

1850	The United States census showed 450 Chinese immigrants in the United States. This number increased to 34,933 in 1860.
	The California legislature passed a discriminatory Foreign Miner's Tax, which forced Chinese immigrants to pay a highly disproportionate share of the state taxes.
1859	Authorities in the Kwangtung Province legalized the recruitment of Chinese laborers.
1868	The United States and China signed the Burlingame Treaty. This treaty affirmed friend-

Important Dates cont.

	ship between the two nations and granted the Chinese the right to travel and live in the United States and Americans the right to trade and travel in China.
1869	The Transcontinental Railroad, linking the West to the East, was completed. Chinese laborers did most of the work on the Pacific portion of the railroad.
	One of the earliest anti-Chinese riots took place in San Francisco.
1871	A White mob in Los Angeles attacked a Chinese community. When the conflict ended, nineteen Chinese were killed and their community was in shambles.
1880	One of the most deplorable anti-Chinese riots occurred in Denver, Colorado.
1882	The Chinese Exclusion Act was passed by Congress. The immigration of Chinese laborers was prohibited for ten years. Subsequent acts renewed the terms of this act, thus excluding Chinese immigrants for decades.
1885	A serious anti-Chinese riot took place in Rock Springs, Wyoming. Twenty-eight Chinese were killed, and many others were wounded and driven from their homes.
1888	The Scott Act prohibited the immigration of Chinese laborers and permitted only officials, teachers, students, merchants, and travelers from China to enter the United States.
1892	The Geary Act excluded Chinese laborers and took away most of the Chinese immigrants' legal rights.
1943	The Chinese Exclusion Act was repealed. However, only a token quota of 105 Chinese immigrants a year were allowed to enter the United States.
1959	Hiram L. Fong, of Hawaii, became the first United States Senator of Asian ancestry.
1965	Congress passed an Immigration Act that

Important Dates cont.

eliminated quotas based on national origins and instituted fair immigration policies; it became effective in 1968. After this act, the number of Chinese immigrating to the United States increased substantially, from 4,057 in 1965 to 14,417 in 1971.

The Immigration

When the news reached the Kwangtung Province in Southeast China that there was a "Golden Mountain" across the Pacific, a number of young men violated both Chinese law and tradition and headed for the promised land. The decision to leave China for a foreign land was a serious one because it was illegal to immigrate and violators could be severely punished. Also, Confucian doctrine, which was an integral part of Chinese life during this period, taught that a young man should value his family above all else and thus should not leave it. However, both the promises of the land of the Mountain of Gold and the severe living conditions in the Toishan district in Kwangtung, from which most of the first Chinese immigrants hailed, helped to push the young immigrants across the Pacific.

Political upheaval, famine, local warfare, excessive taxes, a severely depressed economy, and a rugged terrain in Toishan that was inimical to farming helped to motivate young Chinese males to seek better opportunities in an unknown land where, according to a pervasive myth, one could easily strike gold and return to China a rich man. Most of the Chinese who headed for California were young married men. They were self-proclaimed "sojourners" who intended to earn their fortunes in the United States and return to their families in China. Because of tradition and the rough voyage across the Pacific, their families were left behind.

The journey across the Pacific was rugged and hazardous. Upon their arrival in California, the Chinese immigrants experienced a rude awakening. Although White Americans expressed little overt hostility toward the Chinese when they first started immigrating to the West Coast in substantial numbers in the 1850s, they considered them exotic, strange people. Whites thought that the Chinese were strange because of their traditional Chinese clothing, language, queue hair style (which Whites called pigtails), and skin color. Almost from the beginning, the Chinese were the victims of dehumanizing curiosity and racism. One historian has noted, "From almost the first moment the Chinese landed in San Francisco in the 1850s, they were subjected to harsh treatment. The aim was to exclude them from the United States because of basically *racist* fears and beliefs"[2] [emphasis added].

Labor

In addition to receiving a curious and strange welcome from Californians, the Chinese immigrants found that the mines in which they had to dig for gold had already been thoroughly gone over by White gold diggers. They had to dig for the scraps. However, the Chinese immigrants managed to secure very respectable sums of money by remining White claims. When Congress decided to build a railroad linking the Missouri River to the Pacific Coast in 1862, the Central Pacific issued a call for men to build the western portion of the railroad. Because of the back-breaking work involved in building a railroad over the rugged Western terrain, few Whites would take the work. But the Chinese took up the challenge and almost single-handedly built the Pacific portion of the transcontinental railroad. While the nation celebrated the completion of the railroad on May 10, 1869, 25,000 laborers, most of them Chinese, lost their jobs.[3]

It was not easy for the Chinese immigrants to save money because of the large debts they had made when they arranged to come to California. Most of them came to the United States through a credit-ticket system, which was similar to the indenture system that was used to bring many European immigrants to North America. In this system, a moneyless Chinese could borrow money from a relative or fellow villager to pay for his passage to California. Chinese organizations, such as the Hui Kuan

2. H. Brett Melendy, *The Oriental Americans* (New York: Hippocrene Books, 1972), p. 42.

3. Betty L. Sung, *The Story of the Chinese in America* (New York: Collier Books, 1967), pp. 30, 35, 39.

or *Landsmanner*, collected the money from the immigrant and sent it to the individuals from whom it was borrowed.

The leaders of the Hui Kuan not only collected money from the immigrants, but provided them a place to eat and sleep upon their arrival in San Francisco, and sent gangs of them out to work in the mines. Before the worker received his wages, the amount he owed for his passage was deducted. Because of the credit-ticket system, some immigrants ended up worse off financially than they were before they came to California. Some found that their return to China was indefinitely delayed. What at first promised to be a nation of gold turned out, for many, to be a land of disillusionment and shattered dreams. "The Chinese existed at a poverty level, receiving low wages for their work. Even so, they gained materially a bit more than they had in China. The dream of coming to the Golden Mountain to make a fortune and return home still seemed possible to most. For many, however, this was the impossible dream." [4]

Despite the difficulties the Chinese immigrants experienced, many were able to find enough work in a wide range of occupations that most Whites found unpalatable, such as domestic work, work on railroads, and intensive farming, to save up enough money to return to China to visit their families and to father children, hopefully sons. The immigrants who returned to China usually told about the promises of California but said little about its difficulties. Also, the home folks were very impressed with what seemed like sizable sums of money the sojourners brought back to China. As the news about the Mountain of Gold spread, and immigrants returned home with money or sent money home to their families, the number of Chinese immigrating to California rose tremendously.

Anti-Chinese Agitation

According to the 1860 census, there were 34,933 Chinese in the United States. By 1880, that number had risen to 105,465. Although the increase was sizable, there were still few Chinese immigrating to the United States compared to the number of European immigrants. Between 1820 and 1930, 38 million im-

4. Melendy, *Oriental Americans*, p. 20.

migrants entered the United States, mostly from Europe. However, White racists became alarmed with the number of Chinese entering the United States and a vicious movement developed to keep them out of this country. Although leaders of the anti-Chinese movement claimed that the Chinese could not be assimilated and that they competed unfairly with Whites on the labor market, racism was one of the main forces behind the anti-Chinese movement. As Saxton has pointed out, "the Chinese inherited the long-standing hostility of whites against people of color, particularly blacks. White Californians, conditioned to the notion that Blacks were inferior persons and servile workers, easily transferred these perceptions to the Chinese." [5]

Led by Dennis Kearney and the California Workingmen's party, "The Chinese Must Go" became the rallying cry of the anti-Chinese movement. Leaders of all types joined in the movement to push the Chinese out of the West. Labor leaders were among the most staunch anti-Chinese adovocates. Politicians jumped on the bandwagon in order to gain votes. As the hostility against the Chinese mounted, they became increasingly defenseless. Unlike the Japanese, they did not have a strong nation that could threaten the balance of world power when its citizens in the United States were ill treated.

The anti-Chinese movement began in California but later spread as the Chinese moved to such states as Washington, Oregon, Colorado, and Wyoming. Anti-Chinese activities took the form of racist newspaper stories; violent attacks against defenseless men, women, and children; and highly discriminatory laws aimed primarily at the Chinese, such as the Queues Ordinance, the Laundry Ordinance, and the 1876 Cubic Air Law. One of the most blatantly discriminatory laws was the Foreign Miner's Tax which was passed by the California legislature in 1850. Applied most effectively against the Chinese, it forced them to pay a highly disproportionate share of the taxes collected under the law. Taxes paid by the Chinese largely financed the California state and county governments during this period.[6] The movement to ban the immigration of Chinese culminated with the passage of the Immigration Act of 1882. This bill stopped the

5. Quoted in Melendy, *Oriental Americans*, p. 18.

6. Chun-Hoon, "Teaching the Asian-American Experience," p. 123.

immigration of Chinese laborers for a period of ten years. It represented a victory for the anti-Chinese leaders and was followed by a series of similar bills which drastically reduced Chinese immigration for decades. The number of Chinese entering the United States dwindled from 39,579 in 1882 to 472 in 1893.

Violence and Riots

Violence directed against the Chinese was widespread in the late 1800s. An anti-Chinese riot took place in San Francisco as early as 1869. A White mob in Los Angeles attacked a Chinese community in 1871. When the conflict ended, nineteen Chinese Americans were killed and their community was in shambles. Another anti-Chinese riot exploded in Denver, Colorado in 1880. One Chinese was killed and most of the homes in the Chinese community were wrecked during the riot. A serious anti-Chinese riot occurred in Rock Springs, Wyoming in 1885. Twenty-eight Chinese were killed, fifteen were wounded, and many were driven from their homes. The property destroyed was estimated at $150,000. Most of the White aggressors in these riots went unpunished partly because testimony against a White person by a Chinese was inadmissible in the courts.

Chinese American Communities

The Chinese responded to this violence by moving further eastward, to the Northwest, and by retreating into ethnic communities in urban areas. "By the end of the 19th century, the California Chinese had, for the most part, died off, returned to China, moved eastward or settled into the ghettos of American cities referred to as 'Chinatowns.' There they would remain to the present day." [7]

Despite its outer glitter, life in Chinatown was and is tough and depressing. Since most of the male immigrants did not bring their wives to California and were unable to marry Caucasians, Chinatown was made up primarily of desperate and lonely men who sought their recreation in the form of prostitution, gambling, and opium smoking. Because of the high popu-

7. Stanford M. Lyman, *The Asian in the West* (Reno: Desert Research Institute, 1970), p. 14.

lation of lonely and virile men, and the scarcity of females, prostitution loomed large in Chinatown in the 1800s. It was controlled by the Chinese secret societies that paid off police officials so that they could "safely" practice their business. Competition between the various Chinese societies for power, women, and money was keen, and violence between them often erupted. These conflicts were sensationalized by the White press and were popularized as "tong wars." Such stories made good copy and were eagerly sought by irresponsible journalists. These news stories played into the hands of the anti-Chinese racists and were fully exploited.

Prostitution, "tong wars," gambling, and opium smoking are largely things of the past in Chinatown. However, powerful, antiquated Chinese organizations that care little about the masses still exercise a lot of power. Poverty, squalor, and disease are rampant in some Chinese urban communities. San Francisco's Chinatown has one of the highest population densities in the nation; suicide rates there are three times higher than the national average. The tuberculosis rate in Chinatown is the highest in San Francisco. Many of the women in San Francisco's Chinatown work in the garment industry for outrageously low wages. Housing and education in San Francisco's Chinatown are among the worst in the nation. The power elite in Chinatown, which profits from the misery of the masses, has helped to obscure these outrageous conditions in Chinatown and has publicized its glitter. Chinatown has been described as a "gilded ghetto whose tinseled streets and brightly lit shops barely camouflage a pocket of poverty in the metropolis." [8]

The Chinese American Today

While Chinatown served as a port of entry for most of the earlier immigrants, provided them with a sense of security, ties with the old world culture, and a partial escape from White racism, today the population within these urban districts is rapidly shifting as Chinese Americans acquire higher social class status and join the exodus to the suburbs. Despite the racism they have experienced in the United States, the achievements of Chinese Americans in such areas as education, the sciences, and

8. Ibid., p. 8.

the arts have been tremendous. In 1969, 17.1 percent of Chinese Americans were employed in professional and technical occupations, while only 4.0 percent worked as laborers. The median Chinese-American family income was $10,610 compared with a median of $10,089 for White Americans.* Because of the economic and educational mobility of Chinese Americans, many of them have moved out of Chinatown to other areas within the city. They are still primarily urban dwellers. About 95 percent lived in urban areas in 1970. Almost all poor Chinese, aged bachelors, and recent immigrants, many of whom hail from Hong Kong, live in Chinatown. Other groups, however, also live there. Despite the fact that many Chinese Americans have joined the larger society, the Chinatowns of the nation are still viable communities that satisfy important human and ethnic needs. Even the highly assimilated Chinese American occasionally returns to Chinatown on the weekend for a good ethnic meal or to buy certain Chinese products unavailable in predominantly Anglo-Saxon communities.

The Chinese community has experienced a new influx of immigrants since the passage of the Immigration Act of 1965, which gave Asia a liberal immigration quota. Between 1960 and 1970, the Chinese population in the United States increased 85 percent, while the White American population increased by 12 percent. In 1965 only 4,057 Chinese immigrants entered the United States, while 14,417 came in 1971. In 1970 there were 435,062 Chinese Americans in the United States, making them our second largest Asian-American group.[9]

Youth Rebellion

Like other American youths who are victimized by poverty and oppression, youths in Chinatown have formed social protest groups which, unlike their early ancestors in the United

* *These statistics are adapted from the United States census and include only Chinese Americans living in states with a population of 10,000 or more Chinese-American residents and Chinese-American workers who are age sixteen or older.*

9. These statistics, based on the 1970 United States census, are from Seymour Fersh, "Orientals and Orientation," *Phi Delta Kappan*, 53 (January 1972), pp. 315–16.

States, demand their civil rights and liberties from the White establishment and the old Chinese oligarchy. One such group that was vocal in the 1960s and received a great deal of publicity was the Red Guard party. Modeled after the Black Panther party, the Red Guard party made nonnegotiable demands and asserted its right to defend Chinese-American communities against hostile policemen. The Red Guards were also involved in some rather nonradical but useful community action projects. They sponsored a petition to prevent a Chinese playground from being converted into a garage and started a breakfast program to aid needy children in Chinatown.

The voice of the Red Guard party was rather mute by 1974. However, other community action groups had emerged in Chinatown. Chinese-American college students and social service agencies were working in Chinatown to bring about effective community change. The old oligarchy had lost some of its strength in the Chinese community. The extent to which these individuals and groups will succeed in their efforts to reform American Chinatowns is unclear. However, self-help projects are vigorous in Chinese urban communities throughout the United States.

Japanese Americans: Historical Perspective

Important Dates

1868	One hundred forty-eight Japanese contract laborers arrived in Hawaii.
1869	The unsuccessful Wakamatsu Colony, made up of Japanese immigrants, was established in California.
1906	The San Francisco Board of Education ordered all Asian children to attend a segregated Oriental school.
1907–08	The United States and Japan made the Gentlemen's Agreement, which was designed to reduce the number of Japanese immigrants entering the United States.
1913	The California legislature passed a land bill

Important Dates cont.

	making it difficult for Japanese immigrants to lease land.
1920	The California legislature passed a more stringent land bill to prohibit the Japanese immigrants from securing land.
1924	An immigration bill was passed by Congress which stopped Asian immigration to the United States.
1930	The Japanese American Citizenship League was founded.
1941	Japan attacked Pearl Harbor on December 7.
1942	On February 19, President Franklin D. Roosevelt issued Executive Order 9066, which authorized the internment of Japanese Americans who lived on the West Coast.
1946	The last internment camp was closed.
1948	The Japanese American Evacuation Claims Act, signed by President Harry S. Truman, authorized some compensation for the financial losses incurred by the Japanese Americans during the internment.
1952	The McCarran-Walter Immigration Act was passed by Congress. It ended the total exclusion of Asian immigrants, which had begun with the passage of the Immigration Act of 1924.

The Immigration

Because of overpopulation, depressed farming conditions, and political turmoil in Japan in the late 1800s, its citizens began migrating to Hawaii and the United States mainland in search of better economic opportunities. Although 148 Japanese contract laborers arrived in Hawaii in 1868 to work on the plantations, their emigration violated Japanese law. Japanese immigrants did not arrive in the United States and Hawaii in significant numbers until the Japanese government, because of internal problems, legalized immigration in 1886. There were 55 persons of Japanese ancestry in the United States in 1870; 2,039 in 1890;

and 111,010 in 1920.[10]   The largest number of Japanese immigrants arrived in the United States between 1891 and 1924. About 200,000 came during this period.[11]

After the anti-Chinese forces had successfully stopped Chinese immigration, epitomized by the Chinese Exclusion Act of 1882, there was still a need for seasonal farm laborers in the developing West.   The Japanese immigrants filled the labor void in agriculture and in other areas that had been created by the cessation of Chinese immigration.   Why Whites on the West Coast halted the immigration of one group of Asians and then encouraged the coming of another is a curious and complex historical phenomenon.   However, it was only a matter of time before the anti-Asian forces, already mobilized, began to aggressively and viciously attack the Japanese Americans as they had earlier attacked the Chinese.

Most of the first Japanese immigrants were young men, some of whom were married.   They hoped to earn a small fortune in the United States and return to Japan.   Like the Chinese, however, most of them remained in North America.   There were many similarities in the experiences of Japanese and Chinese immigrants to the United States.   However, there were some significant differences that profoundly influenced the development of the Chinese-American and Japanese-American communities.   Organizations emerged within the Little Tokyos of America, as in early Chinatown, to help the new immigrant secure lodging, food, and jobs.

There were also few women among the first Japanese immigrants.   Like the Chinese, they had to share the women who were available.   However, the man-woman ratio never became as imbalanced within the Japanese-American community as it became in the Chinese community because the Japanese immigrants were able to marry Japanese women, despite the exclusion laws that were directed against Japanese immigrants.   Although the men were in the United States and the women in Japan, marriages were arranged with photographs.   The wives would later join their husbands, whom they had never seen, in the

---

10.   Lyman, p. 66.

11.   Harry H. L. Kitano, *Japanese Americans: The Evolution of A Subculture* (Englewood Cliffs, N. J.; Prentice-Hall, 1969), p. 7fn.

United States. These women became known as "picture brides." Although this type of marriage was vigorously opposed by anti-Japanese groups, it was consistent with Japanese custom and continued until outlawed in Japan in 1920. Many parents of second generation Japanese Americans (Nisei)* were married in a "picture" ceremony. These marriages worked amazingly well, partly because traditionally romantic love had not been a major factor in Japanese marriages. Rather, marriages were more the joining of two families (or *ie*) than two individuals. This Japanese adage cogently expresses this attitude toward marriage: "Those who come together in passion stay together in tears."

Although most of the Issei men were much older than their "picture brides," the fact that they were able to marry helped the Japanese to establish strong families in the United States. Some writers consider the Japanese family the most significant factor in the social and economic mobility of Japanese Americans. Strong families developed early in the Japanese-American community, partly because of the picture bride custom. Because of exclusion laws which prohibited the immigration of Chinese females, family life in the Chinese American community developed slowly. A large and assertive second generation of Japanese Americans emerged because the Issei were able to establish families in the United States. Such a generation did not develop among the Chinese because of their lack of family life for several decades. There were few Chinese women available and Chinese men were unable to marry Whites. The Chinese community, because of exclusion laws, was made up primarily of destitute, lonely, aging, and exploited men for several decades.

When they arrived on the West Coast, the Japanese immigrants worked in a variety of fields, including agriculture, the railroads, domestic work, gardening, small businesses, and industry. Because of job discrimination, they worked mainly in self-employment types of occupations. Consequently, they made their greatest impact in such fields as agriculture, gardening, and small business. Of all of these areas, their accomplishments in agriculture, and especially truck farming, were the most impressive. Much of the land they were able to farm was considered

---

* *Japanese Americans use specific terms to designate each generation:* Issei, Nisei, *and* Sansei *refer to the first, second, and third generations, respectively. These terms are used frequently in this book.*

unarable and largely useless by most White farmers. With a great deal of ingenuity and the use of intensive-farming techniques, the Japanese began to dominate certain areas of California truck farming. They produced 90 percent of the state's peppers, strawberries, celery, and snap beans in 1941. In the same year, they raised a large percentage of California's cucumbers, tomatoes, cabbage, carrots, lettuce, and onions.[12]

The Japanese immigrants were often praised for their industry and eagerness when they first arrived in California. However, their tremendous success in agriculture eventually alarmed and frightened farmers. They no longer saw the Japanese merely as ambitious workers and servants, but as tough competitors in the marketplace. To halt their success and to drive them out of California, White farmers and labor leaders enflamed anti-Asian feelings and warned of a new "Yellow-Peril."

Some familiar faces and organizations, such as Dennis Kearney and the California newspapers, renewed their anti-Asian tactics. Anti-Japanese attitudes were pervasive on the West Coast. Almost every institution was affected. In 1906, the San Francisco Board of Education ordered all Asian-American children, including the Japanese, to attend the segregated "Oriental" school. Japan was upset by this order and considered it a gross insult. Because of Japan's growing military strength, President Theodore Roosevelt thought that the order might cause a serious conflict with Japan. Consequently, he intervened and persuaded the school board to rescind the order.

To help mitigate the pervasive anti-Japanese feelings on the West Coast, the United States and Japan worked out an agreement designed to drastically reduce the immigration of Japanese laborers to the United States. This agreement, which became known as the Gentlemen's Agreement, was completed in 1908. Japan agreed to halt the immigration of laborers to the United States; the United States agreed to end discrimination against the Japanese. After this agreement, the number of Japanese entering the United States was drastically reduced. However, the anti-Japanese movements continued unabated. The most extremist groups wanted nothing less than total exclusion of the Japanese.

12. Melendy, *Oriental Americans*, p. 137

"The Japs Must Go!" became the rallying cry of the anti-Japanese movements. Racist headlines in the press, attacks on Japanese businesses, and other forms of violence took place. The anti-Japanese forces won a major victory when the California legislature passed the Alien Land Bill in 1913. Japanese immigrants were considered "aliens ineligible for citizenship." This bill, designed to drive the Japanese out of farming, prohibited the Issei from leasing land for more than three years. Although the Japanese found this law devastating, they were able, to some extent, to circumvent it. Consequently, it did not have the impact its architects had hoped. Many Issei used their children's names to secure land or obtained land with the help of White friends. In 1920 the California legislature passed a more severe law, which was destined to have the effects the legislators had hoped the 1913 law would have. This law prevented the Issei from leasing land and prohibited them from using their children's names to lease land which they could not legally lease themselves. This law served as the prototype for laws later passed in such states as Arizona, New Mexico, Oregon, Utah, and Wyoming.

Although the Alien Land Law of 1920 successfully reduced the number of Japanese Americans in agriculture, the anti-Japanese movement continued in full force. The groups making up this movement wanted a total victory, which they viewed as a complete halt of Japanese immigration to the United States and the removal of the Japanese from California. They claimed that despite the Gentlemen's Agreement, the picture brides were swelling the Japanese population in the United States and that the Japanese were having an alarming number of children. The phobia of these groups was totally unfounded. The proportion of Japanese immigrants in the United States has always been very small. During the period 1915-24, when the movement to exclude Japanese immigrants was intense, 85,197 Japanese immigrants entered the United States, which made up only 2.16 percent of all immigrants who came to the United States during this period.[13] While a total of 45,533,116 immigrants came to the United States between 1820 and 1971, only 370,033 of these were Japanese. In 1920 there were only 111,010 Japanese immigrants

13. William Petersen, *Japanese Americans* (New York: Random House, 1971), pp. 4–5

in the United States. Thus it was clearly fiction and racism rather than fact that caused alarm about the "swelling" Japanese population in the United States.

The anti-Japanese forces experienced a long awaited victory when the Immigration Act of 1924 was passed. This act fixed quotas for European countries on the basis of the percentages of their immigrants living in the United States. The act, in effect, stopped Asian immigration. "The 1924 immigration act was a major victory for racists, nativists, and exclusionists, and there is little doubt that it was resented by an insulted and bewildered Japan, which having understood that she was to become an important member of the family of nations, did not now understand this slap in the face." [14]

The Internment

On December 7, 1941, Japan attacked Pearl Harbor. Hysteria emerged on the West Coast as the anti-Japanese groups spread rumors about the so-called fifth column and espionage activities among the Japanese.[15] Some Whites argued that all Japanese Americans were still loyal to their mother country; others claimed that you could not tell a "good Jap" from a "bad Jap." Rumors, which spread like wildfire, suggested that the United States was in danger of being attacked by a fleet of Japanese soldiers and that Japanese Americans were helping to plan the attack. A tremendous fear of what came to be known as the "Yellow Peril" haunted the Pacific Coast. Daniels notes that the fear of conquest by Japan was irrational and racist.[16] The press reinforced and perpetuated the fear by printing highly fictionalized and sensationalized news stories about the Japanese "threat."

It is significant to note that California farmers and politicians played key roles in creating and perpetuating myths about the Yellow Peril. The farmers had long wanted to drive the Japanese out of California; politicians used the issue to gain votes and to divert attention from real political and social issues.

14. Kitano, *Japanese Americans*, p. 28.

15. Roger Daniels, *Concentration Camps USA: Japanese Americans and World War II* (New York: Holt, 1971), p. 27.

16. Ibid., p. 29.

It is also worth noting that we know of no sabotage activities in which Japanese Americans were involved during the war. In his perceptive study of the internment, Daniels argues that the decision to remove the Japanese from the West Coast was a political, rather than military decision. Military officials knew during the war that the Japanese on the West Coast were not a security risk. However, because anti-Japanese groups in California urged the removal of the Japanese, it was politically expedient to intern them.[17]

The uproar on the West Coast and the fear which spread throughout other parts of the nation resulted in the issuance of Executive Order No. 9066 by President Franklin D. Roosevelt on February 19, 1942. This order authorized the secretary of war to declare military areas "from which any or all persons may be excluded, and with respect to which, the right of any person to enter, remain in, or leave shall be subject to whatever restrictions the Secretary of War . . . may impose in his discretion."[18] Although mention of the Japanese Americans by name is notably absent from the document, the order was clearly aimed at them. It authorized the secretary of war to remove Japanese Americans from the West Coast (declared a "military area") and to set up federal concentration camps to which they would be forcibly removed. (See Figure 9.1.)

The Japanese were first sent to assembly centers, which served as temporary living quarters. Later, a total of 110,000 Japanese Americans were located in these ten concentration camps: Tule Lake and Manzanar in interior California, Minidoka in Idaho, Topaz in Utah, Poston and Gila River in Arizona, Heart Mountain in Wyoming, Granada in Colorado, and Rohwer and Jerome in Arkansas. Most of the camps were located in desolate and barren areas which had hot weather in the summer and cold weather in the winter. They were fenced in with barbed wire and guarded by soldiers.

The internment had some very adverse effects on the culture

17. This is the major thesis set forth in Daniels, *Concentration Camps USA.*

18. Franklin D. Roosevelt, "Executive Order No. 9033," reprinted in Audrie Girdner and Anne Loftis, *The Great Betrayal: The Evacuation of the Japanese-Americans during World War II* (New York: Macmillan, 1969), pp. 521–22.

THE WRA RELOCATION CAMPS, 1942–1946

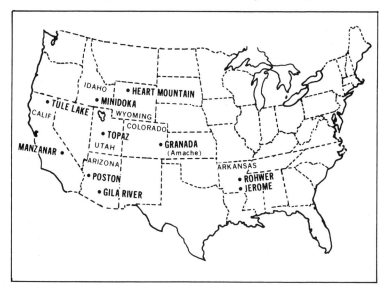

FIGURE 9.1 *Reprinted with permission from Roger Daniels,* Concentration Camps USA: Japanese Americans and World War II *(New York: Holt, Rinehart and Winston, Inc., 1971). Copyright © 1971 by Holt, Rinehart and Winston, Inc.*

and life of the Japanese American. Because of the wide differences in the cultures of Japan and the United States, the Issei and Nisei had been less able to understand each other than most other immigrants and their children. The camp experience increased their alienation. The position of the Issei was further undermined in the camps because often their children, because they were American citizens, were able to get responsible jobs for which the Issei did not qualify. This was a severe blow to the self-image and confidence of the Issei male, since for centuries the oldest Japanese male had been the undisputed head of the household.

Other events greatly undermined the strength and cogency of the Japanese family, which traditionally had been the pivotal force within the Japanese community. The female often made as much money as the male, and the family had to eat in a communal dining room. The father was unable to exercise his usual authority because of these types of situations. Consequently, family solidarity was greatly lessened in the camps.

Widespread conflict developed within the camps over the question of loyalty. The Nisei often questioned the loyalty of the Issei. Japanese nationals accused the leaders of the Japanese American Citizenship League, who cooperated with the War Relocation Authority, of participating in the oppression of the Japanese. In their eagerness to prove their loyalty to the United States government, some Japanese helped federal authorities to conduct witch hunts for "suspected" Japanese. The internment showed how a dehumanizing experience could demoralize a group which had traditionally had high group solidarity and trust and cause mistrust and suspicion within it. Several writers have recently discussed the "advantages" of the internment.[19] However, to discuss the "advantages" of this demoralizing experience would be comparable to discussing the "advantages" of slavery and lynching.

The Japanese American Today

In 1970 there were 591,290 Americans of Japanese descent living in the United States. This is a relatively small percentage of our total population, which was over 200 million in 1970. Japanese immigration was halted by the Immigration Act of 1924 and did not resume until the ban on Asian immigration was lifted when the McCarran-Walter Act was passed in 1952. Although this act set a quota of only 185 Japanese immigrants per year, Asian immigrants were no longer totally excluded.

After World War II most Japanese Americans returned to the West Coast, although many moved to the East and Midwest. However, the Japanese-American population is highly concentrated rather than dispersed. In 1970 more than 80 percent of the Japanese Americans lived in Hawaii and California. Each of these two states had about the same Japanese population. The states of Washington, Illinois, and New York had the next largest concentrations of Japanese Americans. Each state contained about 3 percent of the Japanese-American population.[20] Japanese Americans are primarily urban dwellers. Eighty percent of them lived in urban areas in 1970. After Congress passed the Immigration Reform Act in 1965, the percentage of Japanese

19. Kitano, *Japanese Americans;* Daniels, *Concentration Camps USA.*

20. Fersh, "Orientals and Orientation," p. 315.

Americans increased. The White-American population increased by 12 percent in the decade of 1960–70. The Japanese-American population increased by nearly 30 percent during this same period.[21]

The Japanese Americans have been called the "model" American ethnic minority group because of their success in education, social class mobility, and low levels of crime, mental illness, and other social deviances. Notes Petersen: "By almost any criterion of good citizenship that we choose, not only are Japanese Americans better than any other segment of American society, including native whites of native parents, but they have realized this remarkable progress by their own almost unaided effort. . . . Every attempt to hamper the progress of Japanese Americans, in short, has resulted in enhancing their determination to succeed." [22]

While it is true that most Japanese Americans belong to the middle class and have largely culturally assimilated, it is also true that they are often the victims of racism and discrimination, even though it might be subtle. The Japanese have acquired more schooling since 1940 than any other group in the United States. However, their average income is still below that of Whites.[23] Also, Japanese Americans are rarely found in top administrative positions in business and industry. While the Japanese have attained a high degree of cultural assimilation, their structural assimilation has been limited.* Much of their social and civil life is confined to their ethnic group. Their sense of peoplehood and group solidarity is greatly strengthened by functioning within their ethnic group. Thus structural pluralism greatly benefits both the ethnic individual and the group. Although the Japanese Americans are economically successful, they are rather powerless politically.

Despite the Nisei's disappointment over much of the behavior of the highly assimilated Sansei, they have, more than any other previous generation of Japanese Americans, called atten-

21. Ibid., p. 316.

22. Petersen, *Japanese Americans*, pp. 4–5.

23. Ibid., pp. 113, 120.

* Cultural *and* structural assimilation *are defined and discussed in Chapter 2, pp. 43–45.*

tion to the subtle racism to which they are often the victim and have argued for the right to assert their ethnic culture and identity. The Sansei have also issued a call for psychological liberation and political power. However, it was the noted if quiet achievements of the Issei and Nisei that made it possible for the Sansei to have both the desire and courage to speak out so forcefully today.

Filipino Americans: Historical Perspective

Important Dates

1898	The Philippine Islands were ceded to the United States under the Treaty of Paris which ended the Spanish-American War.
1907	Over 200 Filipino contract laborers were brought to Hawaii by the Hawaiian Sugar Planters Association.
1923–29	A large number of Filipinos immigrated to Hawaii and the United States mainland to work as field laborers.
1927	The Filipino Federation of Labor was founded in Los Angeles. Filipinos became active in the union movement and organized a number of strikes during the 1920s.
1929	An anti-Filipino riot occurred in Exeter, California, in which over 200 Filipinos were assaulted.
1930	Fermin Tobera, who later became a Filipino martyr, was killed in an anti-Filipino riot in Watsonville, California.
1934	Congress passed the Tydings-McDuffie Act. This act promised the Philippines independence and limited Filipino immigration to the United States to fifty per year.
1935	President Franklin D. Roosevelt signed the Repatriation Act on July 11. This act offered free transportation to Filipinos who would return to the Philippines. Those who left

Important Dates cont.

	were unable to return except under the quota system.
1940	Under the terms of the Nationality Act of 1940, Filipino immigrants to the United States could now become citizens through naturalization. American citizenship was extended to other categories of Filipino Americans on July 2, 1946.
1941	Japan attacked the Philippines.
1946	On July 4, 1946, the Philippines became independent.
1970	By 1970, Filipino immigration had increased substantially because of the Immigration Act of 1965. In 1965, 2,545 Filipinos immigrated to the United States, while in 1970, 25,417 came.

The Immigration

The magnet that pulled Filipinos to Hawaii and the United States came primarily from without rather than within. Immigration from the Philippines during the 333 years that the Islands were ruled by Spain was virtually nil. However, when the United States acquired the Philippines after the Spanish-American War in 1898, it was only a matter of time before farmers in Hawaii and the United States would successfully lure Filipinos away from the islands to work as cheap and exploited field hands. Recruiting and transportation agents lured Filipinos away from their homeland with high-pressured propaganda about the promises of Hawaii and the United States. Because of chronic unemployment and widespread poverty in the islands, thousands of Filipinos left their native land in search of the dream.

Since Chinese immigration had come to an abrupt end in 1882, Japanese immigrants had been the main source of cheap labor for plantation owners in Hawaii and big farmers on the United States West Coast. However, the Gentlemen's Agreement of 1907 substantially reduced Japanese immigration, and the Immigration Act of 1924 virtually stopped it. When Japanese immigration had ended, a new source of cheap labor was desired by farmers in Hawaii and in the United States. The United States had recently annexed both Puerto Rico and the Philippines. Each nation was regarded as a promising source of cheap labor. However, the attempt to start large scale immigration from Puerto Rico failed, and the farmers turned to the Philippines, where they had considerable success. The powerful Hawaiian Sugar Planters Association became so alarmed when the Gentlemen's Agreement restricted Japanese immigration in 1907 that it brought over 200 Filipino workers to Hawaii that year. The association wanted to make sure that when Japanese immigration stopped there would be a new source of labor just as abundant and cheap.

Filipino immigration to Hawaii continued and escalated after 1907. However, until the 1920s, most of the Filipino immigrants remained in Hawaii and did not come to the United States mainland. In 1920 there were only 5,603 Filipinos in the United States. However, from 1923, when Filipino immigration to the United States gained momentum, until it reached its peak in 1929, large scale immigration to the mainland occurred. In 1929 alone, 5,795 Filipinos entered California. Between 1907 and 1910, about 150,000 immigrants left the Philippines and headed for Hawaii or the United States.

Although the highly glorified and exaggerated tales spread by recruiting and transportation agents made up the magnet which pulled hundreds of Filipinos from their homeland, the letters and money sent back home by immigrants, as well as the desire to get rich quick, helped to motivate them to leave the poverty stricken Islands.

Filipino immigrants in the United States had some unique group characteristics which were destined to make their lives on the West Coast harsh and poignant. As the third wave of Asian immigrants, they were victims of the accumulated anti-Asian racism. They were also a very young group. According to McWilliams, they were the youngest group of immigrants in United States history. They ranged in age from about 16 to 30. Most, 84.3 percent, were under 30.[24] The immigrants were predominantly male. Few Filipino women immigrated because

24. Carey McWilliams, *Brothers Under the Skin* (Boston: Little, Brown and Company, 1943), p. 232.

female immigration violated tradition. Also, most of the immigrants were sojourners who hoped to return to the Philippines after attaining the riches of America. Like the other Asian sojourners, the longer they stayed in the United States, the more the hope waned that they would ever be able to return home.

The sex ratio was serious, as it was in early Chinese-American communities. In 1930 there was one woman for every 143 men. The Filipino immigrated from a country that was an American colony in which the American myth of "all men are created equal" was perpetuated in the schools. Thus, unlike the other Asian groups, he came to the United States expecting to be treated like an equal. His acceptance of this myth made his adjustment in the United States all the more difficult.

Work

Like other Asian immigrants, the Filipino came to Hawaii and the United States to do work the Anglos disdained and refused to do. They were hired, usually under a contract system, to pick asparagus and lettuce, and to do other kinds of "stoop" field work. In addition to farming, the Filipino, especially after World War II, worked as a domestic. He cooked, washed dishes, and worked as a house servant. Some worked in the fishing industry and in canneries.

The Filipino Community

Unlike the Japanese and Chinese, the Filipino was unable to develop tightly knit ethnic communities. The "Little Manila" districts in cities such as Los Angeles and San Francisco were primarily stopping places for the field hands between seasons and entertainment centers. The Filipino could not establish highly cohesive communities because his jobs kept him moving and because, like the Chinese immigrant, he was unable to have much of a family life because of the paucity of Filipino females.

The types of entertainment and recreation which emerged within Filipino American communities reflected the sociological makeup of young, unmarried males searching for meaning in life within a hostile and racist atmosphere. Prostitution, cockfighting, and gambling were favorite pastimes for the lonely, alienated men. The Filipino-owned dance halls, in which White girls danced and sold or gave other favors to the immigrants, were popular and a source of widespread tension between Filipinos and White men. Whites passed laws prohibiting Filipinos from marrying White women. However, these laws had little effect on biological drives and mutual attraction between White women and Filipino men. Stockton, California, because so many Filipinos settled there, was dubbed the "Manila of the United States." It was the site of much conflict and tension between Filipinos and Whites. Although there were few tightly organized Filipino communities, a strong sense of group solidarity and sense of peoplehood emerged among Filipinos. Strong nationalism, as the gifted Filipino-American writer Carlos Bulosan epitomized,[25] was widespread among Filipinos in the United States.

Anti-Filipino Agitation

Filipinos were the third wave of Asian immigrants to come to the West Coast. Consequently, they inherited all of the anti-Asian prejudice and racism which had accumulated since the Chinese started immigrating to the United States in the 1850s. When Filipino immigration reached significant levels in the 1920s, familiar anti-Asian screams about the "Yellow Peril" were again heard. These anti-Asian movements were, again, led by organized labor and patriotic organizations such as the American Federation of Labor and the Native Sons of the Golden West. The arguments were identical to those that had been made against the Chinese and Japanese: the victims were different but the victimizers the same. Labor groups claimed that Filipinos were "unfair competition"; patriotic groups argued that they were unassimilable and would pollute the "pure" White race. One exclusionist warned, "This mongrel stream is small, but when it is considered how rapidly it multiplies and grows it is clear that the tide must be stemmed before its gets beyond control."[26]

25. Bulosan's works are perceptively discussed in E. San Juan, Jr., *Carlos Bulosan and the Imagination of the Class Struggle* (Quezon City: University of the Philippines Press, 1972).

26. Quoted in Robert A. Divine, *American Immigration Policy, 1924–1952* (New Haven: Yale University Press, 1957).

Labor and nativistic groups had succeeded in halting Chinese and Japanese immigration by urging Congress to pass exclusion laws. However, the Filipinos presented a different problem. They could not be excluded as "aliens" under the provisions of the Immigration Act of 1924 because of their peculiar and ambiguous legal status. Because the United States had annexed the Philippines in 1898, its citizens were not aliens. However, unlike Puerto Ricans, they were not citizens of the United States either. Filipinos were "nationals" or "wards" of the United States. Consequently, they could not be excluded with the immigration laws applied to foreign nations. Representative Richard Welch of California, nevertheless, fought hard to get an outright exclusion act through Congress in 1928. The attempt failed, but Welch succeeded in rallying widespread support for the anti-Filipino cause.

The failure of the Welch bill convinced the leaders of the exclusion movement that they had to try another strategy. The desire for independence within the Philippines had grown intense by the late 1920s. The Philippines independence movement gave the exclusionists new hope for a cause which had become an obsession: to exclude and deport Filipinos. They jumped on the independence bandwagon. If the Philippines became independent, they correctly reasoned, its citizens could be excluded under the provisions of existing immigration laws. The passage of the Tydings-McDuffie Act on March 24, 1934, was a significant victory for the exclusionists.

In addition to promising the Philippines independence, the Tydings-McDuffie Act limited Filipino immigration to the United States to 50 persons per year. This act, as was the intention of its architects, virtually excluded Filipino immigration to the United States. Even this bill did not totally satisfy the exclusionists. They not only wanted Filipino immigration stopped; they wanted them deported. They pushed the so-called Repatriation Act through Congress. President Franklin D. Roosevelt signed the act on July 11, 1935. Under the terms of the act, any Filipino could obtain free transportation back to the Philippines. However, there was an insidious catch to this inducement. Once they returned, they could not reenter the United States. Few Filipinos were seduced by this racist trap. Only about 2,000 returned to the Philippines under the act's provisions.

Riots and Anti-Filipino Violence

Both before and after the Filipino exclusion and deportation acts, anti-Filipino Whites carried out a vicious and active campaign of violence against Filipinos in the Western states. One of the first anti-Filipino riots broke out in Yakima, Washington on September 19, 1928. Some of the most serious riots took place in California, where most Filipino immigrants first settled. On October 24, 1929, Whites attacked and assaulted over 200 Filipinos and did considerable property damage in Exeter, California. Fermin Tobera, a lettuce picker, was killed in a riot which took place in Watsonville, California in January, 1930. Tobera's murder greatly disturbed his native homeland, and a National Humiliation Day was declared in Manila. Some Filipinos felt that Tobera was ruthlessly slain by a "mob of bloodthirsty Americans." [27] Three people were shot in a riot which occurred near Salinas, California in August 1934. An anti-Filipino riot took place as late as June 1939, in Lake County California. "No reparations or indemnities were ever made for these repeated outrages; nor were the culprits ever punished. . . ."[28]

Filipino Americans Today

Filipinos have become the second largest group immigrating to the United States since the passage of the Immigration Act of 1965.* They are exceeded only by Mexican nationals. The number of Filipinos entering the United States increased from 2,545 in 1965 to 25,417 in 1970.[29] The Filipino population in the

---

* Although a large number of Puerto Ricans enter the United States mainland from the island each year, Puerto Ricans are not considered immigrants but migrants because they are United States citizens.

27. Sonia E. Wallovits, "The Filipinos in California," master's thesis, University of Southern California, 1966, p. 124.

28. McWilliams, *Brothers*, p. 240.

29. Earl Caldwell, "Filipinos: A Fast Growing Minority," *New York Times*, March 5, 1971, quoted in Amy Tachiki, Eddie Wong, Franklin Odo, with Buck Wong, eds., *Roots: An Asian American Reader* (Los Angeles: UCLA Asian American Studies Center, 1971), p. 312.

United States increased by 95 percent in the decade of 1960 to
1970, while the White population increased by 12 percent. In
1970 there were 343,060 Filipino Americans. Of these about
40 percent lived in California and 30 percent in Hawaii. The
next highest concentrations lived in New York, Illinois, and
Washington, with about 3 percent each. Most Filipinos, about
75 percent of them, lived in urban areas in 1970.[30]

While most of the Filipinos who came to the United States
in the 1920s were unskilled laborers, quite a few professionals,
such as teachers, doctors, lawyers, and other skilled workers are
among those immigrating from the Philipines today. These immigrants come to the United States to seek jobs which are more
consistent with their training than ones they can get in the Philippines. More persons are trained for professional jobs in the
Phillipines than can find suitable employment.

However, professional Filipino immigrants to the United
States face a number of unique problems because of discrimination, alleged difference in training, and linguistic traits. Many
of them are unable to find jobs in the United States consistent
with their training. Thus, a number of highly trained Filipino
American professionals work as laborers and in service jobs because they are unable to obtain other kinds of work. Many of
those who eventually obtain professional jobs have obtained
additional training at American schools.

The significant number of professionally trained Filipinos
who have immigrated to the United States since the Immigration
Act of 1965 was enacted has substantially changed the social
and demographic characteristics of the Filipino Americans.
Daniels wrote, prior to the publication of the 1970 census, ". . .
Filipinos are the most disadvantaged identifiable immigrant and
immigrant-descended group: they have less formal education,
lower income, and are more heavily concentrated as migrant
laborers than any other segment of the population."[31] The 1970
census data indicate that Daniels' conclusions are inaccurate to-

30. Fersh, "Orientals and Orientation," pp. 315–16.

31. Roger Daniels, "The Asian American Experience," in William H.
Cartwright and Richard L. Watson, Jr., eds., *The Reinterpretation of Ameri-
can History and Culture* (Washington, D. C.: National Council for the
Social Studies, 1973), p. 143.

day.[32] The mean income of Chinese Americans, sixteen and over, in states with 10,000 or more Chinese American population was $5,195 in 1969. Comparable mean incomes for Japanese Americans and Filipino Americans were $6,001 and $4,862 respectively. In 1969, 19 percent of the total number of Japanese Americans who were employed were professional, technical, and kindred workers. Two percent were farm laborers and foremen. Comparable figures for Chinese Americans were 25 percent and 1.3 percent respectively. In the same year, of the total number of Filipino Americans in the Labor force, 24 percent worked as professional, technical and kindred workers, and 7 percent as farm laborers and foremen. (See Table 9.1).

These statistics indicate that the total group characteristics of Filipino Americans, using several important criteria related to income and employment, do not differ substantially from the Japanese Americans and Chinese Americans. Data in the 1970 census suggest that old statistics about the economic and employment characteristics of Filipino Americans must be seriously questioned and revised. However, these summary statistics should not be construed to mean that there is not a substantial lower socioeconomic group of Filipino Americans. Mean figures tend to conceal the extreme characteristics of a population. Most of the Filipino Americans who were members of the lower class in 1960 still are today. However, there are signs that things will improve considerably for Filipino Americans in the future. Increasingly, Filipinos are becoming involved in community action programs and have initiated grass-roots programs which are destined to bolster their economic status and facilitate their current identity quest. The rapidly increasing numbers of Filipino Americans is a potential political asset. If the Filipino community is effectively organized, and there are signs that it will be, it can become a cogent force for political and social change that will substantially improve the Filipino's plight in America.

32. *Japanese, Chinese, and Filipinos in the United States: Subject Report* (Washington, D. C.: U. S. Government Printing Office, 1973). All of the data which follow are based on individuals who are sixteen years and over who live in United States states with 10,000 or more members of the ethnic groups that are the subjects of the data. The data are not based on heads of households. If they were, the mean incomes of all groups would be considerably higher.

Table 9.1

Selected Income and Employment Characteristics of Asian Americans*

	Japanese Americans	Chinese Americans	Filipino Americans
Total employed	263,972	183,562	131,555
Percent employed as professional, technical, and kindred workers	19 percent	25 percent	24 percent
Percent employed as farm laborers and foremen.	2 percent	0.3 percent	7 percent
Percent employed as service workers, except private household	11 percent	20 percent	19 percent
Mean income (based on individuals employed who are 16 or over in selected states)	$6,001	$5,195	$4,862

* This table is based on information reported in *Japanese, Chinese and Filipinos in the United States: Subject Report* (Washington, D. C.: U. S. Government Printing Office, 1973). All of the data are based on individuals who are 16 years and over who live in United States states with 10,000 or more members of the ethnic groups that are the subjects of the data. The data *are not* based on heads of households. If they were, the totals would be quite different.

Teaching Strategies

Concepts such as immigration, discrimination, and cultural diversity are highlighted in the historical overviews. In this part of the chapter, strategies for teaching two concepts, immigration and discrimination, are illustrated. An infinite variety of strategies can be used to teach both concepts. However, these activities are illustrative, and can serve as a guide to teacher planning. While both concepts can and should be taught at all grade levels, we discuss strategies for teaching immigration at the primary and intermediate and upper levels and discrimination at the high school level.

PRIMARY GRADES

CONCEPT: Immigration

Generalization: Asian Americans immigrated to the United States to improve their economic conditions and to fulfill labor needs in Hawaii and in the continental United States.

1. Ask the students if their families have ever moved from one part of the city to another, from one city to another, or from one state to another. Also ask if any students have moved from one country to another. Record their responses on the board or butcher paper. Discuss them.

2. Ask the students *why* their families moved. List their responses on the board or butcher paper. Reasons may include, "My dad had to move because he was out of work. He moved to get a new job"; "We moved because we wanted a bigger house"; "We moved to be closer to relatives"; and "We moved because the building that we were living in was being torn down." Group and classify the reasons why people move. Discuss the reasons.

3. Introduce the concept of immigration. Tell the students that some people not only move from one part of a city to another, or from city to city, or state to state, but from nation to nation. In fact, every group of people in our nation, except American Indians, came to this country from another nation. Say, "When people move from one nation to another we say that they are *immigrating*." Write the word on the board or butcher paper. Ask the students if they have ever

known a family that immigrated. If so, discuss their responses.

4. Explain to the students, using a large primary grade map, that present Americans came from many different lands, including Africa, Australia, Europe, and Asia. Say, "Today, we are going to discuss a family that lived in China (show on map) in 1847 (explain how long ago that was), the Wong family. Before I read the story about the Wong family, let's list some reasons why we think that Mr. Wong may have wanted to leave China and come to the United States." List students' responses on board or butcher paper.

5. Through questioning, bring out that people sometimes move from nation to nation for some of the same reasons that they move from city to city, or state to state, e.g., for work, more money, or to live closer to relatives.

Read the following story to the class and ask the questions which follow.

THE WONG FAMILY

Many, many years ago, in 1847, there lived a family in a land far across the Pacific Ocean in a country called China. The father's name was Mr. Wong. The mother's name was Mrs. Wong. Their three children and Mr. Wong's parents lived with Mr. and Mrs. Wong. The Wongs lived in a tiny village in Southern China called Toishan.

"I think that the rice crop will fail again this year," said Mr. Wong to Mrs. Wong one day as they walked to the house on their way from the rice field after a hard day's work. For three years in a row floods had almost totally destroyed their rice crops. Rice was the main crop and source of food in Toishan. This year another big flood had come, and it seemed like the crop would again be nearly destroyed. Mr. and Mrs. Wong had been working in the field all day trying to save the rice crop.

Mr. and Mrs. Wong were very worried about how they were going to harvest enough rice to feed the family and to pay the high taxes, which had gotten higher and higher each year. The Wongs also had other problems. Their small farm was too little for a family as large as theirs to make a good living. There were too many people in the tiny village and more and more children were born each year. The government was also having troubles. Some people were very upset with the way that the government was running the nation. They had started *rebellions*. (Explain)

The Wong family had just finished dinner when Mr. Chan, a family friend, stopped by the house. Mr. Chan was very excited! He was so excited that he could barely tell the good news he had heard that day in town. "We needn't worry about our crops anymore, about high taxes, or about the trouble with the government!" said Mr. Chan. "Why, why, why?" asked Mr. Wong anxiously. "About 7,000 miles across the ocean there is a land of a Mountain of Gold!" said Mr. Chan. Mr. Chan told Mr. and Mrs. Wong about the great land of gold, and how Mr. Wong could go there, get rich, and come back home. He then showed them a glittering gold nugget that Mr. Lee's son had brought back from the land of gold. Everyone was speechless with excitement! Mr. Chan said that if he and Mr. Wong went to the land of Gold and came back, they would never again have to worry about failing crops. He told Mr. and Mrs. Wong about how much the trip cost, and when the next ship would be leaving for the land of gold from Canton, a city north of Toishan.

Mr. and Mrs. Wong thought for weeks about the land of the Mountain of Gold, and how great it would be if Mr. Wong could go there and get rich! Mr. Wong did not want to tell his parents that he was thinking of leaving China because he knew that custom taught that a son should stay and take care of his family, which included a son's parents in China. Mr. and Mrs. Wong also knew that the family could not go with Mr. Wong if he went, and that Mr. Wong would be harshly punished if he was caught trying to leave the country. It was *illegal* (explain) to leave the country. They also did not know where they would get the money for his trip.

Nearly two months after Mr. Chan's visit, Mr. Wong, Mr. Chan, and some other men who lived in Toishan, left for the land of the Mountain of Gold. The parting of the Wong family was very sad, but Mr. Wong thought that he would get rich and return home in a year or two. The three young Wong children cried when Daddy said good-bye, but they knew that he was trying to make things better for them, mother, and their grandparents.

After a rough 7,000 mile voyage across the ocean, Mr. Wong finally reached the land of the Mountain of Gold. However, when he got to San Francisco, the people thought that he looked strange, and would often say mean things to him. He could not find any gold and had to dig in mines which had already been dug by White men from the Eastern part of the United States. Mr. Wong's dreams were shattered. He was able to send a little money home, but it was many years later before he was able to go back to China to see his family. But Mr. Wong was luckier than some of the other men who went to California from Toishan. Mr. Chan never saw his family back in China again.

Questions

1. In what nation did Mr. and Mrs. Wong live? Point it out on the map.
2. What problems did the Wong family have in China? Why?
3. Why did Mr. Wong decide to come to California (show on map)?
4. Why was California known as the "land of the Mountain of Gold?"
5. What happened to Mr. Wong once he was in California? Why?
6. What do you think happened to his family back in China?

Summarize the lesson by saying, "Let's see if we can summarize what we have learned about why people *immigrate* and why Mr. Wong came to San Francisco." List the children's responses on the board or butcher paper.

INTERMEDIATE AND UPPER GRADES

1. Read to the class, or ask them to read, the selections indicated below. Ask the students to be able to answer these questions when they have finished the readings:

    a) What economic, social, and political problems did the Chinese, Japanese, and Filipinos have in China, Japan, and the Philippines?
    b) What were the labor needs on the West Coast of the United States?
    c) Why did the immigrants leave China, Japan, and the Philippines?

d) Was the United States what they expected? Why or why not?

The Readings Are:

Daniel Chu and Samuel Chu, *Passage to the Golden Gate: A History of the Chinese to 1910*, pp. 23–27.*

Noel L. Leathers, *The Japanese in America*, pp. 11–28.

2. Carefully study the historical summary on Filipino-Americans in this chapter on pages 341–49. Prepare a two-page ditto summarizing the economic, social, and political conditions of the early Filipino immigrants who went to Hawaii and the United States. Assign this ditto to the students as a third reading.

3. After the students have read and discussed each of the three readings, have them complete Table 9.2.

4. When the students have completed the chart, have them

Table 9.2

Data Retrieval Chart on Asian-American Immigrants

	Chinese Immigrants	Japanese Immigrants	Filipino Immigrants
Economic situation in homeland when immigration began			
Political situation in homeland when immigration began			
Social conditions in homeland when immigration began			
Labor needs on U. S. mainland when immigration began			
Labor needs in Hawaii when immigration began			

* *Complete citations for all books cited in this part of the chapter are found in the final part of the chapter, "Materials and Resources."*

summarize and generalize about why many Chinese, Japanese, and Filipinos immigrated to Hawaii and the United States, and about the labor needs which they satisfied in these two nations.

5. Have the students role-play the situation below, which involves a representative of the Hawaiian Farmers Association trying to persuade a Filipino worker to go to Hawaii to work on a sugar plantation in 1910. After the role-playing situation, ask the students the questions that follow. The role descriptions:

Mr. Howard Smith, the Hawaiian Sugar Planters Association Representative

> Mr. Smith has been hired to recruit workers for the association. He realizes that his job depends on his success in recruiting workers. He also realizes that if he truthfully explains the situation in Hawaii, he will get very few workers. He therefore decides to paint a very rosy picture of the work on the sugar plantation in Hawaii. He explains to Mr. Ilanos that the contract is for three years and that the association will pay his transportation from the Philippines to Hawaii.

Mr. Jose Ilanos, a Filipino who lives in the Philippines

> Mr. Ilanos is a young man with a wife and two children. He is a very hard worker. However, in the last few years he has not been able to make enough money to support his family. He has heard about Mr. Smith and is interested in talking to him. However, his wife does not want him to leave the Philippines. Moreover, he has heard from friends that the work in Hawaii is very hard and that the pay is rather low.

Questions

1. Did Mr. Smith succeed in persuading Mr. Ilanos to go to Hawaii to work? Why or why not?
2. If Mr. Ilanos decided to go to Hawaii, do you think that Mrs. Ilanos would go with him? Why or why not?

3. If Mr. Ilanos decided to go to Hawaii, what do you think will happen to him? Why? Do you think that he might eventually immigrate to the United States? Why or why not?
4. If Mr. Ilanos decided to remain in the Philippines, what do you think will happen to him? Why?
5. Were there any other options opened to Mr. Ilanos besides keeping his same job or going to Hawaii to work on the sugar plantations? If there were, what were they? If there were not, why?
6. If you were Mr. Ilanos would you have accepted a contract from Mr. Smith? Why or why not?

Valuing Activity

Read the following story to the class and ask the questions which follow.

FATHER AND SON

Mr. Robert Morimoto is a second generation Japanese American who lives in an upper-middle-class, predominantly White suburban community near Los Angeles. He is a very successful businessman. Mr. Morimoto is proud to be an American and believes that even though our country has problems, any person, regardless of his race, can make it in the United States if he or she really tries. Mr. Morimoto does not like to talk about the years that he spent in the Heart Mountain federal concentration camp in Wyoming during World War II. The internment, he feels, is a thing of the past. Japanese Americans should not dwell on it too much today. Mr. Morimoto is very impatient with those Sansei who talk about the internment all of the time. He feels that they have had it easy, and do not have much right to criticize their country the way that they do.

Mr. Morimoto and his son have a lot of fights because of their different beliefs. Henry is a student at a local university and is president of the Asian-American Student Association on campus. Henry believes that the United States is a racist nation that oppresses all people of color, including the Japanese Americans. He often talks about the internment and harshly criticizes Japanese Americans like his father who try to "sweep it under the rug." Henry believes that all Third World people (by which he means all non-Whites) should join together to fight oppression and racism in America. When they had their last verbal fight, Henry told his father that even though he was successful in business, he had no political power in America, and was yellow on the outiside but was White in the inside. Mr. Morimoto got very upset with Henry. He told Henry that he would either have to start treating him with respect or move out of his house.

Questions

1. Why do you think Mr. Morimoto feels the way he does?
2. Why do you think Henry feels the way he does?
3. Do you think that Henry is treating Mr. Morimoto fairly?
4. Do you think that Mr. Morimoto is treating Henry fairly?
5. If you were Henry, what would you do? Why?
6. If you were Mr. Morimoto, what would you do? Why?

HIGH SCHOOL GRADES

CONCEPT: Discrimination

Generalization: Asian Americans have been the victims of widespread prejudice and highly discriminatory immigration and migration laws.

Initiate this unit by showing the students a film on the internment such as *Guilty by Reason of Race* (or a filmstrip such as *Relocation of Japanese Americans: Right or Wrong?*). After viewing the film or filmstrip, ask the students to write one-sentence reactions to it. Divide the class into groups of three to five to discuss their written reactions to the film or filmstrip. Each group should be asked to develop a written reaction, to be shared later with the entire class, on which all group members can agree.

1. Ask individual students or small groups of students to prepare short research reports on the following topics and present them to the class. When completing their research reports, the students can use the following books:
   Roger Daniels and Harry H.L. Kitano, *American Racism: Exploration of the Nature of Prejudice*
   Carey McWilliams, *Brothers under the Skin*

H. Brett Melendy, *The Oriental Americans*
Betty L. Sung, *The Story of the Chinese in America*

The topics are:

    a) The California Foreign Miner's Tax of 1850
    b) Anti-Chinese riots that took place in the 1800s
    c) The Chinese Exclusion Act of 1882
    d) Anti-Asian groups that developed on the West Coast in the late 1800s and continued through the 1930s, such as the Native Sons of the Golden West
    e) The California Alien Land Laws which prohibited Japanese immigrants from owning or leasing land
    f) The internment of Japanese Americans
    g) The Immigration Act of 1924
    h) Anti-Filipino riots that occurred in the 1920s and 1930s
    i) The Tydings-McDuffie Act of 1934
    j) The Repatriation Act of July 11, 1935

2. When students share their reports, have them list on a master chart (a) ways in which all of the laws and actions were similar, (b) ways in which they were different, and (c) ways in which they discriminated against Asian Americans. Through the use of higher level questions, help the students derive the key generalization stated above.

3. Have your students role-play a session of Congress in which the Chinese Exclusion Act of 1882 is debated. The entire class can participate. However, assign several specific students to lead the debates. For example, ask one student to play the role of a California senator who is very anxious to get reelected, and thus is strongly in favor of the act. Ask another student to argue against the act. Before the role-playing begins, read and discuss the act with the class. It is reprinted in Cheng-Tsu Wu, *"Chink!" A Documentary History of Anti-Chinese Prejudice in America*, pages 70–75. Ditto the act for the class.

    When the main speakers start debating, the other class members can participate both by asking them questions and by arguing on the floor. When the discussion of the act is complete, the students should then vote on it. After the voting, the role-playing should be discussed as well as the actual historical event. The students should discuss why their voting results were similar or different from that of Congress in 1882 and why. In this activity, try to help the students to create the political and social atmosphere of the late 1800s. One way this can be done is to ask each student to pretend that he or she is a senator from a specific state with a particular mandate from his constituency.

4. Ask a group of students to do research and complete Table 9.3.

After the students have completed the chart, ask them to: (1) write a generalization about the percentage of Asian immigrants that came to the United States between 1861 and 1960 and the total number of immigrants that came to the United States; and (2) discuss, using the completed chart, whether White Americans on the West Coast had valid reasons to fear what was called the "Yellow Peril." Ask them to discuss: "If Whites on the West Coast had no valid reasons to fear a Yellow Peril, why do you think that Asian Americans were the victims of so much hostility and harassment?"

Table 9.3
Asian Immigrants in the United States

Period	Number	Percentage of All Immigrants
1861–1880		
1881–1900		
1900–1914		
1914–1925		
1925–1940		
1940–1960		

5. Ask the students to read a book on the internment. Recommended books are:

   Allan R. Bosworth, *America's Concentration Camps*

   Roger Daniels, *Concentration Camps USA: Japanese Americans and World War II*

   Audrie Girdner and Anne Loftis, *The Great Betrayal: The Evacuation of the Japanese Americans during World War II*

6. After they have read a book on the subject, ask them to:

   a) Compare the interpretation of the internment in the book read with the interpretation in a high school American history textbook or some other source.

   b) Discuss why they think that the internment occurred.

   c) Discuss the role of the Japanese American Citizenship League during the internment.

   d) Discuss the roles of the following men in the internment:

      1) President Franklin D. Roosevelt
      2) Secretary of War Henry L. Stimson
      3) Lieutenant General John L. DeWitt
      4) Assistant Secretary of War John J. McCloy
      5) Colonel Karl R. Bendetsen
      6) Major General Allen W. Gullion

7. Role-play a meeting of the men listed above discussing whether the Japanese should be interned during World War II.

8. Discuss the moral implications of the internment, i.e., Should the internment have occurred? Why or why not? Who was responsible for the internment? What does the internment teach us about our society? Do you believe that an ethnic minority group could be interned today? Why or why not? Why were the Japanese interned and not the Germans?

9. To summarize this activity, ask the students to write an essay on "The Meaning of the Internment—Then and Now."

10. Asian-American authors, like other American writers, often express their reactions and experiences with prejudice and discrimination in their writings. Literary works by Asian Americans can provide students with insights that cannot be gained from factual sources. To help your students bet-

ter understand the reactions of Asian Americans to discrimination, have the class read and discuss selections from these books:

a) Shizuye Takashima, *A Child in Prison Camp*. This compelling autobiography about a child's life in a Canadian concentration camp will evoke serious emotions and reflections.

b) Carlos Bulosan, *Sound of Falling Light: Letters in Exile*. A powerful book which chronicles the collective experience of Filipinos in the United States as well as reveals the author's tragic but creative life. Students can easily read and understand Bulosan's letters.

c) Carlos Bulosan, *America Is in the Heart*. This is a poignant, beautiful, and revealing book. It can serve as an excellent springboard for a discussion about anti-Filipino discrmination in the United States.

d) David Hsin-Fu Wand, eds., *Asian-American Heritage: An Anthology of Prose and Poetry*. This anthology includes stories, poetry, essays, and excerpts from novels.

e) Yoshiko Uchida, *Journey to Topaz*. This is a good book for students to read after they have mastered basic knowledge about the internment. This is a fictionalized account of the Sakane family's experiences in the Topaz camp.

Materials and Resources

REFERENCES FOR THE TEACHER

Multiethnic

Chun-Hoon, Lowell K. Y. "Teaching the Asian-American Experience." In James A. Banks, ed. *Teaching Ethnic Studies: Concepts and Strategies*. Washington, D. C.: National Council for the Social Studies 43rd Yearbook, 1973, pp. 118–147.

This unusually perceptive and thoroughly researched chapter gives an excellent historical overview of the experiences of Asian Americans.

Daniels, Roger and Harry H. L. Kitano. *American Racism: Explorations of the Nature of Prejudice.* Englewood Cliffs, N. J. Prentice-Hall, 1970.

By using the experiences of ethnic minority groups, the authors document how racism is endemic in the United States.

Fersh, Seymour. "Orientals and Orientation." *Phi Delta Kappan* 53 (January 1972), pp. 315–18.

An informative, creative, and compassionately written article.

Hill, Herbert. "Anti-Oriental Agitation and the Rise of Working-Class Racism." *Society* 10 (January/February 1973), pp. 43–54.

An informative discussion of racism in organized labor.

Jacobs, Paul, Saul Landau with Eve Pell. *To Serve the Devil, Volume 2: Colonials and Sojourners.* New York: Vintage Books, 1971.

This is an excellent documetary history, with an extensive text by the authors. The tone of the book is hard hitting and refreshingly candid.

Lyman, Stanford M. *The Asian in the West.* Reno: Desert Research Institute, 1970. Special Science and Humanities Publication no. 4.

A scholarly and well-researched study of selected aspects of Chinese-American and Japanese-American institutions and cultures.

Melendy, H. Brett. *The Oriental Americans.* New York: Twayne Publishers, 1972.

An easy-to-read and useful general historical overview of Chinese and Japanese Americans. Contains a useful bibliography.

Sue, Stanley and Nathaniel N. Wagner, eds. *Asian-Americans: Psychological Perspectives.* Ben Lomand, Calif.: Science and Behavior Books, 1973.

An excellent, comprehensive collection of readings which deals with diverse aspects of the Asian American experience.

Sue, Stanley and Harry H.L. Kitano, eds. "Asian Americans: A Success Story." *Journal of Social Issues* 29, no. 2 (1973), special issue.

This is an excellent collection of articles which explore diverse aspects of the experiences of Asian-Americans.

Tachiki, Amy, Eddie Wong, Franklin Odo, with Buck Wong. *Roots: An Asian American Reader.* Los Angeles: UCLA Asian American Studies Center, 1971.

This comprehensive and carefully edited anthology contains articles presenting perspectives on the historical, sociological, and psychological experience of Asian Americans.

Wand, David Hsin-Fu, ed. *Asian-American Heritage: An Anthology of Prose and Poetry.* New York: Pocket Books, 1974.

This anthology includes stories, poetry, essays, excerpts from novels, and other literary selections.

Chinese Americans

Barth Gunther. *Bitter Strength: A History of the Chinese in the United States, 1850–1870.* Cambridge: Harvard University Press, 1964.

A useful and careful study of the early Chinese immigrants to the United States.

Brett, Victor G. and DeBarry Nee, eds. *Longtime California: A Documentary Study of An American Chinatown.* New York: Pantheon, 1972.

This book includes narratives and interviews which reveal the culture and problems of San Francisco's Chinatown.

Cheng-Tsu Wu, ed. *"Chink!": A Documentary History of Anti-Chinese Prejudice in America.* New York: World Publishing, 1972.

A useful collection of documents about anti-Chinese movements in the United States.

Lee, Rose Hum. *The Chinese in the United States.* Hong Kong: Hong Kong University Press, 1960.

This book discusses the social, economic, occupational, and institutional life of Chinese Americans.

Lyman, Stanford M. *Chinese Americans.* New York: Random House, 1974.

An informed study of diverse aspects of Chinese-American life.

Miller, Stuart Creighton. *The Unwelcome Immigrant: The American Image of the Chinese, 1785–1882.* Berkeley: University of California Press, 1969.

In this well-written and scholarly book, Miller provides new perspectives and interpretations of anti-Chinese attitudes and movements in the United States.

Sung, Betty L. *The Story of the Chinese in America.* New York: Macmillan, 1967.

The author presents the story of the Chinese American in a highly interesting and readable style. A popular, not a scholarly history.

Sung, S. W. *Chinese in American Life: Some Aspects Of Their History, Status, Problems, and Contributions.* Seattle: University of Washington Press, 1962.

A comprehensive and well-researched reference on the Chinese in the United States.

Japanese Americans

Bosworth, Allan R. *America's Concentration Camps.* New York: Norton, 1967.

This is a popular account of the internment which both teachers and high school students can read.

Daniels, Roger. *Concentration Camps U.S.A.: Japanese Americans and World War II.* New York: Holt, 1971.

An excellently written, perceptive history of the internment of the Japanese during World War II.

———. *The Politics of Prejudice: The Anti-Japanese Movement in California and the Struggle for Japanese Exclusion.* Gloucester, Mass.: Peter Smith, 1966.

A careful study of the long struggle that took place on the West Coast to exclude the Japanese.

Girdner, Audrie and Anne Loftis. *The Great Betrayal: The Evacuation of the Japanese Americans during World War II.* New York: Macmillan, 1969.

This well-written popular account of the internment conveys the feelings and attitudes of the people involved in a "catacylsmic uprooting."

Grodzins, Morton. *Americans Betrayed: Politics and the Japanese Evacuation.* Chicago: University of Chicago Press, 1949.

Grodzins argues that the internment was caused by pressure groups and West Coast politicians.

Hosokawa, Bill. *Nisei: The Quiet Americans.* New York: William Morrow, 1969.

A popular history stressing the role of the Japanese American Citizenship League.

Kitano, Harry H. L. *Japanese Americans: The Evolution of a Subculture.* Englewood Cliffs, N.J.: Prentice-Hall, 1969.

A useful sociological and historical overview of Japanese Americans.

Petersen, William. *Japanese Americans.* New York: Random House, 1971.

An informative but pedestrian and tedious sociological and historical treatment of Japanese Americans.

Spicer, Edward H., Asael T. Hansen, Katherine Luomala, and Marvin K. Opler. *Impounded People: Japanese-Americans in the Relocation Centers.* Tucson: University of Arizona Press, 1969.

Four former employees of the War Relocation Authority present their interpretation of the internment.

tenBroek, Jacobus, Edward N. Barnhart, and Floyd W. Matson. *Prejudice, War and the Constitution.* Berkeley: University of California Press, 1954.

The authors advance a novel theory to explain the evacuation and present a carefully researched analysis of its origins and stages.

Filipino Americans

Bulosan, Carlos. *Sound of Falling Light: Letters in Exile.* Edited by Dolores S. Feria. Quezon City, Philippines: published by the editor, 1960.

A perceptive and deeply moving collection of the letters and previously unpublished poems by one of the most gifted writers of this century.

Burma, John H. *Spanish-Speaking Groups in the United States.* Durham, N. C.: Duke University Press, 1954.

This book contains a useful chapter on Filipino Americans.

Divine, Robert. *American Immigration Policy, 1924–1952.* New Haven: Yale University Press, 1957.

This book contains a brief but useful history of the development of immigration policy as it relates to citizens of the Philippines.

Grunder, Garel A. and William E. Livezey. *The Philippines and the United States.* Norman: University of Oklahoma Press, 1951.

A useful reference which treats the acquisition of the Philippines by the United States and the subsequent relationship between the two nations.

Jocano, Landa F. *Growing Up in a Philippines Barrio.* New York: Holt, 1969.

An anthropologist analyzes life in a Philippine community, with emphasis on the process of socialization.

Lasker, Bruno. *Filipino Immigration to Continental United States and Hawaii.* Chicago: University of Chicago Press, 1931.

Although this book is dated, it is still valuable for the teacher who needs basic information about the early immigration of Filipinos to Hawaii and the United States mainland.

McWilliams, Carey. *Brothers Under the Skin.* Boston: Little, Brown, 1943.

This book reflects the ethnocentrism and subtle racism of the World War II period. However, the chapter on Filipino Americans is valuable.

Morales, Royal F. *Makibaka: The Filipino American Struggle.* Los Angeles: Mountainview Publishers, Inc., 1974. Available only by direct order from the publisher: 4057 Marchena Drive, Los Angeles, CA 90065.

An important articulation of the contemporary problems and characteristics of Filipinos in the United States.

Munoz, Alfredo N. *The Filipinos in America.* Los Angeles: Mountainview Publishers, Inc., 1971. Available only by direct order from the publisher. See address under Morales entry above.

A general study of the Filipino-Americans.

Nicanir, Precioso M. *Profiles of Notable Filipinos in the U.S.A.* New York: Pre-Mer Publishing Co., 1963.

A useful collection of ninety-one biographical sketches of notable Filipino Americans in New York and New Jersey. A wide range of occupations are covered and the biographies are sufficiently detailed.

San Juan, Epifanio, Jr. *Carlos Bulosan and the Imagination of the Class Struggle.* Quezon City: University of the Philippines Press, 1972.

A brilliant and perceptive study of the writings of the gifted Filipino American writer. This study is especially important because it treats the writings of one of the most talented, yet sadfully neglected, twentieth century writers.

————. *The Radical Tradition in Philippine Literature.* Quezon City, Philippines: Manlapaz Publishing Co., 1971.

A useful discussion of the writings of Jose Rizal, Lope K. Santos, Carlos Bulosan, Amado V. Hernandez, and Jose Maria Sison.

Wallovits, Sonia E. "The Filipinos in California." Master's thesis, University of Southern California, 1966.

This thesis contains some valuable information about Filipino Americans, although the author's racism often juts through the text.

BOOKS FOR STUDENTS

Multiethnic

Asian Writers' Project/Asian Media Project. *Sojourner I, II, III, and IV.* Berkeley: Unified School District, 1972, 1973, 1974.

A collection of original prose, poetry, photographs, and drawings by Asian-American students. Four books are in the series. (High School)

Finkelstein, Milton, Hon. Jawn A. Sandifer, and Elfreda S. Wright. *Minorities U.S.A.* New York: Globe, 1971.

A comprehensive book dealing with ethnic minorities in the United States. A well-written book with study questions. (Intermediate)

Goldberg, George. *East Meets West: The Story of the Chinese and Japanese in California.* New York: Harcourt, 1970.

A well-written and perceptive account of the Chinese and Japanese in America. (Intermediate)

Holland, Ruth. *The Oriental Immigrants in America.* New York: Grosset and Dunlap, 1969.

Although not without flaws, this is a good general history of Japanese and Chinese Americans. (Intermediate)

Hsu, Kai-yu and Helen Palubinskas, eds. *Asian-American Authors.* Boston: Houghton Mifflin, 1972.

This anthology includes literary selections written by Japanese, Chinese, and Filipino authors and a useful chronology of each group. (High School)

Lands and People: The World in Color. New York: Grolier, 1963, vol. 4 and vol. 7.

A fairly good reference source for basic information about China, Japan, Korea, and Mexico. (Upper)

Liang, Yen. *Tommy and Dee-Dee.* New York: Oxford, 1953.

A delightful story, told with words and illustrations, about the many ways in which a boy in China and an African American boy are alike. (Primary)

Milton, Daniel L., and William Clifford. *A Treasury of Modern Asian Stories.* New York: New American Library, 1961.

A highly representative collection of Asian literature. (High School)

Chinese American

Chu, Daniel and Samuel Chu. *Passage to the Golden Gate: A History of the Chinese in America to 1910.* Garden City, N. Y.: Doubleday, 1967.

A readable, detailed history of Chinese Americans. (Intermediate)

Dowdell, Dorothy and Joseph Dowdell. *The Chinese Helped Build America.* New York: Julian Messner, 1972.

An accurate, illustrated, and readable history of Chinese Americans told with the use of a main character. (Intermediate)

Hsu, Francis L. K. *The Challenge of the American Dream: The Chinese in the United States.* Belmont, Calif.: Wadsworth, 1971.

Dr. Hsu examines many aspects of Chinese American culture. The author concludes the text with a discussion of the future of Chinese Americans. (High School)

Jones, Claire. *The Chinese in America.* Minneapolis: Lerner, 1972.

This general history of Chinese Americans includes background information about China and biographies of eminent Chinese Americans. (Upper)

Lenski, Lois. *San Francisco Boy.* New York: Lippincott, 1955.

A readable, amply illustrated story about life in the Chinese community in San Francisco. (Intermediate)

Molnar, Joe. *A Chinese-American Child Tells His Story.* New York: Franklin Watts, 1973.

This book tells the story of a young Chinese-American boy who lives in New York City. Sherman talks about his family, school, hobbies, and cultural heritage. (Intermediate)

Politi, Leo. *Moy Moy.* New York: Scribner's, 1960.

A story about a young Chinese-Amercian girl and her family which centers around the Chinese New Year. It reveals much about Chinese customs and words. Illustrated. (Primary)

Reit, Seymour. *Rice Cakes and Paper Dragons.* New York: Dodd, Mead and Co., 1973.

A story about a Chinese American girl who lives in New York's Chinatown. The story focuses on her interpretation of the Chinese New Year. The plot is weak but the book is informative.

Sung, Betty Lee. *The Chinese in America.* New York: Macmillan, 1972. In this comprehensive history of Chinese Americans, the author skillfully piles mountains of information into a little over 100 pages. An excellent history of the Chinese Americans for young readers. (Intermediate)

Wong, Jade Snow. *Fifth Chinese Daughter.* New York: Harper, 1945. The author shares the joys and cultural conflicts of her youth in San Francisco. This autobiography is both enjoyable and informative. That the author loves and respects her people comes through cogently in the book. (High School)

Japanese American

Bonham, Frank. *Burma Rifles.* New York: Crowell, 1960. This is an exciting adventure story about Jerry Harada and the heroic 5307. The 5307 was a special unit of Japanese Americans who served in the armed forces during World War II. (Intermediate)

Conrat, Maisie and Richard Conrat. *Executive Order 9066: The Internment of 110,000 Japanese Americans.* San Francisco: California Historical Society, 1972. A brilliant, poignant, and deeply moving photo essay of the internment experience. (All Levels)

Haugaard, Kay. *Myeko's Gift.* New York: Abelard-Schuman, 1966. A story about a young Japanese-American girl that can be used to teach children how cruel we often are to people who are different. (Intermediate)

Houston, Jeanne Wakatsuki and James Houston. *Farewell to Manzanar.* Boston: Houghton Mifflin, 1973. A true story focusing on the period during and after World War II. (High School)

Inada, Lawson Fusao. *Before the War: Poems as they Happened.* New York: William Morrow, 1971. An interesting book of poetry. (High School)

Inouye, Daniel K., with Lawrence Elliott. *Journey to Washington.* Englewood Cliffs, N. J.: Prentice-Hall, 1967. A highly readable and worthwhile autobiography of the first Japanese American United States Senator. (Upper)

Ishigo, Estelle. *Lone Heart Mountain.* Los Angeles: published by the author, 1972. Distributed by the Japanese American Curriculum Project, P. O. Box 367, San Mateo, CA 94401 A touching story about life in an American concentration camp. This book is beautifully illustrated with the author's black and white drawings. (Intermediate)

The Japanese American Curriculum Project. *Japanese Americans: The Untold Story*. New York: Holt, 1971.

This is a sensitively told story of the Japanese in America. It focuses on the internment and the attitudes of White Americans prior to it. This book has evoked some controversy. (Intermediate)

Jaynes, Ruth. *Friends! Friends! Friends!* Glendale, Calif.: Bowmar Publishing Corp., 1967.

Kimi is a beautiful little Japanese American girl who has many friends. In this book, we learn who her friends are and what they do together. (Primary)

Kitagawa, Daisuke. *Issei and Nisei: The Internment Years*. New York: Seabury Press, 1967.

A sensitive account of life in an American internment camp. (Upper)

Leathers, Noel L. *The Japanese in America*. Minneapolis: Lerner, 1967.

The author presents a sensitive "American" interpretation of Japanese American history. He cites many famous Japanese Americans and discusses their lives. (Intermediate)

Means, Florence Crannell. *The Moved Outers*. Boston: Houghton Mifflin, 1945.

A moving fictional account of a Japanese-American family experience in an internment camp. (Upper)

Ogawa, Dennis N. *Jan Ken Po*. Honolulu, Hawaii: Japanese American Research Center, 1973.

The experiences of Japanese Americans in Hawaii are treated in this interesting and provocative book. (High School)

Okubo, Mine. *Citizen 13660*. New York: AMS Press, 1966.

An autobiographical account of life in Topaz, which was a concentration camp. Illustrated. (Upper)

Takashima, Shizuye. *A Child in Prison Camp*. Plattsburgh, N. Y.: Tundra Books of Northern New York, 1971.

A touching and poignant autobiographical account of a young girl's experiences in Canada during the internment. The author, a Japanese-Canadian artist, uses outstanding drawings to illustrate the book. (Upper)

Uchida, Yoshiko. *Journey to Topaz*. New York: Scribners, 1971.

A fictionalized account of the Sakane family and their experiences during the evacuation. Illustrated. (Upper)

——— . *Mik and the Prowler*. New York: Harcourt, 1960.

Mik, a young Japanese American boy, grows into a responsible, mature young man during the summer. The story has both mystery and adventure. (Intermediate)

————. *The Magic Listening Cap: More Folk Tales from Japan.* New York: Harcourt, 1955.

Using modern word usage, the author retells fourteen Japanese folktales. Illustrated. (All Levels)

————. *Samurai of Gold Hill.* New York: Scribner, 1972.

The story of a boy who was a member of the first group of Japanese immigrants who settled in the United States. (Upper)

————. *The Sea of Gold and Other Tales from Japan.* New York: Scribner's, 1965.

Children will love reading or listening to these twelve folktales from ancient Japan. (All Levels)

————. *The Promised Year.* New York: Harcourt, 1959.

This story, about a young Japanese girl who moves to San Francisco to live with her aunt and uncle, moves rather slowly and evokes little interest. (Intermediate)

Yashima, Taro. *Umbrella.* New York: Viking, 1958.

A cute story about a girl named Momo. The story revolves around her third birthday gift, an umbrella. Children will enjoy the excitement in the story as well as the brightly colored illustrations. (Primary)

————. *Youngest One.* New York: Viking, 1962.

Bobby, the central character in this story, is a young, shy Japanese-American boy. He finds a new friend, Momo, and begins to reach out. This is a charming story. Illustrated. (Primary)

Filipino Americans

Buaken, Manuel. *I Have Lived with the American People.* Caldwell, Idaho: Caxton Printers, 1948.

This interesting personal account of the author's experiences in the United States raises and answers a number of powerful questions about Filipino Americans. (High School)

Bulosan, Carlos. *America Is in the Heart.* New York: Harcourt, 1943.

A beautiful, poignant book about a young man trying to survive in a hostile, racist land. In this autobiography, Mr. Bulosan illuminates the culture of his people in both the Philippines and the United States. (High School)

————. *The Laughter of My Father.* New York: Harcourt, 1942.

In this collection of vignettes about his family, the author discusses poignant events in a lighthearted manner. (Upper)

Taruc, Luis. *Born of the People.* New York: International Publishers, 1953.

A touching book about life in the Philippines and the conditions that lead to a fight for liberation. (Upper)

Puerto Rican Americans: Concepts, Strategies, and Materials

10

We are opposed to violence, the violence of hungry children, illiterate adults, diseased old people, and the violence of poverty and profit. . . . The time has come to defend the lives of our people against repression and for revolutionary war against the businessmen, politicians, and police. When a government oppresses the people, we have the right to abolish it and create a new one.

Young Lords Party

Introduction

There were over one and a half million Puerto Ricans on the United States mainland in 1971. While most of them lived in eastern cities, large pockets of Puerto Ricans were in such cities as Chicago, Cleveland, Milwaukee, and San Francisco. Content about Puerto Rican Americans should be included in the curriculum because Puerto Ricans are an integral part of American society. Their experience on the mainland can help students to master key social science concepts such as migration, cultural conflict, and cultural diversity.

When studying about Puerto Ricans on the United States mainland, students can compare and contrast their experience with those of other migrant and immigrant groups. In some ways, their migration is similar to the movement of other groups to the United States. They are culturally uprooted, like European immigrants were, when they migrate to the United States. However, their migration is also unique in American history. It started when automation had greatly decreased the need for manual labor in the United States and when Americans had become highly suspicious of "foreigners." Puerto Ricans are United States citizens when they set foot on American soil. Their migration is the first "airborne migration" in American history. Puerto Ricans bring racial attitudes to this country that are considerably more liberal than those they find here. The study of the complex nature of the Puerto Rican migration and experience on the mainland provides students with excellent opportunities to formulate generalizations that are essential components of a sound ethnic studies program.

Puerto Rican Americans: Historical Perspective

Important Dates

1493	Columbus landed on the island of Borinquén, November 19, 1493. Borinquén was the home of the Taino (or Arawak) Indians, the native inhabitants of Puerto Rico.
1508	Juan Ponce de Léon became the Governor of Puerto Rico.
1511	The Puerto Rican Indians unsuccessfully rebelled against Spanish slavery.
1513	African slaves were introduced on Puerto Rican plantations.
1873	Slavery was abolished in Puerto Rico.
1898	Spain ceded Puerto Rico to the United States under the terms of the Treaty of Paris, the treaty which formally ended the Spanish-American War.
1900	Under the terms of the Foraker Act, the United States established a government in

Important Dates cont.

	Puerto Rico in which the president of the United States appointed the governor and the Executive Council. The House of Delegates and the resident commissioner were to be elected by popular vote.
1910	The United States census indicated that there were 1,513 native Puerto Ricans living in the United States.
1917	The Jones Act was passed by the United States Congress. It made Puerto Ricans American citizens and subject to the United States draft. The act also provided for the popular election of both houses of the Puerto Rican legislature.
1920	11,811 persons born in Puerto Rico were living in the United States. That number increased to 58,200 in 1935.
1937	Twenty people were killed in a tragedy known as the "Ponce Massacre" on Palm Sunday. A confrontation between the Puerto Rican police and the Nationalist party took place.
1947	The United States Congress amended the Jones Act of 1917. Puerto Ricans were granted the right to elect their own governor. The governor was given the right to make most of the appointments for high public offices.
1948	Luis Muñoz Marin became the first elected governor of Puerto Rico. He was governor of Puerto Rico until 1964.
1952	On July 25, Governor Luis Muñoz Marin led the inauguration ceremonies establishing the Commonwealth of Puerto Rico or the Associated Free State.
1965	With the passage of the Civil Rights Act of 1965, Puerto Rican Americans were no longer required to pass an English literacy test to vote in the state of New York.

Important Dates cont.

1967	In a plebiscite, Puerto Ricans voted to maintain the Associated Free State status. Statehood and independence were the second and third choices respectively.
1970	Herman Badillo was elected to the U. S. House of Representatives. He was the first Puerto Rican American elected to Congress. Governor Ferré and President Nixon formed an *ad hoc* committee to discuss the United States presidential vote for Puerto Rico.
1971	Cuban representatives to the United Nations proposed a resolution to have United States colonialism in Puerto Rico debated during a meeting of the United Nations Trusteeship Council.
1972	The Popular Democratic party was returned to power in Puerto Rico with the election of Rafael Hernandez Colón as the new governor.

THE ISLAND BACKGROUND

Puerto Rico

Puerto Rico, or "rich port" as it was called by the Spaniards, is a beautiful, small tropical island in the Caribbean Sea. The island, which sits on the top of a large underwater mountain, is smaller than the state of Connecticut. It is about 35 miles wide, a hundred miles long, and is made up of slightly more than 3,400 square miles. Puerto Rico, which has become one of the favorite resting places for American tourists, has one of the highest population densities in the world, 800 people per square mile. Almost 3 million people live on this attractive island.

Puerto Rico's history is just as interesting as its terrain and demography. During the last four centuries, it has suffered an identity crisis and a sense of political alienation because its destiny has been determined by two faraway nations that ruled it like absentee landlords govern a slum. Spain ruled the country from the sixteenth century up to the Spanish-American War in 1898. In 1898 the United States took control. It governed

Puerto Rico awkwardly and ambiguously. Although the Commonwealth of Puerto Rico has existed since July 1952, Puerto Rico's relationship with the United States is still shaky and unclear. Puerto Rico is neither a state nor an independent nation. She is still in search of her identity and destiny. This identity quest is likely to continue for some years to come, especially as cries for independence keep emerging in Puerto Rico, even if they are only voiced by a determined, forceful few.

Since 1917, Puerto Ricans have been citizens of the United States. In the period between the two World Wars, they started migrating to the mainland in large numbers, mainly to New York City. Today, more Puerto Ricans live in New York City than in San Juan, Puerto Rico's capital city. In 1971 about half as many people of Puerto Rican descent lived in the United States as lived in Puerto Rico. There were over 1.5 million Puerto Ricans living in the United States and 2.8 million living on the island. Many mainland Puerto Ricans were born and raised in the United States. The number of Puerto Ricans in the United States is significant, and it increases with each census count. The 1960 census showed almost 900,000 Puerto Ricans in the United States. When the 1970 census was taken, that number had risen to 1,518,000.[1]

The Taino Indians*

Puerto Ricans have three major racial heritages—Indian, African, and Spanish. The island was inhabited by a group of Indians called the Tainos when the Spanish came in the fifteenth century. Because they left no written records, little is known about the Tainos, except what archaeologists have been able to detect from potsherds and skulls. Some social scientists believe that there were about 40,000 Tainos on the island when the Spanish came[2] and that they had straight black hair and copper-colored skin. Their culture was based on farming, hunting, and

1. Bureau of the Census, *Population Characteristics: Selected Characteristics of Persons and Families of Mexican, Puerto Rican, and Other Spanish Origin* (Washington, D. C.: U. S. Government Printing Office, July, 1972).

2. Teresa Maria Babin, *The Puerto Ricans' Spirit.* Translated by Barry Luby. (New York: Collier Books, 1971), p. 154.

* *The* Taino *Indians are also referred to the* Arawak *Indians.*

raising animals. Religion was also an important part of the Taino culture. The Spaniards caught the Indians by surprise and totally without the kinds of weapons they needed to fight men who fought with swords.[3]

The Coming of the Spaniards

In search for a new route to India, Columbus arrived in the Americas in 1492. When he came back to the Americas in 1493, he landed on the island of Borinquén, home of the Taino Indians. Columbus's arrival on the island foreshadowed the Spanish take-over. When Juan Ponce de Léon was made governor of the island in 1508, the Spanish occupation of Puerto Rico was well underway. From the time of the arrival of the Spanish conquistadores, life for the native Indians became increasingly more difficult. Eventually, they were almost totally exterminated. The Spanish set up a kind of slavery, known as the *encomienda system*.[4] Under this system, each Spanish colonizer was given a group of Indians to work for him. The Spanish colonizer was supposed to "teach" the Indians Spanish "culture" in return for their work.

At first, the Indians did not fight back. They thought that the Spaniards were immortal. Eventually, a group of Taino Indians decided to find out if the Spanish were actually immortal. They tried to drown a young Spaniard and succeeded. Once they discovered that the Spaniards died like other men, they started fighting back. A number of Indian rebellions took place in various parts of the island. Many Spaniards were killed in these skirmishes. In addition to rebelling, the Tainos also ran away from the Spanish settlements. The conquistadores searched for them, often with little success. So many Indians were killed by the Spaniards and their diseases, and so many escaped from the island, that by 1777 they had all but disappeared from Puerto Rico.

Spanish Rule

By the late nineteenth century, Puerto Rico was one of the most neglected colonies in the Western Hemisphere. For nearly

3. Kal Wagenheim, *Puerto Rico: A Profile* (New York: Praeger, 1970), pp. 38–41.

4. Ibid., pp. 42–43.

400 years Spain had ruled the colony from across the Atlantic like an absentee landlord and had woefully neglected it. Puerto Rico's last series of Spanish governors were incompetent and autocratic. They ineptly governed the island with an oppressive, heavy hand. When Spain and the United States entered the Spanish-American War in 1898, Spain's 400-year neglect of her small Caribbean colony was painfully visible. The masses of the people were peons, and the country's wealth was concentrated in the hands of the small upper class. No middle class existed. Most of the people were illiterate, and 92 percent of the children were not in school. Contagious diseases were widespread. Public health facilities were almost totally absent. Nearly 80 percent of the draftable Puerto Rican males failed the physical test given by the United States military during World War I.

Spain's neglect and mistreatment of Puerto Rico had led to an aggressive movement for home rule by the 1800s. In 1868, the famous Lares Revolt occurred. A group of independence advocates took the city of Lares and proclaimed it the "Republic of Puerto Rico." The revolt failed but the agitation for home rule continued, even though it was often sporadic and poorly organized. Eventually the movement bore fruits. On November 28, 1897, Puerto Rico was granted autonomy by Spain. This proved to be one of the shortest and most meaningless political changes in history. Barely before the new Puerto Rican government could begin to function, American troops landed on the island and the Spanish-American War began.

The Spanish-American War

Spain declared war on the United States on April 24, 1898. A truce was signed on August 12 of that same year. Spain was a pushover for the United States. The two nations formally ended the war with the Treaty of Paris, signed on December 10, 1898. At the meeting, the United States reigned supreme. Spain ceded the Philippines and Puerto Rico to the United States and gave up rights to Cuba. The United States also acquired American Guam.

As had been the case for 400 years, nobody asked Puerto Rico about her political future. Her fate was determined by the United States and Spain. After the meeting, Puerto Rico lost the little autonomy that Spain had granted her in 1897 and became a United States possession. Puerto Rican independent leaders were shocked and dismayed. They had thought that their neighbor from the North had come to free them from colonialism. It was a rude awakening to discover that the United States, the "citadel of freedom and democracy," was also going to subjugate Puerto Rico just as Spain had done.

United States Rule

When the United States government took control of Puerto Rico in 1898, it had little experience in governing colonies. In fact, "self-determination of nations" had been one of the main ideas voiced by the United States government. However, with the emergence of the doctrine of Manifest Destiny, the United States began to go after foreign lands rather aggressively. She acquired nearly one-third of Mexico's territory in 1848 and increasingly saw how important Caribbean possessions would be to her, both financially and militarily. When the United States entered the Spanish-American War, she hoped to acquire a toehold in the Caribbean Sea.

The United States relationship with Puerto Rico was awkward and ambiguous during the first two years of American rule. Military governors from the United States manned the island. This type of government did not prove satisfactory. Congress attempted to establish a more workable relationship with Puerto Rico in 1900. That year it passed the Foraker Act. Under the terms of this act, Puerto Rico became "the People of Puerto Rico." Puerto Ricans were not American citizens nor was the nation independent. The governor and the Executive Council (the Upper House) were to be appointed by the president of the United States. The House of Delegates (the Lower House) and the resident commissioner were to be chosen by popular election.[5] The resident commissioner's job was to present the island's views on issues in the United States House of Representatives, although he would be unable to vote. Any action taken by the elected House of Delegates could be vetoed by the United States Congress. The Circuit Court of Boston was named the high court for the island. Puerto Rican leaders were shocked by

5. Joseph P. Fitzpatrick, *Puerto Rican Americans: The Meaning of Migration to the Mainland* (Englewood Cliffs, N. J.: Prentice-Hall, 1971), p. 44.

this arrangement, which they correctly interpreted as a slap in the face. They had hoped that when the United States took over the island, its people would be able to decide their own political destiny with a plebiscite. The Foraker Act shattered their hopes.

The Struggle for Self-Governance

Cries for independence were heard throughout Puerto Rico during the sixteen years that the Foraker Act was in effect. Anti-United States feelings continued to grow and spread on the island. The island's factional parties shared the belief that Puerto Rico had been betrayed by the United States. As anti-American feelings escalated, the president and the Congress decided that action had to be taken. The then resident commissioner in Washington, Muñoz Rivera, wanted to poll Puerto Rico's citizens to determine what they felt should be the political status of the island. Muñoz's arguments were ignored. Congress decided to deal with the problem by making Puerto Ricans United States citizens with the Jones Act in 1917. This act only further alienated the Puerto Ricans who wanted self-governance on the island. The act not only "forced" American citizenship on Puerto Ricans, but made them obligated to serve in the United States armed forces. Many Puerto Ricans resented the "forced" American citizenship and the fact that they had no voice in the matter. They could resist American citizenship, but resistance meant that they would lose many benefits and become aliens within their homeland.

The Nationalist Party

The Nationalist party, the radical party which strongly advocated the independence of Puerto Rico, emerged out of the forces that opposed the way in which the United States was handling Puerto Rico's affairs. The party leaders felt, with some justification, that the major Puerto Rican parties were too sympathetic to American interests and that party members could not deal with the United States effectively by using traditional means such as the ballot and appealing to the American conscience. Pedro Albizu Campos emerged as the militant leader of the party. A graduate of Harvard, Albizu knew American politics well. The party's tactics were often violent, and it became a target of the Puerto Rican and American governments, who considered it extreme and dangerous. At a parade which the Nationalist party sponsored on Palm Sunday, March 21, 1937, a shot fired into a crowd resulted in a massacre in the streets of Ponce. In the ruckus, 20 people lost their lives and more than 100 were wounded. Liberation leaders remember this day as the "Ponce Massacre." It symbolizes the independence struggle in Puerto Rico.

LUIS MUÑOZ MARIN: GOVERNOR OF PUERTO RICO, 1948–1964

Between 1900 and 1946 Puerto Rico was headed by a series of fifteen American governors appointed by the president of the United States. With only a few exceptions, they were very unimpressive men. They differed little from the Spaniards who had ruled Puerto Rico prior to 1898. Medical, educational, and economic conditions on the island reflected poor leadership. By 1940 conditions in Puerto Rico were not substantially different than they had been in 1898. Persistent expressions of dissatisfaction with the governors by Puerto Rican leaders led the United States to grant Puerto Rico the opportunity to elect its own governor in 1947. In 1948 Senator Luis Muñoz Marin was elected governor of Puerto Rico. He was the first elected governor in Puerto Rico's history.

The Commonwealth of Puerto Rico

Muñoz was destined to decisively change the course of Puerto Rican history. More changes took place in Puerto Rico during his sixteen years as governor than had taken place during the previous four centuries of Spanish rule. Without question, Muñoz's influence on the island was unprecedented. Like any political leader who gets things done and shapes history, he was a charismatic and controversial figure.

Once in office, Muñoz took a position on the polemical status question. He favored what later became known as the Commonwealth or the Estado Libre Asociado [Free Associated State].

With this status, Puerto Rico would maintain a tie with the United States, but would have a degree of governmental autonomy. Muñoz fought hard to make the Commonwealth a reality. The people approved it in a plebiscite on June 4, 1951. Muñoz led an inauguration ceremony which began the Commonwealth of Puerto Rico on July 25, 1952.

The Commonwealth did not solve the status question, and the controversy continued. Both statehood and independence advocates opposed the new status. Many refused to go to the polls because they claimed that the plebiscite was a hoax since the voters were presented with only two choices. They had to vote either to maintain the status quo or to initiate the proposed Commonwealth. Thus the meaning of the plebiscite was bitterly debated. To this day, the status question is still one of the hottest political issues on the island. It tends to dominate and overshadow other issues.

Urbanization and Operation Bootstrap

Muñoz also set Puerto Rico on a new economic course. He felt that income from the island's three main cash crops—sugar, tobacco, and coffee—was inadequate to support Puerto Rico. Muñoz wanted to industralize the island by luring American manufacturers to set up plants in Puerto Rico. He formed "Operation Bootstrap" to attract American industry to Puerto Rico. He attracted them by offering generous benefits such as lower wages and tax exemptions for up to ten years. Many American companies set up plants in Puerto Rico under this program. Like most changes which Muñoz implemented, the program was both successful and controversial. The changes that Operation Bootstrap stimulated in Puerto Rico have been truly amazing. By 1971 the program had recruited 2,000 plants and $2 million in investments. Income from manufacturing was more than three times that from agriculture, although agriculture was still important in the island's economy. The island's per capita income jumped from $188 a year in 1940 to $1,234 a year in 1969.

However, this success story has been mixed. Urbanization has brought its usual problems in housing and has created new slums and a new poverty class: the urban poor. In 1969 the per capita income in Puerto Rico, while high when compared to Latin American nations, was still only one-third of that in the

United States. The unemployment rate was chronically high. At the same time, it cost more to live in San Juan than in most mainland cities. Clearing land for factories has forced many poor families off the farms into the city slums, which have blossomed with urban growth.

Although urbanization has created a middle class in Puerto Rico and bedroom suburban communities, Muñoz's critics correctly point out that Operation Bootstrap has brought the greatest benefits to the upper class and to American industrialists. American companies take the bulk of the money they earn on the island back to the United States. Urbanization in Puerto Rico, like so many other developments, has done little to change the living conditions of the very poor, except perhaps to show them how to live poor "urban" rather than "rural" style. Despite the mixed blessings that Operation Bootstrap and urbanization have brought to Puerto Rico, it would be premature to make any final judgments about the Muñoz reforms. What is clear now, however, is that his sixteen-year reign made a tremendous difference in the island's present and future.

LIFE ON THE MAINLAND

The Migration

After the United States gained control of Puerto Rico, the stage was set for the mass movement of islanders to the United States mainland. A few Puerto Ricans, such as cigar makers and merchant seamen, had settled in New York before the 1920s; but Puerto Ricans did not begin to migrate to the United States in significant numbers until the 1920s and 1930s. When Mills et al. published their pioneering study in 1950, most Puerto Ricans in New York City had come during the years between the two great World Wars.[6] The number of Puerto Ricans migrating to the United States decreased considerably during World War II because of the closing of transportation routes between New York and Puerto Rico.

6. C. Wright Mills, Clarence Senior, and Rose K. Goldsen, *The Puerto Rican Journey: New York's Newest Migrants* (New York: Harper and Brothers, 1950).

After the war, the number of Puerto Ricans migrating to the United States increased. In 1945, only 22,737 Puerto Ricans came to the United States. That number increased to 101,115 in 1947. Puerto Rican migration to the United States has always reflected economic trends. A significant number of migrants usually return to the island when the mainland economy is depressed. During the Great Depression of the 1930s, the net migration* back to the island reached 8,694 persons in a four-year period.[7] When the United States economy is booming, Puerto Rican migration usually increases and return migration decreases considerably.

The lack of legal barriers is a major factor in Puerto Rican migration to the United States. The Jones Act of 1917 made Puerto Ricans American citizens. As United States citizens, they can move freely from the island to the mainland, and within various parts of the United States. Their migration to the United States is not limited by restrictive quotas, as was the case in Mexico and in the various Asian nations. Many Puerto Ricans take advantage of their freedom of movement and migrate to the United States. Although the movement of Puerto Ricans to the mainland has many of the sociological characteristics of an immigration, Puerto Ricans are technically migrants rather than immigrants because they are citizens of the United States.

Easy transportation to the mainland also facilitates Puerto Rican migration. In the 1930s, Puerto Ricans could make a boat trip from San Juan to New York City in the relatively short period of three and a half days, and for as low as $40.[8] After World War II, plane transportation from the island became much more available and inexpensive. During this period, a migrant could fly from San Juan to New York City for as low as $35.[9] Today, transportation from the island is more convenient and still inexpensive. While the flight from San Juan to New

---

* Net migration *is the difference between the number of Puerto Ricans who enter the United States and the number who leave within a specific time period. It can be a positive (+) or a negative (−) figure.*

7. Ibid., p. 44.

8. Lawrence R. Chenault, *The Puerto Rican Migrant in New York City* (New York: Columbia University Press, 1938), p. 56.

9. Mills et al., *Puerto Rican Journey*, p. 44.

York City took eight bumpy hours in the 1940s, the trip could be made as quickly as two and a half hours and for as low as $62 in 1973. Convenient and inexpensive transportation has not only stimulated migration from the island to the mainland but has helped to make Puerto Ricans transients between the island and the United States. Many Puerto Ricans in New York return to the island to visit relatives, to vacation, or to take care of business for short periods. This ability to move easily back and forth from the island to the mainland has made it more difficult for many Puerto Ricans to settle in the United States because they realize that they can always go "back home" when they encounter problems on the mainland.

The "Americanization" of Puerto Rico since 1898 and economic factors have played major roles in motivating Puerto Ricans to migrate to the United States. Since Puerto Rico became an American colony, United States culture and institutions have profoundly influenced Puerto Rican culture and lifestyles. Americans forced the teaching of English in Puerto Rican schools for years and put textbooks in them which venerated George Washington and Abraham Lincoln rather than Puerto Rican leaders. These books also described the United States as the neighbor to the North in which "democracy and freedom" flourished. American stores such as J. C. Penney and Sears dot the streets in San Juan as they do in Chicago. Many Puerto Ricans who return to the island tell their relatives and friends about the "great" life in New York City. The availability of jobs in New York City during periods of intensive migration, and the higher pay which Puerto Ricans can earn in New York than in San Juan, have also lured many Puerto Ricans from the island to the mainland.

Although the migration of Puerto Ricans from the island to the mainland is similar in many ways to other movements of peoples to the United States, it is unique in several ways. As Fitzpatrick points out, it is the first "air borne migration" in United States history.[10] Puerto Ricans, unlike many of the earlier immigrants, are also American citizens when they arrive in the United States. They bring attitudes toward race that are alien to the United States. They also come at a time when "foreigners" are viewed with strong suspicion and distrust be-

10. Fitzpatrick, *Puerto Rican Americans*, p. 15.

cause automation has eliminated most of the jobs requiring unskilled laborers. Most of the unique characteristics of the Puerto Rican migration have increased rather than mitigated their problems on the mainland. These factors have not, on the whole, helped them to develop ways to cope with the difficulties they encounter in the United States.

Conflict and Adjustment on the Mainland

A dominant theme runs through the careful studies that have been done on Puerto Ricans on the mainland.[11] It relates to the enormous cultural conflicts they experience in the United States. The Puerto Rican, like any other individual, learns norms, values, beliefs, and behavior patterns which enable him or her to adjust to his or her social and cultural environment and to meet his or her survival needs. For the Puerto Rican migrant, there is a right way for a wife to behave, a right way to socialize children, and a right way for a child to respond to his or her parents. There is also a right language to speak. When individuals are socially adjusted, they know the correct ways to behave within their culture and they act out these behavior patterns in their daily life. When individuals either do not know or do not conform to their society's norms and values, we say they are socially and culturally maladjusted. People who are socially maladjusted become confused and alienated and experience identity crises. To a great extent, the Puerto Rican migrant's life on the mainland is like the individual who is experiencing a social crisis because the norms and values that guide his or her behavior conflict with those in the larger environment.

When an individual or group experiences a social crisis, ways to adjust and cope must be learned. One route for a foreign group is to assimilate: to acquire the values and behavior patterns of the dominant culture. Another way is to confine one's activities as much as possible within the ethnic community; another route is to try to live a bicultural life, that is, to conform

11. Among the most important studies of Puerto Rican Americans are those by Mills et al., *Puerto Rican Journey,* Fitzpatrick, *Puerto Rican Americans,* and Elena Padilla, *Up from Puerto Rico* (New York: Columbia University Press, 1958).

to one set of norms and values when interacting with the larger society and another when interacting with one's ethnic group. Puerto Ricans have used all of these tactics to adjust to mainland culture, with varying levels of success.

The Family

The family, which is very important in traditional Puerto Rican culture, experiences a tremendous shock when it is transplanted from Puerto Rico to the mainland. Although traditional Puerto Rican values and mores are undergoing change, even in Puerto Rico, they are much more a part of Puerto Rican culture than American life because values are highly resistant to change. The family is uprooted in the United States because traditional family roles are severely challenged, and most family roles are unable to withstand the challenge. The roles in the Puerto Rican American family are undergoing tremendous change at a very rapid pace. This creates major adjustment problems for Puerto Ricans on the mainland.

No role in the Puerto Rican American family has been more challenged than that of the father. In traditional Puerto Rican culture, the man was the undisputed head of the household. He was also expected to uphold his *machismo* (maleness). The "good woman" was one who obeyed her husband, stayed at home and out of the streets, took care of the children, and worked from "sun up to sun rise." The children were expected to obey their parents, especially their fathers, to stay out of trouble, and to develop a strong loyalty to the family. The family in traditional Puerto Rican culture, like the Italian family, was a highly valued institution. The individual's wants and needs were subservient to those of the family.

On the United States mainland, little societal support is given to these traditional roles. In fact, they are undercut by norms in the larger society. The statuses of the women and children are increased greatly in the United States. The woman is more likely to work than in Puerto Rico and is influenced greatly by American norms toward the role of the woman. The school and the community in America teach children that they should have more freedom, be more aggressive, and should not speak Spanish. The statuses of women and children are increased by the pervasive belief among mainland Puerto Ricans that the government protects them. Thus women get the edge on men in the courts, and children cannot be beaten because if they are their parents will be jailed. Traditional family roles are shattered on the mainland, and the family experiences shocks that cause strains, role conflict, and identity confusion.

Racial Problems

Puerto Ricans experience racial problems in the United States that are unknown in Puerto Rico because *social race* has different meanings in the two cultures.[12] While it is more desirable to be White than Black in Puerto Rico, and Whites are more likely to be members of the upper classes, social-class status in Puerto Rico is often as important as race. Upper-class Whites tend to exclude both poor Whites and poor Blacks from their social gatherings. However, poor Whites and poor Blacks tend to mix rather freely. Whites tend to marry other Whites, although intermarriage occurs more often in Puerto Rico than in the United States. While race influences social interactions in Puerto Rico as in the United States, racial segregation has never been legalized on the island as it has been in the United States. Also, to be Black in Puerto Rico is much less a handicap than to be Black in the United States. Blacks can and do enter the upper class. When they do, their race becomes less important in their social relationships.

Puerto Ricans on the mainland are forced to fit into one of two racial categories, Black or White. These categories are often meaningless in the Puerto Rican community. Puerto Ricans, both on the island and the mainland, recognize and use a number of racial categories, such as *blanco* [Whites], *prieto* [dark-skinned], *negro* [Blacks], and *trigueño* [tan].[13] Other words they use to make color distinctions among themselves are *Idio, Grifo,* and *de Color.*[14] When determining an individual's color, Puerto Ricans consider his or her hair color and texture, as well as his or her skin color. Also, an individual's color classi-

12. Padilla provides an excellent explanation of this concept in *Up from Puerto Rico,* pp. 69–75.

13. Wagenheim, *Puerto Rico,* p. 147.

14. Padilla, *Up from Puerto Rico,* p. 76.

fication is determined primarily by his or her physical traits rather than by the color of his or her parents or relatives. Within one family may be individuals who are considered *blanco*, *negro*, and *trigueño*.

The different ways in which color is recognized and treated on the mainland causes problems for the Puerto Rican migrant, especially for those who are intermediate in skin color. In their community, they are neither Black nor White; but they are often considered Black by outsiders. This causes the intermediate individual to feel alienated from both the White and Black communities in the United States. Puerto Rican migrants who are intermediate in color experience more adjustment problems in the United States than individuals who are clearly identified as either Black or White.[15]

The Puerto Rican American Community

Since they first started migrating to the United States, most Puerto Ricans have settled in New York City. However, the number of Puerto Rican migrants settling in other mainland cities has increased sharply in recent years. In 1950, 80 percent of the Puerto Rican population in the United States lived in New York City. By 1970 that number had declined to 70 percent.[16] There were about one million Puerto Ricans in New York City in 1970. However, pockets of Puerto Ricans lived in many other United States cities, stretched as far apart as Chicago and San Francisco; 120,000 lived in Chicago, 15,000 in Cleveland, and 20,500 in San Francisco.[17] Puerto Ricans tend to be dispersed within cities as they are within the nation. While there are pockets of Puerto Ricans in certain areas of New York City, such as East Harlem and South Bronx, the Puerto Rican population in New York is dispersed rather than highly concentrated.

Even though the Puerto Rican population tends to be spread out in cities, there are pockets of Puerto Ricans in American cities that constitute ethnic neighborhoods. The Puerto Rican

15. Mills et al., *Puerto Rican Journey*, p. 133.

16. Fitzpatrick, *Puerto Rican Americans*, p. 10.

17. Ronald J. Larsen, *The Puerto Ricans in America* (Minneapolis: Lerner Publications, 1973), p. 41.

community is usually a poor community, with the characteristics of people who are poor. In New York City, Puerto Ricans are at the bottom of the educational and economic ladder. They are highly concentrated in those jobs the poor usually get, such as hotel and restaurant work and jobs in the garment industry. Large numbers of Puerto Ricans are also operatives, kindred and nonhousehold service workers. A significant number, especially among the later generations, have entered clerical and sales fields or have become skilled craftsmen.[18] Many Puerto Ricans experience downward occupational mobility when they migrate to the mainland.[19]

The sound of Spanish, bodegas, travel agencies, and Pentecostal storefront churches are familiar sounds and sights in most Puerto Rican-American neighborhoods. Although Puerto Rican American culture is decidedly different from Puerto Rican culture—even the Spanish they speak differs—certain parts of the old culture are retained on the mainland. Hispanos, as many Eastville Puerto Ricans refer to themselves,* usually speak Spanish at home and English when talking with outsiders. To get the foods to prepare favorite ethnic dishes, such as rice and beans, fried plaintains, or dried codfish, the wife shops at the bodegas, the little corner grocery stores usually run by Puerto Ricans. Herbs and plants needed to cure illnesses or to fight the "evil eye" can be bought at the botanicas. Tickets for an air trip back home are purchased at the local travel agency, perhaps on easy terms. The Pentecostal Church, a fast-growing institution in Puerto Rican American communities, serves the spiritual needs of the migrants. The Puerto Rican community, with its bodegas, bontanicas, and Pentecostal churches, like ethnic communities of the past, help to ease the cultural shock for the migrant and serve as a "transition" for him or her as he or she prepares to function in the larger society.

Community Organizations

Although organized action groups have not traditionally been a large part of the Puerto Rican community on the main-

18. Fitzpatrick, *Puerto Rican Americans*, p. 61.

19. Mills et al., *Puerto Rican Journey*, pp. 66 and 69.

* *In her study,* Up from Puerto Rico, *Padilla calls the New York community "Eastville."*

land, a number of them have emerged in recent years. These organizations range in nature from the education-oriented Aspira to the militant Young Lords party. However, these diverse groups share a common goal: to improve the lives of Puerto Ricans in the United States. Each organization is contributing to this goal in its unique way. The Puerto Rican Forum, organized in 1957, is one of the most influential and effective groups in New York City. Its activities are diverse. The Forum is involved in community development as well as educational projects. The Puerto Rican Community Development Project, another effective organization, sponsors programs such as job training and drug prevention projects. Aspira is involved primarily in programs to encourage Puerto Rican youths to enter college. Many newly arrived Puerto Rican migrants are served by The Puerto Rican Family Institute, which was organized by a group of Puerto Rican social workers in New York City.

One of the best-known community organizations is the Young Lords party. Founded in 1969, the party is tightly organized and is similar to the Black Panther party. It has several branches in New York City. The party attempts, through its community programs and projects, to help liberate Puerto Ricans from oppression and to protect the Puerto Rican community. It has initiated free breakfast and lead poisoning detection programs for Puerto Rican youths, become involved in the welfare rights movement, and organized community health projects. The Young Lords party has become known as a militant group because of its strong stand on issues such as "self-determination," "liberation," and "community control." In its "13 Point Program and Platform" the party spells out ways in which it is dedicated to the "liberation of all oppressed people." [20]

Viable organizations such as the Puerto Rican Forum, Aspira, and the Young Lords party, will have a tremendous impact on the development of the Puerto Rican community on the mainland.

The Future

Occupational mobility has increased markedly among Puerto Ricans in recent years. There are other signs that the Puerto

20. Michael Abramson and the Young Lords party, *Palante: Young Lords Party* (New York: McGraw-Hill, 1971), p. 150.

Rican-American community is undergoing healthy change. Historically, Puerto Rican migrants have shied away from American politics and have depended on the Commonwealth offices in New York and Chicago to present their views to policymakers. However, the younger generation of Puerto Ricans, unlike their parents, are demanding cultural integrity as well as political power, and are taking steps to get both. They played pivotal roles in demanding rights for Puerto Ricans in the demonstrations at City College in New York in the late 1960s. The political power that Puerto Rican groups attain may decisively shape both their present and future on the mainland.

Teaching Strategies

To illustrate how content related to the Puerto Rican experience can be incorporated into an inquiry-conceptual curriculum, we have identified three key concepts related to the Puerto Rican experience and sample strategies for teaching them. Strategies are presented for teaching cultural conflict, racial problems, and colonialism for the primary, intermediate and upper, and high school grades, respectively.

PRIMARY GRADES

CONCEPT: Cultural Conflict

Generalization: The Puerto Rican migrant family in the United States experiences many conflicts and problems because it encounters new norms, values, and roles on the mainland that conflict with those in Puerto Rico.

1. Read the following case study to the students and ask the questions which follow. During the discussion of the story, help the children to state the above generalization in their own words.

THE RAMOS FAMILY

Mr. and Mrs. Ramos and their two children, Maria 3 and Carlos 7, live in New York City in an area called El Barrio. The Ramos family moved to New York two years ago from San Juan,

Puerto Rico. When the family lived in San Juan, Mr. Ramos worked in a factory. Mrs. Ramos stayed at home and took care of the children and house.

Both Mr. and Mrs. Ramos were happy living in San Juan until some of their relatives moved from San Juan to New York City. First, Mrs. Ramos's two sisters, whom she liked very much, moved to New York. Later, Mr. Ramos's brother moved to New York. They missed their relatives very much. They wanted to be able to see them more often. Mr. and Mrs. Ramos decided to go to New York to pay their relatives a visit.

When Mr. and Mrs. Ramos arrived in New York to visit, their relatives were very glad to see them. Mrs. Ramos kissed her two sisters. She told them about all the news back home. Her sisters told her about New York City. They liked it very much. Mrs. Ramos became very excited about New York City as she listened to her sisters talk about it. Mr. Ramos and his brother were also very glad to see each other. Mr. Ramos told his brother how the family was doing in San Juan. Mr. Ramos's brother told him about how good things were in New York. He told Mr. Ramos that he could make twice as much money in New York City as he made in San Juan! Mr. and Mrs. Ramos enjoyed New York City for two weeks. When they left, they had decided that they were going to move to New York City as soon as they got back home!

When the Ramos family got to New York again, things were not as nice as they thought they would be. The family was not as happy as it had been in San Juan. They had to live with Mr. Ramos's brother for two months because they could not find a nice apartment right away. When they did find one, it cost much more than they had paid for rent in San Juan. Mr. Ramos looked a long time before he could find a job. To help the family pay its bills, Mrs. Ramos got a job in a garment factory. Mrs. Ramos was the only person in the family working. She began to make more and more decisions for herself, Carlos, and Maria. In Puerto Rico, Mr. Ramos had made most of the decisions for everyone in the family.

Mr. Ramos spent most of each day looking for a job. He spoke good Spanish but many companies would not hire him because he spoke little English. Since Mrs. Ramos was working and Mr. Ramos was job hunting, Carlos and Maria had to spend a lot of time without either parent. Sometimes they would get into trouble with the neighborhood children.

Carlos got very sad when he started to school. He was a top student in Puerto Rico. However, he did poorly in school in New York. He could not read the books that were printed in English, a language which he did not know at all. He fell further and further behind in school each week. The teacher called him "Carl" instead of "Carlos." The children teased him because he spoke "funny." Carlos tried hard to speak English, even at home. His parents wanted him to speak Spanish at home so that they could understand him.

After looking for three months, Mr. Ramos found a job in a hotel. The family then moved into their own apartment. Things got better then. Mr. Ramos wanted Mrs. Ramos to quit her job and stay at home with the children. Mrs. Ramos wanted to keep working because she felt that it took more money to live in New York than in San Juan. Sometimes the family wished that they had stayed in San Juan.

The Ramos family has now been in New York City for two years. They are much happier now, but they still miss their friends and relatives in San Juan. Mr. Ramos understands why Mrs. Ramos wants to work. Carlos is speaking better English and getting better grades in school. The family is planning to visit Puerto Rico during the Christmas season. Carlos is counting the days until Christmas!

Questions

1. Why did the Ramos family move from San Juan to New York City?
2. Was New York City like the family expected it to be? Why or why not?
3. What problems did each of the family members have in New York City that they did not have in San Juan?
4. Which family member faced the greatest problems in New York? Why?
5. Which family member faced the least problems in New York? Why?
6. What problems do you think the family faced in New York City that are not brought out in the story? Why?

7. How do you think the family will feel about New York a year from now? Do you think that the family will move back to Puerto Rico? Why or why not?

Read *The Boy Who Wouldn't Talk* by Louis Kalb Bouchard* to your students. This is a story about a boy who has trouble adjusting to life in New York City. He and his family recently moved to New York from Puerto Rico. Carlos does not like New York and wants to go back to Puerto Rico. Life in New York is very strange to him. The language and customs are very different from those in Puerto Rico. After reading the story to the class, ask the following questions:

1. Why did Carlos dislike living in New York City?
2. What did he do about his situation? Do you think this was right? Why or why not?
3. How did Carlos's family and friends react to what he did?
4. What would you have done if you had been Carlos? Why?

INTERMEDIATE AND UPPER GRADES

CONCEPT: Racial Problems

Generalization: Puerto Rican migrants in the United States experience numerous racial and identity problems because racial concepts and norms on the mainland differ from those on the island.

1. Find old copies of picture magazines such as *Ebony, Tan, Life,* and *Look.* Locate pictures of people who look (a) obviously Caucasian, (b) obviously Negroid, (c) like fair skinned Afro-Americans. Mount these pictures on cardboard.
2. Show the students three of the pictures, one which will fit into each of the categories described above. Ask the students to name the "race" of the person in each picture. They will most likely say that one of the pictured persons is "White," and that the other two are "Black" or "Negro."

* *Complete citations for all books cited are found in the "Materials and Resources" section of this chapter, beginning on p. 403.*

Ask, "Why do we use only two categories to classify the people in these pictures?" With the use of careful questions, bring out the idea that in the United States any person, regardless of his or her physical appearance, is considered "Black" or "Negro" if he or she has any *known* African ancestry.

3. Show the class mounted pictures of (a) a fair skinned Afro-American male adult, (b) a fair skinned Afro-American female adult, (c) a dark skinned Afro-American male child, (d) a female child who looks Caucasian.

4. Ask the students to name the "race" of each of the pictured persons. After discussing their responses, tell the class that the pictures represent a Puerto Rican family that recently moved from San Juan to New York City. In the pictures are mom, dad, brother, and sister. Point out that while we may call the parents and the son "Black," Puerto Ricans have words to describe each color. Introduce these words. They would call the parents *Trigueño*, the son *Negro* or *De Color*, and the daughter *Blanco*. Tell the students that in Puerto Rico "color" has a special meaning that is very different from its meaning in the United States. Ask the students what race would the different family members belong to in the United States and why. Through questioning, bring out that all of them would be considered "Black" or "Negro" and why.

5. Ask, "Now that the family is in New York City, what kinds of racial problems might they encounter?" "Why?" Through questioning bring out that mother and father will be considered "Black" on the mainland while they were intermediates (Trigueños) in Puerto Rico. Discuss with the class the kinds of identity and social problems that the couple will face on the mainland and how they might cope with them. Ask the class:

   a) How do you think mother and father will feel when mainland Whites call them "Black" or "Negro?" Why?

   b) How do you think they will feel when Afro-Americans call them "Black?" Do you think they will identify with the Black struggle for civil rights? Why or why not?

c) Do you think they will want to be called "White" or "Black?" Why? What problems might they encounter when seeking to obtain their preferred racial identification? Why? How might they go about solving them?

With these and other questions, bring out the generalization that Puerto Rican migrants to the mainland who are intermediate in color have serious racial and adjustment problems because they are neither White nor Black in Puerto Rico but are forced to be "Black" on the mainland. Ask the class these valuing questions: Do you think that it is right to consider intermediates on the mainland "Blacks?" Why or why not? Do you think they should be considered "White?" Why or why not? If you were an intermediate Puerto Rican on the mainland, would you want to be considered "White" or "Black?" Why? When asking valuing questions such as these, accept all responses and maintain an open classroom atmosphere.

Ask the class these questions:

a) What special identity and racial problems might the son have in his family? In school? In the community? Why? How might he deal with them?
b) What special racial and identity problems might the daughter have in the family? In school? In the community? Why? How might she deal with them?

Read the following case study to the class and ask the questions which follow.

Mr. Díaz and Mr. Seda on the Mainland

Mr. Díaz looks Caucasian. In Puerto Rico he and Mr. Seda, who is *de color*, were very close friends. They both now live in New York City. When they first came to New York City, they would visit each other often, as they had done in Puerto Rico. Eventually Mr. Díaz started visiting Mr. Seda less and less and would often act unfriendly when Mr. Seda came to visit him, especially when his White friends were over. Mr. Díaz's White friends would always give Mr. Seda strange looks when he came over. Mr. Díaz began to understand that in New York City he was expected to mix socially with Whites only. Now, Mr. Díaz never visits Mr. Seda, and Mr. Seda goes to Mr. Díaz's house very seldom. When he does, he stays only a very short time. The last time that Mr. Seda visited Mr. Díaz's home, Mr. Díaz left in the middle of the visit with a White American friend. He told Mr. Seda that he and his White American friend had to go out and take care of some important business.

Questions

1. What is the main problem in this case study?
2. What kind of relationship did Mr. Díaz and Mr. Seda have in Puerto Rico?
3. Why did their relationship change when they moved to the mainland?
4. If you were Mr. Díaz, would you act as he acted when he moved to the mainland? Why or why not?
5. If you were Mr. Seda, would you act as he acted when he moved to New York City? Why or why not?

Valuing Exercises

Ask the students to independently complete these open-ended sentences. After they have completed them, discuss their responses and summarize the lesson by highlighting the generalization about the racial problems Puerto Rican migrants experience on the United States mainland.

a) Mr. Díaz should _____.
b) Mr. Seda should _____.
c) Mr. Diaz values _____ more than _____.
d) Mr. Seda values _____ more than _____.
e) If I were Mr. Díaz, I would _____.
f) If I were Mr. Seda, I would _____.

HIGH SCHOOL GRADES

CONCEPT: Colonialism

Generalization: Since the late fifteenth century, Puerto Rico has been controlled by foreign powers. This has caused rebellions, political ambiguity, and instability on the island.

1. Ask the students to read a selection about the Arawak Indians prior to 1493. Before asking them to do the reading, give them a copy of the questions below. Tell them to be able to respond to these questions when they have finished their reading. After the students have completed the reading assignment, discuss the questions. The following books include information about the Arawak (or Taino) Indians:

    Morton J Golding, *A Short History of Puerto Rico.*
    Ronald J. Larsen, *The Puerto Ricans in America* (for less able readers).
    Kal Wagenheim, *Puerto Rico: A Profile.*

Questions

    a) How did the Arawaks obtain food?
    b) What kind of political system did they have?
    c) What kind of religion did they have?
    d) What was a typical day like for (1) an Arawak adult female, (2) an Arawak adult male, (3) Arawak children?
    e) What kinds of relationships did the Arawaks have with other American Indian groups?
    f) What kinds of weapons did the Arawaks use when they were at war with other Indian tribes?

2. Divide the class into research groups and ask them to prepare and give short reports on each of these topics. They should be encouraged to present their reports to the class in the form of debates, simulations, role-play situations, and with the use of visual aids such as charts and graphs.

    a) Columbus's trips to North America and his relationship with the native populations.
    b) The establishment of Spanish domination in Puerto Rico in the 1500s.
    c) The *encomienda* system of slavery which the Spanish

established in Puerto Rico during the early years of
domination.

d) Ways in which the Arawaks resisted Spanish colonization by rebelling and running away.

e) Spanish domination in Puerto Rico in the 1600s, 1700s,
and 1800s.

f) *Grito de Lares* of 1868.

g) The political, economic, and social status of Puerto
Rico in 1898.

h) The Spanish-American War (causes and events).

i) The Treaty of Paris, 1898.

j) The American takeover of Puerto Rico in 1898.

After the students have a basic understanding of Puerto
Rican history up to 1898, they can then become involved in
activities such as the ones below to gain a better understanding of the island's political and economic status today.

3. Ask the students to pretend that they are members of the
United States Congress in 1898. Spain has just ceded Puerto
Rico to the United States. Their job is to decide on specific
political and economic policies for their new territory. They
must spell out a plan for governing the island and get it
approved by majority vote. After this exercise is completed,
ask the students to compare their plan with the plan the
United States used to govern Puerto Rico during the first two
years of American rule and with the plan delineated in the
Foraker Act of 1900. Ask the students to discuss the similarities and differences in the three plans and possible reasons
for them.

4. Ask the students to research the positions advocated by the
following political parties regarding the political status of
Puerto Rico:

a) The Independence party (Independence)

b) The New Progressive party (Statehood)

c) The Popular party (Commonwealth)

After their research, ask three students to role play an
advocate of each of the status positions. The advocate of
each position should argue his or her position in front of the
class. The three speakers will debate the status question and

answer questions posed by the class. After the debate and discussion, each class member will vote for one of the three positions: (1) the Commonwealth, (2) statehood, or (3) independence. After the voting, conduct a class discussion in which the class will compare their choice with the choice made by the citizens of Puerto Rico in a plebiscite held in 1967.* The students should discuss the reasons for the similarities and differences in their choice and the choice made by Puerto Rican citizens.

5. Ask a group of students to role-play a discussion between the individuals named below about what should be the future of Puerto Rico. Conduct a class discussion about the role-play situation when it ends.

   a. Pedro Albizu Campos
   b. Luis Muñoz Marin
   c. Luis A. Ferré
   d. Rafael Hernandez Colon
   e. A United States businessman who is president of a company that owns several factories in Puerto Rico.
   f. A southern United States senator
   g. A United States congressman from the Midwest

Since the Spanish colonized Puerto Rico in the sixteenth century, there have been uprisings and rebellions against oppression on the island. Ask the students to prepare a short research paper on forms of resistance to oppression in Puerto Rico since the sixteenth century. Make sure that they note resistance as exemplified by: (1) the Arawak Indians, (2) the Lares Rebellion of 1868, (3) the Nationalist party, and (4) the university student uprisings in Puerto Rico in the 1960s. After the students have completed and discussed their papers, ask them to write and present a dramatization about "The Struggle for Home Rule in Puerto Rico." They can invite another class or their parents and friends to attend the presentation.

---

* *See page 376 of this chapter.*

Materials and Resources

REFERENCES FOR THE TEACHER

Especially Recommended

There are a number of books on Puerto Rico and Puerto Rican Americans. They vary widely in quality and in their approach to the topic. Most teachers are very busy and find it necessary to read only a few carefully selected books. While a number of books are annotated in this section, we would like to call your attention to several. The teacher will need to read at least one book about the island since a knowledge of its history and culture is essential for understanding Puerto Ricans on the mainland. The best general and most readable book on the island is Kal Wagenheim's *Puerto Rico: A Profile*. The most comprehensive recent study of Puerto Ricans on the mainland is *Puerto Rican Americans: The Meaning of Migration to the Mainland,* by Joseph P. Fitzpatrick. A third book which is essential reading for the teacher is Elena Padilla's *Up from Puerto Rico.* It is an excellent anthropological study of a Puerto Rican community in New York City. It portrays the positive aspects of Puerto Rican American culture and presents an insightful theoretical perspective for viewing it.

Teachers who have the time and inclination should examine some of the more technical and popular books in the following bibliography. However, the author feels that the three books described above are must reading for the teacher who wishes to integrate content about Puerto Rican Americans into his or her curriculum.

Abramson, Michael and The Young Lords Party. *Palante: Young Lords Party.* New York: McGraw-Hill, 1971.

A deeply moving book about the emergence and struggle of the Young Lords Party. Through essays and powerful photographs, the party members reveal their history, goals, fears, aspirations, and tragic confrontations with the establishment. Although this book is an excellent resource, it may evoke controversy in some school settings, both because of its language and the topics discussed. The teacher should examine this book carefully before assigning it to students.

Arán, Kenneth, Herman Arthur, Ramón Colón, and Harvey Goldberg. *Puerto Rican History and Culture: A Study Guide and Curriculum Outline.* New York: United Federation of Teachers, 1973.

A useful guide for elementary and high school teachers that includes content, approaches, and activities.

Babín, Teresa Maria. *The Puerto Ricans' Spirit.* Translated by Barry Luby. New York: Collier Books, 1971.

This is a good book that includes a sketch of the island and treatment of the fine arts, folklore, and historical and contemporary literature of Puerto Rico. It contains a useful detailed chronology of Puerto Rican history.

Burma, John H. *Spanish-Speaking Groups in the United States.* Durham, N. C.: Duke University Press, 1954.

Burma includes a chapter on "The Puerto Ricans in New York" which relies heavily on the earlier study by Mills, Senior, and Goldsen. This chapter is dated as well as replete with overstatements and oversimplifications.

Chenault, Lawrence R. *The Puerto Rican Migrant in New York City.* New York: Columbia University Press, 1938.

This pioneering study of Puerto Ricans in New York City is informative, lucid, and of historical interest.

Cordasco, Francesco and Eugene Bucchioni, eds. *Puerto Rican Children on the Mainland: A Source Book for Teachers.* Metuchen, N. J.: Scarecrow Press, 1968.

A useful and informed collection of articles and studies that treats diverse aspects of Puerto Rican culture on the mainland. Particular attention is given to the problems which Puerto Rican children experience in mainland schools.

———. *The Puerto Rican Experience: A Sociological Sourcebook.* Totowa, N. J.: Littlefield Adams, 1973.

An excellent collection of excerpts from books, magazines, and journal articles that deals with many aspects of Puerto Rican life both on the mainland and on the island.

Cordasco, Francesco. *The Puerto Ricans, 1493–1973: A Chronology and Fact Book.* Dobbs Ferry, N. Y.: Oceana Publications, 1973.

An informative and useful reference book.

Cordasco, Francesco, with Gugene Bucchioni and Diego Castellanos. *Puerto Ricans on the United States Mainland.* Totowa, N. J.: Rowman and Littlefield, 1972.

A bibliography of reports, texts, critical studies, and related materials.

Fitzpatrick, Joseph P. *Puerto Rican Americans: The Meaning of Migration to the Mainland.* Englewood Cliffs, N. J.: Prentice-Hall, 1971.

The most up-to-date, comprehensive and well-done general sociological study of Puerto Ricans on the mainland that is currently available. The book is both informed and sensitive. However, the author is a staunch assimilationist and sees assimilation as "the way" for Puerto Ricans on the mainland.

Glazer, Nathan and Daniel P. Moynihan. *Beyond the Melting Pot: The Negroes, Puerto Ricans, Jews, Italians and Irish of New York City.* 2nd ed. Cambridge, Mass.: The M. I. T. Press, 1970.

This book contains a chapter on Puerto Ricans in New York City that is as much speculation and opinion as social science but is nevertheless worth reading.

Golding, Mortin J. *A Short History of Puerto Rico.* New York: Signet, 1973.

A popular history of Puerto Rico which is suitable for use with high school students. Available in paperbound edition.

Handlin, Oscar. *The Newcomers: Negroes and Puerto Ricans in A Changing Metropolis.* Garden City, N. Y.: Doubleday, 1959.

In this useful historical study of ethnic groups in New York City, Handlin describes the experiences of the city's White immigrants and points out how Black and Puerto Rican migrants are significantly different from the immigrants of the first 300 years of the city's history.

Lewis, Gordon K. *Puerto Rico: Freedom and Power in the Caribbean.* New York: Monthly Review Press, 1963.

A comprehensive and detailed history of Puerto Rico written from a refreshingly perceptive and sympathetic point of view.

Lopez, Alfredo. *The Puerto Rican Papers.* Indianapolis, Indiana: Bobbs-Merrill, 1973.

An informative reference book on the Puerto Rican experience.

Mills, C. Wright, Clarence Senior, and Rose K. Goldsen. *The Puerto Rican Journey: New York's Newest Migrants.* New York: Harper and Brothers, 1950.

Although considerably dated, this early study of Puerto Ricans in New York City is both informative and insightful.

Padilla, Elena. *Up from Puerto Rico.* New York: Columbia University Press, 1958.

An excellent anthropological study of a New York Puerto Rican community by a perceptive and sensitive anthropologist. This book is more than an ethnographic description. The author uses sociological and anthropological theory to interpret the experiences of Puerto Rican Americans. The themes of cultural variation and conflict within the Puerto Rican community that are documented throughout the book make it especially worthwhile.

Petrullo, Vincenzo. *Puerto Rican Paradox.* Philadelphia: University of Pennsylvania Press, 1947.

This polemical, journalistic, and didactic account of Puerto Rico focuses on its relationship with the United States mainland. The accuracy of this book is questionable.

Rand, Christopher. *The Puerto Ricans.* New York: Oxford University Press, 1958.

A journalistic treatment of Puerto Ricans on the mainland that is replete with simplistic generalizations and detrimental stereotypes.

Senior, Clarence. *The Puerto Ricans: Strangers—Then Neighbors.* Chicago: Quadrangle Books, 1961.

The author compares the experiences of various American ethnic groups, gives an overview of nativistic movements, and presents an incredibly hopeful view of the Puerto Rican's plight on the mainland. This book is much too "American" and simplistic.

Sexton, Patricia Cayo. *Spanish Harlem: An Anatomy of Poverty.* New York: Harper and Row, 1965.

This book, which attempts to provide a sound description of a New York Puerto Rican community and to delineate recommendations for social action programs, is readable but a failure. It is "popular" sociology, with all of the inherent limitations and problems that result when a popular approach is used to explain complex social phenomena. Because of the nature of the content, the book is considerably dated.

Silen, Juan Angel. *We the Puerto Rican People.* Translated by Cedric Belfrage. New York: Monthly Review Press, 1971.

For many reasons, this is a significant book. In a series of incisive and terse essays, Silen discusses colonization as a decisive force in Puerto Rican history. He traces the emergence of Spanish and later American dominance of the island. This is a deeply compassionate and hard-hitting book. However, it is not without flaws. It does not read very smoothly, probably because the translation is not the best. Like any forensic book, it is highly partisan. However, Silen's views merit deep pondering by teachers and students in the United States.

Vivó, P. ed. *The Puerto Ricans: An Annotated Bibliography.* New York: R. R. Bowker, 1973.

This bibliography consists of 2,600 entries, most of which are in English.

Wagenheim, Kal, and O. J. de Wagenheim, eds. *The Puerto Ricans: A Documentary History.* New York: Praeger, 1973.

A useful and informative collection of historical documents.

Wagenheim, Kal. *Puerto Rico: A Profile.* New York: Praeger, 1970.

A very informative and well-written popular book that treats various aspects of Puerto Rico. It is better than most popular books and includes chapters on Puerto Rican history, economy, government, culture, and the settlement on the mainland. It contains a useful chronology of Puerto Rican history. This book is an excellent source for both teachers and high school students.

Wakefield, Dan. *Island in the City.* Boston: Houghton Mifflin, 1959.

A journalistic account of Puerto Ricans in New York City. The author uses too many dramatic, catchy phrases. However, the book does give the reader an emotional tie-in with Puerto Ricans on the mainland. The author explores their living conditions and the racism they have to face. Wakefield, however, misses the essence of Puerto Rican life. His view of Puerto Rican culture and life is distorted by his cultural and racial blinders.

BOOKS FOR STUDENTS

Problems in Selecting Books for Students

Selecting books about Puerto Ricans for students is very difficult. There are very few excellent books on the topic. A number of problems recur in juvenile books about Puerto Ricans.

Many books focus on the poverty and the lack of family stability in the Puerto Rican American home. This occurs even when this information is unrelated to the story. Some authors seem to feel that a story about Puerto Ricans must emphasize their poverty in order to be authentic. This type of book creates or reinforces the belief that all Puerto Rican families are poor and unstable.

Other books focus on some deviant aspect of the protagonist's personality such as his or her inability to relate to other children. The character seems abnormal. The reader of this type of book may conclude that Puerto Rican children are strange and different.

Aspects of Puerto Rican culture, such as the use of herbs, are portrayed as exotic in many books. There is a tendency to show Puerto Rican lifestyles as old fashioned, while Anglo-Saxon values and culture are portrayed as worthwhile and modern. Children in these kinds of stories are unhappy as long as they accept Puerto Rican culture. As soon as they reject their culture and assimilate into the dominant society they become happy. Students who read these kinds of stories may feel that Puerto

Ricans should melt into Anglo-Saxon society and that the problems they face are created by themselves, or that they are the direct result of the Puerto Ricans' refusal to give up their culture.

History books tend to gloss over the Indian and African components of Puerto Rican culture. They also concentrate on the poverty of the island. The role played by the United States in Puerto Rico is often overdrawn. The United States is frequently portrayed as the savior of the island. Little attention is devoted to the problems in Puerto Rico which were created by United States domination. Some of the books also have factual errors.

Illustrations should also be noted when selecting books. Instead of showing the wide diversity of racial and physical types among Puerto Rican people, illustrations often consist of Anglo children colored light brown.

Teachers should be aware of all of these flaws and try to select books that do not have them. Since so few books meet our criteria, teachers should point out and discuss these points with their students both before and after the books are read. Students should also learn how to evaluate books.

In their early study of Puerto Rican Americans, the teacher should provide his or her students with a general overview of Puerto Ricans on the island and the mainland. Ronald J. Larsen's *The Puerto Ricans in America* is a very readable book which gives an historical overview of Puerto Rico and sets the stage for more specific readings.

This book can be followed up with Louis Kalb Bouchard's *The Boy Who Wouldn't Talk*. This book can be used to show students some of the conflicts faced by Puerto Ricans who migrate from the island to the mainland. Cultural conflict is an important aspect of the Puerto Rican experience on the mainland.

The Island of Puerto Rico

Belpré, Pura. *Dance of the Animals.* New York: Frederick Warne, 1972.
   A truly delightful Puerto Rican folktale about how the goat got his stump tail. Well illustrated with color drawings. (All Levels)

―――― . *The Tiger and The Rabbit and Other Tales.* New York: Lippincott, 1965.

An excellent collection of Puerto Rican folktales. They range from the fanciful to the humorous. Students of all ages will enjoy these tales that are set in Puerto Rico. (All Levels)

Bowen, David, Jr., *The Island of Puerto Rico.* New York: Lippincott, 1968.

A reasonably good history of Puerto Rico. However, Bowen has a tendency to oversimplify. The book focuses on modern history and deals with the economy, geography, and politics of the island. The early period of Puerto Rican history is covered briefly. (Upper)

Brau, M. M. *Island in the Crossroads: The History of Puerto Rico.* Garden City, N. Y.: Doubleday, 1968.

A readable and somewhat comprehensive history of the island. However, the book concentrates on the Spanish role in Puerto Rican history and de-emphasizes the African and Indian influences. The information about the American influence in Puerto Rican history is biased. (Intermediate)

Colorado, Antonio J. *The First Book of Puerto Rico.* New York: Franklin Watts, 1965.

This book is concerned with modern Puerto Rico. It deals with the geography, politics, and culture of the island. It also contains a glossary of Spanish words. The text is boring and sometimes inaccurate. The black and white photographs are okay. (Intermediate)

Page, Homer. *Puerto Rico: The Quiet Revolution.* New York: Viking Press, 1963.

A pictorial essay on contemporary Puerto Rico. The text presents a negative image of Puerto Rican Indians and most Puerto Ricans of African descent. The pictures are technically good, although they evoke little feeling in the reader. The captions are separated from the pictures. (All Levels)

Kurtis, Arlene Harris. *Puerto Ricans: From Island to Mainland.* New York: Julian Messner, 1969.

This history of Puerto Rico is told through the eyes of fictional characters. It is well illustrated and quite readable. However, the book contains inaccuracies and questionable interpretations. It contains a glossary of Spanish words used in the text. (Intermediate)

Manning, Jack. *Young Puerto Rico.* New York: Dodd, Mead, 1962.

This book deals with life in Puerto Rico as seen through the eyes of children. The text has inaccuracies. However, the book does contain some beautiful pictures of Puerto Rican children. Illustrated. (Intermediate)

Rivera, Geraldo. *Puerto Rico: Island of Contrasts.* New York: Parents Magazine Press, 1973.

A general description of the island of Puerto Rico for young readers. (Primary)

Rollins, Frances. *Getting to Know Puerto Rico.* New York: Coward-Mc-Cann, 1967.

An unfortunate modern overview of Puerto Rico. This overview is told from an American point of view. The United States is portrayed as the savior of the stricken island. (Primary)

Schloat, G. Warren, Jr. *Maria and Ramon: A Girl and Boy of Puerto Rico.* New York: Alfred A. Knopf, 1966.

This book contains a brief history of Puerto Rico. It concentrates on two modern families, those of Maria and Ramon. This book has the usual American biases and paints a rosy picture of Puerto Rico without discussing the problems that the people face. Illustrated with photographs. (Intermediate)

Sterling, Philip and Maria Brau. *The Quiet Rebels.* Garden City, N. Y.: Doubleday, 1968.

An interesting biography of four of Puerto Rico's famous leaders. The biographies focus on the men's efforts to help their people. They are informative and readable. However, they sometimes gloss over some of the problems faced by Puerto Ricans and the role played by the United States in Puerto Rico's oppression. Good illustrations. (Upper)

Tor, Regina. *Getting to Know Puerto Rico.* New York: Coward-McCann, 1955.

This is a very "American" interpretation of Puerto Rico. It presents Puerto Rico as a stricken island and the United States as its savior. The illustrations are poor. (Intermediate)

Weeks, Morris, Jr. *Hello Puerto Rico.* New York: Grosset and Dunlap, 1972.

A modern account of Puerto Rico. This book emphasizes the island's problems and the means used by the United States to solve them. It dismisses the contributions made by the Spanish, Indians, and Africans. A shorter part of the book deals with Puerto Ricans on the mainland. This section is handled somewhat more sensitively. The author shows how racism and discrimination cause problems for Puerto Ricans. (Upper)

Life on the Mainland

Allyn, Paul. *The Picture Life of Herman Badillo.* New York: Franklin Watts, 1972.

This biography of the first person of Puerto Rican ancestry elected to the United States Congress is very readable and well illustrated. It can be an inspiration to Puerto Rican children and help other children to appreciate the contributions Puerto Ricans have made to American life. (Intermediate)

Barth, Edna. *The Day Luis Was Lost.* Boston: Little, Brown, 1971.

This is a good story about Luis, a young Puerto Rican boy who recently migrated to the United States and his efforts to grow up. The story deals with how Puerto Ricans from the Island have to adapt to new lifestyles when they arrive in the United States. The illustrations are good. (Primary)

Belpre, Pura. *Santiago.* New York: Frederick Warne, 1969.

This is a delightful story about a young boy named Santiago Roman. Santiago shares his most cherished possession, a picture of his pet chicken, Selina, with his friends at school, thus convincing doubtful Ernie that Seline really exists. The story presents a positive image of a Puerto Rican child and his family. The color illustrations compliment the text. (Primary)

Bouchard, Lois Kalb. *The Boy Who Wouldn't Talk.* Garden City, N. Y.: Doubleday, 1969.

Carlos Vega is a sensitive young boy. He and his family recently moved to New York City. This change is especially hard on Carlos. The traffic, language, and customs are foreign to him. Carlos does not like New York. He wants to go back to Puerto Rico. He deals with his cultural conflict by refusing to talk. This story can show children how it feels to be in a strange place. Illustrated with drawings. (Intermediate)

Brahs, Stuart. *An Album of Puerto Ricans in the United States.* New York: Franklin Watts, 1973.

A comprehensive treatment of Puerto Ricans on the United States mainland. (Upper)

Buckley, Peter. *I Am from Puerto Rico.* New York: Simon & Schuster, 1971.

Federico Ramirez tells us what it is like to live in New York and Puerto Rico. This book gives some insight into life in rural Puerto Rico. It is illustrated with black and white photographs. The photographs alone could be used to tell the story. (Upper)

Campion, Nardi Reeder. *Casa Means Home.* New York: Holt, 1970.

Lorenzo longs to live in Puerto Rico. His life in East Harlem is dull and lonely. He eventually gets a chance to visit his grandparents in Puerto Rico for a summer. This book can be used to teach students about alienation felt by people when they move to a new area. The author does not show many positive family interactions and focuses too much on pathologies. Illustrated. (Intermediate)

Cole, Mary. *Summer in the City.* New York: Kenedy and Sons, 1968.

This is the story of a community-centered program. The book opens with a chapter on the 1967 Puerto Rican riot in New York and continues with chapters on people and events surrounding the program. The book tries to emphasize the positive aspects of Puerto Rican culture as seen from a White point of view. The role of the Catholic church in the Puerto Rican community is highlighted. (High School)

Cooper, Paulette, ed. *Growing Up Puerto Rican.* New York: Arbor House, 1972.

A collection of short, sensitively written autobiographies by Puerto Rican Americans, which highlight problems. Because of the emphasis on the negative aspects of Puerto Rican life in these accounts, they can reinforce stereotypes. There are also a number of anti-Black statements in them. The subject matter discussed, such as sex, may restrict or prohibit the use of this book in many schools. (High School)

Kesselman, Wendy. *Joey.* New York: Lawrence Hill and Co., 1972.

A photographic essay about a young Puerto Rican boy's adjustment to life in New York City. (All Levels)

Larsen, Ronald J. *The Puerto Ricans in America.* Minneapolis, Minn.: Lerner Publications, 1973.

A very readable and interesting history of Puerto Rico and Puerto Ricans on the mainland. The part of the book that deals with U. S.-Puerto Rican relations is "American" biased. The final chapter contains biographies of several distinguished Puerto Rican Americans. A very good reference book. Illustrated. (Upper)

Lexau, Joan M. *Jose's Christmas Secret.* New York: Dial Press, 1963.

Jose, a ten-year-old boy, assumes the role of the man of his family and provides his mother with a needed and wonderful Christmas gift. Jose is a strong, positive character who will inspire his readers. The family portrayed is strong, although the setting and certain points that the author brings out are stereotypic and somewhat over drawn. (Intermediate)

Matilla, Alfredo and Ivan Silen, eds. *The Puerto Rican Poets: Los Poetas Puertorriquenos.* New York: Bantam, 1972.

This bilingual anthology includes a wide range of poems penned by Puerto Rican poets. (High School)

Mayerson, Charlotte Leon, ed. *Two Blocks Apart.* New York: Holt, 1965.

Two teenagers, one a Puerto Rican American and the other a middle class Anglo-American, who live two blocks apart in the same New York community, speak freely about the separate worlds in which they live. (High School)

Shearer, John. *Little Man in the Family.* New York: Delacorte, 1972.

A sad but hopeful story about a Puerto Rican child and an Anglo child. This photographic essay will force students to ask many questions about our society. (All Levels)

Thomas, Piri. *Down These Mean Streets.* New York: Signet, 1967.

A touching autobiography of a young Puerto Rican American who is the victim of racism and poverty. The author tells how he fell into bad company, started using drugs, went to prison, and then eventually won a place for himself in society. The book deals with controversial areas such as drugs and sex. The teacher should read this book to determine whether it is suitable for use within his or her particular school and class. (High School)

————. *Savior, Savior, Hold My Hand.* Garden City, N. Y.: Doubleday, 1972.

This book is a sequel to *Down These Mean Streets.* It begins with Mr. Thomas returning to the barrio from prison. The author faces many problems, some old, others new. However, he also discusses many pleasant moments in this part of his life, such as meeting and dating his future wife. The author writes extremely well and many readers will find the book worthwhile. Because of the author's candor and subject matter, teachers should read this book carefully before asking students to read it. (High School)

Talbot, Toby. *My House Is Your House.* New York: Cowles, 1970.

Juana is a young girl who finds that she and her family are going to be displaced by urban renewal. She has only been in New York City five years and her New York home is the only she knows. The story deals with her anxiety and unhappiness about being forced from her home. The author unnecessarily discusses stereotypic pathologies commonly associated with Puerto Rican American life. This adds nothing to the book. Illustrated with color drawings. (Intermediate)

Weiner, Sandra. *They Call Me Jack: The Story of A Boy from Puerto Rico.* New York: Pantheon, 1973.

A moving and informative account of the life of a young Puerto Rican boy in New York City. This is a well-written and candid book. (All Levels)

Cuban Americans
and Native Hawaiians:
Concepts, Strategies,
and Materials*

Cuban Americans

*If in things concerning my country I should be given a choice
above all others . . . this would be the good I would choose: I
should want the cornerstone of our Republic to be the devotion
of Cubans to the dignity of man.*

José Martí

INTRODUCTION

The influx of Cubans on the American scene has supplied the
United States with one of its newest immigrant populations.
Their arrival provided another major element to the diverse
Spanish-speaking ethnic groups already in the United States,
such as Mexican Americans and Puerto Rican Americans.

Cuban Americans are a group with low visibility, since their

* *Chapter contributed by Charles F. Diaz, social studies teacher, Palm
Beach County (Florida) Public Schools, and doctoral candidate, Florida
Atlantic University.*

relocation has occurred almost exclusively in a few large urban areas. In 1974 they numbered well over one-half million persons. The largest Cuban-American community was found in Miami, Florida. It was over a quarter million. The next largest concentration was found in the New York City metropolitan area; 89,596 Cuban Americans lived in New York state.

The Cubans' brief history on American soil shares some common elements with older and more established immigrant groups. Yet there are many unique differences that distinguish their exodus. Most Cubans have migrated to the United States since the Castro revolution of 1959. Those that came did so almost invariably because they felt threatened by the political situation they experienced in Cuba. This contrasts with most other American immigrants who came to the United States searching primarily for economic promise.

Another characteristic of the Cuban influx is that those who left the island in search of a political haven are not a representative sample of the Cuban population at large. A demographic study showed that, "a disproportionate number of refugees come from the middle and upper strata of pre-revolutionary society." [1] People in the lower socioeconomic strata who opposed the revolution had fewer tools at their disposal to turn their dissatisfaction into some viable action.

Those who managed to reach the United States share one characteristic almost without exception: they are vehemently anti-Communist. Anything that hints of support for communism in any form will be strongly opposed by most Cuban Americans. Such a reaction is quite predictable, since communism is perceived as a concrete threat, rather than as a nebulous philosophy. Cuban immigrants are particularly sensitive to political developments, especially any concerning their native land.

The Cuban immigrant has generally accepted and lived by the predominant American ethos that hard work will ultimately be rewarded. Considering the deprived economic conditions that most started with, the results have been notable, if not drastic. Their accomplishments will probably lead them to be touted as a "model minority," much like their Japanese American counterparts. Yet the success of Cubans should not be con-

---

1. Richard R. Fagen, Richard A. Brody and Thomas J. O'Leary, *Cubans in Exile* (Stanford, California: Stanford University Press, 1968), p. 16.

strued to obscure the general plight of Spanish-speaking Americans. Generally, this success has not occurred without hardship, nor should their accomplishments imply that Cuban Americans do not have problems. The Cuban immigrant community has a very high percentage of elderly citizens, as well as working wives. Also, the cohesive nature of Cuban family life has sometimes suffered because of economic pressures.

To obtain a full understanding of the Cuban-American experience, we must explain the circumstances that caused their exodus. For most, leaving was a painful but, from their point of view, necessary move that they had to experience. For some, existence in exile is anguish, and they have failed to accept the permanence of their new surroundings.

Cuban Americans: Historical Perspective

Important Dates

1959   Fidel Castro took over the reigns of power in Cuba from the government of dictator Fulgencio Batista.

1961   Diplomatic relations between the United States and Cuba were severed.
The Cuban exile brigade 2506 landed at the Bay of Pigs, on the southern coast of Cuba, in an ill-fated attempt to overthrow the Castro regime.

1962   Commercial airflights between the U. S. and Cuba were ended. Immigration to the United States became strictly clandestine.
The Cuban missile crisis prompted President Kennedy to blockade Cuba. The Soviet Union eventually withdrew the missiles from Cuban soil.

1965   Beginning of the Cuban Refugee Airlift program. Flights from Cuba to Miami, Florida, were sponsored by the United States government.

Important Dates cont.

1973   Termination of the Cuban Refugee Airlift
          program. Immigration to the United States
          returned to a clandestine status or through a
          third country such as Spain or Mexico.

Cuban Americans: Life in Cuba

On January 1, 1959, the city of Havana, Cuba rocked with
the effects of a drastic change. The regime of Dictator Fulgencio Batista had been deposed by "la Revolución," led by a
bearded young rebel named Fidel Castro. His triumphal entry
into the capital city was seen by nearly everyone as the coming
of a new messiah. His popularity was more than that of a political figure; he had all the markings of a charismatic leader.

Promises of economic prosperity and of uniting the Cuban
people were among the many he made. The synthesis of the
Castro revolution took place in a slow, deliberate series of steps
to the delight of some and the disillusionment of others. The
Agrarian Reform confiscated large holdings of land in private
hands. This land became government property, and farmers
became government employees.

As the course of the revolution drifted politically left, a
marked polarization of Cuban society began to occur. A person
either supported the revolution or he or she was thought of as
a *gusano* [worm]. The latter was a parasite to progress, and the
revolution was better off without him or her. True to the Cuban
sense of humor, the expression *abrir los ojos* [see the light]
marked a person who took exception to revolutionary policies.
These political divisions permeated the family unit and caused
bitter disagreements between relatives who advocated the revolution and those who opposed it. Many of these rifts still remain
today. The Cuban revolution affected everyone, regardless of
his or her place in society. Fundamental changes reached the
economic, political, social, and religious sectors of Cuban life.

Cubans who were pondering the decision to leave did not
do so on the basis of the experiences of others; rather, they had
been affected personally and felt threatened in some way. This
painful decision to leave was made by many families who did

not want to see their children indoctrinated by a Marxist ideology, nor live under that system.

Leaving entailed many sacrifices. Invariably, there were relatives left behind. This point is particularly significant when the close-knit nature of the extended Cuban family is realized. This made it even more difficult to break from the family unit. Forfeit of all possessions was another factor to consider. Everything a person had worked for in a lifetime would find its way into government hands. Also, there was the prospect of starting all over again in a strange environment. For most, this was to happen without command of the English language. Despite all these difficulties, over a half-million Cubans felt threatened enough to choose exile.

The Cuban exodus was aided greatly by a United States policy that gave them a preferred status. There was no quota limiting the number of Cubans seeking asylum in the United States.

Departure

Prohias and Casal have identified three stages in the migration of Cubans to the United States. They are: "a *first stage*, between January, 1959, and October, 1962, when commercial flights between Cuba and the United States were available; a *second stage*, between October, 1962, and December, 1965, with a corresponding slowdown of the migration rate as Cubans had to resort to unconventional means (small boats, rafts, etc.) or to flights through third countries to come to the United States; a *third stage*, with daily airflights between Varadero and Miami throughout most of the period." [2] The third stage, which was known as the Cuban Refugee Airlift, was terminated in January 1973. Since then, refugees have had to revert to the unconventional means used in the second stage.

The trauma of leaving varied greatly with the particular experience. Leaving by commercial airline in 1960 was fairly conventional. However, escaping in a small boat was done by jeopardizing one's life. Also, the date of departure determined

2. Rafael J. Prohias and Lourdes Casal, *The Cuban Minority in the U. S.*, Cuban Minority Planning Study (Florida Atlantic University, Boca Raton, Florida, 1973), p. 12.

how much difficulty an exile would encounter in leaving the Island. "The records of the Miami Cuban Refugee Center show 10,000 arrivals in 1,002 small boats since 1961, a figure which becomes about 12,000 by including those not registered with the Center. It has been estimated that for every one who wins freedom three die." [3] Many Americans have heard of Cubans reaching our shores in small boats, but little publicity is given to the fact that many never made it after encountering a patrol boat or drifting away in the Gulf Stream current.

Adaptation to American Life

Most immigrants to the United States have come with the unwavering conviction of making this country their permanent home. Many Cubans arrived here with the thought of returning to their homeland as soon as the political climate changed. Although very grateful to the United States for their asylum, their ultimate plans were not in this country. Thus they did not feel the need to assimilate into the mainstream culture. With the passing of time, only the most optimistic clung exclusively to this point of view. It became apparent that the Castro regime showed strong signs of longevity, and exiles should adapt to their new environment.

The adaptation of Cubans to American life has not been easy in many cases. This process has been more extensive in areas where the Cuban population is small. In a city like Miami, with its large Cuban community, it is possible to lead a life without crossing the boundaries of the ethnic neighborhood. Naturally, assimilation is not imperative under such circumstances. One major change has been to forsake the more leisurely mood of the Cuban lifestyle. "Conversion to the pace of American life has threatened to disrupt the traditional Cuban way of life. The initial cultural shock was compounded by the dizzying social changes under way in this country that perplexed most Americans." [4]

One of the problems encountered by Cuban parents was

3. Mario Lazo, *Dagger in the Heart! American Policy Failures in Cuba* (New York: Twin Circle Publishing Company, 1968), p. 413.

4. *New York Times*, 21:4, April 16, 1971.

having their children adhere to the Cuban system of social customs. This was stricter than the one their American peers enjoyed. This situation does not differ greatly from the one faced by other immigrant groups as their children drifted away from the older customs.

Where Cubans resettled in large numbers, they were received in a variety of ways. A former Cuban lawyer related his impression in the following manner: "There are many people in Miami who still resent the Cubans settling here," he said, "but for the most part, since we have been the most successful immigrants in American history, Americans find it hard to look down their noses at us because we arrived here loaded with American characteristics. We are just too outgoing and enterprising and hardworking for them to stay mad at us."[5]

Economically, Cubans have done very well, all factors considered. Their median family income in 1973 ($9,371), although much higher than the Puerto Rican ($6,185), or the Mexican ($7,486), was still lower than the United States median income ($10,285).[6] Part of their economic position is due to the extremely high percentage of Cuban women in the work force.

When they tried to pursue their former occupations in the United States, most Cubans ran into difficulty. The main obstacle to white-collar employment was mastery of the English language, which many did not possess. In the professional fields, degrees earned in Cuba were often not recognized, and individuals frequently returned to college if they wanted to get work related to their training in Cuba.

Since their arrival from Cuba, there has been a catastrophic loss of occupational status among Dade County (Miami) Cubans. A 1966 survey showed that the percentage of unskilled laborers doubled, while the percentage of professionals, proprietors, technicians, and managers suffered a 4 to 1 reduction.[7] Today's figure should not be so drastic, but one must assume that a fair degree of loss in occupational status remains.

The typical exile family received some assistance from the

5. Ibid.

6. Prohias and Casal, *Cuban Minority*, p. 61.

7. Ibid., p. 65.

Cuban Refugee program as a new arrival. Afterward, they took whatever employment was immediately available in hope that their preferred work could be obtained later. When the concentration of Cubans in the Miami area grew to be substantial, the government started a resettlement program. This program offered jobs and one month's rent free for agreeing to move outside Florida.

The process of adaptation has also been slowed by the disproportionate representation of older Cubans in exile. This took place primarily because older people faced fewer restrictions in trying to leave the island. Therefore the average age of Cuban immigrants is much higher than what would be found in a normal population. The senior citizens find it more difficult to adjust to the American setting than younger exiles. Yet they provide a necessary day-care function that allows many Cuban women to join the labor force.

Politically, Cubans have tended to support the more conservative candidates. This is not surprising, since they have lived through an experience where something that began as liberalism progressed steadily into communism. As more Cubans become American citizens through naturalization, they may become a strong voting bloc. This is likely to happen when they realize the potential of the ethnic vote in America and become more highly acculturated and politicized. The ethnic vote has always played a major role in American politics. There is no reason why Cubans will not, in time, wield their power in the political arena. Above all, the Cuban American yearns for political stability and security.

Recently, Miami Cubans have been trying to assert some political influence, particularly in the area of public education. They feel that there is a gross imbalance between the percentage of Cuban students in the Dade County (Miami) school system and the number of Cuban teachers and administrators. Another point of contention is the use of federal impact funds designed to aid the Cuban student. These funds were allocated for the sole purpose of helping the Cuban student bridge the language gap. Many Cubans feel that not all of these funds were spent for their stated purpose.

The emphasis on the Cuban "success" story has clouded many of the problems that still grip the immigrant. This shroud of accomplishment has affected both Cubans and other Americans in obscuring the needs of the less successful refugee.

The Cuban American Today

Never before in our history has such a massive wave of political exiles found a haven on American shores. The uniqueness of this migration stands out from other immigrant groups. They are generally a people who were fairly successful previously and stepped into a very success-oriented environment.

Prohias and Casal note, "A cursory reading of the studies surveyed seems to indicate that Cubans have adjusted well to life in the United States and that, after the initial influx which caught Miami by surprise, they have not been a social problem. Early studies found Cubans to be low in all indices of social disorganization or maladjustment."[8] Their statement suggests that the process of acculturation is taking place, however slowly. As in the case of the Japanese Americans, the amount of cultural assimilation has exceeded the degree of structural assimilation.* Where large Cuban settlements occur, a great deal of the social and civic life still centers around the ethnic community. In Miami, theaters show films in Spanish; there are Latin civic clubs and a Latin Chamber of Commerce. Miami has become a bilingual city.

The average Cuban exile has gone through a great psychological transition, the severity of which correlates strongly with his or her age at the time of leaving. It is quite difficult to portray accurately and fully the trauma involved. There are many cases of former professional men in Cuba who had to begin again in middle age as unskilled workers. This change required some mature adjustment to cope with the new situation. Some parents sent their children to the United States hoping that they could follow in the near future. In many cases their hopes were realized; other parents still remain in Cuba.

It would be pure conjecture to estimate how many Cubans would return to their native land if the Castro regime were replaced by one that was more palatable to them. Many have put

8. Ibid., p. 6.

* Cultural *and* Structural assimilation *are defined and discussed in Chapter 2, pp. 43–45.*

down roots in this country that cannot be severed. Others would find the lure of a "free Cuba" irresistible, even though they may be well established here in the United States. Despite what political events may or may not occur in Cuba, a sizable number of exiles is here to stay. Today Cuban Americans are the third largest Spanish-speaking group in the United States, Mexican Americans and Puerto Rican Americans being the first and second largest. Unlike these two other groups, Cubans do not have a militant segment to fight oppression. Whatever militancy exists is confined to anti-Castro efforts. Almost all Cubans are very thankful to have found a haven in the United States. Therefore they are not as likely to criticize the government as are groups who do not feel this indebtedness. The Cuban experience to date indicates that they have been a viable and beneficial inclusion to American Society. This pattern can be expected to continue.

One factor marks the Cuban exile, regardless of whether his or her hopes are to remain in the United States or to return to Cuba some day. That element is a fervent desire to see his or her native land free from communism.

THE NATIVE HAWAIIANS

You must not think that this is anything like olden times, that you are the only chiefs and can leave things as they are. Smart people have arrived from the great countries that you have never seen. They know our people are few in number and living in a small country; they will eat us up.

David Malo, 1837

Introduction

In 1778 Captain James Cook's expedition landed on the Sandwich Islands, later to be known as the Hawaiian chain. There they found an island kingdom of close to one-half million people living an undisturbed life. Since that date, Hawaiian history has been fraught with a benevolent paternalism by Europeans and Americans to the detriment of native Hawaiians. This story is a trail of broken promises and exploitation which is very similar to the poignant plight of American Indians.

Until foreigners started coming to Hawaii, the native Hawaiians did not have a word for *race*. There were two groups, Hawaiians and strangers. They called themselves *kanakas* and referred to strangers as *haoles*. This total unimportance of race was to change with the European influence. The word *haole* took on the meaning of White instead of stranger, as Whites became more prevalent on the islands. Hawaiian leaders were forced to deal with an alien White economic, social, and legal system which they were simply unprepared to use.

Native Hawaiians: Historical Perspective

Important Dates

1778	The beginning of European contact. Captain James Cook's expedition landed on the Hawaiian Islands.
1795	The rise to power of King Kamehameha I. This marked the beginning of the Kamehameha dynasty.
1819	The first missionaries arrived in Hawaii from New England.
1835	King Kamahameha III granted an American firm the first long-term lease for a sugar plantation.
1848	The Great Mahele; all of the land on the islands was divided between the king and 245 chiefs.
1893	Queen Liliuokalani was overthrown in a bloodless revolution led by American planters. The Republic of Hawaii was established, with Sanford B. Dole as president. This government lasted until annexation by the United States.
1898	Hawaii was annexed by the United States.
1920	The Hawaiian Homes Commission was

Native Hawaiians: Before European Contact

The survival of Hawaiians depended on a communal effort to reap the maximum benefits from the islands' scarce resources. A very small percentage of the land was arable; consequently, sharing was almost a necessity. The islands were governed by the *ali'i*, who were powerful chiefs. The power of these chiefs was legitimized by the priests, or *kahuna*, who interpreted the religious doctrine set forth in the *kapu*. The common people, or *maka'ainana*, were extremely devoted to their chiefs. Each chief was the supreme ruler over his territory. Although sharing was a predominant belief, there was a considerable difference between the lifestyles of the chiefs and the common people.

There were two Hawaiian customs that would lead to inevitable conflict with *haoles* in the future. One was a system of barter, where products were exchanged from one island to another. The Hawaiians did not use currency and therefore the accumulation of wealth as we know it was unknown. The other custom was the notion that land belonged to everyone and could not be owned. The earliest visitors to the islands found the natives very willing to share whatever they had. After all, that was the Hawaiian way.

European Contact

The propensity of Hawaiians to share eventually helped to seal their demise. Besides providing provisions for ships, Hawaiians were quite willing to share their women, and Whites were eager to become intimate with them. These casual contacts over a long period of time had a decimating effect on the island's population. The venereal disease introduced by the European sailors found little natural resistance among the Hawaiians. Along with the measles, cholera, and alcoholism, the deadly toll was taken.

An estimated one-half million persons inhabited the Hawaiian Islands at the time of European contact. By 1840, only about 100,000 remained. Many native Hawaiians were naturally alarmed at what was taking place due to contact with the *haoles*. One of the spokesmen who espoused this point of view was David Malo, a noted Hawaiian writer, who once said, "The ships of the white man have come, and smart men have arrived from the great countries. . . . They know our people are few in number and living in a small country; they will eat us up."[9] His prophecy came true eventually, but at the time it fell on deaf ears. When David Malo died, he was buried at his request high on a mountainside, as far away from the *haoles* who destroyed his land as possible.

The paternalism of *haoles* began with sea captains who needed the islands as a place to replenish supplies and repair their ships. Often, chiefs were given a few metal items in return for supplies. As the commercialism grew and the chiefs saw more European goods, there began to be a demand for these items that were absent before. Some chiefs became avaricious, and forced their subjects to work even harder to satisfy their demands for foreign goods. Sandalwood, which is indigenous to the islands, became an item traders sought. They would later transport it to China, where it would be sold at high profits.

The ascension to power of King Kamehameha I marked the rise of the Kamehameha dynasty. "One of Kamehameha's greatest qualities was his ability to attract many white men to his service and retain their loyalty for years or even a lifetime."[10] This practice proved disastrous in the long run, because often the advisor had his interests ahead of the people he represented.

Besides the traders and the confidants of chiefs, another group entered the Hawaiian scene to lend its paternalistic hand. In 1820 the first group of missionaries arrived in the islands from New England. Their goal was to "Christianize" the natives, but

9. Paul Jacobs and Saul Landau, with Eve Pell, *To Serve the Devil, Volume 2: Colonials and Sojourners* (New York: Vintage, 1971), p. 22.

10. A. Grove Day, *Hawaii and Its People* (New York: Meredith Press, 1968), p. 44.

in most cases their influence far surpassed the religious realm. Jacobs and Landau write: "Under increased influence of the missionaries of the king, more *haoles* were given the right to lease land for commercial enterprises. But these men did not want merely to lease the land; they wanted to own it outright so they could then sell or lease it to others."[11] This notion of landownership was diametrically opposed to traditional Hawaiian custom. Yet the *maha'ainana* (common people) accepted the decisions of the king without retort. Soon there began to develop a *haole* industrialist class whose only interest was its own financial gains. The businessmen never worried because the missionaries' influence was ever-increasing. Thus their positions as feudal landlords were safe.

Annexation

To paint a picture of something other than imperialistic motives by the United States in annexing Hawaii would be doing a severe injustice to the facts. The American militaristic minds saw Hawaii as a coaling station for our Pacific fleet. As Jacobs and Landau point out, "The strength and influence of the pro-annexation Americans grew in Hawaii and on the mainland, where the concept of expansion and 'manifest destiny' was attracting a growing number of adherents."[12] The latter doctrine, having reached our Pacific shore, seemed to have its sights set on Hawaii.

The first attempt at the deposition of the monarchy came on January 17, 1893. This coup was supported by American troops (although not officially) and it was led by Sanford B. Dole, a *haole* planter. The overthrow of Queen Liliuokalani was one from which Hawaiians never recovered. The queen did not order her troops to battle the insurgents because she trusted the fairness of the United States. After losing her throne, the queen wrote a desperate plea to President Cleveland to be restored, but it was ignored. The Republic of Hawaii was established, with Sanford B. Dole as its first and only president. Annexation by the United States was imminent. In 1898 the islands became

11. Jacobs and Landau with Pell, *To Serve the Devil*, p. 26.

12. Ibid., p. 29.

a part of the territorial possessions of the United States. Manifest Destiny had triumphed again. The *haole* who had once come as a guest had managed to usurp the entire kingdom.

Richard Olney, the secretary of state at that time, summed up the whole situation this way: "Hawaii is ours," he said, "but as I look back upon the first steps in this miserable business and as I contemplate the means used to complete the outrage, I am ashamed of the whole affair."[13]

The Hawaiians Today

In 1971 there were about 15,000 *pure-blooded* Hawaiians* from the nearly half-million that once inhabited the islands. They compose less than 2 percent of the present population. These cold statistics tell the story of a people who have been crowded out of a way of life by more powerful forces.

The average native Hawaiian falls far below his White counterpart in the area of economic prosperity. He or she generally lives in a community whose facilities are substandard. Many poverty-stricken Hawaiians are forced to eke out an existence from the land or to become objects of curiosity for tourists' cameras.

Present-day Hawaii is a polyglot of peoples with varied backgrounds. There are sizable communities of Chinese and Japanese Americans. There is a Korean-American population that originally came over to work in the pineapple and sugar cane estates. Filipinos and Portuguese also came as agricultural workers. The latest inclusion, the Samoan, is at the bottom of the social and economic ladder. There are also a few thousand Blacks in Hawaii, as well as the still-dominant *haole*. The White and Asian American form the nucleus of today's power structure. This myriad of cultures has combined to yield a surprisingly stable society. Although Hawaii is often touted as a paradise of racial harmony, that is a misrepresentation to some degree. True, it may be more harmonious than most places on earth, but it still falls short of its billing.

13. Theon Wright, *The Disenchanted Isles* (New York: Dial Press, 1972), p. 21.

* *However, 99,958 people in the United States, excluding Alaska, indicated that they were members of the* Hawaiian *race in the 1970 Census.*

The future of racial distinctions in Hawaii is open to debate. The native Hawaiian's outmarriage rate is the highest of any group.[14] This population seems destined to be dissolved among the larger racial stocks. Meanwhile, tourists marvel at native dances and feasts, and the Hawaiians dream of a time when these islands were theirs.

Teaching Strategies

The concept of expansion can be illustrated in many ways. The native Hawaiians provide a classic case of the displacement of a native population because they were an obstacle to the expanding forces. Their story can be related to other native inhabitants that suffered a similar fate.

The Cuban refugee poses a unique case study in American immigration. Political exile is the exception rather than the usual reason for immigrating to the United States. Therefore the Cuban refugee provides an interesting comparison and contrast to other American immigrants.

CONCEPT: Expansion

Generalization: As a nation expands to obtain territory, often the rights of the native population are not protected.

1. After giving the students sufficient background information about the native Hawaiian, ask them to make a list of factors that apply to the native Hawaiian and the American Indian. These factors can include both past and present situations. Afterward, these points may be grouped, classified, and discussed.
2. Organize your students into small groups. Present them with this hypothetical situation: One person in the group would be chosen to supervise and control the financial affairs of all the members. What problems may develop with such an arrangement? A tape could be made of their reactions. Later, this tape could be replayed and compared to what took place between American advisors and Hawaiian rulers.
3. Role-play the following situation which takes place in Ha-

14. William L. Abbott, "Trapped in a Mystique," *Nation*, 208 (February 3, 1969), p. 147.

waii in 1875. The *haole* advisor to the King is trying to persuade him to grant some land to Mr. Farmer, a prospective planter. Kaeo opposes the entire proposition. After the role-playing situation, ask the students the questions that follow. The role descriptions:

> *King Kamehameha:* He is indecisive over what to say to the planter. Yet he respects greatly the advice of his *haole* counsel, Mr. George Bennett.
>
> *George Bennett:* Advisor to the king and a good friend of Mr. Farmer's, whose interests he protects. He has been a missionary for nearly twenty years.
>
> *Floyd S. Farmer:* Planter and business tycoon. He intends to start pineapple plantations in Hawaii because of the predictably warm weather.
>
> *Kaeo:* A native Hawaiian and a member of the king's court. He vehemently opposes the granting of any more land to *haoles.*

Questions

1. Did George Bennett succeed in persuading the king to grant the land to Mr. Farmer? If so, why? If not, why not?
2. Was Kaeo successful in his opposition to the land deal? Why or why not?
3. Did Mr. Farmer tell the king his plans for using native labor? Why or why not?
4. Did the king decide to grant the land lease to Mr. Farmer? If he did, what were his reasons? If he did not, why not?
5. Did Mr. Bennett use his position as a missionary to help his argument? Why or why not?

CONCEPT: Immigration

Generalization: Cuban immigrants were victims of a political system that caused them to choose self-imposed exile.

1. Divide your class into small groups and instruct them as follows: Your family is forced to move to a country where the language and customs are alien. Each of you is allowed to take only a small amount of clothes. All of your other possessions are left behind and forfeited, since you cannot return. Describe what your life might be like where you are

going. What clothing would you take with you? Why? How well do you think your family would fare? What adjustments would all of you have to make? The students' reactions could be taped or written. The taping would provide more spontaneous responses. Afterward, compare and discuss reactions among groups.

2. After sufficient background information is presented, ask each student to write an essay titled, "If I Had Been a Cuban in 1959, What Would I Have Done?"

3. Organize a debate in which one side takes the position that deposing the Castro regime is feasible and the other feels it is impossible.

Read the following story to the class and ask the questions that follow.

THE PINA FAMILY

Ernesto Pina was a fisherman who lived in Cardenas, on the north coast of Cuba. He and his wife, Iliana, had never been wealthy, but fishing had always provided for the necessities of life. Ernesto always seemed to be able to return with fish of one type or another.

They had been happy to see the tyrant Batista deposed by the Castro revolution. Ernesto felt that Fidel Castro had the interests of the "little man" like himself at heart. One day when he returned to the fishery to sell his catch, Ernesto was informed that part of it would go to the government. Officials said that his fish would be exported and goods received in return would help the revolution. Ernesto did not want to be considered greedy, but he needed his entire catch to support his family. At the risk of being caught, he would hide some fish and sell them privately to friends.

The family's only son, Jose, was sixteen and had been forced to join the militia. Neither parent liked this, but it could not be helped.

One night Ernesto and Iliana were talking and she suggested going to the United States. Yet both knew that they could not depart legally, since Jose was of military age. Obviously, they

could not leave their only son behind. So the three decided to
try to escape in the fishing boat one night. They knew they
would be shot in the water if discovered but decided to run the
risk anyway.

The eventful night came, and the Pina family slipped away
from the harbor. Ernesto was sailing the craft because he did
not want the noise of the engine to be heard. He had been quite
careful to wait for the proper tide and a moonless night. After
a short time, they heard an engine; the sound kept coming closer.
It was the shore patrol! He lowered the sail quickly and they
hid in the bottom of the boat. The patrol boat passed within
fifty yards, but had not spotted them. They had been saved by
the darkness!

When morning came, Ernesto started his small engine because the breeze had faded. He hoped for the best because he
did not have much gasoline. After two days at sea, he was beginning to worry. His family was sunburned, he was out of gasoline, and he had not yet spotted the Florida coast. Yet they
kept their faith. They were lucky to be seen by a United States
Coast Guard cutter which towed them into port.

As the three stepped off the boat on to American soil, they
each said a prayer for having been so fortunate.

Questions

1. If you had been one of the Pina family and found yourself
   in their circumstances, would you have taken the risk they
   did? Why or why not?
2. What problems did Mr. Pina encounter that made him decide to leave Cuba?
3. Why didn't the Pina family attempt to leave Cuba by legal
   means?
4. What kind of future do you foresee for the Pina family in
   the United States?

Have each student (either in writing or orally) describe the cir-
circumstances of a political situation in the United States that
would cause him or her to escape to a foreign nation which would
involve risking his or her life.

Read the following story to the class and ask the questions that
follow.

THE REYES FAMILY

Carlos Reyes was a successful lawyer in Havana in 1959, the time of the takeover of Fidel Castro. Like most other people, he saw the new government as the future salvation of his country. He was ready to do his part for the revolution.

As the years wore on, he began to see some changes that disturbed him. Being a criminal lawyer, he saw a drastic reduction in the civil liberties of the public at large.

His wife, Maria, was having an increasingly difficult time buying food to prepare well-balanced meals for the family. She naturally complained about this, but only in the privacy of their own home. If she were not careful, these complaints might be heard by the informant who lived on her block and she would be labeled a "counter-revolutionary."

Their two daughters, Gloria and Cecilia, were receiving daily lessons in Marxism at the school. These classes were mandatory for all students. The girls naturally saw a conflict between this philosophy and what they were taught at home, but they did not mention it to anyone at school.

Mr. Reyes had been having second thoughts about the revolution for quite some time. In 1967 he decided to leave, so he placed his family on the list for the Cuban Refugee Airlift. In doing so, he knew that all of his property would be forfeited to the government upon departure.

Before leaving, he was sent to the country to harvest sugar cane. This was a necessary task that would befall those who chose to exit. For eight months Carlos did the back-breaking agricultural work he had never done before. A typical day lasted from four in the morning till sunset.

Finally, in 1970, the magic day arrived when his turn had come on the next flight to Miami. Before leaving, the family surrendered rings, watches, and any other items of value. Each person brought only the clothes he or she could fit in a small suitcase.

Regardless of the circumstances, they were all very grateful to be in the United States. They received lodging and food from the Refugee Center, as well as a small amount of money. Having no trade, and speaking little English, Carlos Reyes began to work as a dishwasher in a restaurant. His former legal profession was useless now. The family had to adjust to these hard times. It was not easy, but they managed to get by.

Today, four years later, the Reyes family lives in a small apartment in Miami, and have even bought an automobile. Although their lifestyle is hardly luxurious, they are grateful for their new freedom.

Questions

1. Identify on a map the place where the Reyes family used to live.
2. What were some of the reasons why Mr. Reyes decided to leave Cuba?
3. Why do you think the Cuban government made it difficult for people to leave the island?
4. How would you have felt if you had been Carlos Reyes and you had been forced to cut sugar cane before leaving?
5. How do you think Mr. and Mrs. Reyes reacted to their daughters' receiving classes in communism?
6. How do you think the change from lawyer to dishwasher affected Mr. Reyes? His wife and children?
7. How do you think the Reyes' daughters adjusted to school in Miami?

Tell the students, "Pretend that you are one of the members of the Reyes family. Describe in a paragraph (or brief essay) your feelings upon landing on American soil from Cuba."

Materials and Resources

REFERENCES FOR THE TEACHER

Cuban Americans

Although there is a great deal of published literature on Cuba and the Cuban revolution, there is a comparative dearth of material on the Cuban exile in America. Most of the literature available on the Cuban refugee is not in published form. A lot of it appears in unpublished theses, dissertations, and reports. This information is not easily accessible, and perhaps more publishing about Cuban Americans will be done in the future.

One obvious resource would be to bring a Cuban exile into the classroom to relate his or her experiences. This may or may not be possible depending upon the geographic area in which you teach. Most of the following are easily available sources for all teachers.

Alexander, Tom. "Those Amazing Cuban Emigrees." *Fortune* 74 (October 1966), pp. 144–49.

Article dealing with the success of Cuban immigrants.

Burt, Al. "Miami: The Cuban Flavor." *The Nation* (March 8, 1971), pp. 299–302.

An article about the impact of Cubans and their lifestyle in the Miami area.

Fagen, Richard R., Richard A. Brody, and Thomas J. O'Leary. *Cubans in Exile.* Stanford, California: Stanford University Press, 1968.

The main published source on Cubans in Miami, Florida, and their reasons for leaving Cuba. Complete with demographic information on the Cuban exodus.

Lazo, Mario. *Dagger in the Heart!* New York: Twin Circle Publishing Company, 1968.

Very descriptive source about how Cuba fell into Communist hands.

Linehan, Edward J. "Cuba's Exiles Bring New Life to Miami." *National Geographic* 144 (July 1973), pp. 68–95.

Excellent article with many photographs. This would be a good source for students to peruse.

Prohias, Rafael J. and Lourdes Casal. *The Cuban Minority in the U. S.* Cuban Minority Planning Study, SRS Grant No. 08–P–55933/4–01, Florida Atlantic University, Boca Raton, Florida, 1973.

The only comprehensive nationwide study done on Cubans in the United States. This work is extremely thorough in all aspects. It is the only source with unique demographic information. It is available on loan from the Florida Atlantic University library.

Senior, Clarence O. *Our Citizens from the Caribbean.* St. Louis, Mo.: McGraw-Hill, 1965.

Includes a chapter on the Cuban exiles.

Walsh, Bryan O. "Cubans in Miami." *America* (February 26, 1966), pp. 286–89.

This article deals with the Cuban Refugee program and the impact of Cubans in the Miami area.

Native Hawaiians

Most of the information about native Hawaiians is found in general sources about Hawaii. With perseverance, their story can be pieced together.

Abbott, William L. "Trapped in a Mystique." *Nation* 208 (February 3, 1969), pp. 146–49.

This is not an historical account. The author takes a look at the different elements that compose present-day Hawaii.

Jacobs, Paul, and Saul Landau, with Eve Pell. *To Serve the Devil, Volume 2: Colonials and Sojourners.* New York: Vintage, 1971, pp. 3–63.

Contains an extremely informative chapter on the native Hawaiians.

Lind, Andrew W. *Hawaii, The Last of the Magic Isles.* Toronto, Canada: Oxford University Press, 1969.

Very interesting source dealing primarily with race relations. A book students are more likely to read than most.

Simpich, Frederick. *The Anatomy of Hawaii.* Toronto, Canada: Coward, McCann, and McGeoghan, 1971.

A very descriptive account from the earliest days of Hawaii. Contains an excellent table of contents.

Wright, Theon. *The Disenchanted Isles.* New York: Dial Press, 1972.

This work dwells primarily on the political changes that swept the islands during the 1950s (the deposition of the old order).

BOOKS FOR STUDENTS

Hawaiians

Bailey, Bernadine. *Hawaii.* Chicago, Illinois: Albert Whitman and Company, 1964.

A very brief and readable source on Hawaii for young children. (Primary)

Bauer, Helen. *Hawaii, The Aloha State.* Garden City, New York: Doubleday and Company, 1960.

A well-written and detailed account of Hawaiian history. It is also amply illustrated. (Intermediate)

Bianchi, Lois. *Hawaii in Pictures.* New York: Sterling Publishing Co., 1965.

This book is divided into sections on the land, people, history, and economy of Hawaii. It has many illustrations. (Intermediate)

Epstein, Sam and Beryl. *The First Book of Hawaii.* New York: Franklin Watts, 1961.

A series of stories incorporating facts about Hawaii. Its narrative style should hold the students' interest. (Intermediate)

Ferguson, Edna J. *Hawaii, Life in America.* Grand Rapids, Michigan: Fideler Co., 1966.

An elementary social studies text about Hawaii. It is fraught with misrepresentations of Hawaiian history. However, it contains some useful information. (Intermediate)

Lipkind, William. *Boy of the Islands.* New York: Harcourt, 1954.

A fictional adventure story about a native Hawaiian boy before the coming of the Europeans. (Primary)

Swenson, Juliet. *Hawaii.* New York: Holt, 1963.

An elementary source on the Hawaiian Islands and their history. It is well illustrated. (Primary)

Cuban Americans *

Eiseman, Alberta. *Mañana Is Now: The Spanish-Speaking in the United States.* New York: Atheneum, 1973.

A good general history of Puerto Rican Americans, Mexican Americans, and Cuban Americans. This book is well written and is a good introduction to the experiences of Spanish-speaking groups in the United States. (High School)

* *We were unable to locate any books for young people that dealt exclusively with Cuban Americans.*

Multiethnic Units: Concepts and Teaching Strategies

Chapters 1 through 11 include content about American ethnic groups, descriptions of exemplary teaching strategies, and annotated bibliographies. Part I discusses goals of ethnic studies, key concepts for ethnic studies programs, and ways to organize the instructional program. Chapters 5 through 11 deal with content about ethnic groups and strategies that can be incorporated into the school curriculum. This chapter is designed to highlight and summarize the major points discussed in the book and to illustrate how the teacher can use the information and strategies described in the other chapters to implement and evaluate multiethnic units which focus on two or more ethnic groups. The major components of a sample multiethnic unit are presented to illustrate the steps involved in unit construction.

Identifying Key Concepts

When planning a multiethnic unit, the teacher should first decide which key concepts he or she will use to organize the unit. As stated in Chapter 4, these concepts should be high-level ones related to the structure of the social sciences, such as scarcity (economics), culture (anthropology), and power (political science). The teacher should also select a key concept from each of the social science disciplines so that his or her unit will be interdisciplinary. The rationale for making units interdisciplinary is presented in Chapters 3 and 4. We have selected the following key concepts for the sample unit discussed in this chapter:

DISCIPLINE	KEY CONCEPT
Anthropology	cultural assimilation
Economics	economic status
Geography	ethnic community
History	immigration
Political Science	social protest
Psychology	identity
Sociology	discrimination

Identifying Key and Intermediate-Level Generalizations

After the teacher has identified organizing concepts, key generalizations related to each of the concepts should be chosen. Ideally, the teacher should identify a key or universal generalization for each concept, and then an intermediate-level generalization for each concept. A universal generalization applies to all cultures, times, and peoples (see Chapter 4). An intermediate-level generalization is limited in its application to a particular nation, subculture, or time period.[1] Thus a generalization that applies only to the United States is an intermediate-level generalization. In our examples below, we identify a universal generalization and an intermediate-level generalization for our first concept, cultural assimilation, but only intermediate-level generalizations for other key concepts. We are taking this short cut to save space.

KEY CONCEPT: Cultural Assimilation

Key or Universal Generalization: Whenever a minority group comes into contact with a dominant culture, it is usually expected to acquire the culture and values of the dominant group.

1. Hilda Taba, Marcy C. Durkin, Jack R. Fraenkel, and Anthony H. McNaughton, *A Teacher's Handbook to Elementary Social Studies: An Inductive Approach,* 2nd ed., (Reading, Mass.: Addison-Wesley, 1971).

Intermediate-Level Generalization:	In the United States, ethnic minority groups are expected to acquire the culture and values of the dominant Anglo-American culture.
KEY CONCEPT:	Economic Status
Intermediate-Level Generalization:	Because of racial discrimination and other factors, members of American minority groups are often paid low wages for their work. Consequently, most of them are members of the lower socioeconomic classes.
KEY CONCEPT:	Ethnic Community
Intermediate-Level Generalization:	American ethnic groups that have strong ethnic identities and characteristics usually live in ethnic neighborhoods and communities.
KEY CONCEPT:	Immigration
Intermediate-Level Generalization:	Most ethnic groups came to America and moved within it to improve their economic conditions. However, some ethnic groups were either forced to America or were forced to move from one region of the United States to another.
KEY CONCEPT:	Social Protest
Intermediate-Level Generalization:	Throughout their experiences in the United States, ethnic minorities have resisted discrimination and oppression in various ways.
KEY CONCEPT:	Identity
Intermediate-Level Generalization:	In recent years, ethnic groups in the United States have become increasingly aware of their ethnic identities and have expressed them in various ways.
KEY CONCEPT:	Discrimination
Intermediate-Level Generalization:	Most American ethnic groups have been the victims of various kinds of discrimination. Nonwhite ethnic groups still experience discrimination in contemporary American society.

Deciding Which Ethnic Groups to Include in the Unit

After the key and intermediate-level generalizations have been identified, the teacher should decide which ethnic groups will be included in the unit. While we argued in Part I that ethnic studies programs should include all ethnic groups, a teacher, for a variety of reasons, might want particular units to focus on specific ethnic groups. Because of the teacher's interests or those of his or her students, or because of the availability of materials, the teacher might want his or her first ethnic studies unit to focus on Afro-Americans, Mexican Americans, Native Americans, and Puerto Rican Americans, and other units to focus on other ethnic groups, such as Italian Americans, Filipino Americans, and Cuban Americans. While the total ethnic studies program, as well as the entire curriculum, should include content about all American ethnic groups, specific units might justifiably be more limited in scope. We are including Afro-Americans, Mexican Americans, Puerto Rican Americans, Chinese Americans, and Native Americans in the exemplary unit outlined in this chapter.

Identifying Subgeneralizations

After the ethnic groups to be included in the unit have been identified, the teacher should then identify subgeneralizations (see Chapter 4) related to each of the key concepts and to each of the ethnic groups chosen for study. Subgeneralizations are low-level statements which explain how the experiences of specific groups are related to the key concepts and generalizations. In our examples below, we have identified subgeneralizations for each of the key concepts as they relate to Afro-Americans, one of the ethnic groups chosen for study in our sample unit. However, in an actual unit, the teacher should identify subgeneralizations for each of the groups chosen for study.

Ethnic Group: Afro-Americans

Cultural Assimilation: To attain economic and social mobility, Afro-Americans must acquire the behavior, values, and norms of the dominant middle-class culture in the United States.

Economic Status: Because of job discrimination, low education levels, and other factors, most Afro-Americans are members of the lower socioeconomic classes.

Ethnic Community: Most Afro-Americans live in ethnic communities called "ghettos" by the dominant society. However, as individual Afro-Americans attain higher social status and higher levels of cultural assimilation, they tend to move out of their ethnic communities.

Immigration: While other ethnic groups who immigrated to America came voluntarily to improve their economic conditions, Afro-Americans were forced to come to America as slaves.

Social Protest: Since they were first captured on the West Coast of Africa, Afro-Americans have systematically protested against oppression and discrimination. Their forms of protest have reflected the times in which they occurred.

Identity: In the 1960s, Afro-Americans attempted to shape a new identity and to reject the view of themselves that had been perpetuated by the dominant society.

Discrimination: Since they landed in America, Afro-Americans have been the victims of racism and discrimination. Discrimination against Afro-Americans has taken different forms in various historical periods.

Teaching Strategies

When the subgeneralizations for each ethnic group have been identified, the teacher is then ready to write the strategies and identify the materials for teaching each of the subgeneralizations. One helpful format is for the teacher to divide a sheet of paper as illustrated in Table 12.1 and list the concepts and generalizations on one side and the activities and materials on the other. In the lesson plan in Table 12.1, we illustrate how content about Mexican Americans, one of the ethnic groups chosen for study in our sample unit, can be used to teach the concept of social protest at the senior high school level.

Helping Students to Derive the Key Generalizations

In order to formulate the key generalizations in the unit, the students must be given opportunities to compare and contrast the experiences of different ethnic groups. Students cannot derive key generalizations by studying one ethnic group. Rather, high-

Table 12.1
Key Ideas and Teaching Strategies

Key Ideas	Activities
KEY CONCEPT: Social Protest *Key Generalization:* When individuals and groups are victims of oppression and discrimination, they tend to protest against their situation in various ways.	1. To give the students a general overview of Mexican-American history, show them a film, such as *Chicano*, distributed by BFA Educational Media, Monica, CA. Before showing the film, ask the students to be able to discuss these questions after they have seen it:
Intermediate-Level Generalization: Throughout their experiences in the United States, ethnic minorities have resisted discrimination and oppression in various ways.	a) What major problems have Mexican Americans experienced in the United States? b) What actions have been taken by Mexican American individuals and groups to eliminate the discrimination which they have experienced?
Low-Level Generalization: Mexican Americans have resisted Anglo discrimination and oppression since Anglo-Americans conquered and occupied the Southwest.	2. Ask a group of students to prepare reports that reveal the ways in which the following men led organized resistance to Anglo-Americans in the 1800s: Juan N. Cortina Juan Jose Herrerra Juan Patron The class should discuss these men when the reports are presented. A good reference for this activity is, Rodolfo Acuña, *Occupied America: The Chicano's Struggle Toward Liberation.*
	3. Ask a group of students to prepare a report to be presented in class which describes Chicano involvement in strikes and unions between 1900 and 1940. When this report is presented, the students should discuss ways in which strikes and union activities were forms of organized resistance. Helpful sources for this exercise are:

Table 12.1 (Cont.)
Key Ideas and Teaching Strategies

Key Ideas	Activities
	Matt S. Meier and Feliciano Rivera, *The Chicanos: A History of Mexican Americans;* Carey McWilliams, *North From Mexico.*
	4. Ask the students to research the goals, tactics, and strategies used by the following Mexican-American civil rights groups: Order of the Sons of America, League of United Latin-American Citizens, The Community Service Organization, The American G. I. Forum, Federal Alliance of Free Cities, and Crusade for Justice. Ask the students to write several generalizations about the activities of these groups.
	5. Ask the students to research these questions: a) How is the "Chicano" movement similar to other Mexican-American protest movements? b) How are its goals and strategies different? c) When did the movement emerge? d) What long-range effects do you think the movement will have? Why?
	6. Ask the students to read and dramatize the epic poem of the Chicano movement, *I Am Joaquin,* by Rodolfo Gonzales.
	7. Ask the students questions that will enable them to summarize and generalize about how Mexican Americans have resisted Anglo discrimination and oppression in both the past and in contemporary American society. A good teacher

Table 12.1 (Cont.)
Key Ideas and Teaching Strategies

Key Ideas	Activities
	reference for kinds of questions to ask students is Francis P. Hunkins, *Questioning Strategies and Techniques* (Boston: Allyn and Bacon, 1972).
	8. Conclude the unit by viewing and discussing the film, *I Am Joaquin,* distributed by El Teatro Campesino, San Juan Bautisa, CA.

level generalizations can be derived only when students use data from several groups. At various points during the teaching of multiethnic units, the teacher should give the students ample opportunities to compare and contrast the experiences of various ethnic groups, and to formulate the key generalizations.

A simple device that enables students to compare and contrast the experiences of various ethnic groups and to derive key generalizations is the data retrieval chart. This device allows students to log in the data they have found in answer to a series of questions related to the key concepts in the unit. Its chief value is that it can be easily expanded to include two or more data samples. The data retrieval chart enables students to ask the same kinds of questions about a number of ethnic groups. Thus comparisons and contrasts can be readily made. A data retrieval chart related to our sample unit is presented in Table 12.2.

DETERMINING UNIT OBJECTIVES

Multiethnic units should have clearly stated objectives so that the teacher can effectively evaluate instruction and student learning. Multiethnic units should have two major types of objectives, cognitive and affective. *Cognitive objectives* are those related to the mastery of knowledge and skills. *Affective objectives* are related to student attitudes and values.

Table 12.2

Comparative Study of Ethnic Groups

Key Concepts and Questions	Native Americans	Mexican Americans	Afro-Americans	Chinese Americans	Puerto Rican Americans
Cultural Assimilation Level Within group?					
Economic Status High or Low?					
Ethnic Community To what extent?					
Immigration Reasons?					
Social Protest Forms?					
Identity Kinds of expressions?					
Discrimination What kinds does group experience?					

Cognitive Objectives

Throughout this book, we have recommended the conceptual approach to instruction, in which the teacher determines the key concepts and generalizations to be taught and then selects content related to ethnic groups to be used in teaching the concepts and generalizations. In the conceptual approach, the teacher emphasizes the mastery of concepts and generalizations rather than the mastery of specific facts. Facts are important only to the extent that they are necessary to help students to learn key concepts and generalizations.

When the teacher identifies the key concepts and generalizations for a unit, he or she has already largely determined the cognitive objectives of the unit, although they have not been specifically stated. In the sample unit discussed in this chapter, the key concepts chosen for study are cultural assimilation, economic status, ethnic community, immigration, social protest, identity, and discrimination. A major objective of this unit is for the students to demonstrate their understandings of each of these concepts. However, since *understanding* is a word which means different things to different people, we must state the objective in *behavioral* terms so that its meaning will be more precise. To do this, we use an action word in the objective. Action words often used in behavioral objectives include:

recall	recite	describe
identify	compare	contrast
apply	analyze	observe

Our conceptual objective for this unit can be stated this way:

a) The student will be able to identify examples and nonexamples of the key concepts in the unit.
b) The student will be able to state examples and non-examples of the key concepts in the unit.

Other major unit objectives relate to the key generalizations in the unit and the method of inquiry used to derive them. At the conclusion of the unit, the students should be able to state or write the key generalizations in their own words as well as to use the method of scientific inquiry to derive them. The objec-

tive related to the method of inquiry is a skill objective. The
method of inquiry involves these basic steps:[2]
  a) problem statement
  b) statement of hypotheses
  c) definition of terms (conceptualization)
  d) evaluation and analysis of data
  e) testing hypotheses (deriving generalizations)

The teacher can write objectives that relate to any or all of the
skills involved in the process of inquiry. Below are objectives
related to the basic steps of scientific inquiry:
     When presented a problem such as, "What are the basic
     causes of racial and ethnic discrimination?" the student
     will be able to:

  a) state relevant hypotheses
  b) collect pertinent data
  c) evaluate the data (tell whether it is valid and reli-
     able; state whether it is related to the problem)
  d) write a tentative generalization
  e) revise the generalization when presented with addi-
     tional data related to the problem.

Affective Objectives

Objectives related to feelings, attitudes, and values pose special problems for the teacher. Although teachers in traditional
classrooms usually had as one of their major objectives the development of democratic attitudes in students, current theory and
research about value teaching and learning has raised some serious questions about traditional approaches to value education.[3]
Contemporary value education theorists question the validity of
trying to inculcate specific values in students and argue that
traditional approaches to value education have not been very

2. For a detailed discussion of the steps in scientific inquiry see James
A. Banks, with Ambrose A. Clegg., Jr., *Teaching Strategies for the Social
Studies* (Reading, Mass.: Addison-Wesley, 1973), pp. 41–75.

3. See Maurice P. Hunt and Lawrence P. Metcalf, *Teaching High School
Social Studies*, 2nd ed., (New York: Harper and Row, 1968), and Louis E.
Raths, Merrill Harmin, and Sidney B. Simon, *Values and Teaching: Working With Values in the Classroom* (Columbus, Ohio: Charles E. Merrill,
1966).

successful in helping students to attain a system of clarified beliefs on which they are willing to act.

Most students have many negative as well as confused and conflicting feelings and attitudes about racial and ethnic groups. The goal of the affective component of an ethnic studies program should be to help students to determine how their values conflict, identify values alternatives, predict the consequences of alternative values, and freely choose a set of values on which they are willing to act. In other words, the teacher should help the students to critically examine their values, determine how they conflict, and derive a system of clarified values that can guide their actions. We are assuming that standards can guide a person's behavior only if they have been freely chosen from alternatives and after thoughtful consideration of the alternatives. If teachers and other adults force values upon students, the students will not prize the values, and the forced standards will have little effect on their behavior when they are out of the presence and influence of authorities. Like cognitive objectives, affective objectives should be stated in behavioral terms so that they can be successfully evaluated. The following value objectives are based on the Banks valuing model that was presented in outline form in Chapter 4.[4]

a) The student will be able to define and recognize value problems.

b) The student will be able to describe value-relevant behavior.

c) The student will be able to list values exemplified by behavior described.

d) The student will be able to identify conflicting values in behavior described.

e) The student will be able to state hypotheses about the sources of values analyzed.

f) The student will be able to list alternative values to those exemplified by behavior observed.

g) The student will be able to state hypotheses about the possible consequences of the values analyzed.

h) The student will be able to state value preferences.

i) The student will be able to state reasons, sources, and possible consequences of his or her value choices.

4. Banks, with Clegg, *Teaching Strategies*, pp. 445–77.

Using Multimedia Resources

In previous chapters we stressed the use of written materials in the exemplary teaching strategies because books are the easiest resources for most teachers to obtain. However, whenever possible, the teacher should use other media when teaching ethnic studies, such as records, films, filmstrips, photographs, and slides. In recent years, a number of multimedia materials have been produced that can be used to teach ethnic studies. Many professional organizations as well as commercial publishers issue catalogs that list, and often annotate, available multimedia resources related to ethnic studies. The Anti-Defamation League of B'nai B'rith publishes an annual *Catalog of Audio-Visual Materials*. This publication can be obtained free from either the national office or a regional office of the league. The National Education Association also publishes a list of multimedia resources it produces. Some excellent multimedia resources are listed in the catalogs of commercial firms such as Scholoat Productions in Tarrytown, New York. An annotated list of films and filmstrips is found in Appendix B.

While catalogs and bibliographies are helpful in locating multimedia resources, it is imperative that the teacher preview multimedia materials before using them in his or her class. Most commercial firms will send materials for examination on a trial basis. Previewing multimedia resources is a time-consuming task. Unfortunately, however, there is no other way to make sure that they will contribute to the teacher's instructional goals and depict ethnic groups accurately and sensitively. Multimedia resources are often expensive to rent or purchase and are frequently difficult to obtain when they are needed by the teacher. However, in most metropolitan areas there is at least one good public library that has an excellent collection of A-V materials which can be borrowed without charge. Teachers should take advantage of the many excellent services provided by the public libraries in their communities. Photographs are usually easier to obtain than films, filmstrips, and records. They can be cut from magazines such as *Ebony* and *Sepia* and can be purchased from publishers for a reasonable price. There are many sets of commercial photographs available that deal with American ethnic groups. Afro-Am Publishing Company and the Johnson Publishing Company both publish sets of photographs on Black Americans.

Using Community Resources

Every community has resources the teacher can use to enrich his or her ethnic studies lessons. One of the most helpful community resources is the ethnic organization. Ethnic organizations such as the Anti-Defamation League of B'nai B'rith, the National Association for the Advancement of Colored People, the Japanese American Citizenship League, and the Puerto Rican Forum provide a number of services, many of them without charge, which can help a teacher to strengthen his or her ethnic studies program. These organizations issue publications that describe and annotate teaching materials (usually available free upon request) and will often provide speakers for a class or school that are specialists on particular ethnic groups.

Some ethnic organizations, such as the Japanese American Curriculum Project, Inc. and the Indian Historian Press, exist solely for the purpose of developing books and other materials that can be used as teacher references and as student resources. Materials published by ethnic organizations, and annotated bibliographies issued by them, merit special attention in the school ethnic studies program. Within every ethnic community, there are a wide diversity of opinions and attitudes. However, there are certain feelings and points of view which are usually shared within the ethnic community but which are frequently unknown by authors of books about ethnic groups or by librarians and teachers who select books for the school or public library. Paying close attention to the publications issued by ethnic organizations can enable the teacher to select books and materials that more accurately reflect ethnic cultures and perspectives.[5]

There are other community resources the teacher should use when teaching ethnic studies. Most colleges and universities have programs in Afro-American studies as well as professors on

5. A list of minority group publishers and their current addresses can be obtained from the Council on Interracial Books for Children, 1841 Broadway, New York, N. Y., 10023. *The Bulletin*, published periodically by the council, is an excellent source for information about books written by ethnic minorities.

their staffs who teach courses related to other American ethnic groups. Many colleges and universities also have departments or divisions of Mexican-American, Puerto Rican-American, and Asian-American Studies. The professors who teach in these types of programs are academic specialists on the various ethnic groups and are often members of minority groups. The teacher can draw upon the services of these specialists when planning and teaching ethnic studies lessons. They are an important human resource which should not be overlooked. Heads of ethnic organizations, who are social activists, can also be invited to speak to the class or the school. They can present knowledge and points of view which are essential in a sound ethnic studies program.

Evaluation

If both the cognitive and affective objectives have been stated in behavioral terms, the evaluation of ethnic studies units will be greatly facilitated. To determine whether students can recognize examples and nonexamples of concepts such as racial discrimination and social protest, the teacher can give the students lists containing examples and nonexamples of discrimination and social protest and ask them to indicate which are examples of the concepts and which are nonexamples. Below is a list containing examples and nonexamples of racial discrimination. Note that the student must have a mastery of factual knowledge about the court cases and events in order to be able to determine which items on the list are examples and nonexamples of racial discrimination. However, the major goal of the exercise is to test the student's ability to recognize examples and nonexamples of one of the key concepts, racial discrimination:

Directions:

Below are some events and court cases we have studied. Indicate those which are examples of racial discrimination by placing an "X" in front of them. Mark those which are nonexamples of discrimination with "N."

    _____the Civil Rights Act of 1964
    _____the *Plessy* vs. *Ferguson* decision, 1896

_____the March on Washington, 1963

_____Jim Crow laws

_____the Brown decision, 1954

_____the Detroit race riot, 1943

_____the Immigration Act of 1924

_____the Geary Act, 1892

To determine whether students can use the method of social inquiry to derive key generalizations related to concepts such as immigration, social protest and ethnic community, the teacher can give them graphs, statistics, maps, selected readings, and other kinds of data, and ask the students key questions which will enable them to formulate and write out the generalizations.

Many types of sources and exercises, a number of which are described in the books by Simon et al. and Raths et al.[6] can be used to determine whether students are able to recognize value problems, identify value conflicts, and to state their own values. These include the valuing sheet, the values grid, the value survey, role-playing exercises, literary selections, photographs, open-ended stories, and essays written by the students. Some of these types of materials and exercises are discussed in Chapter 4 in the section dealing with valuing goals and strategies.

Evaluating the Total Multicultural Program

Ethnic studies content and materials should be an integral part of the total school program and environment. When trying to determine the quality of multicultural education in their school, the instructional and administrative staff can use the rating scale in Table 12.3. When completed, this scale will give the staff a rough estimate of the general quality of the school multicultural program. This information will better enable the staff to identify recommendations to guide actions to make the school environment more culturally pluralistic. In areas where the school program is already outstanding, the findings derived by using the scale can provide the staff with needed positive reinforcement.

6. Sidney B. Simon, Leland W. Howe, and Howard Kirschenbaum, *Values Clarification: A Handbook of Practical Strategies for Teachers and Students* (New York: Hart Publishing Co., 1972); Raths et al. *Working with Values in the Classroom.*

Table 12.3
*Evaluating the Total Multicultural Program**

* Directions for using this rating scale: *Check "na" if the answer to the question is "not at all." Check "1" if the answer is "yes but very little." Check "5" if the answer is "yes, that aspect of our program is outstanding." Check the numbers from 2 to 4 if the response is somewhere between the extremes. By adding the points when you have finished rating your school, you can get a rough estimate of the general quality of your total multicultural educational program. "na" = 0 points. 80 is the total number of points possible.*

		na	1	2	3	4	5
1.	Is information about American ethnic groups included in *all* of the courses in the school, including the social studies, English, literature, physical education, home economics, and science?	na	1	2	3	4	5
2.	Is there a procedure for evaluating the treatment of ethnic groups in textbooks before they are adopted for use in the school? If so, to what extent is it effective?	na	1	2	3	4	5
3.	Are there pictures of minority groups in the classrooms and in the halls of the schools?	na	1	2	3	4	5
4.	Do the calendars in the school include information about ethnic holidays and outstanding Americans of ethnic origin?	na	1	2	3	4	5
5.	Do the foods that are served in the school cafeteria reflect the ethnic diversity of American life? If so, in what ways? ———	na	1	2	3	4	5
6.	Do school assemblies and plays reflect the ethnic diversity of American life? If so, to what extent?	na	1	2	3	4	5
7.	Are the teachers and administrators provided in-service workshops and activities where they can acquire content about American ethnic cultures and ways to teach about them?	na	1	2	3	4	5

Table 12.3 (Cont.)
Evaluating the Total Multicultural Program

		na	1	2	3	4	5
8.	Does the school's professional library include books about American ethnic groups and ways to teach about them? (See the "Ethnic Studies Basic Library" on page 460–61.)	na	1	2	3	4	5
9.	Does the school's library include an ample number of books about American ethnic groups for all grade levels? If so, have the books been evaluated for their sensitivity to ethnic groups?	na	1	2	3	4	5
10.	Does the school library subscribe to ethnic magazines such as *Ebony, Indian Historian, Amerasia Journal* and *El Grito?* (See list of ethnic periodicals in Appendix C.)	na	1	2	3	4	5
11.	Is there, or has there been, a curriculum committee created to devise ways to integrate the entire school curriculum with ethnic content? If so, did the committee solicit the help of specialists in ethnic studies?	na	1	2	3	4	5
12.	Are individuals from the various ethnic organizations within the community or in nearby communities frequently invited to speak to classes and in school assemblies?	na	1	2	3	4	5
13.	Does the school offer elective courses in ethnic studies? If so, what are they? ——————— Do they provide the student with a range of courses that include information about all American ethnic groups, including Puerto Rican Americans, Filipino Americans, Cuban Americans, and Korean Americans?	na	1	2	3	4	5
14.	Do school holidays and celebrations reflect the ethnic diversity of American life? If so, what specific ethnic holidays are celebrated? ——————— How are they celebrated? ———————	na	1	2	3	4	5

Table 12.3 (Cont.)
Evaluating the Total Multicultural Program

15. Do bulletin boards and other displays in the school reflect the ethnic diversity of American life? If so, in what ways?	na	1	2	3	4	5
16. Does the school district have an ample supply of films, filmstrips, records, and other multimedia resources on American ethnic groups? If so, have they been evaluated for ethnic sensitivity?	na	1	2	3	4	5

TOTAL SCHOOL SCORE ————
RECOMMENDED ACTIONS:
1.
2.
3.
4.
5.

The Teacher and Ethnic Studies

The teacher is the most important variable in the ethnic studies program. His or her attitudes toward ethnic studies and ethnic cultures are crucial. Many teachers, especially White teachers, may fear teaching ethnic content, particularly if their classes include ethnic minorities. This problem might be compounded if minority students in their classes express or show negative attitudes toward learning about their cultural heritages, which sometimes happens. Teachers might also be intimidated by those who argue that White teachers cannot and should not teach about Afro-Americans, Native Americans, Chicanos, and that they can never know the experiences of ethnic minority groups who are victims of institutional racism in America.

The teacher should clarify his or her attitudes toward ethnic minorities before he or she tries to teach about them. Teachers who have negative or condescending attitudes toward ethnic minorities do more harm than good when they teach ethnic content. Research suggests that teacher attitudes are revealed to students even when teachers are unaware of their negative feelings.[7] Teachers who are unsure about their racial and ethnic attitudes should test them by reading some of the books recommended in earlier chapters and by enrolling in a human relations or ethnic studies workshop. If local workshops are not available, the teacher should take a course in ethnic studies at a local college or university. A human relations workshop or an ethnic studies course will give the teacher the opportunity to express his or her feelings and perceptions, compare them with the attitudes of other teachers, and clarify his or her racial feelings.

Once a teacher is keenly aware of his or her racial attitudes and is satisfied that they are basically positive toward American ethnic minorities, he or she should staunchly defend both his or her right and his or her responsibility to teach ethnic content. It is true that White teachers will never know what it means to be Black, Chicano, or Native American in contemporary American society, just as members of these groups will never know what it means to be White. It is also true that members of ethnic groups can present students with perspectives and points of view which the White teacher will be unable to present to them. However, ethnic content is legitimate knowledge which should be taught in the school. We should approach the teaching of ethnic content the way in which we approach the teaching of other content in the social sciences and humanities. We do not assume that a teacher must have lived during medieval times in order to effectively teach medieval history, or that a teacher has to be Italian in order to teach about the Renaissance in Italy. For many years, Black teachers have successfully taught European history. Likewise, we are not justified in arguing that only Blacks can teach about Blacks or that only Chicanos can teach about Mexican Americans. While it is desirable, for many reasons, for school districts to recruit and hire as many minority teachers as possible, White teachers, as well as Black and Mexican-American teachers, have a professional, and I feel moral, responsibility to teach about all American ethnic groups and to integrate ethnic content into their regular curricula and courses.

7. James A. Banks, "Racial Prejudice and the Black Self-Concept," in James A. Banks and Jean D. Grambs, eds., *Black Self-Concept: Implications for Education and Social Science* (New York: McGraw-Hill, 1972), pp. 5–35; for suggested strategies for examining and changing racial attitudes, see George Henderson, *Human Relations: From Theory to Practice* (Norman: University of Oklahoma, 1974).

A teacher who is sensitive and knowledgeable, regardless of his or her ethnic or racial group, can teach any subject effectively. However, it is important for students to be exposed to the points of view and perceptions of members of the various ethnic groups. This can be done by selecting sensitive and powerful teaching materials written by ethnic authors and using the types of community resources discussed earlier in this chapter. Many excellent books written by ethnic authors are annotated in Chapters 5 through 11. Records, films, sound filmstrips, and ethnic periodicals (see Appendix C) can also be used to present the perspectives of ethnic groups to students. Knowledgeable and informed teachers can also interpret many of these viewpoints to students. However, there is no substitute for students reading and listening to such viewpoints themselves.

Sensitive and knowledeable teachers who approach their teaching with integrity and openness can defend their right to teach ethnic content to any individual or group. Such teachers can convince ethnic students that they have a right and a responsibility to teach about ethnic cultures. Usually when a teacher claims that ethnic content is being resisted by minority students, it is because the teacher has presented ethnic content in a condescending way, has not clarified his of her feelings toward minority groups, or has not established a norm in the classroom that respects and tolerates cultural and ethnic differences. It is unrealistic to expect minority group students to be eager to study and examine their cultural heritages in a classroom atmosphere in which Anglo-Saxon culture is held up as the ideal and in which ethnic minority cultures are demeaned in subtle or overt ways.

The need for teachers to be intellectually competent before they embark upon teaching ethnic content cannot be overemphasized. The teacher who is serious about wanting to teach ethnic content should read at least one book on each major American ethnic group and one general source on ethnicity in American society. The "Ethnic Studies Basic Library" at the end of this chapter contains books, all but one of which are available in paperbound volumes, that are strongly recommended. Every school should have a basic ethnic studies library for its professional staff.

We do not mean to suggest that teachers can read a few

books and become an expert in ethnic studies, or a specialist on a particular ethnic group. Becoming an ethnic studies specialist, in any sense, takes many years of study, research, and thinking. While I am recommending that all classroom teachers integrate ethnic content into their regular courses, I feel that specialized courses on ethnic groups or particular ethnic groups, such as a Black Studies course or a Chicano Studies course, should only be taught by a teacher who has specialized in ethnic studies. A person who has successfuly functioned within an ethnic culture is more likely to have the kind of sensitivity needed to teach a specialized ethnic studies course effectively.

The Challenge of Ethnic Studies

No one who has seriously studied American ethnic groups can underestimate the difficulties involved in learning about them. Trying to learn the truth about American ethnic groups involves much unlearning of facts and interpretations that we learned in school and much new learning. A good part of the knowledge that most of us learned in school contained myths created by social scientists and historians who strongly identified with the dominant culture and who felt a need, whether conscious or not, to justify the discrimination and racism which American minority groups experienced. Studying and teaching about ethnic cultures will involve, for most teachers, intellectual and emotional confrontations with many of the feelings and beliefs which they cherish about American society.

To fully understand the nature of American society and the role that ethnicity plays within it, teachers will have to reconceptualize their views of America. For example, the United States is usually studied as an extension of European social and political institutions. However, Native Americans were in America centuries before Columbus. To view America merely as an extension of European institutions does violence to Native American institutions and cultures. Ethnic studies demands that teachers and students reconceptualize their views of the winning of the West, the meaning of slavery, the purpose of American expansion in the late 1800s, and the nature of democracy as it is practiced in contemporary American society.

The intellectual and emotional confrontations which ethnic

studies will require of teachers and students will help them to attain more humanistic views of America's oppressed ethnic minorities and to break out of their own ethnic encapsulations. Ethnic studies will teach them that there are other ways of living and being, and that to be racially and ethnically different does not mean that one is inferior or superior. More humanistic views of other cultures are imperative within our increasingly interdependent and ethnically polarized world. Humanistic views of other groups and cultures may help to create the kind of racial and ethnic harmony that our society must have to survive in the twenty-first century.

Ethnic Studies Basic Library

AFRO-AMERICANS

Franklin, John Hope. *From Slavery to Freedom: A History of Negro Americans.* New York: Vintage, 1969.

ASIAN AMERICANS

Chinese Americans

Hsu, Francis L. K. *The Challenge of the American Dream: The Chinese in the United States.* Belmont, Calif.: Wadsworth, 1971.

Filipino Americans

Morales, Royal S. *Makibaka: The Pilipino American Struggle.* Los Angeles: Mountainview Press, 1974.*

Japanese Americans

Kitano, Harry H. L. *Japanese Americans: The Evolution of a Subculture.* Englewood Cliffs, N. J.: Prentice-Hall, 1969.

MEXICAN AMERICANS

Meier, Matt S. and Feliciano Rivera, *The Chicanos: A History of Mexican Americans.* New York: Hill and Wang, 1972.

* *Available in clothbound edition only.*

NATIVE AMERICANS

Josephy, Alvin M., Jr. *The Indian Heritage of America.* New York: Bantam, 1968.

PUERTO RICAN AMERICANS

Fitzpatrick, Joseph. *Puerto Rican Americans: The Meaning of Migration to the Mainland.* Englewood Cliffs, N. J.: Prentice-Hall, 1971.

EUROPEAN AMERICANS

Handlin, Oscar. *The Uprooted: The Epic Story of the Great Migrations that Made the American People.* New York: Grosset and Dunlap, 1951.

GENERAL

Banks, James A., ed. *Teaching Ethnic Studies: Concepts and Strategies.* Washington, D. C.: National Council for the Social Studies, 1973.

————. *Teaching Strategies For Ethnic Studies.* Boston: Allyn and Bacon, 1975.

Evaluation Guidelines for Multicultural/Multiracial Education. Arlington, Virginia: National Study of School Evaluation, 1973.

Gordon, Milton. *Assimilation in American Life: The Role of Race, Religion, and National Origins.* New York: Oxford University Press, 1964.

Appendixes

Ethnic Groups in American History: a Chronology of Key Events

A

1513	Juan Ponce de León landed on the Florida peninsula while on route from Puerto Rico. The relationship between Europeans and Indians north of Mexico began.
1519	Hernán Cortéz, the Spanish conquistadore, and a group of Spaniards arrived in the region that is now Mexico.
1565	The Spaniards established the St. Augustine colony in Florida, the first settlement organized by Europeans in present-day United States.
1619	The first Blacks arrived in the English North American colonies.
1620	The Pilgrims came to America from England on the *Mayflower* and established a settlement at Plymouth, Massachusetts.
1637	More than 500 Native Americans were killed by the colonists in a massacre known as the Pequot War.
1654	The first Jewish immigrants to North America settled in New Amsterdam to escape persecution in Brazil.
1683	German immigrants settled in Pennsylvania.
1718	The Scotch-Irish began immigrating to North America in large numbers.
1754–63	The French and Indian War took place.

1798   A Federalist-dominated Congress enacted the Alien and Sedition Acts to crush the Republican party and to harass aliens.

1812   The War of 1812, a war between the United States and Britain, caused deep factions among the Indian tribes because of their different allegiances.

1815   The first mass immigrations from Europe to North America began.

1830   Congress passed a Removal Act, which authorized the removal of Indians from the east to the west of the Mississippi.

1831   Nat Turner led a slave revolt in which nearly sixty Whites were killed.

1836   Mexico's President Santa Anna and his troops defeated the Texans at the Alamo. Six weeks later Santa Anna was defeated by Sam Houston and his Texan troops at San Jacinto.

1845   The United States annexed Texas, which had declared itself independent from Mexico in 1836. This was one of the key events which led to the Mexican-American War.

1846–48   A series of potato blights in Ireland caused thousands of its citizens to immigrate to the United States.

1846   On May 13, 1846, the United States declared war on Mexico and the Mexican-American War began.

1848   The United States and Mexico signed the Treaty of Guadalupe Hidalgo that ended the Mexican-American War. Mexico lost nearly half of her territory, and the United States acquired most of the territory that makes up its southwestern states.

1850   The California legislature passed a discriminatory Foreigner Miner's Tax that forced Chinese immigrants to pay a highly disproportionate share of the state taxes.

1855   Castle Garden, an immigration station, opened in New York City

The antiforeign Know-Nothing Movement reached its zenith and had a number of political successes in the 1855 elections. The movement rapidly declined after 1855.

1859   Juan N. Cortina, who became a United States citizen under the provisions of the Treaty of Guadalupe Hidalgo, led a series of rebellions against Anglo-Americans in the Southwest.

1863 On January 1, 1863, President Abraham Lincoln issued the Emancipation Proclamation, which freed slaves in those states still fighting the Union.

1864 Nearly 300 Cheyennes were killed in a surprise attack at Sand Creek, Colorado. This event is known as the Sand Creek Massacre.

1869 The Transcontinental railroad, linking the West to the East, was completed. Chinese laborers did most of the work on the Pacific portion of the railroad.

The unsuccessful Wakamatsu Colony, made up of Japanese immigrants, was established in California.

1871 A White mob in Los Angeles attacked a Chinese community. When the conflict ended, nineteen Chinese were killed and their community was in shambles.

1876 In the disputed Hayes-Tilden election, the Democrats and Republicans made a political bargain which symbolized the extent to which Northern Whites had abandoned Southern Blacks.

Sioux tribes, under the leadership of Sitting Bull, wiped out Custer's Seventh Cavalry at Little Big Horn. This was one of the last victories for Native American tribes.

1882 The Chinese Exclusion Act was enacted by Congress. Another congressional immigration act established a head tax of fifty cents and excluded lunatics, convicts, idiots, and those likely to become public charges.

1885 A serious anti-Chinese riot took place in Rock Springs, Wyoming. Twenty-eight Chinese were killed, and many others were wounded and driven from their homes.

1886 The Apache warrior, Geronimo, surrendered to United States forces in September 1886. His surrender marked the defeat of the Southwest tribes.

The Haymarket Affair in Chicago greatly increased the fear of foreign "radicals" and stimulated the growth of nativistic sentiments in the United States.

The Statue of Liberty was dedicated as nativism soared in the United States.

1887 Congress passed the Dawes Severalty Act which was

designed to partially terminate the Indian's special relationship with the United States government.

1888 The Scott Act prohibited the immigration of Chinese laborers and permitted only officials, teachers, students, merchants, and travelers from China to enter the United States.

1890 Three hundred Sioux were killed in a massacre at Wounded Knee Creek in South Dakota.

1891 Eleven Italian Americans were lynched in New Orleans during the height of American nativism, after being accused of murdering a police superintendent.

1892 Ellis Island opened and replaced Castle Garden as the main port of entry for European immigrants.

1893 Queen Liliuokalani of Hawaii was overthrown in a bloodless revolution led by American planters.
The Republic of Hawaii was established, with Stanford B. Dole as president.

1896 In a historic decision, *Plessy* vs. *Ferguson*, the Supreme Court ruled that "separate but equal" facilities were constitutional.

1898 Hawaii was annexed to the United States.
Under the terms of the Treaty of Paris, the treaty which ended the Spanish-American War, the United States acquired Puerto Rico, Guam, and the Philippines. Cuba became independent of Spain but was placed under United States tutelage.

1900 With the Foraker Act, the United States established a government in Puerto Rico in which the president of the United States appointed the governor and the Executive Council.

1901–10 Almost 9 million immigrants entered the United States, most of whom came from Southern and Eastern Europe.

1908 The United States and Japan made the Gentlemen's Agreement, which was designed to reduce the number of Japanese immigrants entering the United States.

1910 The National Association for the Advancement of Colored People (NAACP) was organized.
A Mexican revolution caused many Mexican peasants

to immigrate to the United States looking for jobs. Other immigrants came to escape political turmoil and persecution.

1913   The California legislature passed a land bill which made it very difficult for Japanese immigrants to lease land.

1917   Thirty-nine Afro-Americans were killed in a bloody riot in East St. Louis, Missouri.

A comprehensive immigration bill was enacted that established a literacy test for entering immigrants.

The Jones Act was passed by the United States Congress. It made Puerto Ricans United States citizens and subject to the United States draft.

1920   The Hawaiian Homes Commission was started to benefit the native Hawaiian. Very little of the land involved was used for its stated purpose.

The number of persons born in Puerto Rico and living in the United States was 11,811. That number increased to 58,200 in 1935.

1924   The Johnson-Reed Act established extreme quotas on immigration and blatantly discriminated against Southern and Eastern European and non-White nations.

1925   A large number of Filipinos began to immigrate to Hawaii and the United States mainland to work as field laborers.

1927   The Filipino Federation of Labor was organized in Los Angeles.

1928   The League of United Latin American Citizens was formed in Harlingen, Texas.

1929   An anti-Filipino riot occurred in Exeter, California, in which over 200 Filipinos were assaulted.

1930   The Japanese American Citizenship League was organized.

1934   Congress passed the Tydings-McDuffie Act. This act promised the Philippines independence and limited Filipino immigration to the United States to fifty per year.

1935   President Franklin D. Roosevelt signed the Repatriation Act. The act offered free transportation to Filipinos who would return to the Philippines. Those who left were unable to return to the United States except under a severe quota system.

1942   On February 19, 1942, President Franklin D. Roosevelt issued Executive Order 9066, which authorized the internment of Japanese Americans who lived on the West Coast.

The United States and Mexico made an agreement that authorized Mexican immigrants to work temporarily in the United States. This project is known as the *bracero* program.

1943   White violence directed at Afro-Americans led to a serious riot in Detroit, in which thirty-four people were killed.

The anti-Mexican "zoot suit" riots took place in Los Angeles during the summer.

1946   On July 4, 1946, the Philippines became independent.

1954   The Refugee Relief Act permitted 5,000 Hungarian refugees to enter the United States.

In a landmark decision, *Brown* vs. *Board of Education*, the Supreme Court ruled that school segregation was inherently unequal.

The United States Immigration and Naturalization Service began Operation Wetback, a massive program to deport illegal Mexican immigrants.

1959   Fidel Castro took over the reigns of power in Cuba from the government of Fulgencio Batista. After this, many Cuban refugees entered the United States.

Hawaii become the fiftieth state of the United States.

1960   On February 1, 1960, the sit-in movement, which desegregated public accommodation facilities throughout the South, began in Greensboro, North Carolina.

1961   The National Indian Youth Council was organized.

1962   Commercial air flights between the United States and Cuba ended. Immigration from Cuba to the United State became strictly clandestine.

1963   Over 2,000 people participated in a "March on Washington for Freedom and Jobs."

1964   The Civil Rights Act of 1964, the most comprehensive civil rights bill in American history, was enacted by Congress and signed by President Lyndon B. Johnson.

1965   With the passage of the Civil Rights Act of 1965, Puerto Rican Americans were no longer required to pass an English literacy test to vote in New York state.

A new immigration act, which became effective in 1968, abolished the national origins quota system and greatly liberalized American immigration policy. Immigration from non-European nations greatly increased after this act was enacted.

A grape strike led by Cesar Chavez and the National Farm Workers Association began in Delano, California, a town in the San Joaquin Valley.

Rodolfo "Corkey" Gonzales formed the Crusade for Justice in Denver. This important civil rights organization epitomized the Chicano movement that emerged in the 1960s.

The Cuban Refugee Airlift program began. Flights from Cuba to Miami, Florida were sponsored by the United States government. The program was terminated in 1973.

1965–68   A series of rebellions took place in American cities in which Afro-Americans expressed their frustrations and discontent.

1966   Stokely Carmichael issued a call for "Black Power" during a civil rights demonstration in Greenwood, Mississippi.

1970   Herman Badillo was elected to the U. S. House of Representatives. He was the first Puerto Rican American elected to Congress.

1972   More than 8,000 delegates attended the first National Black Political Convention in Gary, Indiana.

1973   Afro-Americans were elected mayors in Detroit, Atlanta, Los Angeles, and other cities.

Selected Films and Filmstrips on American Ethnic Groups

FILMS

All the Way Home. Producer/Distributor: Fellowship of Reconciliation, Nyack, N. Y., 1964.

A fictionalized drama about a Black couple's attempts to purchase a home in a White community.

The American Indian Speaks. Producer/Distributor: Encyclopedia Britannica Educational Corporation, Chicago, 1973.

Powerful questions about Indian survival are explored in this film. Case studies focus on the Muskogee, Creek, Rosebud Sioux, and the Nisqually.

Chicano. Distributor: BFA Educational Media, Monica, Calif., 1971.

This film presents important information about the Chicano movement and raises significant questions about cultural pluralism in the United States.

Children of the Fields. Producer: Bobwin Associates, Inc. Distributor: Xerox Films, Middletown, Conn.

A revealing film about the children of migrant workers.

The Chosen People. Distributor: Anti-Defamation League of B'nai B'rith, New York, N. Y.

An effective dramatization of the problems of anti-Semitism in an American community.

Diary of a Harlem Family. Producer/Distributor: Indiana University Audiovisual Center.

The frustrations and problems of a Harlem family are poignantly depicted in this film.

Geronimo Jones. Producer/Distributor: Learning Corporation of America, New York, New York.

An excellent film about an Indian boy's search for identity and attempt to function successfully within two cultures.

Guilty by Reason of Race. Producer/Distributor: NBC Educational Enterprises, New York, 1972.

An award winning TV documentary film about the problems of Japanese Americans during World War II and after.

How the West Was Won . . . and Honor Lost. Producer/Distributor: McGraw-Hill Textfilms, New York.

A powerful film presentation of the betrayal of the Indian through broken treaties and removal.

I Am Joaquin. Distributor: El Teatro Campesino. San Juan Bautisa, Calif., 1970.

The epic poem of the Chicano movement is dramatized in this film.

Island in America. Producer/Distributor: Anti-Defamation League of B'nai B'rith, New York, N. Y.

The cultural, social, and economic life of Puerto Rican Americans is the subject of this film.

The Loon's Necklace. Producer: Crawley Films Limited; Distributor: Encyclopedia Britannica Films, Inc., Chicago, Ill.

A dramatization of the North American Indian legend which tells how the loon, a water bird, got its white neckband.

Martin Luther King: Montgomery to Memphis. Producer/Distributor: Anti-Defamation League of B'nai B'rith, New York, N. Y.

A documentary film study of the great civil rights leader.

Mexican Americans: Invisible Minority. Distributor: Indiana University Audio-Visual Center.

An excellent film in two parts which depicts the problems and aspirations of Mexican Americans.

Mexican Americans: Quest for Equality. Producer/Distributor: Anti-Defamation League of B'nai B'rith, New York, N. Y.

Various aspects of Mexican-American communities are discussed by Dr. Ernesto Galarza in this film.

Nisei: Pride and the Shame. Distributor: Japanese American Citizenship League, Los Angeles.

An overview of the internment is presented in this film.

Nothing but a Man. Producer/Distributor: Benchmark Films, Inc., New York, N. Y.

A powerful film about a Black man's search for dignity and respect.

Of Black America: Black History: Lost, Stolen or Strayed. Producer/Distributor: Columbia Broadcasting System, New York, N. Y., 1968.
A revealing film about Black-White relations in America that is skillfully narrated by Bill Cosby.

Of Black America: Portrait in Black and White. Producer/Distributor: Columbia Broadcasting System, New York, N. Y., 1968.
Based on a nationwide survey, this is an informative film about Whites' attitudes toward Blacks and how Blacks feel about Whites.

Segregation Northern Style. Distributor: Anti-Defamation League of B'nai B'rith, New York, N. Y.
This CBS documentary film deals with the problems encountered by Blacks when trying to buy homes in White communities.

To Live Together. Producer/Distributor: Anti-Defamation League of B'nai B'rith, New York, N. Y.
The difficulties experienced by children at an interracial summer camp is the subject of this film.

Treaties Made, Treaties Broken. Producer/Distributor: McGraw-Hill Textfilms, New York, 1970.
This film focuses on the Treaty of Medicine Creek of 1854 which guarantees the Indians in Washington state fishing and other rights to the land. The controversy which has surrounded the treaty is highlighted.

You Are On Indian Land. Producer/Distributor: McGraw-Hill Films, New York.
This film effectively deals with confrontation between Indians and White law officials.

Who Are the American Jews? Producer/Distributor: Anti-Defamation League of B'nai B'rith, New York, N. Y.
A general study of the American Jewish community is presented in this film.

FILMSTRIPS

Afro-American History. Producer/Distributor: Encyclopedia Britannica Educational Corporation, Chicago, Ill. 7 filmstrips, sound, color.
This set of filmstrips presents a general view of Afro-American history.

America, Melting Pot: Myth or Reality? Distributor: Social Studies School Service, Culver City, Calif. Color, sound.
This filmstrip raises questions about the melting pot and cultural assimilation in America.

The American Indian: A Study in Depth. Producer/Distributor: Schloat Productions. Tarrytown, N. Y. 6 color filmstrips, sound.

Titles in this series include *Before Columbus, After Columbus, Growing Up, Religions, Arts and Culture, The American Indian Today.*

Black Leaders of the Twentieth Century. Producer/Distributor: International Book Corp., Miami, Fla. 10 filmstrips, color and sound.
The biographies of Black leaders in diverse fields are presented in this series.

Black Political Power. Distributor: Social Studies School Service, Culver City, Calif. 6 filmstrips, sound.
This series presents views by Black politicians as well as an analysis of Black politics in America.

The Black Rabbits and the White Rabbits: An Allegory. Producer/Distributor: Schloat Productions, Tarrytown, N. Y. 41 frames, sound.
When the black rabbits are subjugated by the white rabbits in this filmstrip, the black rabbits rebel and overthrow the white rabbits.

Children of the Inner City. Producer/Distributor: Society for Visual Education, Inc., Chicago, Ill. 6 filmstrips.
Family stories of children from six different ethnic groups are told in this series.

Exploding the Myths of Prejudice. Producer/Distributor: Schloat Productions, Tarrytown, N. Y. 48 frames, sound.
Authored by an anthropologist, this filmstrip attempts to shatter pervasive myths about prejudice.

The First Americans. Producer/Distributor: The New York Times, New York, N. Y. Sound.
Key issues and problems of contemporary American Indians are explored in this filmstrip.

Growing Up Black. Producer/Distributor: Schloat Productions. Tarrytown, N. Y. 4 color sound filmstrips, each average 60 frames.
Afro-Americans reveal the anguish of being Black in America in this filmstrip.

The Harlem Renaissance and Beyond. Producer/Distributor: Guidance Associates, Inc., Pleasantville, N. Y. 2 sound filmstrips.
Vital aspects of the Black cultural renaissance are presented in this series.

The History of the Black Man in the United States. Producer/Distributor: Educational Audiovisual, Pleasantville, N. Y. 8 sound filmstrips.
This series covers the history of the Black man in America from the colonial period to the present.

How to Close Open Housing. Producer: Sunburst Communications. Distributor: Social Studies School Service, Culver City, Calif. 1 color sound filmstrip.

The story of a wealthy black rabbit who faces difficulties when he tries to buy a house in a neighborhood of white rabbits.

Immigration: The Dream and the Reality. Producer/Distributor: Schloat Productions, Tarrytown, N. Y. 6 color sound filmstrips.

Titles in this series include *The Dream, The Reality, No Irish Need Apply, Little Italy, You Belong to Germany,* and *The Japanese Nightmare.*

Indian Cultures of the Americas. Producer/Distributor: Encyclopedia Britannica Educational Corporation, Chicago, Ill. 6 color filmstrips, sound.

A variety of visuals are used to present vital phases in the development of Indian cultures in both North and South America.

The Japanese Americans: An Inside Look. Producer/Distributor: Japanese American Curriculum Project, San Mateo, California.

In these two filmstrips, Japanese Americans highlight many of their problems and hopes.

Judaism. Distributor: Social Studies School Service, Culver City, Calif. 2 color sound filmstrips.

Judaism and Jewish holidays are discussed in this filmstrip.

La Raza: A History of Mexican-Americans. Producer/Distributor: Multi-Media Productions, Inc., New York, N. Y. 24 sound filmstrips.

Titles in this series include *The Mexican Heritage, The Pioneer Heritage, Conflict of Cultures,* and *The Awakening.*

Los Puertorriquenos. Producer/Distributor: Schloat Productions. Tarrytown, N. Y. 2 color sound filmstrips.

A wide variety of Puerto Rican Americans reveal diverse aspects of their lives in this series.

Minorities Have Made America Great. Producer/Distributor: Schloat Productions. Tarrytown, N. Y. 12 color filmstrips in two sets, sound.

Titles in this series include *Negroes, Jews, Italians, Irish, American Indians, Orientals,* and *Mexican Americans.*

Prejudice in America: The Japanese Americans. Producer/Distributor: Japanese American Curriculum Project, San Mateo, Calif.

This series of four filmstrips focus on the wartime evacuation and the contemporary problems of Japanese Americans.

Relocation of Japanese-Americans: Right or Wrong? Distributor: Social Studies School Service, Culver City, Calif., 1971.

This filmstrip on the internment was written by an eminent scholar, Dr. Harry H. L. Kitano.

Rush Toward Freedom. Producer/Distributor: Schloat Productions. Tarrytown, N. Y. 8 color sound filmstrips; each average 115 frames.

These eight filmstrips focus on various aspects of the civil rights movement among Afro-Americans.

Scapegoating/Impact of Prejudice: Understanding Prejudice. Producer: Sunburst Communications. Distributor: Social Studies School Service, Culver City, Calif. 2 color sound filmstrips.

Case studies are used to explain the nature of scapegoating.

Seeds of Hate: An Examination of Prejudice. Producer/Distributor: Schloat Productions, Tarrytown, N. Y. 2 color sound filmstrips.

Various aspects of prejudice are examined in this filmstrip, such as segregation, discrimination, scapegoating, and stereotyping.

Stereotyping/Master Race Myth: Understanding Prejudice. Producer: Sunburst Communications. Distributor: Social Studies School Service, Culver City, Calif. 2 color filmstrips, sound.

Various dimensions of prejudice are explained in this filmstrip.

Ethnic Periodicals:
A Selected List

C

Throughout this book, I have emphasized the need for teachers to view the experiences of ethnic groups from the groups' perspectives and points of view. I suggested earlier that one way to do this is to have students compare the treatment of ethnic groups in their basal textbooks with accounts about ethnic groups in books written by ethnic authors. I also indicated how multimedia resources can be effectively used to bring unique ethnic viewpoints into the classroom. Another important resource can be used to help students to view the contemporary experiences of ethnic groups from diverse perspectives: the ethnic periodical. Hundreds of ethnic newspapers, magazines, and newsletters are published each week, month, and year. Ethnic periodicals are valuable resources that the teacher can use to teach about the contemporary experiences of ethnic groups, to show the variety of opinions within ethnic communities, and to illustrate how ethnic viewpoints often differ from those in the Anglo-American press. Ethnic periodicals also cover many events related to ethnic groups which are ignored, for a variety of reasons, by the Anglo-American press.

To help the teacher select ethnic periodicals for use in the classroom or for his or her own use, a selected list of such publications follow. No such list of periodicals can be totally satisfactory to every reader. Without a doubt, some favorite titles have been omitted. However, I would like to make the criteria that I used in compiling the list explicit. I tried to select periodicals that (1) reflect the various perspectives within ethnic groups, (2) would appeal to general readers, (3) were published in English, and (4) were recommended by members of the various ethnic groups. More comprehensive lists of ethnic periodicals are found in the guides listed below. The *Ulrich* guide is, by far, the most comprehensive, and can be found in the reference section of any good library. It has a special section on "Ethnic Interests" periodicals. In addition to the types of periodicals listed below, hundreds of ethnic periodicals are published in local communities. The teacher should become aware of those published in his or her community.

Recommended Guides to Periodicals

Ayer Directory of Publications. Philadelphia, Pa.: Ayer Press, 1974.

Katz, Bill, *Magazines for Libraries*, 2nd ed. New York: R. R. Bowker, 1972.

The Standard Periodical Directory. New York: Oxbridge Publishing Co., 1973.

Ulrich's International Periodicals Directory, 15th ed. New York: R. R. Bowker, 1974.

Wynar, Lubomyr R. *Encyclopedic Directory of Ethnic Newspapers and Periodicals in the United States.* Littleton, Colorado: Libraries Unlimited, 1972.

Multiethnic Periodicals

Ethnicity (Quarterly)
Academic Press, Inc.
111 Fifth Avenue
New York, New York 10003

International Migration Review (Quarterly)
Center for Migration Studies of New York, Inc.
209 Flagg Place
Staten Island, New York 10304

Interracial Books for Children (8 issues per year)
Council on Interracial Books for Children, Inc.
1841 Broadway
New York, New York 10023

Journal of Ethnic Studies (Quarterly)
College of Ethnic Studies
Western Washington State College
Bellingham, Washington 98225

Phylon (Quarterly)
The Atlanta University Review of Race and Culture
Atlanta University
223 Chestnut Street
Atlanta, Georgia 30314

Race (Quarterly)
Oxford University Press
Press Road, Neasden Lane
London, N. W. 10

Afro-American Periodicals

Black World (Monthly)
Johnson Publishing Company
820 South Michigan Avenue
Chicago, Illinois 60605

The Black Scholar (Monthly, except July and August)
The Black World Foundation
Box 908
Sausalito, CA 95965

Ebony (Monthly)
Johnson Publishing Company (address above)

Journal of Black Studies (Monthly)
Sage Publications, Inc.
275 S. Beverly Drive
Beverly Hills, CA 90210

Journal of Negro History (Quarterly)
Association for the Study of Negro Life and History
1407 14th Street, N. W.
Washington, D. C. 20005

Negro History Bulletin (Monthly)
Association for the Study of Negro Life and History (address above)

Asian American Periodicals

Amerasia Journal (Twice annually)
Asian American Studies Center Publications
Box 24A43
Los Angeles, CA 90004

Bulletin of Concerned Asian Scholars (Quarterly)
9 Sutter Street, Suite 300
San Francisco, CA 94104

Bridge Magazine (Every 2 months)
Basement Workshop

54 Elizabeth Street
New York, New York 10013

East West (Weekly-Chinese American)
East/West Publishing Company
758 Commercial Street
San Francisco, CA

Filipino American World (Monthly)
800 Southern Avenue, S. E.
Room 408
Washington, D. C. 20032

Girda (Monthly)
Girda, Inc.
P. O. Box 18046
Los Angeles, CA 90018

Pacific Citizen (Weekly)
Japanese American Citizenship League
125 Weller Street
Los Angeles, CA 90012

Philippine American (Monthly)
395 Broadway
New York, New York 10013

Philippines Mail (Monthly)
Box 1783
Salinas, CA 93901

Mexican American Periodicals

Aztlan: Chicano Journal of the Social Sciences and the Arts (Quarterly)
Chicano Studies Center
Campbell Hall
University of California
405 Hilgard
Los Angeles, CA 90024

El Grito: A Journal of Contemporary Mexican American Thought (Quarterly)
Quinto Sol Publications
Box 9275
Berkeley, CA 94709

Journal of Mexican American History
P. O. Box 13861
Santa Barbara, CA 93107

Native American Periodicals

Akwesasne Notes (Monthly)
State University of New York at Buffalo

Program in American Studies
Buffalo, New York 14214

American Indian Culture Center Journal (Quarterly)
3231 Campbell Hall
University of California
Los Angeles, CA 90024

Indian Historian Quarterly (Quarterly)
Indian Historical Society, Inc.
1451 Masonic Avenue
San Francisco, CA 94117

Indian Voice (Monthly)
Native American Publishing Company
Box 2033
Santa Clara, CA 95051

Warpath (Monthly)
United Native Americans, Inc.
Box 26149
San Francisco, CA 94126

Puerto Rican American Periodicals

Palante (Twice monthly)
Young Lords Party
352 Willis Avenue
Bronx, New York 10454

Rican (Quarterly)
Rican Jorunal, Inc.
Box 11039
Chicago, Illinois 60611

European American Periodicals

American-Scandinavian Review (Quarterly)
American-Scandinavian Foundation
127 E. 73rd Street
New York, New York 10021

Commentary (Monthly)
American Jewish Committee
165 East 56th Street
New York, New York 10022

The Greek American (Semimonthly)
Greekam Publication, Inc.
251 West 42nd Street
New York, New York 10036

Italian American Review (Quarterly)
Italian Historical Society of America
111 Columbia Hts.
Brooklyn, New York 11201

Jewish Currents (Monthly)
Jewish Currents, Inc.
22 East 17th Street, Suite 601
New York, New York 10003

Jewish Spectator (Monthly)
250 West 57th Street
New York, New York 10019

Polish American Studies (Twice annually)
Polish American Historical Association
Polish Museum of America
984 Milwaukee Avenue
Chicago, Illinois 60622

Slovak Americans (Weekly)
313 Ridge Avenue
Middletown, PA 17057

Criteria for Evaluating the Treatment of Minority Groups and Women in Textbooks and Other Learning Materials*

D

Educators have a major responsibility for the kind and quality of textbooks and other curriculum materials used in the learning-teaching process.

As responsible and dedicated educators in a democracy, we must bring our influence and strength and commitment and wisdom to bear. We must insist upon the production, selection, and use of the finest learning materials that our writers and artists are capable of creating for the education of all our children —male and female, black and white, rich and poor, rural and urban and suburban, Catholic and Protestant and Jewish, Indian and Oriental and Spanish-speaking—all of our children without exception.

Textbooks and other instructional materials are vitally important to learners and their learning. These materials are relevant to the students' life experiences, or they are not. These ma-

* Developed by Max Rosenberg. Reprinted, with permission, from *Educational Leadership,* vol. 31 (November 1973), pp. 108–109. Copyright © 1973 by the Association for Supervision and Curriculum Development.

terials give the students the clear feeling that this education is intended for them, or it is not. These materials make the students aware that they are part of the mainstream of American education and American life, or that they are not. Curriculum materials profoundly affect learners and their learning—in the way they view themselves and their social groups; in the way they think about their roles and future, and about the society and its future; in the way they are motivated to work and play and learn and live.

All textbooks and other curriculum materials should be examined, analyzed, and evaluated with care and thought, to ensure that they meet the highest standards both in subject area content and in their treatment of women and minority groups. Books and other materials which do not meet these highest standards should certainly be rejected.

Following is a list of 20 criteria which can serve as significant guidelines for educators in the process of selecting textbooks and other curriculum materials. While not all of the criteria will be applicable in every case, the questions raised do focus upon basic considerations in the learning materials that we use in the education or miseducation of our children.

Does this textbook or learning material in both its textual context and illustrations: Yes   No

1. Evidence on the part of writers, artists, and editors a sensitivity to prejudice, to stereotypes, to the use of material which would be offensive to women or to any minority group?   ☐   ☐

2. Suggest, by ommission or commission, or by overemphasis or underemphasis, that any sexual, racial, religious, or ethnic segment of our population is more or less worthy, more or less capable, more or less important in the mainstream of American life?   ☐   ☐

3. Utilize numerous opportunities for full, fair, accurate, and balanced treatment of women and minority groups?   ☐   ☐

4. Provide abundant recognition for women and minority groups by placing them frequently in positions of leadership and centrality?   ☐   ☐

5. Depict both male and female adult members of

minority groups in situations which exhibit them Yes No
as fine and worthy models to emulate? □ □

6. Present many instances of fully integrated human groupings and settings to indicate equal status and nonsegregated social relationships? □ □

7. Make clearly apparent the group representation of individuals—Caucasian, Afro-American, Indian, Chinese, Mexican American, etc.—and not seek to avoid identification by such means as smudging some color over Caucasian facial features? □ □

8. Give comprehensive, broadly ranging, and well-planned representation to women and minority groups—in art and science, in history and mathematics and literature, and in all other areas of life and culture? □ □

9. Delineate life in contemporary urban environments as well as in rural or suburban environments, so that today's city children can also find significant identification for themselves, their problems and challenges, and their potential for life, liberty, and the pursuit of happiness? □ □

10. Portray sexual, racial, religious, and ethnic groups in our society in such a way as to build positive images—mutual understanding and respect, full and unqualified acceptance, and commitment to ensure equal opportunity for all? □ □

11. Present social group differences in ways that will cause students to look upon the multi-cultural character of our nation as a value which we must esteem and treasure? □ □

12. Assist students to recognize clearly the basic similarities among all members of the human race, and the uniqueness of every single individual? □ □

13. Teach the great lesson that we must accept each other on the basis of individual worth, regardless of sex or race or religion or socioeconomic background? □ □

14. Help students appreciate the many important contributions to our civilization made by members of the various human groups, emphasizing that every human group has its list of achievers,

thinkers, writers, artists, scientists, builders, and   Yes   No
political leaders?   ☐   ☐

15. Supply an accurate and sound balance in the matter of historical perspective, making it perfectly clear that all racial and religious and ethnic groups have mixed heritages, which can well serve as sources of both group pride and group humility?   ☐   ☐

16. Clarify the true historical forces and conditions which in the past have operated to the disadvantage of women and minority groups?

17. Clarify the true contemporary forces and conditions which at present operate to the disadvantage of women and minority groups?   ☐   ☐

18. Analyze intergroup tension and conflict fairly, frankly, objectively, and with emphasis upon resolving our social problems in a spirit of fully implementing democratic values and goals in order to achieve the American dream for all Americans?   ☐   ☐

19. Seek to motivate students to examine their own attitudes and behaviors, and to comprehend their own duties and responsibilities as citizens in a pluralistic democracy—to demand freedom and justice and equal opportunity for every individual and for every group?   ☐   ☐

20. Help minority group (as well as majority group) students to identify more fully with the educational process by providing textual content and illustrations which give students many opportunities for building a more positive self-image, pride in their group, knowledge consistent with their experience; in sum, learning material which offers students meaningful and relevant learning worthy of their best efforts and energies?   ☐   ☐

This author's criteria are not in effect a rating scale. You may however want to judge your present learning materials by these criteria. Unless you are able to answer "Yes" to all of these questions, you may feel there is room for improvement—or even a need to select new textbooks and other instructional materials.

Index

53, 59–63, 71–72, 74, 76–
77, 81–82, 94
Discrimination, 82–83, 358, 440–
442, 446
generalization, 358, 440, 442
legal, 326–327
Displaced Persons Act, 202
Divide-and-conquer tactics, 149
Dole, Sanford B., 427
Domhoff, G. William, 78
Douglass, Frederick, 241
Downe, John, 213
Driver, Harold E., 119
DuBois, W.E.B., 251, 254

Economic:
exploitation, 63
key concepts, 60–63, (table)
94
problems of society, 61
status, 440, 442, 446
generalization, 440, 442
Education:
ethnic minority, 14
Eiseman, Alberta, 211, 212
Emancipation Proclamation, 245
Emigration, 187
Employment, of ethnic minority,
14–15, 61–62, 73
Empresario grants, 290
Encomienda system, 378
Endresen, Guri, 213
English immigrants, 194–195, 212
Environmental determinism, 63
Environmental perception, 64–65
Essien-Udom, E. U., 79
Estevan (Estevanico), 234, 289
Ethclass, defined, 44
Ethnic community, 440, 442, 446
generalization, 440, 442
Ethnic enclave, 64–67
Ethnic group, defined, 10–11
Ethnic groups:
comparing, (table) 446
importance in curriculum, 8
selecting for curriculum, 441
Ethnic institution, generalization,
101
Ethnicity:
in America, 5–8, 180

in politics, 5–6
Ethnic literacy, 20, 87, 321
test, 129–131
Ethnic minority groups:
compared, 11–12
defined, 12–13
Ethnic studies:
basic library for, 460–461
challenge of, 459–460
content, acquiring, 116–121
curriculum planning, 17–18, 92–
128
lesson planning, 37–38
programs, problems in, 9, 17
purpose, 11, 18–22, 27–29, 50
value component, 103–115
who should study, 18–20
Ethnic Studies Basic Library, 458,
460–461
Ethnocentrism, 58–60
European Americans. See also
Immigration.
acquiring content about, 120–
121
Anglo-Saxon cultural
dominance, 194–195
assimilation and acculturation
process, 205–208
books about, 221–228
democracy, founding of, 187–
188
generalizations about, 97
ghetto, 190–191
immigrants, diversity, 185–186
immigration, reasons for, 185–
187
mother country, attitude toward,
193–194
occupations, 190
passage to America, 188–190
politics, 191–194, 202–205
population, 205
1960–1970, 340
1970, 348
religious freedom, 187–188
Southern and Eastern European
immigrants, 195–197
teaching strategies, 208–220
valuing activity, 217–218
Evaluation, 452–456
Executive Order No. 9066, 337

DATE DUE

DISPLAY			
MAR 8 '77			
FEB 18 '78			
NOV 14 '78			
NOV 16 '78			
MAY 22 '78			
MAY 21 '79			
GAYLORD			PRINTED IN U.S.A.